VXLAN Fabric with BGP EVPN Control Plane
Design Considerations

Copyright © Toni Pasanen, All rights reserved.

First edition – 9 September 2020

About the Author:

Toni Pasanen. CCIE No. 28158 (RS), Distinguished Engineer at Fujitsu Finland. Toni started his IT-carrier in 1998 at Tieto, where he worked as a Service Desk Specialist moving via the LAN team to the Data Center team as a 3rd. Level Network Specialist. Toni joined Teleware (Cisco Learning partner) in 2004, where he spent two years teaching network technologies focusing on routing/switching and MPLS technologies. Toni joined Tieto again in 2006, where he spent the next six years as a Network Architect before joining Fujitsu. In his current role, Toni works closely with customers helping them in selecting the right network solutions not only from the technology perspective but also from the business perspective. He is also the author of books *"Virtual Extensible LAN – VXLAN: The Practical Guide to Understand VXLAN Solution - 2019"* and *"LISP with VXLAN in Campus Fabric - 2020"*

About this book

The intent of this book is to explain various design models for Overlay Network and Underlay Network used in VXLAN Fabric with BGP EVPN Control-Plane. The first two chapters are focusing on the Underlay Network solution. The OSPF is introduced first. Among other things, the book explains how OSPF flooding can be minimized with area design. After OSPF there is a chapter about BGP in the Underlay network. Both OSPF and BGP are covered deeply and things like convergence are discussed. After the Underlay Network part, the book focuses on BGP design. It explains the following models: (a) BGP Multi-AS with OSPF Underlay, this chapter discusses two design models – Shared Spine ASN and Unique Spien ASN, (b) BGP-Only Multi-ASN where both direct and loopback overlay BGP peering models are explained, (c) Single-ASN with OSPF Underlay, (d) Hybrid-ASN with OSPF Underlay – Pod-specific shared ASN connected via Super-Spine layer using eBGP peering, (e) Dual-ASN model where leafs share the same ASN and spines share their ASN. Each of the design model chapters includes a "Complexity Map" that should help readers to understand the complexity of each solution. This book also explains BGP ECMP and related to ECMP, the book also covers ESI Multihoming. The last chapter introduces how two Pods, can also be geographically dispersed DCs, can be connected using Layer 3 only DCI with MPLS.

I am using 5-stage Clos topology throughout the book. Some solutions are though explained by using only three switches for the sake of simplicity. I am also using IP-Only Underlay Network with Ingress-Replication, so this book does not cover Underlay Network Multicast solution. Besides, I am not covering DCI using Layer 2 Border Gateway (BGW) or Overlay Tenant Routing Multicast solution in this book because those, among the Underlay Multicast solutions, are covered in my first book "Virtual Extensible LAN – VXLAN: A Practical Guide to VXLAN solution" that is available at Amazon and Leanpub.

I wanted to keep the focus of the book fairly narrow and concentrate on the Control-Plane design and functionality. Please be aware that this book does not give any recommendation to which solution is the best and which is not. It is the readers' responsibility to find that out and selects the best solution for their needs. The book includes 66 full-color images, 260 configuration/show command examples, and 32 packet captures.

Who should read the book

The target audience for this book are persons how would like to understand the differences of these models from not only configuration perspective but also understand what those works. The book explains the OSPF and BGP quite deeply, so if you are preparing to certification exam including these two routing protocols, you might find this book beneficial.

Disclaimers

The content of this book is based on the author's own experience and testing results. This book is meant to be neither actual design nor an implementation guide. After reading this book, readers should do their technology validation before using it in a production environment.

Table of Contents

Table of Contents vi

Chapter 1: Underlay Network with OSPF 1

  Introduction 1
  Infrastructure AS Numbering and IP Addressing Scheme 1
  OSPF Neighbor Process 2
    OSPF Neighbor Process: Init 3
    OSPF Neighbor Process: ExStart 7
    OSPF Neighbor Process: Exchange and Full 9
  Shortest-Path First (SPF)/Dijkstra Algorithm 18
    SPF Run – Phase I: Building a Shortest-Path Tree 19
    First iteration round 20
    Second iteration round 21
    Third iteration round 24
    SPF Run – Phase II: Adding Leafs to Shortest-Path Tree 25
  Convergence 26
    Flood reduction with multiple OSPF Areas 30
    OSPF summarization in ABR 40
    Removing OSPF Router from the Datapath 43
  LSA and SPF timers 47
    LSA Throttling Timer 47
    Flood Pacing Timer 49
    LSA Group Pacing Timer 50
  Summary 51
  References 52

Chapter 2: Underlay Network with BGP 53

  Introduction 53
  Infrastructure AS Numbering and IP Addressing Scheme 54
  BGP Configuration 55
    Leaf Switches 55
    Spine Switches 56
    Super-Spine Switches 56
  BGP Neighbor Process 57
    Idle 57
    Connect 57
    Active 57
    Finalizing negotiation of the TCP connection 58
    OpenSent and OpenConfirm 61
    Established 61
  BGP NLRI Update Process 65
    RIB to Adj-RIB-Out (Pre-Policy) 65
    Adj-RIB-Out (Pre) to Adj-RIB-Out (Post) 65
    Adj-RIB-In (Post) to Adj-RIB-In (Pre) 66
    Adj-RIB-In (Pre) to Loc-RIB 66

Loc-RIB to RIB 66
BGP Update: Unreachable Destination 70
MRAI Timer 71
BGP AS-Path Prepend 71
OSPF and BGP Comparison 75
References 78

Chapter 3: BGP Multi-AS with OSPF Underlay 79

Introduction 79
Inter-Switch Link IP addressing 80
Underlay Network Routing with OSPF 81
Overlay Network BGP L2VPN EVPN Peering 83
Adding L2VN segment 86
Routing comparison: Spine Sharing ASN vs. Unique ASN 88
  Spine Switches Sharing ASN 88
  All Switches in Unique ASN 94
BGP convergence: Group of Spines in the same AS 101
BGP convergence: All switches in unique AS 106
Complexity Chart of Multi-ASN Design with OSPF Underlay 113
  Spines in shared ASN – OSPF Underlay 113
  All switches in unique ASN - OSPF Underlay 114
References 115

Chapter 4: BGP Only Multi-ASN Design 117

Introduction 117
Underlay: Direct Peering – Overlay: Loopback 117
Underlay: Direct Peering – Overlay: Direct Peering 125
Complexity Chart Multi-ASN Design with eBGP Underlay 132
  Direct Underlay Peering – Loopback Overlay Peering 132
  Direct Underlay Peering – Direct Overlay Peering 133

Chapter 5: Single AS Model with OSPF Underlay 135

Introduction 135
Configuration 136
BGP Policy and BGP Update Configuration 136
  Leaf Switches 136
  Spine Switches 137
  Super-Spine Switches 138
Verification 140
  BGP L2VPN EVPN Peering 140
  BGP Table Verification 140
  Inconsistency Problem with Received Route Count 142
  Fixing the Problem 148
  Re-checking of BGP Tables 151
  NVE Peering 154
  MAC Address Table and L2RIB 156
  Data-Plane Testing 158
Complexity Chart 159
  Single-AS Design with OSPF Underlay 159

Chapter 6: Hybrid AS Model with OSPF Underlay 161

Introduction 161
Configuration 162
  Leaf – BGP Policy and BGP Update settings 162
  Spine - BGP Adjacency and BGP Update settings 163
  SuperSpine - BGP Adjacency and BGP Update settings 166
Verification 170
Complexity Chart of Hybrid-ASN Design 187
  Direct Underlay Peering – Loopback Overlay Peering 187

Chapter 7: Dual-AS Model with OSPF Underlay 189

Introduction 189
Configuration 190
  BGP Adjacency Policy 190
  BGP Update Message Modification 190
  BGP Loop Prevention Adjustment 191
Verification 193
  BGP peering 193
  BGP table 193
  L2RIB 196
  MAC Address Table 197
Complexity Chart of Hybrid-ASN Design with OSPF Underlay 198

Chapter 8: ESI Multi-Homing 199

Introduction 199
ESI Multihoming Configuration 200
Designated Forwarder fo L2BUM 202
Mass-Withdraw 206
Load-Balancing 214
References 217

Chapter 9: ECMP process 219

ECMP process 219

Chapter 10: L3-Only Inter-Pod Connection 229

Introduction 229
MPLS Core Underlay Routing with IS-IS. 230
IS-IS Configuration 231
IS-IS Verification 231
MPLS Label Distribution with LDP 233
  MPLS LDP Configuration 235
  MPLS Verification 235
  MPLS Control-Plane Operation - LDP 237
  MPLS Data-Plane Operation – Label Switching 238
BGP VPNv4 Peering 240
  BGP VPNv4 Configuration 240
  BGP VPNv4 Peering Verification 241
BGP L2VPN EVPN Peering 242

BGP VPNv4 Configuration 242
BGP L2VPN EVPN Peering Verification 243
Adding Tenant to Border Leafs 244
Tenant Configuration 244
Verification 246
Control-Plane: End-to-End Route Propagation 246
Data-Plane: Label Switching Path 251
Data-Plane: ICMP Request 253

Appendix A: Chapter 10 device configurations 255

Chapter 1: Underlay Network with OSPF

Introduction

The foundation of a modern Datacenter fabric is an Underlay Network and it is crucial to understand the operation of the Control-Plane protocol solution used in it. The focus of this chapter is OSPF. The first section starts by introducing the network topology and AS numbering scheme. The second section explains how OSPF speakers connected to the same segment become fully adjacent. The third section discusses the process of how OSPF speakers exchange Link State information and build a Link-State Database (LSDB) which is used as an information source for calculating Shortest Path Tree (SPT) towards each destination using the Dijkstra algorithm. The focus of the fourth section is an OSPF LSA flooding process. It strat by explaining how local OSPF speaker sends Link State Advertisements wrapped inside a Link-State Update message to its adjacent router and how receiving OSPF speakers a) installs information into LSDB, b) Acknowledge the packet, and c) floods it out of OSPF interfaces. The fifth section discusses of LSA and SPF timers. At the end of this chapter, there are OSPF related configurations from every device.

Infrastructure AS Numbering and IP Addressing Scheme

Figure 1-1 illustrates an AS numbering and an IP addressing scheme used throughout this book. All Leaf switches have dedicated BGP Private AS number while spine switches in the same cluster share the same AS number. Inter-Switch links use Unnumbered IP addressing using (interface Loopback 0) which is also used as OSPF Router-Id. OSPF type for Inter-Switch link is point-to-point so there is no DR/BDR election process. Leaf switches also have interface Loopback 30 that is used as a VTEP (VXLAN Tunnel End Point) address. Loopback 30 IP addresses are advertised by Leaf switches. All Loopback interfaces are in OSPF passive interface mode. At this stage, all switches belong to OSPF Area 0.0.0.0.

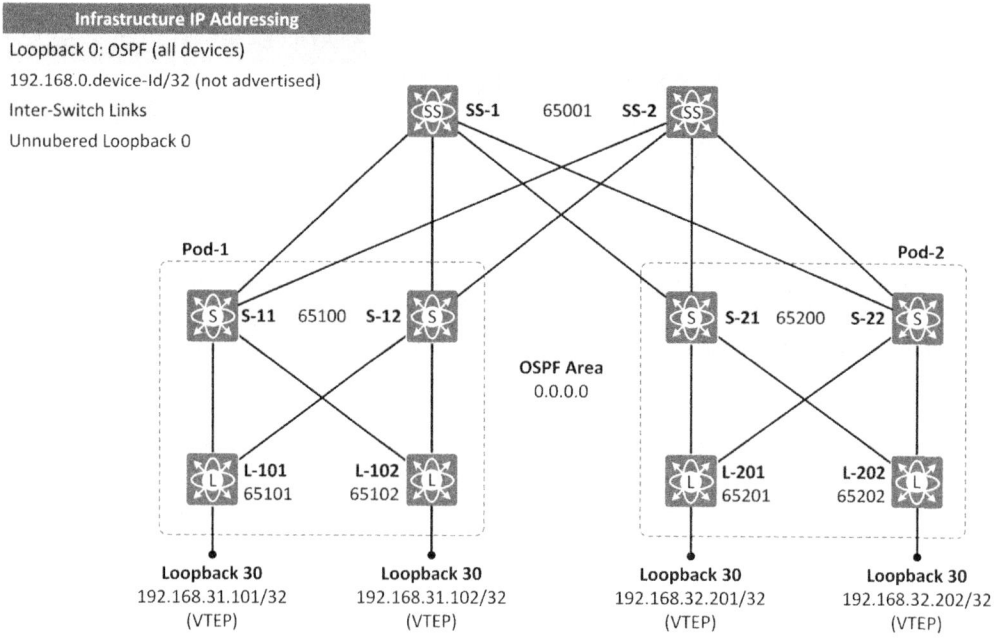

Figure 1-1: *AS Numbering and IP Addressing Scheme.*

I'm using only two Leaf and Spine switches per Pod for simplicity but the model scales out and you can have more switches within Pods.

OSPF Neighbor Process

The OSPF neighbor process is explained by using three switches; L-101, S-11, and L-102. At the starting point, the interface towards Spine-11 on Leaf-101 is down while Spine-11 and Leaf-102 are fully adjacent and their Link State Databases are synchronized.

OSPF Neighbor Process: Init

Phase 1. The interface E1/1 is brought UP on Lef-101 (1a). Leaf-101 receives three valid OSPF Hello messages from Spine-11 before Leaf-101 itself sends the first OSPF Hello message to Spine-11 (1b-d). These messages don't have Leaf-101 listed as an "Active Neighbor". This means that Leaf-101 can't be sure if Spine-11 knows its existence and that is why the state of the OSPF Finite State Machine (FSM) is INIT. When S-11 receives the OSPF Hello message sent by Leaf-101 (1e), it can now use the OSPF RID of Leaf-101 in the "Active Neighbor" field in the next OSPF hello message (1f). When Leaf-101 sees its own OSPF RID in the received message, it knows that Spine-11 has heard its OSPF Hello message and now the OSPF FSM state can be set to EXSTART. The OSPF process on Leaf-101 is shown in debug 1-1. Captures 1-1 to 1-3 show the actual packets exchange between Leaf-101 and Spine-11.

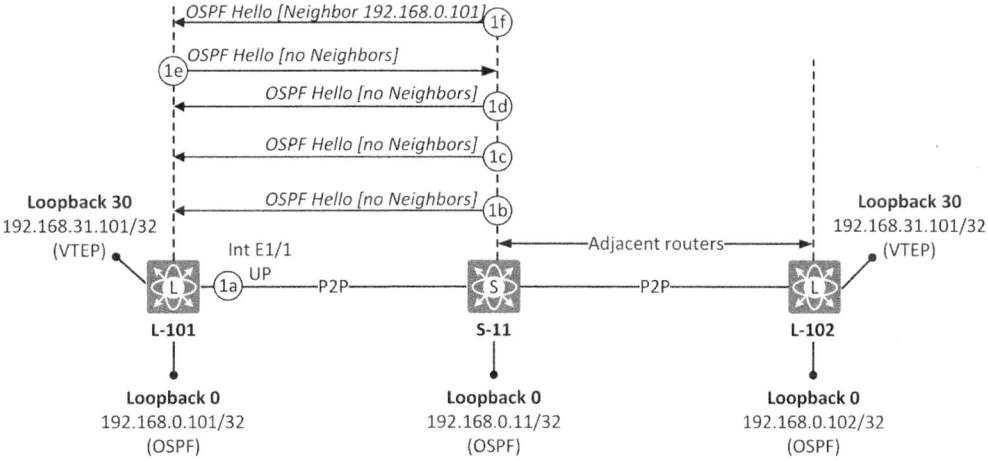

Figure 1-2: *OSPF Neighbor Process: Init-One Way-Two Way.*

```
        Scheduling hello for Ethernet1/1
          Hello timer start succeeded
      Created new neighbor 192.168.0.11
  Nbr 192.168.0.11 FSM start: old state DOWN, event HELLORCVD
  Nbr 192.168.0.11 FSM state changed from DOWN to INIT, event HELLORCVD
Nbr 192.168.0.11: DOWN --> INIT, event HELLORCVD
  Nbr 192.168.0.11 FSM start: old state INIT, event TWOWAYRCVD
  Nbr 192.168.0.11 FSM state changed from INIT to EXSTART, event ADJOK
Nbr 192.168.0.11: INIT --> EXSTART, event TWOWAYRCVD
  Nbr 192.168.0.11 FSM start: old state EXSTART, event HELLORCVD
Nbr 192.168.0.11: EXSTART --> EXSTART, event HELLORCVD
  Nbr 192.168.0.11 FSM start: old state EXSTART, event TWOWAYRCVD
Nbr 192.168.0.11: EXSTART --> EXSTART, event TWOWAYRCVD
  Nbr 192.168.0.11 FSM start: old state EXSTART, event HELLORCVD
Nbr 192.168.0.11: transitioning to OneWay - did not find ourselves
  Nbr 192.168.0.11 FSM start: old state EXSTART, event ONEWAYRCVD
  Nbr 192.168.0.11 FSM state changed from EXSTART to INIT, event ONEWAYRCVD
Nbr 192.168.0.11: EXSTART --> INIT, event ONEWAYRCVD
  Nbr 192.168.0.11 FSM start: old state INIT, event HELLORCVD
Nbr 192.168.0.11: INIT --> INIT, event HELLORCVD
Nbr 192.168.0.11: transitioning to OneWay - did not find ourselves
  Nbr 192.168.0.11 FSM start: old state INIT, event ONEWAYRCVD
Nbr 192.168.0.11: INIT --> INIT, event ONEWAYRCVD
  Nbr 192.168.0.11 FSM start: old state INIT, event HELLORCVD
Nbr 192.168.0.11: INIT --> INIT, event HELLORCVD
Nbr 192.168.0.11: transitioning to OneWay - did not find ourselves
  Nbr 192.168.0.11 FSM start: old state INIT, event ONEWAYRCVD
Nbr 192.168.0.11: INIT --> INIT, event ONEWAYRCVD
  Nbr 192.168.0.11 FSM start: old state INIT, event HELLORCVD
Nbr 192.168.0.11: INIT --> INIT, event HELLORCVD
  Nbr 192.168.0.11 FSM start: old state INIT, event TWOWAYRCVD
  Nbr 192.168.0.11 FSM state changed from INIT to EXSTART, event ADJOK
Nbr 192.168.0.11: INIT --> EXSTART, event TWOWAYRCVD
```

Debug 1-1: *Debug OSPF Adjacency detail on Leaf-101.*

Capture 1-2 shows the first OSPF Hello message sent by Spine-11. The source IP address is the OSPF RID while the destination IP address is 224.0.0.5 (AllSPFRouters). The OSPF Hello messages are targeted only to the connected network segment (TTL 1). Not that the packet is automatically marked with DSCP CS6, and in case of link congestion, these packets are prioritized over unclassified traffic. However, this has no impact if there is no QoS-policy defined between links (which is usually the case in DC). OSPF runs over IP (protocol 89) and it doesn't use either TCP (like BGP and LDP) or UDP (like VXLAN) as a transport protocol. The OSPF Hello message validation process verifies that all highlighted fields in capture 1-1 match receivers OSPF settings while the source OSPF RID must be different than OSPF RID used by the receiver. In case of some of these rules are not meat, the OSPF adjacency is not formed.

```
Internet Protocol Version 4, Src: 192.168.0.11, Dst: 224.0.0.5
    0100 .... = Version: 4
    .... 0101 = Header Length: 20 bytes (5)
    Differentiated Services Field: 0xc0 (DSCP: CS6, ECN: Not-ECT)
    Total Length: 64
    Identification: 0xa1b4 (41396)
    Flags: 0x0000
    ...0 0000 0000 0000 = Fragment offset: 0
    Time to live: 1
    Protocol: OSPF IGP (89)
    Header checksum: 0x7638 [validation disabled]
    [Header checksum status: Unverified]
    Source: 192.168.0.11
    Destination: 224.0.0.5
Open Shortest Path First
    OSPF Header
        Version: 2
        Message Type: Hello Packet (1)
        Packet Length: 44
        Source OSPF Router: 192.168.0.11
        Area ID: 0.0.0.0 (Backbone)
        Checksum: 0x3aec [correct]
        Auth Type: Null (0)
        Auth Data (none): 0000000000000000
    OSPF Hello Packet
        Network Mask: 0.0.0.0
        Hello Interval [sec]: 10
        Options: 0x02, (E) External Routing
        Router Priority: 1
        Router Dead Interval [sec]: 40
        Designated Router: 0.0.0.0
        Backup Designated Router: 0.0.0.0
```

Capture 1-1: *The First OSPF Hello Message Sent by Spine-11.*

Capture 1-2 shows the OSPF Hello packet sent by Leaf-101.

```
Internet Protocol Version 4, Src: 192.168.0.101, Dst: 224.0.0.5
Open Shortest Path First
    OSPF Header
        Version: 2
        Message Type: Hello Packet (1)
        Packet Length: 44
        Source OSPF Router: 192.168.0.101
        Area ID: 0.0.0.0 (Backbone)
        Checksum: 0x3a92 [correct]
        Auth Type: Null (0)
        Auth Data (none): 0000000000000000
    OSPF Hello Packet
        Network Mask: 0.0.0.0
        Hello Interval [sec]: 10
        Options: 0x02, (E) External Routing
        Router Priority: 1
        Router Dead Interval [sec]: 40
        Designated Router: 0.0.0.0
        Backup Designated Router: 0.0.0.0
```

Capture 1-2: *The First OSPF Hello Message Sent by Leaf-101.*

Capture 1-3 shows OSPF Hello packet send by Spine-11 after it has received the first OSPF Hello packet from Leaf-101. At this stage, Spine-11 uses Leaf-101 OSPF RID in the "Active Neighbor" field.

```
Internet Protocol Version 4, Src: 192.168.0.11, Dst: 224.0.0.5
Open Shortest Path First
    OSPF Header
        Version: 2
        Message Type: Hello Packet (1)
        Packet Length: 48
        Source OSPF Router: 192.168.0.11
        Area ID: 0.0.0.0 (Backbone)
        Checksum: 0x79da [correct]
        Auth Type: Null (0)
        Auth Data (none): 0000000000000000
    OSPF Hello Packet
        Network Mask: 0.0.0.0
        Hello Interval [sec]: 10
        Options: 0x02, (E) External Routing
        Router Priority: 1
        Router Dead Interval [sec]: 40
        Designated Router: 0.0.0.0
        Backup Designated Router: 0.0.0.0
        Active Neighbor: 192.168.0.101
```

Capture 1-3: *The Fourth Hello Message Sent by Spine-11*

OSPF Neighbor Process: ExStart

Phase 2a. Now the OSPF FSM state on Leaf-101 has moved from INIT to EXSTART. The purpose of EXSTART is to decide which router controls the Database synchronization process and to set a random starting sequence number. Because Leaf-101 has higher OSPF RID it takes control. Leaf-101 sends an empty DBD (DataBase Descriptor) with Init (I) bit, More (M) bit, and Master/Slave (MS) bit all set to one. The I-bit indicates that this is the first DBD packet, M-bit indicates that there is more DBD packet to come (this one is empty), and MS-bit indicates that Leaf-101 wants to take the controller role for the rest of the adjacency processes.

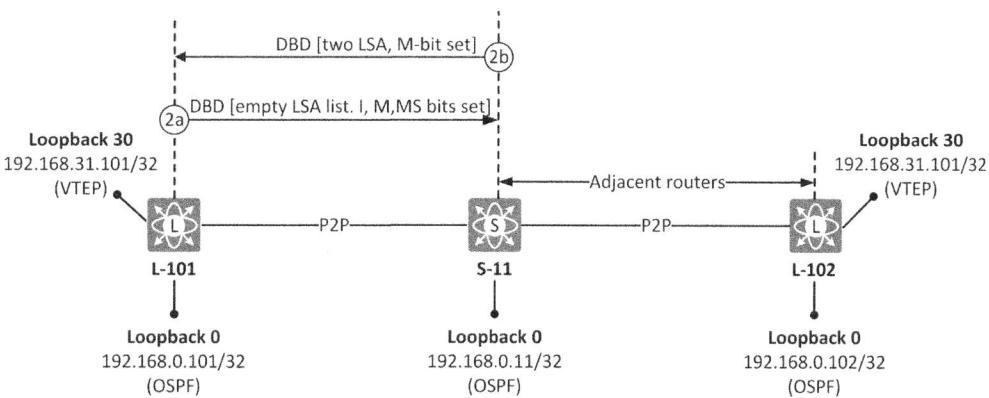

Figure 1-3: *OSPF Neighbor Process: Exstart.*

Debug 1-2 shows the adjacency process on Leaf-101. Note that ddbits 0x7 in binary mode is 0000 0111 where three rightmost bits indicate I, M, and MS-bits.

```
Sending DBD to 192.168.0.11 on Ethernet1/1
Sent DBD with 0 entries to 192.168.0.11 on Ethernet1/1
  mtu 1500, opts: 0x42, ddbits: 0x7, seq: 0x5aec6dfa
  Got DBD from 192.168.0.11 with 2 entries
    seqnr 0x5aec6dfa, dbdbits 0x2, mtu 1500, options 0x42
    We are MASTER, 192.168.0.11 is slave
    Nbr 192.168.0.11 FSM start: old state EXSTART, event NEGDONE
      Preparing DBD exchange for nbr 192.168.0.11, 135/5
```
Debug 1-2: *Debug OSPF Adjacency detail on Leaf-101 - ExStart.*

Capture 1-4 shows the DBD packet send by Leaf-101

```
Internet Protocol Version 4, Src: 192.168.0.101, Dst: 224.0.0.5
Open Shortest Path First
    OSPF Header
        Version: 2
        Message Type: DB Description (2)
        Packet Length: 32
        Source OSPF Router: 192.168.0.101
        Area ID: 0.0.0.0 (Backbone)
        Checksum: 0x2c06 [correct]
        Auth Type: Null (0)
        Auth Data (none): 0000000000000000
    OSPF DB Description
        Interface MTU: 1500
        Options: 0x42, O, (E) External Routing
        DB Description: 0x07, (I) Init, (M) More, (MS) Master
            .... 0... = (R) OOBResync: Not set
            .... .1.. = (I) Init: Set
            .... ..1. = (M) More: Set
            .... ...1 = (MS) Master: Yes
        DD Sequence: 1525444090
```

Capture 1-4: *The First Database Description (DD) Sent by Leaf-101.*

Phase 2b. Spine-11 accepts that Leaf-101 can take control of the OSPF neighbor process for now on. It sends its DBD (capture 1-5) to Leaf-101 where I-bit and MS-bit are cleared and two Type-1 LASs (Router-LSA) are listed. The sequence number of DBD is the same as what was used by Leaf-101 on its first DBD message. Debug 1-3 shows the OSPF adjacency process on Leaf-101 when receiving the DBD from Spine-11. FSM state is changed from EXSTRAT to EXCHANGE meaning the OSPF LSDB synchronization process has now been started. Leaf-101 has neither LSA information in its LSDB so it adds those into the LS Request list.

```
Nbr 192.168.0.11 FSM state changed from EXSTART to EXCHANGE, event NEGDONE
Nbr 192.168.0.11: EXSTART --> EXCHANGE, event NEGDONE
Got DBD from 192.168.0.11 with 2 entries
seqnr 0x5aec6dfa, dbdbits 0x2, mtu 1500, options 0x42
Found 192.168.0.11(0x1)192.168.0.11 (0x80000003) (0xc1ad) (65) in DBD
Added 192.168.0.11(0x1)192.168.0.11 (0x80000003) (0xc1ad) (65)(D) to request list
Found 192.168.0.102(0x1)192.168.0.102 (0x80000004) (0xff13) (65) in DBD
Added 192.168.0.102(0x1)192.168.0.102 (0x80000004) (0xff13) (65)(D) to request list
Added 2 out of 2 LSAs to request list
```

Debug 1-3: *Debug OSPF Adjacency Detail on Leaf-101 - ExStart.*

```
Internet Protocol Version 4, Src: 192.168.0.11, Dst: 224.0.0.5
Open Shortest Path First
    OSPF Header
        Version: 2
        Message Type: DB Description (2)
        Packet Length: 72
        Source OSPF Router: 192.168.0.11
        Area ID: 0.0.0.0 (Backbone)
        Checksum: 0x6316 [correct]
        Auth Type: Null (0)
        Auth Data (none): 0000000000000000
    OSPF DB Description
        Interface MTU: 1500
        Options: 0x42, O, (E) External Routing
        DB Description: 0x02, (M) More
            .... 0... = (R) OOBResync: Not set
            .... .0.. = (I) Init: Not set
            .... ..1. = (M) More: Set
            .... ...0 = (MS) Master: No
        DD Sequence: 1525444090
    LSA-type 1 (Router-LSA), len 36
        .000 0000 0100 0001 = LS Age (seconds): 65
        0... .... .... .... = Do Not Age Flag: 0
        Options: 0x02, (E) External Routing
        LS Type: Router-LSA (1)
        Link State ID: 192.168.0.11
        Advertising Router: 192.168.0.11
        Sequence Number: 0x80000003
        Checksum: 0xc1ad
        Length: 36
    LSA-type 1 (Router-LSA), len 48
        .000 0000 0100 0001 = LS Age (seconds): 65
        0... .... .... .... = Do Not Age Flag: 0
        Options: 0x02, (E) External Routing
        LS Type: Router-LSA (1)
        Link State ID: 192.168.0.102
        Advertising Router: 192.168.0.102
        Sequence Number: 0x80000004
        Checksum: 0xff13
        Length: 48
```

Capture 1-5: *Database Description (DD) Sent by Spine-11.*

OSPF Neighbor Process: Exchange and Full

Phase 3. L-101 sends a Link State Request to S-11 (3a) where it requests LSAs from 192.168.0.11 and 192.168.0.102 (debug 1-4, capture 1-6). It also sends the Database Description of its LSDB (debug 1-5, capture 1-7). This one now includes description while the first DBD was only used for Master/Slave selection and sequence number generation. S-11 replies to LS Request by sending an LS Update packet, where it described the requested LSA in detail (debug 1-6, capture 1-8).

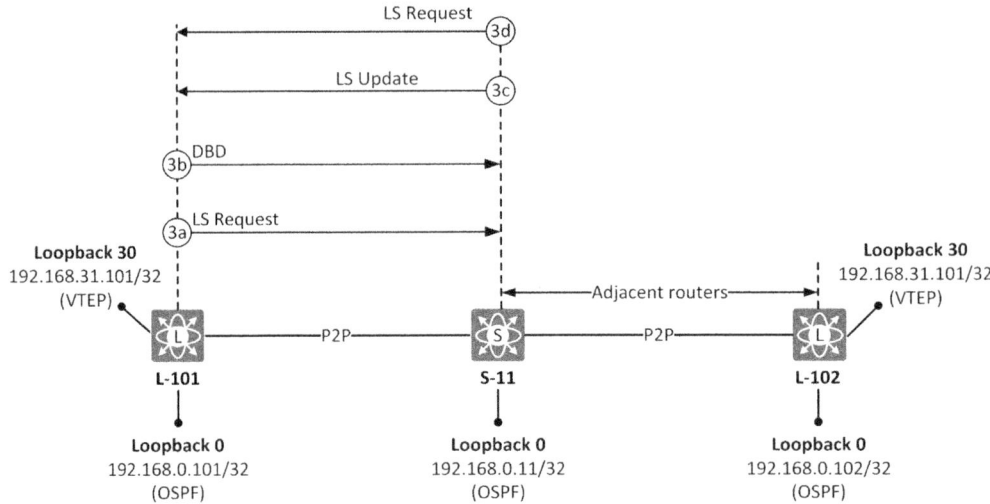

Figure 1-4: *OSPF Neighbor Process: Exstart.*

Debug 1-4 shows how L-101 builds an LS Request based on previously received DBD packet from S-11.

```
Building LS Request packet to 192.168.0.11
     Add 192.168.0.11(0x1)192.168.0.11 (0x80000003) (0xc1ad) (65)(D) to LSR
     Add 192.168.0.102(0x1)192.168.0.102 (0x80000004) (0xff13) (65)(D) to LSR
Built LS Request packet for 192.168.0.11 with 2 entries
```
Debug 1-4: *Debug OSPF Adjacency Detail on Leaf-101 – Link State Request.*

Debug 1-5 shows the process of how L-101 generates its DB Description.

```
Sending DBD to 192.168.0.11 on Ethernet1/1
       Add 192.168.0.101(0x1)192.168.0.101 (0x80000003) (0x5d67) (1300)(0) to DBD
     Filled DBD to 192.168.0.11 with 1 entries
Sent DBD with 1 entries to 192.168.0.11 on Ethernet1/1
   mtu 1500, opts: 0x42, ddbits: 0x3, seq: 0x5aec6dfb
  Got DBD from 192.168.0.11 with 0 entries
   seqnr 0x5aec6dfb, dbdbits 0, mtu 1500, options 0x42
  Got DBD from 192.168.0.11 with 0 entries
   seqnr 0x5aec6dfb, dbdbits 0, mtu 1500, options 0x42
Sending DBD to 192.168.0.11 on Ethernet1/1
     Filled DBD to 192.168.0.11 with 0 entries
Sent DBD with 0 entries to 192.168.0.11 on Ethernet1/1
   mtu 1500, opts: 0x42, ddbits: 0x1, seq: 0x5aec6dfc
```
Debug 1-5: *Debug OSPF Adjacency Detail on Leaf-101 – DB Description.*

Debug 1-6 shows how L-101 receives the LS Request from S-11.

```
Recv LSR from Nbr 192.168.0.11
  Got DBD from 192.168.0.11 with 0 entries
    seqnr 0x5aec6dfc, dbdbits 0, mtu 1500, options 0x42
  Got DBD from 192.168.0.11 with 0 entries
    seqnr 0x5aec6dfc, dbdbits 0, mtu 1500, options 0x42
  Nbr 192.168.0.11 FSM start: old state EXCHANGE, event EXCHDONE
  Nbr 192.168.0.11 FSM state changed from EXCHANGE to FULL, event EXCHDONE
```

Debug 1-6: *Debug OSPF Adjacency Detail on Leaf-101 – Receiving LSR from S-11.*

Debug 1-7 illustrates the process of how L-101 answers the LS request sent by S-11 as well as how the OSPF adjacency is now completed (Exchange to Full).

```
Nbr 192.168.0.11: EXCHANGE --> FULL, event EXCHDONE
  Answering LSR from 192.168.0.11
    1 requests in LSR (1 left)
  Building reply LSU to 192.168.0.11
    Found requested LSA 192.168.0.101(1)192.168.0.101 for 192.168.0.11
    Added 192.168.0.101(0x1)192.168.0.101 (0x80000003) (0x5d67) (1300)(O)
  Built reply LSU with 1 LSAs for 192.168.0.11 84 bytes
  Nbr 192.168.0.11 FSM start: old state FULL, event HELLORCVD
  Nbr 192.168.0.11: FULL --> FULL, event HELLORCVD
  Nbr 192.168.0.11 FSM start: old state FULL, event TWOWAYRCVD
  Nbr 192.168.0.11: FULL --> FULL, event TWOWAYRCVD
```

Debug 1-7: *Debug OSPF Adjacency detail on Leaf-101 – LSR and LU process.*

Capture 1-6 shows the LS Request sent by L-101 where it asks full description of links connected to S-11 (192.168.0.11) and L-102 (192.168.0.102).

```
Open Shortest Path First
  OSPF Header
    Version: 2
    Message Type: LS Request (3)
    Packet Length: 48
    Source OSPF Router: 192.168.0.101
    Area ID: 0.0.0.0 (Backbone)
    Checksum: 0x3938 [correct]
    Auth Type: Null (0)
    Auth Data (none): 0000000000000000
  Link State Request
    LS Type: Router-LSA (1)
    Link State ID: 192.168.0.11
    Advertising Router: 192.168.0.11
  Link State Request
    LS Type: Router-LSA (1)
    Link State ID: 192.168.0.102
    Advertising Router: 192.168.0.102
```

Capture 1-6: *Link-State Request from L-101 to S-11.*

Capture 1-7 shows the DataBase Description message sent by L-101 to S-11. DBD message only contains the OSPF RID of sending router, not any link information connected in it.

```
Open Shortest Path First
    OSPF Header
        Version: 2
        Message Type: DB Description (2)
        Packet Length: 52
        Source OSPF Router: 192.168.0.101
        Area ID: 0.0.0.0 (Backbone)
        Checksum: 0xc535 [correct]
        Auth Type: Null (0)
        Auth Data (none): 0000000000000000
    OSPF DB Description
    LSA-type 1 (Router-LSA), len 36
        .000 0101 0001 0100 = LS Age (seconds): 1300
        0... .... .... .... = Do Not Age Flag: 0
        Options: 0x02, (E) External Routing
        LS Type: Router-LSA (1)
        Link State ID: 192.168.0.101
        Advertising Router: 192.168.0.101
        Sequence Number: 0x80000003
        Checksum: 0x5d67
        Length: 36
```
Capture 1-7: *DB Description from L-101 to S-11.*

Capture 1-8 illustrates the LS Update sent by S-11 as a reply to LS Request from L-101. LS Update detailed information about the links and their type of both S-11 (the first Router-LSA) and L-102 (the second Router-LSA).

```
Open Shortest Path First
    OSPF Header
        Version: 2
        Message Type: LS Update (4)
        Packet Length: 112
        Source OSPF Router: 192.168.0.11
        Area ID: 0.0.0.0 (Backbone)
        Checksum: 0x0c82 [correct]
        Auth Type: Null (0)
        Auth Data (none): 0000000000000000
    LS Update Packet
        Number of LSAs: 2
        LSA-type 1 (Router-LSA), len 36
            .000 0000 0100 0010 = LS Age (seconds): 66
            0... .... .... .... = Do Not Age Flag: 0
            Options: 0x02, (E) External Routing
            LS Type: Router-LSA (1)
            Link State ID: 192.168.0.11
            Advertising Router: 192.168.0.11
            Sequence Number: 0x80000003
            Checksum: 0xc1ad
            Length: 36
```

```
            Flags: 0x00
            Number of Links: 1
            Type: PTP       ID: 192.168.0.102   Data: 0.0.0.3           Metric: 40
               Link ID: 192.168.0.102 - Neighboring router's Router ID
               Link Data: 0.0.0.3
               Link Type: 1 - Point-to-point connection to another router
               Number of Metrics: 0 - TOS
               0 Metric: 40
      LSA-type 1 (Router-LSA), len 48
            .000 0000 0100 0010 = LS Age (seconds): 66
            0... .... .... .... = Do Not Age Flag: 0
            Options: 0x02, (E) External Routing
            LS Type: Router-LSA (1)
            Link State ID: 192.168.0.102
            Advertising Router: 192.168.0.102
            Sequence Number: 0x80000004
            Checksum: 0xff13
            Length: 48
            Flags: 0x00
            Number of Links: 2
            Type: Stub      ID: 192.168.31.102  Data: 255.255.255.255 Metric: 1
               Link ID: 192.168.31.102 - IP network/subnet number
               Link Data: 255.255.255.255
               Link Type: 3 - Connection to a stub network
               Number of Metrics: 0 - TOS
               0 Metric: 1
            Type: PTP       ID: 192.168.0.11    Data: 0.0.0.3           Metric: 40
               Link ID: 192.168.0.11 - Neighboring router's Router ID
               Link Data: 0.0.0.3
               Link Type: 1 - Point-to-point connection to another router
               Number of Metrics: 0 - TOS
               0 Metric: 40
```

Capture 1-8: *Link-State Update from S-11 to L-101.*

At this stage, L-101 is fully adjacent to S-11 just like L-102.

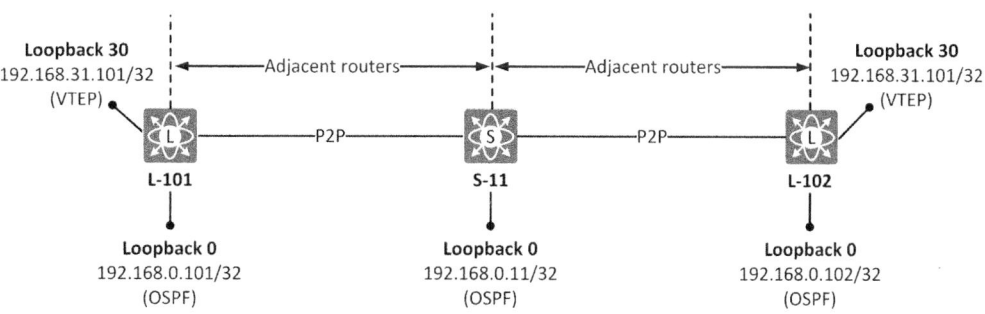

Figure 1-5: *OSPF Neighbor Process: Full Adjacency.*

Example 1-1 shows that the OSPF LSDB now contains all Link-State information about all links connected to both S-11 and L-102. Examples 1-2 show the OSPF LSDB of L-102 and example 1-3 shows the OSPF LSDB of S-11.

```
L-101# sh ip ospf database detail
      OSPF Router with ID (192.168.0.101) (Process ID UNDERLAY-NET VRF default)

             Router Link States (Area 0.0.0.0)

 LS age: 1393
 Options: 0x2 (No TOS-capability, No DC)
 LS Type: Router Links
 Link State ID: 192.168.0.11
 Advertising Router: 192.168.0.11
 LS Seq Number: 0x80000007
 Checksum: 0x4220
 Length: 48
  Number of links: 2

   Link connected to: a Router (point-to-point)
   (Link ID) Neighboring Router ID: 192.168.0.102
   (Link Data) Router Interface address: 0.0.0.3
     Number of TOS metrics: 0
       TOS   0 Metric: 40

   Link connected to: a Router (point-to-point)
   (Link ID) Neighboring Router ID: 192.168.0.101
   (Link Data) Router Interface address: 0.0.0.4
     Number of TOS metrics: 0
       TOS   0 Metric: 40

 LS age: 1391
 Options: 0x2 (No TOS-capability, No DC)
 LS Type: Router Links
 Link State ID: 192.168.0.101
 Advertising Router: 192.168.0.101
 LS Seq Number: 0x80000008
 Checksum: 0xfd14
 Length: 48
  Number of links: 2

   Link connected to: a Stub Network
    (Link ID) Network/Subnet Number: 192.168.31.101
    (Link Data) Network Mask: 255.255.255.255
     Number of TOS metrics: 0
       TOS   0 Metric: 1

   Link connected to: a Router (point-to-point)
   (Link ID) Neighboring Router ID: 192.168.0.11
   (Link Data) Router Interface address: 0.0.0.3
     Number of TOS metrics: 0
       TOS   0 Metric: 40

 LS age: 1399
 Options: 0x2 (No TOS-capability, No DC)
 LS Type: Router Links
 Link State ID: 192.168.0.102
 Advertising Router: 192.168.0.102
 LS Seq Number: 0x80000009
 Checksum: 0xf518
```

```
  Length: 48
   Number of links: 2

    Link connected to: a Stub Network
     (Link ID) Network/Subnet Number: 192.168.31.102
     (Link Data) Network Mask: 255.255.255.255
      Number of TOS metrics: 0
       TOS   0 Metric: 1

    Link connected to: a Router (point-to-point)
     (Link ID) Neighboring Router ID: 192.168.0.11
     (Link Data) Router Interface address: 0.0.0.3
      Number of TOS metrics: 0
       TOS   0 Metric: 40
```

Example 1-1: *Link State Database on Leaf-101.*

```
L-102# sh ip ospf data detail
       OSPF Router with ID (192.168.0.102) (Process ID UNDERLAY-NET VRF default)

               Router Link States (Area 0.0.0.0)

  LS age: 1677
  Options: 0x2 (No TOS-capability, No DC)
  LS Type: Router Links
  Link State ID: 192.168.0.11
  Advertising Router: 192.168.0.11
  LS Seq Number: 0x80000007
  Checksum: 0x4220
  Length: 48
   Number of links: 2

    Link connected to: a Router (point-to-point)
     (Link ID) Neighboring Router ID: 192.168.0.102
     (Link Data) Router Interface address: 0.0.0.3
      Number of TOS metrics: 0
       TOS   0 Metric: 40

    Link connected to: a Router (point-to-point)
     (Link ID) Neighboring Router ID: 192.168.0.101
     (Link Data) Router Interface address: 0.0.0.4
      Number of TOS metrics: 0
       TOS   0 Metric: 40

  LS age: 1677
  Options: 0x2 (No TOS-capability, No DC)
  LS Type: Router Links
  Link State ID: 192.168.0.101
  Advertising Router: 192.168.0.101
  LS Seq Number: 0x80000008
  Checksum: 0xfd14
  Length: 48
   Number of links: 2

    Link connected to: a Stub Network
     (Link ID) Network/Subnet Number: 192.168.31.101
     (Link Data) Network Mask: 255.255.255.255
      Number of TOS metrics: 0
       TOS   0 Metric: 1
```

```
    Link connected to: a Router (point-to-point)
    (Link ID) Neighboring Router ID: 192.168.0.11
    (Link Data) Router Interface address: 0.0.0.3
      Number of TOS metrics: 0
        TOS   0 Metric: 40

  LS age: 1681
  Options: 0x2 (No TOS-capability, No DC)
  LS Type: Router Links
  Link State ID: 192.168.0.102
  Advertising Router: 192.168.0.102
  LS Seq Number: 0x80000009
  Checksum: 0xf518
  Length: 48
   Number of links: 2

    Link connected to: a Stub Network
    (Link ID) Network/Subnet Number: 192.168.31.102
    (Link Data) Network Mask: 255.255.255.255
      Number of TOS metrics: 0
        TOS   0 Metric: 1

    Link connected to: a Router (point-to-point)
    (Link ID) Neighboring Router ID: 192.168.0.11
    (Link Data) Router Interface address: 0.0.0.3
      Number of TOS metrics: 0
        TOS   0 Metric: 40
```

Example 1-2: *Link State Database on Leaf-102.*

```
        S-11# sh ip ospf database detail

OSPF Router with ID (192.168.0.11) (Process ID UNDERLAY-NET VRF default)

              Router Link States (Area 0.0.0.0)

  LS age: 1524
  Options: 0x2 (No TOS-capability, No DC)
  LS Type: Router Links
  Link State ID: 192.168.0.11
  Advertising Router: 192.168.0.11
  LS Seq Number: 0x80000007
  Checksum: 0x4220
  Length: 48
   Number of links: 2

    Link connected to: a Router (point-to-point)
    (Link ID) Neighboring Router ID: 192.168.0.102
    (Link Data) Router Interface address: 0.0.0.3
      Number of TOS metrics: 0
        TOS   0 Metric: 40

    Link connected to: a Router (point-to-point)
    (Link ID) Neighboring Router ID: 192.168.0.101
    (Link Data) Router Interface address: 0.0.0.4
      Number of TOS metrics: 0
        TOS   0 Metric: 40

  LS age: 1524
  Options: 0x2 (No TOS-capability, No DC)
```

```
LS Type: Router Links
Link State ID: 192.168.0.101
Advertising Router: 192.168.0.101
LS Seq Number: 0x80000008
Checksum: 0xfd14
Length: 48
 Number of links: 2

  Link connected to: a Stub Network
   (Link ID) Network/Subnet Number: 192.168.31.101
   (Link Data) Network Mask: 255.255.255.255
    Number of TOS metrics: 0
      TOS   0 Metric: 1

  Link connected to: a Router (point-to-point)
   (Link ID) Neighboring Router ID: 192.168.0.11
   (Link Data) Router Interface address: 0.0.0.3
    Number of TOS metrics: 0
      TOS   0 Metric: 40

LS age: 1529
Options: 0x2 (No TOS-capability, No DC)
LS Type: Router Links
Link State ID: 192.168.0.102
Advertising Router: 192.168.0.102
LS Seq Number: 0x80000009
Checksum: 0xf518
Length: 48
 Number of links: 2

  Link connected to: a Stub Network
   (Link ID) Network/Subnet Number: 192.168.31.102
   (Link Data) Network Mask: 255.255.255.255
    Number of TOS metrics: 0
      TOS   0 Metric: 1

  Link connected to: a Router (point-to-point)
   (Link ID) Neighboring Router ID: 192.168.0.11
   (Link Data) Router Interface address: 0.0.0.3
    Number of TOS metrics: 0
      TOS   0 Metric: 40
```

Example 1-3: *Link State Database on S-11.*

Shortest-Path First (SPF)/Dijkstra Algorithm

Dijkstra/SPF algorithm is used for calculating a Shortest-Path Tree (SPT) topology in OSPF Area. A router starts the process by setting itself as a root of the STP tree. At the first stage, the router builds a Shortest-Path Tree between routers by using the Type-1 Link Description (point-to-point) which describes links to neighbor routers in Router LSA. When the Shortest-Path Tree is formed, the router calculates the distance to subnets connected to each router by using the Link Type-3 (Stub) Link Description in Router LSA.

Routers have two lists related to SPT calculation. The *Candidate List* (also known as a Tentative List) is the list that includes all routers that are currently examined by the router. The *Tree List* (also called Path or Known List) is the list, which includes all the routers participating in a final Shortest-Path Tree. Besides, a Link State Database (LSDB) is a source from where the information is pulled to calculation.

The next section describes the SPT calculation process from L-101 perspectives.

SPF Run – Phase I: Building a Shortest-Path Tree

Figure 1-6 shows the initial situation where L-101 starts the Shortest-Path Tree calculation. L-101 inserts itself into the Candidate list with cost 0 and with next-hop pointing to itself. S-11, S-12, and L-102 are in Unknown-list at this phase. The Path-list is empty at the initial stage.

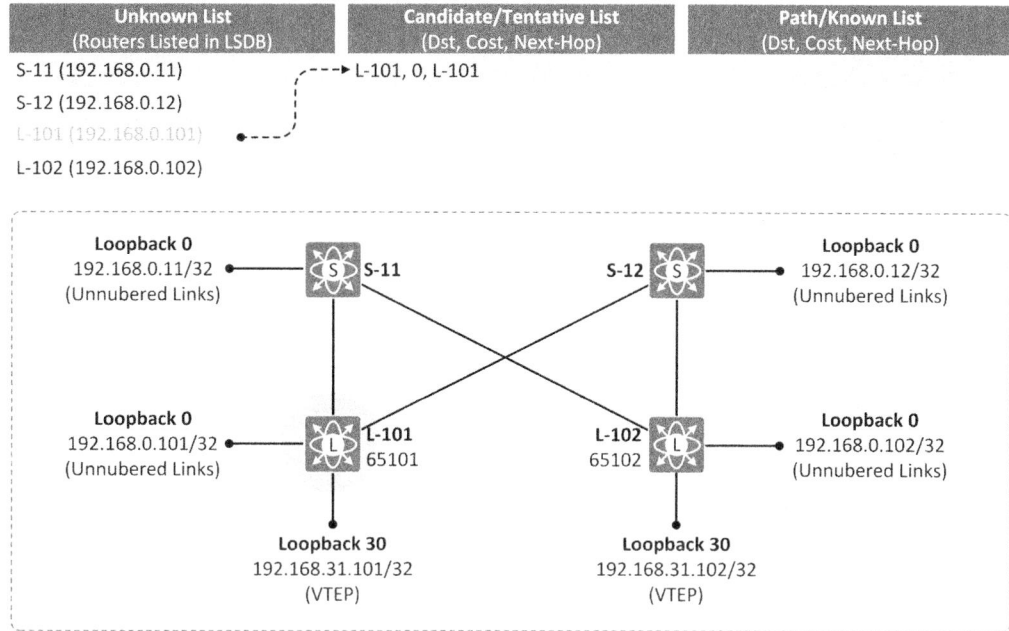

Figure 1-6: *Shortest Path Calculation-1 st. Iteration round.*

```
L-101# sh ip ospf data
        OSPF Router with ID (192.168.0.101) (Process ID UNDERLAY-NET VRF default)

                Router Link States (Area 0.0.0.0)

Link ID          ADV Router       Age      Seq#        Checksum Link Count
192.168.0.11     192.168.0.11     235      0x80000006  0x441f   2
192.168.0.12     192.168.0.12     2        0x80000006  0x342d   2
192.168.0.101    192.168.0.101    224      0x80000006  0x3036   3
192.168.0.102    192.168.0.102    3        0x80000006  0x2a39   3
```

Example 1-4: *Link State Database on L-101.*

First iteration round

Figure 1-7 shows the first SPF iteration round. L-101 inserts itself to the Path List. L-101 examines its self-originated Router LSAs. It starts from the first Link Description (LD) found from the LSA. First LD is Link Type-3 (Stub) so it is ignored and used after the shortest path has been calculated. The next entry describes the link to S-12 (Link Type-1). L-101 moves S-11 into the Candidate list with cost 40. The last LD describes the link to S-11. L-101 move also S-11 to the Candidate List. L-102 is still in the Unknown-list.

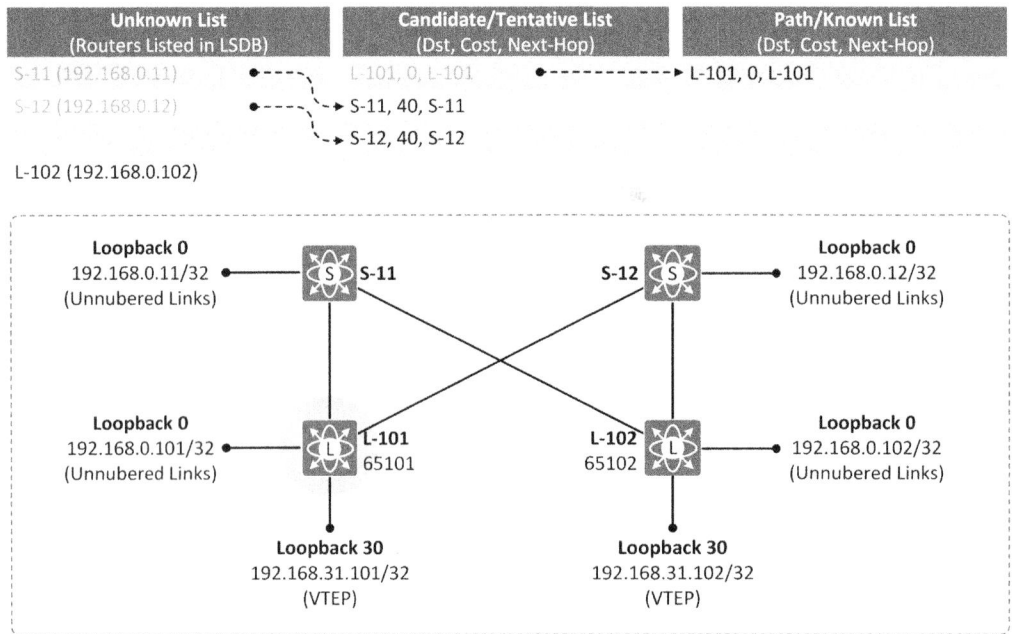

Figure 1-7: *Shortest Path calculation-The First Iteration round.*

Example 1-5 shows the detailed LSDB of L-101. The first Link Description (LD) describes the interface Loopback 30 that is will later be used as an NVE Interface IP address (Network Virtualization Edge). It is ignored from the SPT calculation process due to its type "Stub network". Remember that in the first phase we are forming Shortest Path Tree, and when that is done, we can calculate the best path to each destination.

```
L-101# sh ip ospf database 192.168.0.101 detail
        OSPF Router with ID (192.168.0.101) (Process ID UNDERLAY-NET VRF default)

                Router Link States (Area 0.0.0.0)

  LS age: 301
  Options: 0x2 (No TOS-capability, No DC)
  LS Type: Router Links
  Link State ID: 192.168.0.101
  Advertising Router: 192.168.0.101
  LS Seq Number: 0x80000005
  Checksum: 0x3235
  Length: 60
   Number of links: 3

    Link connected to: a Stub Network
      (Link ID) Network/Subnet Number: 192.168.31.101
      (Link Data) Network Mask: 255.255.255.255
       Number of TOS metrics: 0
        TOS   0 Metric: 1

    Link connected to: a Router (point-to-point)
     (Link ID) Neighboring Router ID: 192.168.0.12
     (Link Data) Router Interface address: 0.0.0.2
       Number of TOS metrics: 0
        TOS   0 Metric: 40

    Link connected to: a Router (point-to-point)
     (Link ID) Neighboring Router ID: 192.168.0.11
     (Link Data) Router Interface address: 0.0.0.3
       Number of TOS metrics: 0
        TOS   0 Metric: 40
```

Example 1-5: *Detailed Link State Database on L-101.*

Second iteration round

L-101 moves Both S-11 and S-12 to the Path-list due to their equal metric. They both have two point-to-point links in their OSPF LSDB. The link to L-101 itself is ignored because L-101 has a better cost for that link (connected). Links to L-102 have an equal cost on both switches so L-101 adds the L-102 into the Candidate list with next-hop set to both S-11 and S-12.

Unknown List (Routers Listed in LSDB)	Candidate/Tentative List (Dst, Cost, Next-Hop)	Path/Known List (Dst, Cost, Next-Hop)
		L-101, 0, L-101
	S-11, 40, S-11	→ S-11, 40, S-11
	S-12, 40, S-12	→ S-12, 40, S-12
L-102 (192.168.0.102)	→ L-102, 80, S-11 and S-11 [ECMP]	

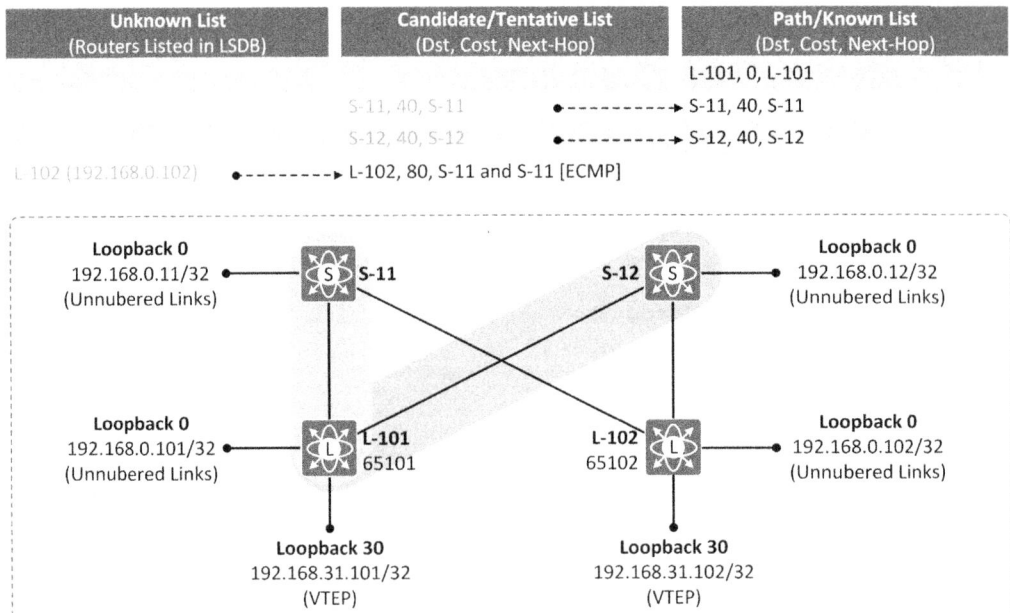

Figure 1-8: *Shortest Path Calculation-Second Iteration round.*

```
L-101# sh ip ospf data 192.168.0.11 detail
      OSPF Router with ID (192.168.0.101) (Process ID UNDERLAY-NET VRF default)

              Router Link States (Area 0.0.0.0)

  LS age: 354
  Options: 0x2 (No TOS-capability, No DC)
  LS Type: Router Links
  Link State ID: 192.168.0.11
  Advertising Router: 192.168.0.11
  LS Seq Number: 0x80000007
  Checksum: 0x4220
  Length: 48
   Number of links: 2

    Link connected to: a Router (point-to-point)
    (Link ID) Neighboring Router ID: 192.168.0.102
    (Link Data) Router Interface address: 0.0.0.3
      Number of TOS metrics: 0
        TOS   0 Metric: 40

    Link connected to: a Router (point-to-point)
    (Link ID) Neighboring Router ID: 192.168.0.101
    (Link Data) Router Interface address: 0.0.0.4
      Number of TOS metrics: 0
        TOS   0 Metric: 40
```

Example 1-6: *Router Links of S-11 installed into LSDB of L-101.*

```
L-101# sh ip ospf data 192.168.0.12 detail
        OSPF Router with ID (192.168.0.101) (Process ID UNDERLAY-NET VRF default)

                Router Link States (Area 0.0.0.0)

  LS age: 135
  Options: 0x2 (No TOS-capability, No DC)
  LS Type: Router Links
  Link State ID: 192.168.0.12
  Advertising Router: 192.168.0.12
  LS Seq Number: 0x80000007
  Checksum: 0x322e
  Length: 48
   Number of links: 2

    Link connected to: a Router (point-to-point)
    (Link ID) Neighboring Router ID: 192.168.0.102
    (Link Data) Router Interface address: 0.0.0.3
      Number of TOS metrics: 0
        TOS   0 Metric: 40

    Link connected to: a Router (point-to-point)
    (Link ID) Neighboring Router ID: 192.168.0.101
    (Link Data) Router Interface address: 0.0.0.4
      Number of TOS metrics: 0
        TOS   0 Metric: 40
```

Example 1-6: *Router Links of S-12 installed into LSDB of L-101.*

Third iteration round

L-101 moves L-102 to the Path-list. The LSDB of L-102 contains two point-to-point links, one to S-11 and the other one to S-12. L-101 already has links to these routers so both links are ignored. Also, the Stub link pointing to L-102 Loopback 30 is ignored at this phase. Now the Shortest-Path is ready.

Unknown List (Routers Listed in LSDB)	Candidate/Tentative List (Dst, Cost, Next-Hop)	Path/Known List (Dst, Cost, Next-Hop)
		L-101, 0, L-101
		S-11, 40, S-11
		S-12, 40, S-12
	L-102, 80, S-11 and S-11 [ECMP] ----▶	L-102, 80, S-11 and S-11 [ECMP]

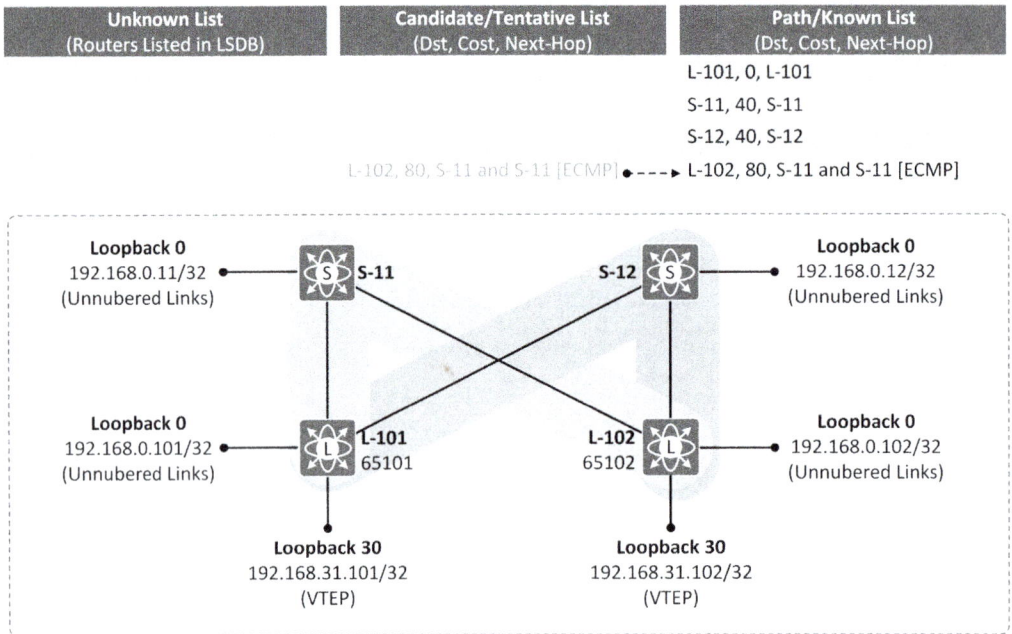

Figure 1-9: *Shortest Path calculation-Third Iteration round.*

```
L-101# sh ip ospf data 192.168.0.102 detail
        OSPF Router with ID (192.168.0.101) (Process ID UNDERLAY-NET VRF default)

                Router Link States (Area 0.0.0.0)

  LS age: 1107
  Options: 0x2 (No TOS-capability, No DC)
  LS Type: Router Links
  Link State ID: 192.168.0.102
  Advertising Router: 192.168.0.102
  LS Seq Number: 0x80000007
  Checksum: 0x283a
  Length: 60
   Number of links: 3

    Link connected to: a Stub Network
     (Link ID) Network/Subnet Number: 192.168.31.102
     (Link Data) Network Mask: 255.255.255.255
      Number of TOS metrics: 0
       TOS   0 Metric: 1

    Link connected to: a Router (point-to-point)
     (Link ID) Neighboring Router ID: 192.168.0.12
     (Link Data) Router Interface address: 0.0.0.2
      Number of TOS metrics: 0
       TOS   0 Metric: 40

    Link connected to: a Router (point-to-point)
     (Link ID) Neighboring Router ID: 192.168.0.11
     (Link Data) Router Interface address: 0.0.0.3
      Number of TOS metrics: 0
       TOS   0 Metric: 40
```

Example 1-7: *Router Links of L-102 installed into LSDB of L-101.*

SPF Run – Phase II: Adding Leafs to Shortest-Path Tree

In the first phase, L-101 forms a Shortest-Path Tree (SPT) by using the Dijkstra/SPF algorithm. In the second Phase, Stub Networks used as an interface NVE IP address, are added into SPT. Once again L-101 starts by examining its self-originated Router LSA. It has a Link Description about Stub Network 192.168.31.101/32 in its LSDB, which is moved into RIB as directly connected. S-11 and S-12 do not have any Stub-Networks in their LSDB. L-102, however, has a Stub-Network 192.168.31.102/32. The SPT between L101 and L-102 includes two equal-cost paths via S-11 and S-12 and the network is inserted into RIB with two next-hop addresses. This means that traffic from L-101 to destination 192.168.31.102 will get flow-based load-balancing forwarding behavior.

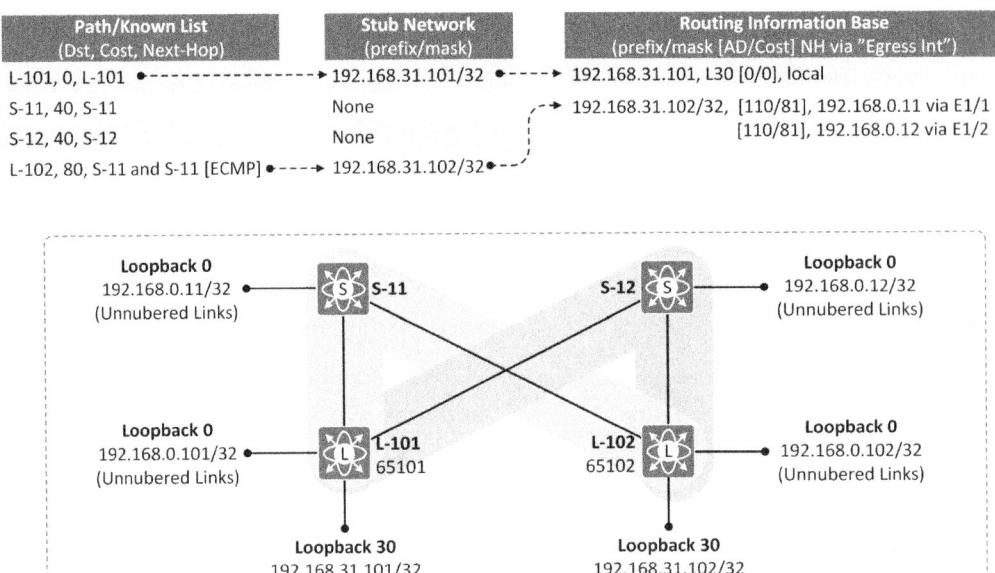

Figure 1-10: *Shortest Path calculation-Second Phase: Stub-Networks.*

Note! You may wonder how the flow-based load-balancing works in VXLAN Fabric because of the source and destination IP addresses for VXLAN encapsulated packets between two VTEPs are always the same (depending on traffic direction). VXLAN uses UDP as a transport-layer protocol which is connectionless by nature that though has a source-port field in its header that is not used for application recognizer for return traffic like with reliable transport protocol TCP. The UDP source port in the VXLAN header is filled with the original source-port used by the application by the sending host.

Convergence

Whenever there is a link state change in OSPF Area, it triggers an LSA flooding process and an SPF calculation. In figure 1-11, the link between L-202 and S-22 fails. Both S-22 and L-202 reacts to this event running full SPF calculation. They both also send LS Update out of the each OSPF interface using AllSPFRouter multicast address 224.0.0.5 as a destination IP address. When adjacent OSPF speakers receive LS Updates, they run SPF and floods the LS Update further out of their OSPF interfaces. This process goes on like a wave through the whole OSPF area.

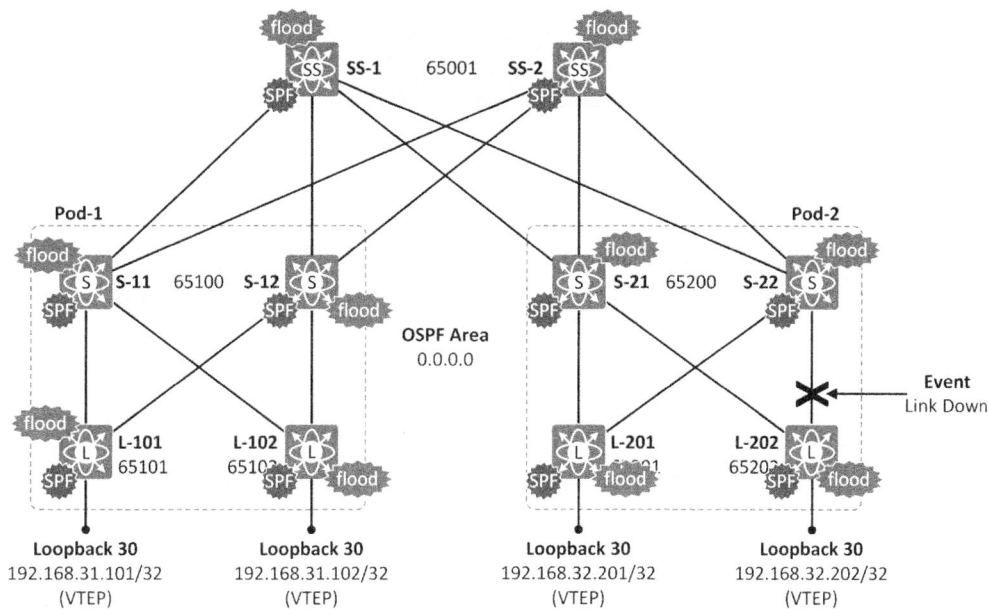

Figure 1-11: *Effect of Single Link Failure.*

We can verify this from L-101. Example 1-8 shows the LSDB of L-101 before link failure. The highlighted rows show the Router Link information of S-22 (Age 748 seconds) and L-202 (Age 749 seconds). The sequence number of S-22 is 0x8000007 and the link count is four. The sequence number of L-202 is 0x8000006 and the link count is three.

```
L-101# sh ip ospf database
        OSPF Router with ID (192.168.0.101) (Process ID UNDERLAY-NET VRF default)

              Router Link States (Area 0.0.0.0)

Link ID          ADV Router       Age         Seq#       Checksum Link Count
192.168.0.1      192.168.0.1      1547        0x80000004 0xee80   3
192.168.0.2      192.168.0.2      1546        0x80000004 0xde8e   3
192.168.0.11     192.168.0.11     1540        0x80000004 0x481d   2
192.168.0.12     192.168.0.12     1547        0x80000006 0xd348   4
192.168.0.21     192.168.0.21     1553        0x80000006 0xa29e   4
192.168.0.22     192.168.0.22     748         0x80000007 0x90ad   4
192.168.0.101    192.168.0.101    1544        0x80000004 0x3434   3
192.168.0.102    192.168.0.102    1544        0x80000004 0x2e37   3
192.168.0.201    192.168.0.201    1551        0x80000004 0x1511   3
192.168.0.202    192.168.0.202    749         0x80000006 0x0b16   3
```

Example 1-8: *OSPF LSDB of L-101 before link failure between S-22 and L-202.*

Example 1-9 illustrates that so far SPF calculation has run 125 times.

```
L-101# sh ip ospf | sec Area
   Area BACKBONE(0.0.0.0)
        Area has existed for 04:54:33
        Interfaces in this area: 3 Active interfaces: 3
        Passive interfaces: 0  Loopback interfaces: 0
        No authentication available
        SPF calculation has run 125 times
         Last SPF ran for 0.010751s
        Area ranges are
        Number of LSAs: 10, checksum sum 0x49e50
```

Example 1-9: *SPF calculation count on L-101 before link failure between S-22 and L-202.*

Example 1-10 shows the link failure can be seen in LSDB of L-101. The age of the Router Link entries is now 55 seconds and the link count is reduced by one.

```
L-101# sh ip ospf database
        OSPF Router with ID (192.168.0.101) (Process ID UNDERLAY-NET VRF default)

                Router Link States (Area 0.0.0.0)

Link ID         ADV Router      Age         Seq#       Checksum Link Count
192.168.0.1     192.168.0.1     1643        0x80000004 0xee80   3
192.168.0.2     192.168.0.2     1643        0x80000004 0xde8e   3
192.168.0.11    192.168.0.11    1636        0x80000004 0x481d   2
192.168.0.12    192.168.0.12    1644        0x80000006 0xd348   4
192.168.0.21    192.168.0.21    1650        0x80000006 0xa29e   4
192.168.0.22    192.168.0.22    55          0x80000008 0x604a   3
192.168.0.101   192.168.0.101   1640        0x80000004 0x3434   3
192.168.0.102   192.168.0.102   1641        0x80000004 0x2e37   3
192.168.0.201   192.168.0.201   1647        0x80000004 0x1511   3
192.168.0.202   192.168.0.202   55          0x80000007 0x8552   2
```

Example 1-10: *OSPF LSDB of L-101 before link failure between S-22 and L-202.*

We can also that the SPF calculation has now run 127 times.

```
L-101# sh ip ospf | sec Area
   Area BACKBONE(0.0.0.0)
        Area has existed for 04:56:14
        Interfaces in this area: 3 Active interfaces: 3
        Passive interfaces: 0  Loopback interfaces: 0
        No authentication available
        SPF calculation has run 127 times
         Last SPF ran for 0.001635s
        Area ranges are
        Number of LSAs: 10, checksum sum 0x4e829
```

Example 1-11: *SPF calculation count on L-101 after link failure between S-22 and L-202.*

Capture 1-9 shows the Link State Update sent by S-12. If we compare the flooding process of OSPF to the traditional ethernet L2BUM traffic flooding process there is (at least) one significant difference. Technically OSPF speaker does not flood the actual received LS Update. LS Update has always been sent to non-routable Multicast address 224.0.0.5 with TTL set to 1, so the original LS Update is only targeted to OSPF speakers in the same network segment. We can see from the capture below that the sending OSPF router is S-12 (192.168.0.12) while the Advertising Router is L-202 (192.168.0.202).

```
Open Shortest Path First
    OSPF Header
        Version: 2
        Message Type: LS Update (4)
        Packet Length: 76
        Source OSPF Router: 192.168.0.12
        Area ID: 0.0.0.0 (Backbone)
        Checksum: 0x0c27 [correct]
        Auth Type: Null (0)
        Auth Data (none): 0000000000000000
    LS Update Packet
        Number of LSAs: 1
        LSA-type 1 (Router-LSA), len 48
            .000 0000 0000 0100 = LS Age (seconds): 4
            0... .... .... .... = Do Not Age Flag: 0
            Options: 0x02, (E) External Routing
            LS Type: Router-LSA (1)
            Link State ID: 192.168.0.202
            Advertising Router: 192.168.0.202
            Sequence Number: 0x80000007
            Checksum: 0x8552
            Length: 48
            Flags: 0x00
            Number of Links: 2
            Type: Stub     ID: 192.168.32.202  Data: 255.255.255.255 Metric: 1
            Type: PTP      ID: 192.168.0.21    Data: 0.0.0.3         Metric: 40
```

Capture 1-9: *LS Update sent by S-12 captured on L-101.*

When L-101 receives the LS Update from S-12 it sends an LS Acknowledge message to S-12. This is how OSPF does a reliable LS Update process. The same LS Update process happens also with S-11 and L-101 but it is not described here.

```
Open Shortest Path First
    OSPF Header
        Version: 2
        Message Type: LS Acknowledge (5)
        Packet Length: 44
        Source OSPF Router: 192.168.0.101
        Area ID: 0.0.0.0 (Backbone)
        Checksum: 0xb249 [correct]
        Auth Type: Null (0)
        Auth Data (none): 0000000000000000
    LSA-type 1 (Router-LSA), len 48
        .000 0000 0000 0111 = LS Age (seconds): 7
```

```
            0... .... .... .... = Do Not Age Flag: 0
        Options: 0x02, (E) External Routing
        LS Type: Router-LSA (1)
        Link State ID: 192.168.0.202
        Advertising Router: 192.168.0.202
        Sequence Number: 0x80000007
        Checksum: 0x8552
        Length: 48
```

Capture 1-10: *LS Update sent by S-12 captured on L-101.*

The effect of single link failure described in the previous section is not the only event that triggers the flooding process. OSPF LSAs have a fixed 3600 seconds (one hour) lifetime that can not be changed. However, OSPF routers refreshed each self-originated LSAs every 1800 seconds (half-hour). Imagine that we have Datacenter with 1000, with eight uplinks in each device. If we run single are OSPF in Underlay, there is almost continuous LSA flooding. This though does not trigger SPF calculation but if there is a link failure, each of those 1000 switches will run SPF calculation. The flooding process can be seen as a problem with OSPF in large scale Datacenter.

Flood reduction with multiple OSPF Areas

Figure 1-12 shows the OSPF Area design where links between Spine and Leaf switches within Pods belongs to regular, non-backbone OSPF areas (Pod 1 in area 0.0.0.1 and Pod 2 in area 0.0.0.2) and links between Spine and Super-Spine belongs to backbone Area 0.0.0.0. Spine switches in both Pods now become OSPF Area Border Routers (ABR). ABR does not forward any Router LSA (Type-1) or Network LSA (Type-2) between areas. Note that Type-2 is irrelevant in DC since we are only using P2P links where there is no DR/BDR election. What ABR does is that it sends Summary-LSA (Type-3) between areas where it describes the Intra-Area networks. In that sense OSPF routers also advertise routing information (use me as a next-hop for the network x.x.x.x/y) even though OSPF routers inside an area advertise only Link-State information without any kind of routing information.

ABRs S-21, as an example, originates the Summary LSAs (Type-3) about networks located in area 0.0.0.2 and floods it into Area 0.0.0.0. Summary LSA describes the networks and S-21 own cost without having any link-state information included in it. In this sense, when using multiple OSPF areas, the OSPF as a Link-State protocol turns into a Distance-Vector protocol, routers within one area have no visibility about the structure of another area.

In this area design, the link failure between S-22 and L-202 only has a local effect. The LS Updates caused by topology change stays within the OSPF Area 0.0.0.2 and only switches within Pod-2 run the SPF calculation. Neither Super-Spine in area 0.0.0.0 nor Spine in OSPF Area 0.0.0.1 does not run SFP algorithm, they just update the cost information into LSDB and RIB based on a new Summary-LSA received from ABR S-22. This way we can reduce flooding and split the network into smaller failure domains.

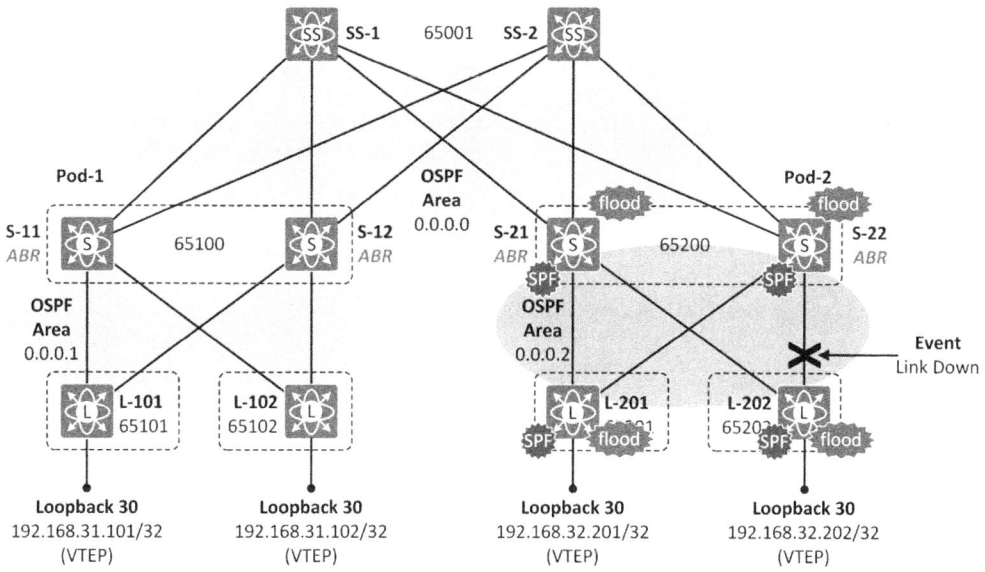

Figure 1-12: *OSPF Area design.*

If we now take a look at the OSPF LSDB in SS-1 we can see that all Loopback 30 addresses are now seen as Summary Network LSA. But why Link-Id 192.168.32.202 is still advertised by S-22 even though the link to next-hop switch L-202 is down?

```
SS-1# sh ip ospf data
        OSPF Router with ID (192.168.0.1) (Process ID UNDERLAY-NET VRF default)

                Router Link States (Area 0.0.0.0)

Link ID         ADV Router      Age     Seq#       Checksum Link Count
192.168.0.1     192.168.0.1     854     0x80000006 0xd6e7   4
192.168.0.2     192.168.0.2     850     0x80000007 0xc4f6   4
192.168.0.11    192.168.0.11    1087    0x80000005 0x6cc3   2
192.168.0.12    192.168.0.12    1084    0x80000005 0x5cd1   2
192.168.0.21    192.168.0.21    851     0x80000005 0xcb50   2
192.168.0.22    192.168.0.22    846     0x80000004 0xbd5d   2

                Summary Network Link States (Area 0.0.0.0)

Link ID         ADV Router      Age     Seq#       Checksum
192.168.31.101  192.168.0.11    1247    0x80000003 0xb619
192.168.31.101  192.168.0.12    1244    0x80000003 0xb01e
192.168.31.102  192.168.0.11    1257    0x80000003 0xac22
192.168.31.102  192.168.0.12    1244    0x80000003 0xa627
192.168.32.201  192.168.0.21    621     0x80000003 0x83dc
192.168.32.201  192.168.0.22    626     0x80000003 0x7de1
192.168.32.202  192.168.0.21    611     0x80000004 0x77e6
192.168.32.202  192.168.0.22    16      0x80000005 0x9279
```

Example 1-12: *LSDB on SS-1 in Area Design.*

The reason is simple. The LSAs are flooded inside an area 0.0.0.2, so eventually flooded Router LSA about 192.168.32.202/32 ended up into OSPF LSDB of S-22. This is a normal LSDB synchronization process with Link-State protocols, all Intra-area router must have an identical OSPF LSDB. The metric shown in LSDB of S-22 about LSA 192.168.32.202 is now 121 while in a stable situation it was 41. This is because the metric is increased by every OSPF routers along the path. The originating router L-202 floods the LSA with its own metric 1 out of its OSPF interfaces. S-21 receives the LS Update and it adds its link cost of an interface where the LSA was received into total metric when installing the LSA into LSDB (In our example network the cost is 40 in each link). Then S-21 runs the SPF algorithm, updates its RIB if necessary, and floods the LS Update out of its OSPF enabled interface to L-201. L-201 installs received LSA into LSDP with metric 81 (received 41 metric plus own link cost 40). Then it runs the SPF algorithm, updates its RIB if necessary, and floods the LSA out its OSFP interface. This way the LSA originated by L-202 eventually end up to LSDB of S-22 with metric 121. In addition to the intra-area flooding process, both ABRs S-21 and S-22 generate Summary LSAs and send those out of their interface attached to the backbone area 0.0.0.0. They are using the same metric in LSAs as what they have in their OSPF LSDB.

BGP EVPN Design Consideration 33

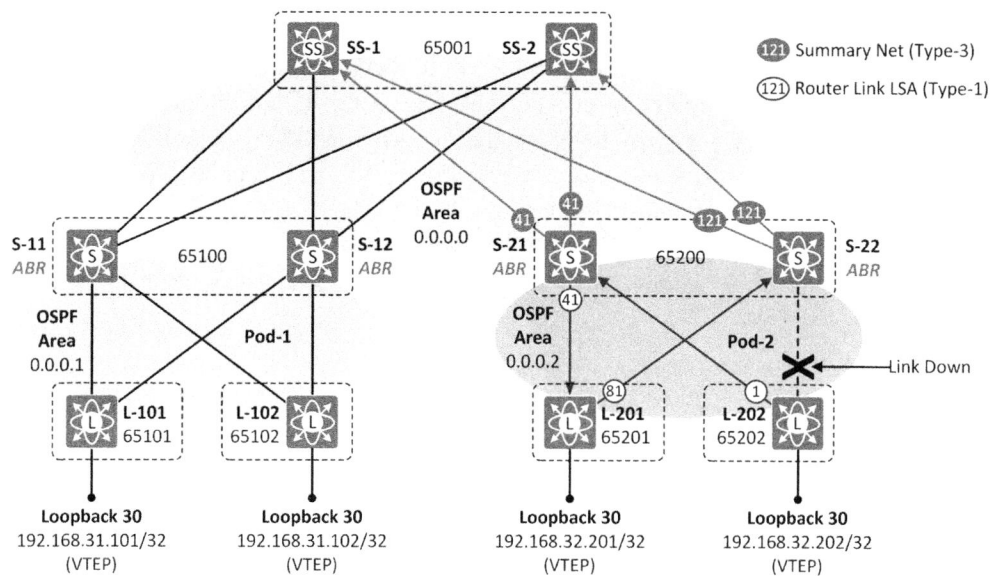

Figure 1-13: *The Flooding Propagation of Router LSA 192.168.32.202/32.*

When SS-1 receives the Summary LSA from ABR S-21 and S-22, it installs both LSAs into OSPF LSDB as is without any modification. Example 1-13 shows that Summary LSA from the ABR S-21 has metric 41 while the Summary LSA from the ABR S-22 has metric 121.

```
SS-1# sh ip ospf data sum 192.168.32.202 detail
        OSPF Router with ID (192.168.0.1) (Process ID UNDERLAY-NET VRF default)

                Summary Network Link States (Area 0.0.0.0)

    LS age: 646
    Options: 0x2 (No TOS-capability, No DC)
    LS Type: Network Summary
    Link State ID: 192.168.32.202 (Network address)
    Advertising Router: 192.168.0.21
    LS Seq Number: 0x80000004
    Checksum: 0x77e6
    Length: 28
    Network Mask: /32
        TOS:   0 Metric: 41

    LS age: 51
    Options: 0x2 (No TOS-capability, No DC)
    LS Type: Network Summary
    Link State ID: 192.168.32.202 (Network address)
    Advertising Router: 192.168.0.22
    LS Seq Number: 0x80000005
    Checksum: 0x9279
    Length: 28
    Network Mask: /32
        TOS:   0 Metric: 121
```

Example 1-13: *Summary Net on LSDB of SS-1.*

The overall metric (received and link cost) to destination 192.168.32.202/32 via S-21 is the best so it is installed into the RIB. The cost installed into RIB is 81 [cost in received LSA = 41] + [cost to reach the advertising ABR = 40]. If we compare intra-area Router LSAs and inter-area Summary LSAs we can see that the Router LSA describes the advertising routers Links which are used as a source of information when building a Shortest Path Tree. The Summary LSA, in turn, hides the source of information and advertises itself as a next hop for the network described in LSA.

```
SS-1# sh ip route 192.168.32.202/32 | b 192
192.168.32.202/32, ubest/mbest: 1/0
    *via 192.168.0.21, Eth1/4, [110/81], 00:55:54, ospf-UNDERLAY-NET, inter
```
Example 1-14: *RIB of SS-1.*

Example 1-15 shows the cost to ABRs on the SS-1 perspective.

```
SS-1# sh ip ospf UNDERLAY-NET border-routers
OSPF Process ID UNDERLAY-NET VRF default, Internal Routing Table
Codes: i - Intra-area route, I - Inter-area route

intra 192.168.0.11 [40], ABR, Area 0.0.0.0, SPF 122
     via 192.168.0.11, Eth1/1
intra 192.168.0.12 [40], ABR, Area 0.0.0.0, SPF 122
     via 192.168.0.12, Eth1/2
intra 192.168.0.21 [40], ABR, Area 0.0.0.0, SPF 122
     via 192.168.0.21, Eth1/4
intra 192.168.0.22 [40], ABR, Area 0.0.0.0, SPF 122
     via 192.168.0.22, Eth1/3
```
Example 1-15: *SS-1 costs to ABRs.*

Figure 1-14 illustrates the Summary LSA propagation process from backbone area 0.0.0.0 to to area 0.0.0.1 (Pod-1). SS-1 and SS-2 flood Summary LSA received from both ABRs S-21 and S-22 to ABRs S-11 and S-12. ABR S-11 and S-12 generate a Summary LSA into Area 0.0.0.1 of LSA generated by S-21 due to its better metric.

```
SS-1# sh ip ospf data summary 192.168.32.0 detail
        OSPF Router with ID (192.168.0.1) (Process ID UNDERLAY-NET VRF default)

                Summary Network Link States (Area 0.0.0.0)

  LS age: 490
  Options: 0x2 (No TOS-capability, No DC)
  LS Type: Network Summary
  Link State ID: 192.168.32.0 (Network address)
  Advertising Router: 192.168.0.21
  LS Seq Number: 0x80000002
  Checksum: 0x67c3
  Length: 28
  Network Mask: /24
        TOS:    0 Metric: 41

  LS age: 296
  Options: 0x2 (No TOS-capability, No DC)
  LS Type: Network Summary
  Link State ID: 192.168.32.0 (Network address)
  Advertising Router: 192.168.0.22
  LS Seq Number: 0x80000003
  Checksum: 0x8256
  Length: 28
  Network Mask: /24
        TOS:    0 Metric: 121
```

Example 1-31: *The Detailed LS information on SS-1.*

After making aggregation in all ABRs, the LSDB of SS-1 has only four Summary LSAs in its LSDB (example 1-32) while without aggregation there were eight Summary LSAs as can be seen in example 1-12 in page 32.

```
SS-1# sh ip ospf database
        OSPF Router with ID (192.168.0.1) (Process ID UNDERLAY-NET VRF default)

                Router Link States (Area 0.0.0.0)

Link ID         ADV Router       Age       Seq#        Checksum Link Count
192.168.0.1     192.168.0.1      530       0x80000009  0xd0ea   4
192.168.0.2     192.168.0.2      535       0x8000000c  0x105e   3
192.168.0.11    192.168.0.11     763       0x80000008  0x66c6   2
192.168.0.12    192.168.0.12     761       0x80000008  0x56d4   2
192.168.0.21    192.168.0.21     582       0x80000009  0xc354   2
192.168.0.22    192.168.0.22     575       0x80000007  0x08b2   1

                Summary Network Link States (Area 0.0.0.0)

Link ID         ADV Router       Age       Seq#        Checksum
192.168.31.0    192.168.0.11     92        0x80000002  0xae87
192.168.31.0    192.168.0.12     71        0x80000002  0xa88c
192.168.32.0    192.168.0.21     1300      0x80000002  0x67c3
192.168.32.0    192.168.0.22     725       0x80000004  0x5dca
```

Example 1-32: *The OSPF LSDB of SS-1.*

Also, the RIB of SS-1 has now only one route advertised by each ABR.

```
SS-1# sh ip route
IP Route Table for VRF "default"
'*' denotes best ucast next-hop
'**' denotes best mcast next-hop
'[x/y]' denotes [preference/metric]
'%<string>' in via output denotes VRF <string>

192.168.0.1/32, ubest/mbest: 2/0, attached
    *via 192.168.0.1, Lo0, [0/0], 02:15:16, local
    *via 192.168.0.1, Lo0, [0/0], 02:15:16, direct
192.168.31.0/24, ubest/mbest: 2/0
    *via 192.168.0.11, Eth1/1, [110/81], 00:01:35, ospf-UNDERLAY-NET, inter
    *via 192.168.0.12, Eth1/2, [110/81], 00:01:13, ospf-UNDERLAY-NET, inter
192.168.32.0/24, ubest/mbest: 2/0
    *via 192.168.0.21, Eth1/4, [110/81], 00:21:43, ospf-UNDERLAY-NET, inter
    *via 192.168.0.22, Eth1/3, [110/81], 00:12:08, ospf-UNDERLAY-NET, inter
```

Example 1-33: *The RIB of SS-1.*

One thing that can also be done in ABRs is to use ***not-advertise*** keyword at the end of an ***area [area-id] range [network/mask]*** command. By doing this we can restrict the whole area (Pod) from the Datacenter fabric but that is another story.

Removing OSPF Router from the Datapath

Every now and then there will be a need for some router maintenance operation such as software upgrades. One major advantage of networks build by using Layer 3 only is that it is possible to remove a device from the data-path before taking it out of service. With OSPF this can be done by advertising LSAs with infinite metric 65535. When adjacent OSPF speakers receive LSA with infinite metrics, they will replace the previous LSA with this new one which is not used for SPF calculation. This way the advertising OSPF speaker is removed from the data-path in a controlled manner. This is not possible with Layer 2 Control-Plane protocol namely Spanning-Tree. Spanning-Tree does not have build-in mechanisms for this kind of signaling. The same applies to Port-Channel, removing a port from the port-group can't be signaled beforehand. Even though a Virtualized Switching System has its mechanism for OS upgrade, it is much more complex and more disruptive than the OSPF process described in this section.

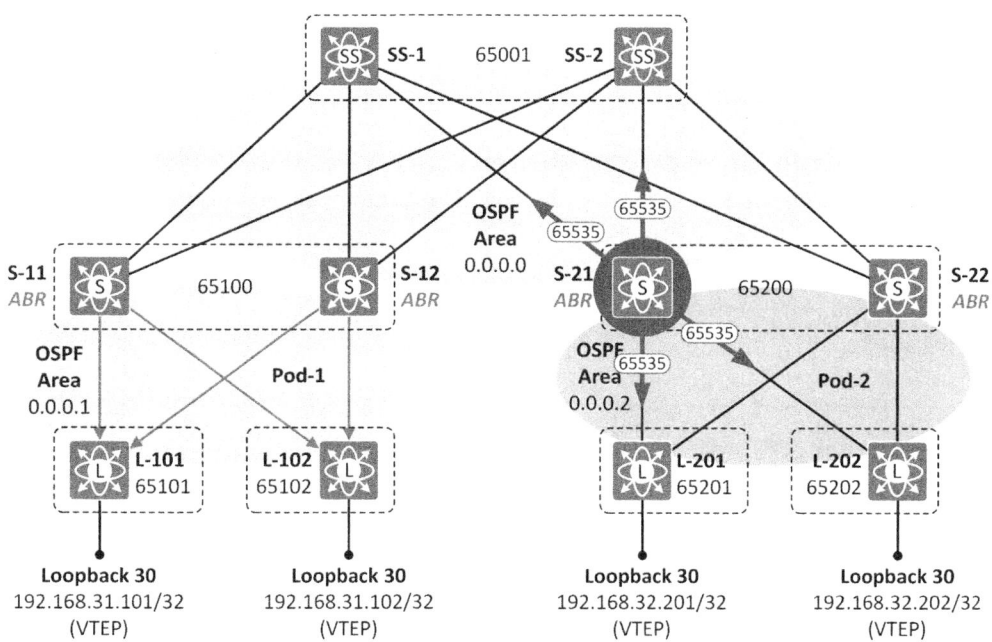

Figure 1-15: *Taken S-21 Out of the Data-Path in a controlled manner with max-metric.*

Example 1-34 shows the RIB of L-201 in a stable situation. All egress traffic is load-balanced between S-21 and S-22.

```
L-201# sh ip route
IP Route Table for VRF "default"
'*' denotes best ucast next-hop
'**' denotes best mcast next-hop
'[x/y]' denotes [preference/metric]
'%<string>' in via output denotes VRF <string>

192.168.0.201/32, ubest/mbest: 2/0, attached
    *via 192.168.0.201, Lo0, [0/0], 02:08:56, local
    *via 192.168.0.201, Lo0, [0/0], 02:08:56, direct
192.168.31.101/32, ubest/mbest: 2/0
    *via 192.168.0.21, Eth1/1, [110/161], 00:00:37, ospf-UNDERLAY-NET, inter
    *via 192.168.0.22, Eth1/2, [110/161], 00:03:04, ospf-UNDERLAY-NET, inter
192.168.31.102/32, ubest/mbest: 2/0
    *via 192.168.0.21, Eth1/1, [110/161], 00:00:37, ospf-UNDERLAY-NET, inter
    *via 192.168.0.22, Eth1/2, [110/161], 00:03:04, ospf-UNDERLAY-NET, inter
192.168.32.201/32, ubest/mbest: 2/0, attached
    *via 192.168.32.201, Lo30, [0/0], 02:08:56, local
    *via 192.168.32.201, Lo30, [0/0], 02:08:56, direct
192.168.32.202/32, ubest/mbest: 2/0
    *via 192.168.0.21, Eth1/1, [110/81], 00:00:37, ospf-UNDERLAY-NET, intra
    *via 192.168.0.22, Eth1/2, [110/81], 00:03:04, ospf-UNDERLAY-NET, intra
```
Example 1-34: *The RIB of L-201.*

Now we take S-21 out of the data-path by using ***max-metric router-lsa*** command under its OSPF process. We can see that S-21 now advertises its P2P link information with infinitive metric 65535. The same operation applies with Summary LSA sent out to area 0.0.0.0.

```
Internet Protocol Version 4, Src: 192.168.0.21, Dst: 224.0.0.5
Open Shortest Path First
    OSPF Header
    LS Update Packet
        Number of LSAs: 1
        LSA-type 1 (Router-LSA), len 48
            .000 0000 0000 0001 = LS Age (seconds): 1
            0... .... .... .... = Do Not Age Flag: 0
            Options: 0x02, (E) External Routing
            LS Type: Router-LSA (1)
            Link State ID: 192.168.0.21
            Advertising Router: 192.168.0.21
            Sequence Number: 0x80000008
            Checksum: 0xa72c
            Length: 48
            Flags: 0x01, (B) Area border router
            Number of Links: 2
            Type: PTP     ID: 192.168.0.202   Data: 0.0.0.3      Metric: 65535
            Type: PTP     ID: 192.168.0.201   Data: 0.0.0.4      Metric: 65535
```
Capture 1-12: *LS Update sent by S-21 generated by S-21 into Area 0.0.0.2.*

Example 1-35 shows that the OSPF LSDB includes Router LSAs from S-21 but now with infinitive metric 65535.

```
L-201# sh ip ospf database 192.168.0.21 detail
        OSPF Router with ID (192.168.0.201) (Process ID UNDERLAY-NET VRF default)

                Router Link States (Area 0.0.0.2)

  LS age: 7
  Options: 0x2 (No TOS-capability, No DC)
  LS Type: Router Links
  Link State ID: 192.168.0.21
  Advertising Router: 192.168.0.21
  LS Seq Number: 0x8000000c
  Checksum: 0x9f30
  Length: 48
  Area border router
   Number of links: 2

    Link connected to: a Router (point-to-point)
    (Link ID) Neighboring Router ID: 192.168.0.202
    (Link Data) Router Interface address: 0.0.0.3
      Number of TOS metrics: 0
       TOS   0 Metric: 65535

    Link connected to: a Router (point-to-point)
    (Link ID) Neighboring Router ID: 192.168.0.201
    (Link Data) Router Interface address: 0.0.0.4
      Number of TOS metrics: 0
       TOS   0 Metric: 65535
```

Example 1-35: The OSPF *LSDB of L-201 After "max-metric router lsa" Command on S-21.*

However, L-201, due to the infinitive metric, removes S-21 as a next-hop for any destination from its RIB.

```
L-201# sh ip route
IP Route Table for VRF "default"
'*' denotes best ucast next-hop
'**' denotes best mcast next-hop
'[x/y]' denotes [preference/metric]
'%<string>' in via output denotes VRF <string>

192.168.0.201/32, ubest/mbest: 2/0, attached
    *via 192.168.0.201, Lo0, [0/0], 02:09:15, local
    *via 192.168.0.201, Lo0, [0/0], 02:09:15, direct
192.168.31.101/32, ubest/mbest: 1/0
    *via 192.168.0.22, Eth1/2, [110/161], 00:03:23, ospf-UNDERLAY-NET, inter
192.168.31.102/32, ubest/mbest: 1/0
    *via 192.168.0.22, Eth1/2, [110/161], 00:03:23, ospf-UNDERLAY-NET, inter
192.168.32.201/32, ubest/mbest: 2/0, attached
    *via 192.168.32.201, Lo30, [0/0], 02:09:15, local
    *via 192.168.32.201, Lo30, [0/0], 02:09:15, direct
192.168.32.202/32, ubest/mbest: 1/0
    *via 192.168.0.22, Eth1/2, [110/81], 00:03:23, ospf-UNDERLAY-NET, intra
```

Example 1-36: *The RIB of L-201 After "max-metric router lsa" Command on S-21.*

This is a standard to signal adjacent OSPF speakers that "hey neighbors, don't send any user data to me anymore". The same behavior can also be done by putting the device in maintenance mode by using the command *isolate* under the OSPF process or putting the device in maintenance mode by using global configuration command *system mode maintenance* that starts a script that gracefully puts every Control-Plane protocol into maintenance mode. Example 1-37 illustrates this process with OSPF.

```
S-21(config)# system mode maintenance

Following configuration will be applied:

router ospf UNDERLAY-NET
  isolate

Do you want to continue (yes/no)? [no] yes

Generating before_maintenance snapshot before going into maintenance mode

Starting to apply commands...

Applying : router ospf UNDERLAY-NET
Applying :   isolate2020 Jul  1 12:31:58.916066 ospf: UNDERLAY-NET [2139]
Maintenance mode is Enabled


Maintenance mode operation successful.

Waiting 120 seconds to allow network re-routing to occur before releasing CLI
.2020 Jul  1 12:32:02 S-21 %$ VDC-1 %$ %MMODE-2-MODE_CHANGED: System changed to
"maintenance" mode.
.....................done
```
Example 1-37: *Starting Maintenace Mode on S-21.*

Note that the OSPF adjacency is not affected.

```
S-21(maint-mode)(config)# sh ip ospf neighbors
OSPF Process ID UNDERLAY-NET VRF default
Total number of neighbors: 4
Neighbor ID     Pri State              Up Time  Address         Interface
192.168.0.201     1 FULL/ -            01:07:55 192.168.0.201   Eth1/1
192.168.0.202     1 FULL/ -            01:07:50 192.168.0.202   Eth1/2
192.168.0.1       1 FULL/ -            01:07:51 192.168.0.1     Eth1/3
192.168.0.2       1 FULL/ -            01:07:52 192.168.0.2     Eth1/4
```
Example 1-38: *OSPF Adjacencies in Maintenance Mode on S-21.*

LSA and SPF timers

This section introduces timers related to Link-State Advertisement and Shortest Path Calculation. Even though these timers can and should be used with default values, it is good to understand what these timers are used for. I am going to use the same old example of link failure between S-22 and L-202 but instead of a link-down event, we now have a flapping link.

LSA Throttling Timer

LSA Throttling Timer helps In a situation where one of the connected links is unstable by delaying self-originated LSAs. Figure 1-16 illustrates the situation from the S-22 perspective (note that flapping link also affects to L-202). The first flap will cause S-22 to send LSA out of OSPF interfaces based on *LSA Throttling Start Time* which default value in NX-OS is 0.00ms. This means that the first LSA will be sent without any delay. *LSA Throttling Hold Time* related to the second LSA defines the actual delay meaning the second LSA will be sent 1000 ms after the first one. The delay of sending the third LSA is calculated by 2 * Hold Time, so in our example, the third LSA will be sent 2 seconds after the second one. The delay of sending the fourth LSA is calculated by 4 * Hold Time, so in our example, the fourth LSA will be sent 4 seconds after the second one. If there is a fifth interface flapping event, the LSA generation is a delay based on *LSA Throttling Maximum Wait Time* that defines the maximum delay for self-originated LSAs. The default values for LSA throttling are (1) Start Time: 0.00 ms, (2) Hold Time: 5000 ms, and (3) Maximum Wait: 5000 ms. I just use Hold Time 1000 ms for the sake of simplicity in this example. The timers will be restarted after 2 * Maximum Wait Time has been elapsed without link failure. Note that L-201 rejects the LSAs about the same instance if they are received at the interval smaller than 1000ms (MinLSArrival).

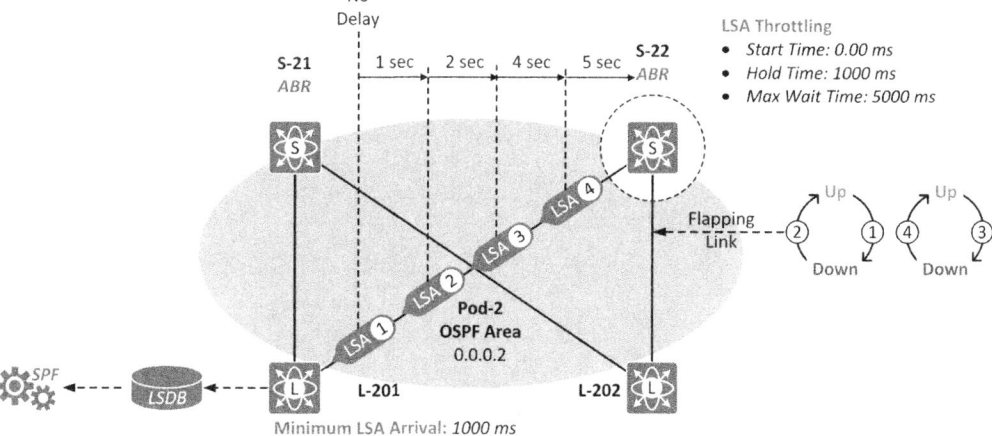

Figure 1-16: *LSA Throttling and MinLSArrival Timers.*

SPF Throttling Timer

SPF Throttling Timer delays the SPF calculation. It uses the same kind of exponential backoff timer than what is used with LSA Throttling. *SPF Throttling Delay Time* defines the time to delay SPF calculation when the first LSA is received. In our example, L-201 waits 200 ms after the first LSA is received. After 200 ms it runs the SPF algorithm. If the next LSA arrives within the next 5000 ms (Maxi Wait Time), L-201 waits 1000 ms for the consequent LSA before the next SPF run. And the same process recurs, if the next LSA arrives within the next 5000 ms, L-201 now delays SPF run by 2000 ms (2 * Hold Time) ms for consequent LSAs. The next delay will be 4000 ms (4 * Hold Time). The SPF Throttling Maximum Wait Time defines the maximum delay between consequence SPF runs. This way L-201 can include more than just one network change in a single SPF calculation. Note that the LSDB is locked during the SPF calculation and LSAs received during calculation will be buffered.

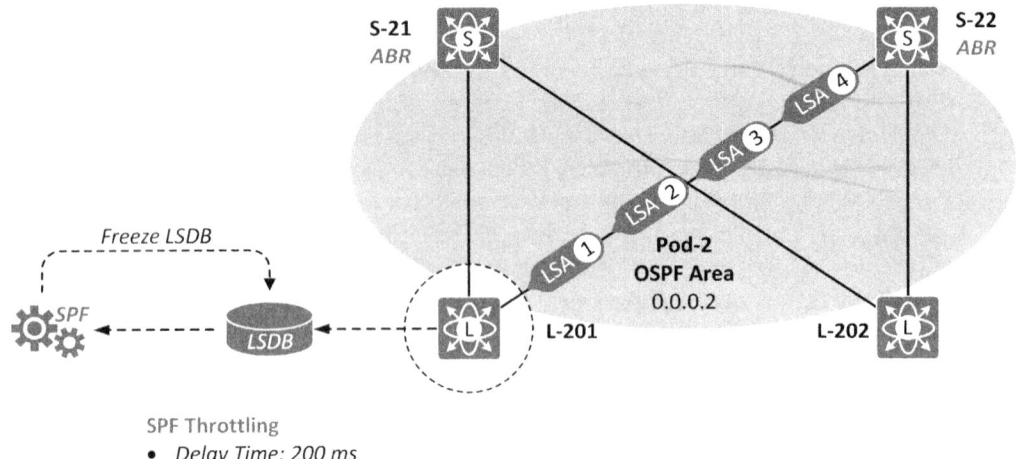

SPF Throttling
- Delay Time: 200 ms
- Hold Time: 1000 ms
- Max Wait Time: 5000 ms

Figure 1-17: *SPF Throttling Timers.*

Flood Pacing Timer

The two consecutive LSAs received from adjacent OSPF speakers are paced by the *Flood Pacing Timer* which default time is 33 ms. In figure 1-18, L-201 floods LSAs received from its adjacent OSPF routers S-22, at the interval of 33 ms out its OSPF interface. You might wonder why this is important because L-201 floods LSAs only from S-22 to S-21 and another way around and those LSAs flooding interval is paced to 33 ms. Also, S-21 and S-22 use LSA throttling for their self-originated LSAs. So it looks like there never will be any need for Flood Pacing Timer. However, in reality, there might be 20 Leaf/ToR switches in one Pod and six Spine switches, then we have a totally different situation, and the need for Flood Pacing Timer is more obvious.

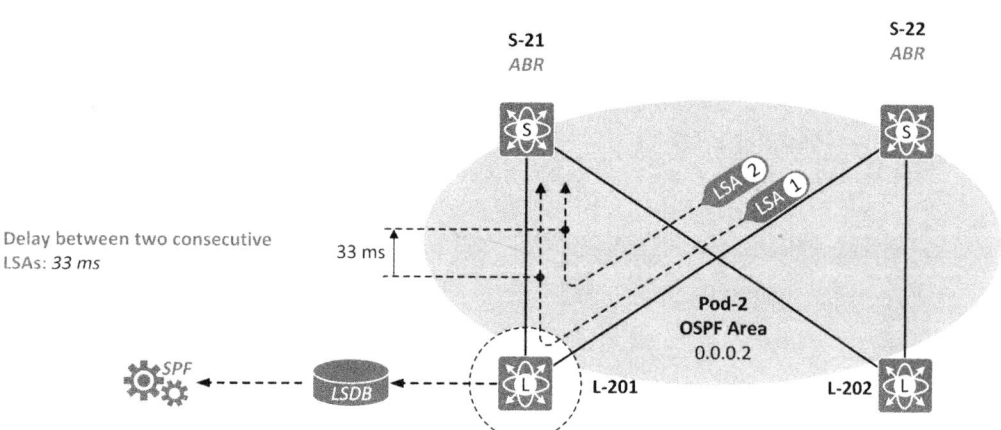

Figure 1-18: *Flood Pacing Timer.*

LSA Group Pacing Timer

All Link-State entries in OSPF LSDB has an individual aging time. The aging time is set to zero by the OSPF speaker that owns the link when the link comes up for the first time. Then it is advertised out of OSPF interfaces. The aging time increases by one every second. In addition, adjacent routers increase aging time by one when they flood the LSA further. The maximum aging time for each LS is 3600 seconds and if the max-age is reached, the LS is removed from the LSDB. The max-age time, however, should not be seen because OSPF uses *Link State Refresh* timer to refresh self-originated LSAs when their age reaches 1800 seconds (Max-Age/2). Advertising each LS individually when its timer reaches 1800 seconds is insufficient and could generate a huge amount of flooding traffic. The solution for this is the *LSA Group Pacing Timer*. In figure 1-19, L-201 has three self-originated LS information in its LSDB. When LS-1 aging time reaches 1800 seconds, L-201 starts the LSA Group Pacing Timer that delays the LSA by 10 seconds. When eight seconds have been elapsed, also LS-2 reaches an aging time in 1800. Then after two seconds, L-201 sends an LSA that carries both LS-1 and LS-2 out of its OSPF interfaces. The LS-3 will be advertised later when its aging time reaches 1800 seconds.

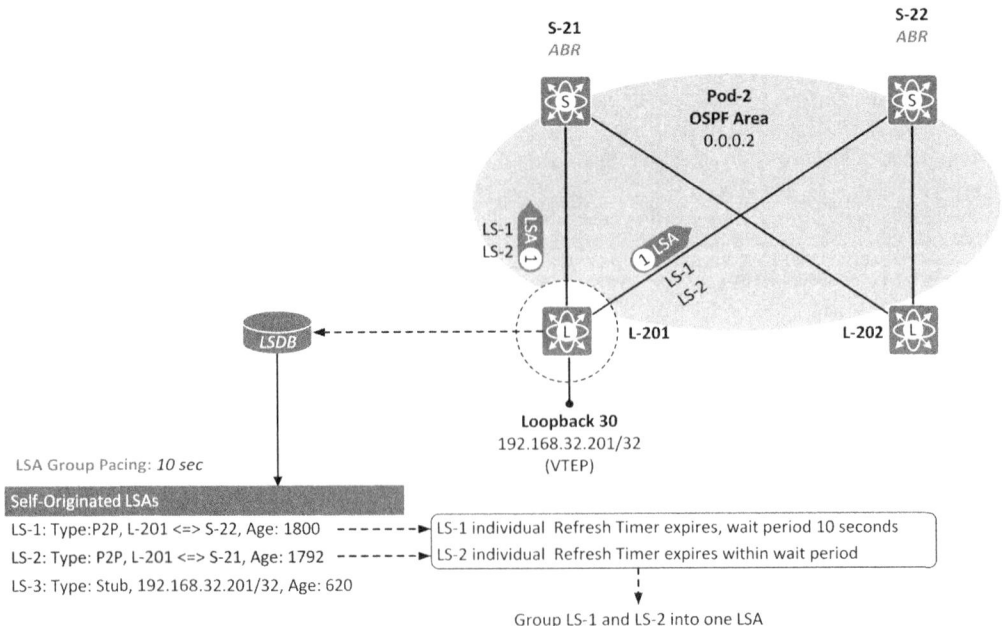

Figure 1-19: *LSA Group pacing.*

Default SPF and timer values used in Cisco NX-OS is described in example 1-39.

```
L-101# sh ip ospf UNDERLAY-NET

Routing Process UNDERLAY-NET with ID 192.168.0.101 VRF default
Routing Process Instance Number 1
Stateful High Availability enabled
Graceful-restart is configured
  Grace period: 60 state: Inactive
  Last graceful restart exit status: None
Supports only single TOS(TOS0) routes
Supports opaque LSA
Administrative distance 110
Reference Bandwidth is 40000 Mbps
SPF throttling delay time of 200.000 msecs,
  SPF throttling hold time of 1000.000 msecs,
  SPF throttling maximum wait time of 5000.000 msecs
LSA throttling start time of 0.000 msecs,
  LSA throttling hold interval of 5000.000 msecs,
  LSA throttling maximum wait time of 5000.000 msecs
Minimum LSA arrival 1000.000 msec
LSA group pacing timer 10 secs
Maximum paths to destination 8
Number of external LSAs 0, checksum sum 0
Number of opaque AS LSAs 0, checksum sum 0
Number of areas is 1, 1 normal, 0 stub, 0 nssa
Number of active areas is 1, 1 normal, 0 stub, 0 nssa
Install discard route for summarized external routes.
Install discard route for summarized internal routes.
Default Passive Interface is enabled
  Area (0.0.0.1)
        Area has existed for 00:53:10
        Interfaces in this area: 3 Active interfaces: 3
        Passive interfaces: 0  Loopback interfaces: 0
        No authentication available
        SPF calculation has run 11 times
          Last SPF ran for 0.001415s
        Area ranges are
        Number of LSAs: 8, checksum sum 0x443aa
```

Example 1-39: *Default OSPF Timers.*

Summary

This chapter explains how OSPF speakers form adjacency and how they run SPF and forms the RIB. This chapter also describes how we can minimize the flooding by splitting the Underlay Network into multiple OSPF areas as well as how we can use summarization between areas. The last part of this section introduces timers related to SPF and LSA.

References

[RFC 2328]   J. Moy., "OSPF Version 2", RFC 2328, April 1998.

OSPF and IS-IS: Choosing an IGP for Large-Scale Networks
ISBN 0-321-16879-8 – Jeff Doyle

Chapter 2: Underlay Network with BGP

Introduction

The focus of this chapter is to explain the BGP Multi-AS Underlay Network design in BGP EVPN/VXLAN Fabric. It starts by explaining the BGP configuration because this way explanation can be done by using show and debug command as well as taking packet captures. The next section discusses of BGP adjacency process and its related states (Idle, Connect/Active, OpenSent, Open Confirm and Established). After that, this chapter explains the BGP routing by discussing how connected routes are sent from RIB to Loc-RIB and from there to Adj-RIB-Out (Pre/Post). This section also introduces how NLRIs received within BGP Update eventually ends up into the RIB of receiving BGP speaker. Besides, this chapter shortly introduces the MRAI timer as well as a non-disruptive device maintenance solution.

Infrastructure AS Numbering and IP Addressing Scheme

The AS-numbering scheme used in this chapter is the same as what was used in chapter 1 but instead of using unnumbered interfaces, each inter-switch interface now has an IP address assigned to it. It is possible to use the Unnumbered interface also with BGP using IPv6 Link-Local addressing [RFC 5549]. However, this solution is not supported by all vendors.

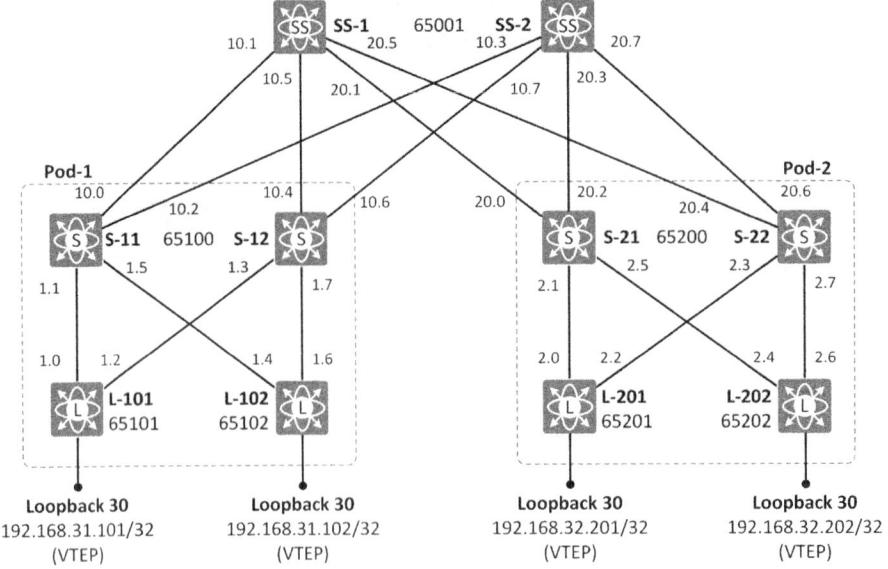

Figure 2-1: *IP addressing Scheme.*

BGP Configuration

Leaf Switches

Example 2-1 shows the BGP configuration of Leaf-101. It has BGP IPv4 peering with S-11 and S-12. BGP is allowed to install eight next-hops with the equal AS-Path length per destination into the BGP Loc-RIB table. In our example, value two would fulfill the requirements but using 8 paths there is no need to change the value when additional spine switches are implemented in the network. The loopback interface that is used in the VXLAN header is redistributed by using a route-map. It could also be redistributed into BGP by using a network clause under the IPv4 address-family but using route-maps we have less unique configuration parameters per VTEP switch. This simplifies the automation. To be able to install multiple paths to one destination, there has to be (a) equal AS-Path attribute count, (b) Equal AS-Path attributes listed in each path. This default behavior means that if the AS-Path count is the same but there are different AS-Path attributes, the paths are not used to load-balance traffic to the destination. This can be relaxed by using the command **bestpath as-path multipath-relax** under the BGP process. In our example, this is not necessary but I have used it because I will demonstrate also the design where Spines have their unique BGP AS-number in chapter 3 (which may not be the best design model. I will explain why later).

```
feature bgp
!
route-map VTEP-TO-BGP permit 10
  match interface loopback30
    redistribute direct route-map VTEP-TO-BGP
!
router bgp 65101
  bestpath as-path multipath-relax
  address-family ipv4 unicast
    redistribute direct route-map VTEP-TO-BGP
    maximum-paths 8
  neighbor 10.10.1.1
    remote-as 65100
    address-family ipv4 unicast
  neighbor 10.10.1.3
    remote-as 65100
    address-family ipv4 unicast
```

Example 2-1: *Leaf-101 BGP configuration.*

Spine Switches

Example 2-2 shows the BGP configuration of S-11 and S-12. Instead of statically configured BGP peering with any Leaf or Super-Spine switches, Spine-11 is passively waiting for BGP connection from BGP speakers using source address from the network 10.10.0.0/16 and which are located in the BGP AS listed in route-map. This shortens the BGP configuration of Spine switches because there is no need for building individual BGP peering configuration with every Leaf switches within the pod, and with Super-Spine switches. Commands *bestpath as-path multipath-relax* and *maximum-paths 8* are also used in Spine switches and Super-Spine switches.

```
feature bgp
!
route-map Dynamic-BGP-AS-List permit 10
  match as-number 65001, 65101, 65102
!
router bgp 65100
  bestpath as-path multipath-relax
  address-family ipv4 unicast
    maximum-paths 8
  neighbor 10.10.0.0/16 remote-as route-map Dynamic-BGP-AS-List
    address-family ipv4 unicast
```
Example 2-2: *Spine-11 BGP configuration.*

Super-Spine Switches

Example 2-3 shows the BGP configuration of SS-1. It has BGP IPv4 peering with all Spine-switches. It also has the same BGP ECMP related commands that are already discussed.

```
feature bgp

router bgp 65001
  bestpath as-path multipath-relax
  address-family ipv4 unicast
    maximum-paths 8
  neighbor 10.10.10.0
    remote-as 65100
    address-family ipv4 unicast
  neighbor 10.10.10.4
    remote-as 65100
    address-family ipv4 unicast
  neighbor 10.10.20.0
    remote-as 65200
```

```
    address-family ipv4 unicast
 neighbor 10.10.20.4
    remote-as 65200
    address-family ipv4 unicast
```

Example 2-3: Super-*Spine-1 BGP configuration.*

BGP Neighbor Process

BGP Adjacency negotiation goes through the Idle, Connect/Active, OpenSent, OpenConfirm, and Established states. This section describes each of these states and the events that trigger changes from one state to another. Figure 2-2 illustrates the processes up to TCP-session establishment.

Idle

In the Idle state, the local BGP speaker is waiting for the Start-event. It does not accept incoming BGP connection from the peer, nor allocate any BGP resources to the peer. For the reaction to the Start-event, the local BGP speaker will start the initialization of TCP connection either actively or passively.

Connect

ManualStart (event 1): An administrator starts the BGP peer connection manually. After that, the local system starts sending and listening to TCP SYN from/to port 179. This event can be started e.g. with basic BGP neighbor configuration under the BGP process. This is what happens in L-101.

AutomaticStart (event 3): Same as Event 1, except the event starts automatically. This could happen for example if the administrator of the remote BGP speaker clears the BGP peering with the local system.

For the reaction to the event 1 (ManualStart) and event 3 (AutomaticStart), the BGP-FSM changes state from Idle to Connect, where the local system is waiting for the TCP-connection to be completed.

Active

ManualStart_with_PassiveTcpEstablishment (event 4): BGP connection started manually by an administrator, but the local system waits for a TCP SYN packet to port 179 from the remote BGP speaker. This can be done e.g. by setting transport mode to passive (1) or by using BGP Dynamic Neighbor solution (2). S-11 uses the BGP Dynamic Neighbor solution.

(1) neighbor 2001:DB8::915:9 transport connection-mode passive
(2) bgp listen range 10.10.0.0/16 remote-as route-map Dynamic-BGP-AS-List

AutomaticStart_with_PassiveTcpEstablihment (event 5): The local system waits passively the TCP connection from a remote peer as in event 4. The start event happens automatically like in event 3.

Reaction to either event 4 (ManualStart_with_PassiveTcpEstablishment) or event 5 (AutomaticStart_ with_PassiveTcpEstablishment) the state is changed from Idle to Active where the local system is passively waiting for a TCP-connection to be completed.

Finalizing negotiation of the TCP connection

Finalizing the TCP connection from either Connect/Active state follows the same procedure. In our example, there are four events related to the TCP three-way handshake started by an active peer L-101. The events related to the TCP 3-way Handshake process are described below:

TcpConnection_Valid (Event 14): This event occurs when the local system receives a TCP Connection Request (TCP SYN) from the peer BGP speaker with a valid source address (configured as a neighbor) and it is destined to the address that the local system uses as a source in BGP negotiation. In addition, the destination TCP port should be 179.

Tcp_CR_Invalid (Event 15): This event occurs when the local system receives a TCP Connection Request (TCP SYN) from the remote BGP speaker and the validity check does not pass.

Tcp_CR_Acked (Event 16): This event indicates that the local system has sent an ACK message to the remote peer as a confirmation of the SYN-ACK message sent by the remote peer.

TcpConnectionConfirmed (Event 17): This event indicates that the local system has received ACK messages from the peer BGP speaker.

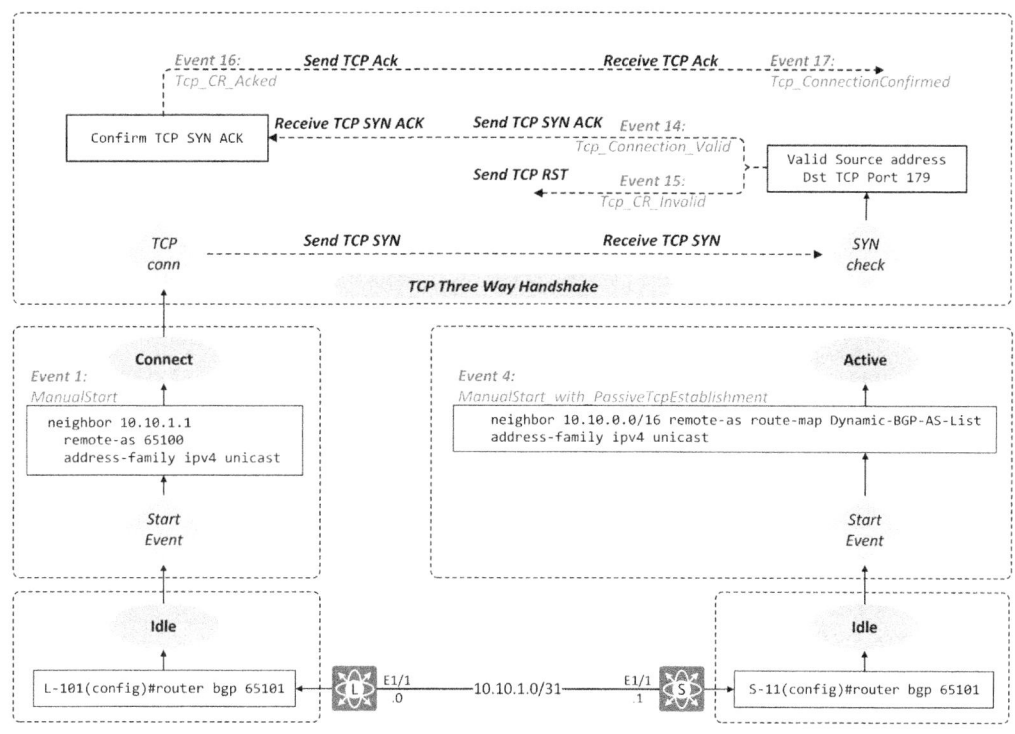

Figure 2-2: *BGP Adjacency: Idle – Connect/Active (Establishing TCP Connection).*

Capture 2-1 shows the TCP-SYN message sent by L-101. The destination TCP port is 179, and the source port has randomly generated number 20376. L-101 generates the sequence number 1716573727. This number increased by the *Next sequence number value* (1) is the value that L-101 expects to be seen in the SYN-ACK message from S-11.

```
Internet Protocol Version 4, Src: 10.10.1.0, Dst: 10.10.1.1
Transmission Control Protocol, Src Port: 20376, Dst Port: 179, Seq: 0, Len: 0
    Source Port: 20376
    Destination Port: 179
    [Stream index: 1]
    [TCP Segment Len: 0]
    Sequence number: 0    (relative sequence number)
    Sequence number (raw): 1716573727
    [Next sequence number: 1    (relative sequence number)]
    Acknowledgment number: 0
    Acknowledgment number (raw): 0
    1010 .... = Header Length: 40 bytes (10)
    Flags: 0x002 (SYN)
    Window size value: 29200
    [Calculated window size: 29200]
    Checksum: 0x3cca [unverified]
    <snipped for brevity>
```

Capture 2-1: *BGP Adjacency – TCP SYN from L101 to S-11.*

Capture 2-2 shows the SYN-ACK message sent by S-11. It uses TCP source port 179 while the destination port is set to 20376. S-11 uses the same value in its Acknowledgement number field than what L-101 used as a Sequence number in its SYN message.

```
Internet Protocol Version 4, Src: 10.10.1.1, Dst: 10.10.1.0
Transmission Control Protocol, Src Port: 179, Dst Port: 20376, Seq: 0, Ack: 1, Len: 0
    Source Port: 179
    Destination Port: 20376
    [Stream index: 1]
    [TCP Segment Len: 0]
    Sequence number: 0    (relative sequence number)
    Sequence number (raw): 1088502133
    [Next sequence number: 1    (relative sequence number)]
    Acknowledgment number: 1    (relative ack number)
    Acknowledgment number (raw): 1716573728
    1010 .... = Header Length: 40 bytes (10)
    Flags: 0x012 (SYN, ACK)
    Window size value: 28960
    [Calculated window size: 28960]
    Checksum: 0xd01c [unverified]
    <snipped for brevity>
```
Capture 2-2: *BGP Adjacency – TCP SYN-ACK from S-11 to L-101.*

When L-101 receives SYN-ACK from S-11, it finalizes the connection by sending ACK messages back to S-11. As in previous steps, the Acknowledgement number is the Sequence number received in SYN-ACK increased by one.

```
Internet Protocol Version 4, Src: 10.10.1.0, Dst: 10.10.1.1
Transmission Control Protocol, Src Port: 20376, Dst Port: 179, Seq: 1, Ack: 1, Len: 0
    Source Port: 20376
    Destination Port: 179
    [Stream index: 1]
    [TCP Segment Len: 0]
    Sequence number: 1    (relative sequence number)
    Sequence number (raw): 1716573728
    [Next sequence number: 1    (relative sequence number)]
    Acknowledgment number: 1    (relative ack number)
    Acknowledgment number (raw): 1088502134
    1000 .... = Header Length: 32 bytes (8)
    Flags: 0x010 (ACK)
    Window size value: 7300
    [Calculated window size: 29200]
    [Window size scaling factor: 4]
    Checksum: 0x537e [unverified]
        <snipped for brevity>
```
Capture 2-3: *BGP Adjacency – TCP ACK from L-101 to S-11.*

OpenSent and OpenConfirm

After successful TCP negotiation, the BGP speakers exchange BGP OPEN messages to ensure that, they use the same version of BGP, their BGP RIDs don't overlap, the peer BGP AS number is the same that is used in with this BGP speaker, and that they support the same set of capabilities (*Event 19 - BGPOpen*). They also compare *HoldTime* (that is used also when calculating *KeepAliveTime*) values and they choose the smaller one if values are not the same. If the check is fine, the state will be changed to *OpenConfirm*, and the local system sends a KEEPALIVE message to the remote peer. After receiving a KEEPALIVE message from the remote peer as a response to event 26 (KeepAliveMsg), the local system finalizes the BGP connection and changes the BGP state from *OpenSent* to *Established*.

Established

In this state, BGP peering is up and running and BGP neighbors can send and receive UPDATE, KEEPALIVE, and NOTIFICATION messages. All received UPDATE messages are validated. An example of the validation is a next-hop reachability checking. The Next-hop address must be other than the receiving BGP speaker's address. If peers are directly connected eBGP neighbors, the next-hop address has to be either the sender's IP address that is used in BGP neighbor negotiation or it has to be from the same network segment than the receivers IP-address (e.g. in the case of BGP redirect). The last rule is relaxed in an Overlay Network in BGP EVPN Fabric where spine switches are configured to retain the original next-hop for L2VPN EVPN afi NLRIs advertised within BGP Update. The reason for that is that the next-hop is used in the VXLAN tunnel header as a destination IP address that is used by spine switches when they route packets between VTEPs.

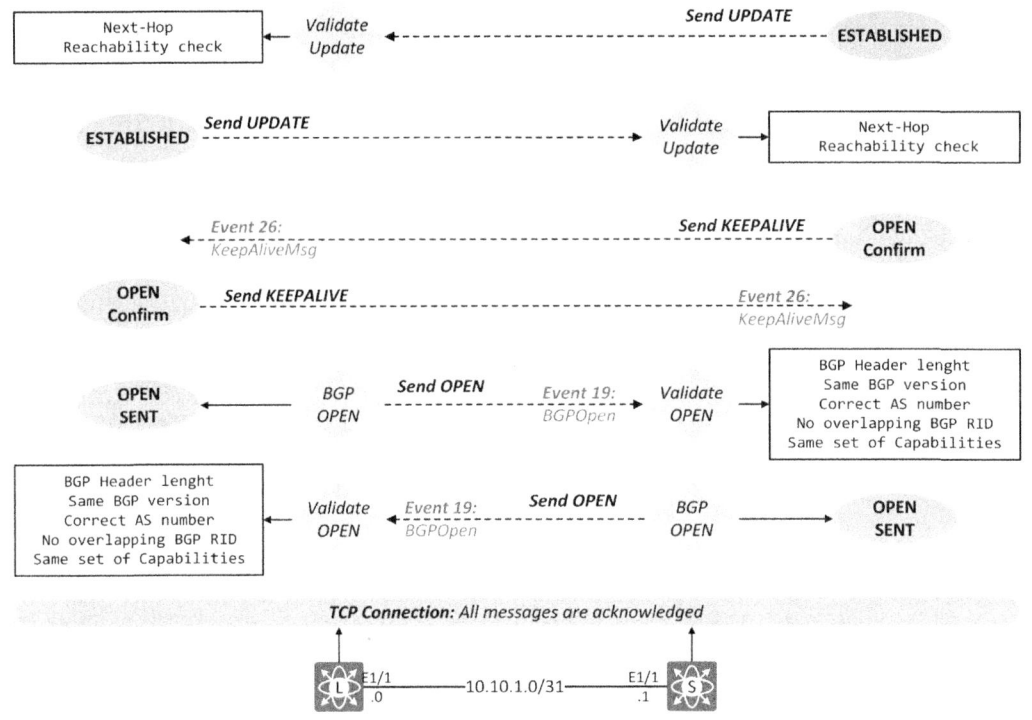

Figure 2-3: *BGP Adjacency – OpenSent, OpenConfirm, and Established.*

Captures from 2-4 to 2-9 show the BGP Open message exchanged between L-101 and S-11.

```
Internet Protocol Version 4, Src: 10.10.1.1, Dst: 10.10.1.0
Transmission Control Protocol, Src Port: 179, Dst Port: 20376, Seq: 1, Ack: 1, Len: 70
<snipped>
Border Gateway Protocol - OPEN Message
    Marker: ffffffffffffffffffffffffffffffff
    Length: 70
    Type: OPEN Message (1)
    Version: 4
    My AS: 65100
    Hold Time: 180
    BGP Identifier: 192.168.0.11
    Optional Parameters Length: 41
    Optional Parameters
```

Capture 2-4: *BGP Adjacency – BGP Open Message sent by S-11.*

```
Internet Protocol Version 4, Src: 10.10.1.0, Dst: 10.10.1.1
Transmission Control Protocol, Src Port: 20376, Dst Port: 179, Seq:1, Ack:71, Len: 70
    <snipped>
Border Gateway Protocol - OPEN Message
    Marker: ffffffffffffffffffffffffffffffff
    Length: 70
    Type: OPEN Message (1)
    Version: 4
    My AS: 65101
    Hold Time: 180
    BGP Identifier: 192.168.0.101
    Optional Parameters Length: 41
    Optional Parameters
```

Capture 2-5: *BGP Adjacency – BGP Open Message sent by L-101.*

```
Internet Protocol Version 4, Src: 10.10.1.1, Dst: 10.10.1.0
Transmission Control Protocol, Src Port: 179, Dst Port: 20376, Seq:71, Ack:90, Len: 19
    <snipped>
Border Gateway Protocol - KEEPALIVE Message
    Marker: ffffffffffffffffffffffffffffffff
    Length: 19
    Type: KEEPALIVE Message (4)
```

Capture 2-6: *BGP Adjacency – BGP KeepAlive Message sent by S-11.*

```
Internet Protocol Version 4, Src: 10.10.1.0, Dst: 10.10.1.1
Transmission Control Protocol, Src Port: 20376, Dst Port: 179, Seq:71, Ack:71, Len: 19
    <snipped>
Border Gateway Protocol - KEEPALIVE Message
    Marker: ffffffffffffffffffffffffffffffff
    Length: 19
    Type: KEEPALIVE Message (4)
```

Capture 2-7: *BGP Adjacency – BGP KeepAlive Message sent by L-101.*

```
Transmission Control Protocol, Src Port: 179, Dst Port: 20376, Seq:90, Ack:90, Len: 48
    <snipped>
Border Gateway Protocol - UPDATE Message
    Marker: ffffffffffffffffffffffffffffffff
    Length: 29
    Type: UPDATE Message (2)
    Withdrawn Routes Length: 0
    Total Path Attribute Length: 6
    Path attributes
        Path Attribute - MP_UNREACH_NLRI
            Flags: 0x80, Optional, Non-transitive, Complete
            Type Code: MP_UNREACH_NLRI (15)
            Length: 3
            Address family identifier (AFI): IPv4 (1)
            Subsequent address family identifier (SAFI): Unicast (1)
            Withdrawn routes (0 bytes)
Border Gateway Protocol - KEEPALIVE Message
    Marker: ffffffffffffffffffffffffffffffff
    Length: 19
    Type: KEEPALIVE Message (4)
```

Capture 2-8: *BGP Adjacency – BGP Update and KeepAlive Message sent by S-11.*

```
Internet Protocol Version 4, Src: 10.10.1.0, Dst: 10.10.1.1
Transmission Control Protocol, Src Port:20376, Dst Port: 179, Seq:90, Ack:138, Len:109
    <snipped>
Border Gateway Protocol - UPDATE Message
    Marker: ffffffffffffffffffffffffffffffff
    Length: 61
    Type: UPDATE Message (2)
    Withdrawn Routes Length: 0
    Total Path Attribute Length: 38
    Path attributes
        Path Attribute - ORIGIN: INCOMPLETE
            Flags: 0x40, Transitive, Well-known, Complete
            Type Code: ORIGIN (1)
            Length: 1
            Origin: INCOMPLETE (2)
        Path Attribute - AS_PATH: 65101
            Flags: 0x40, Transitive, Well-known, Complete
            Type Code: AS_PATH (2)
            Length: 6
            AS Path segment: 65101
        Path Attribute - MULTI_EXIT_DISC: 0
            Flags: 0x80, Optional, Non-transitive, Complete
            Type Code: MULTI_EXIT_DISC (4)
            Length: 4
            Multiple exit discriminator: 0
        Path Attribute - MP_REACH_NLRI
            Flags: 0x90, Optional, Extended-Length, Non-transitive, Complete
            Type Code: MP_REACH_NLRI (14)
            Length: 14
            Address family identifier (AFI): IPv4 (1)
            Subsequent address family identifier (SAFI): Unicast (1)
            Next hop network address (4 bytes)
            Number of Subnetwork points of attachment (SNPA): 0
            Network layer reachability information (5 bytes)
                192.168.31.101/32
                    MP Reach NLRI prefix length: 32
                    MP Reach NLRI IPv4 prefix: 192.168.31.101
Border Gateway Protocol - UPDATE Message
    Marker: ffffffffffffffffffffffffffffffff
    Length: 29
    Type: UPDATE Message (2)
    Withdrawn Routes Length: 0
    Total Path Attribute Length: 6
    Path attributes
        Path Attribute - MP_UNREACH_NLRI
            Flags: 0x80, Optional, Non-transitive, Complete
            Type Code: MP_UNREACH_NLRI (15)
            Length: 3
            Address family identifier (AFI): IPv4 (1)
            Subsequent address family identifier (SAFI): Unicast (1)
            Withdrawn routes (0 bytes)
Border Gateway Protocol - KEEPALIVE Message
    Marker: ffffffffffffffffffffffffffffffff
    Length: 19
    Type: KEEPALIVE Message (4)
```

Capture 2-9: *BGP Adjacency – BGP Update and KeepAlive Message sent by L-101.*

BGP NLRI Update Process

Figure 2-4 illustrates the process of how BGP Network Layer Reachability Information (NLRI) about L-101 loopback 31 is propagated from L-101 to S-11.

RIB to Adj-RIB-Out (Pre-Policy)

The IP address 192.168.31.101/32 of Loopback 31 is redistributed from the RIB to the BGP Loc-RIB using route-map. When the route is redistributed from the RIB to the Loc-RIB, the route itself is encoded as MP_REACH_NLRI Path Attribute with other IPv4 Unicast peer specific BGP Path Attributes, such as ORIGIN, AS_PATH, and MED. The IPv4 address 192.168.31.101/32 is then sent from Loc-RIB to Adj-RIB-Out (Pre-Policy) of all BGP peers witch L-101 has IPv4 Unicast (AFI 1/SAFI 1) peering and are either eBGP, iBGP, RR-Client or Confederation peers. The reason why I mentioned all those four peer types is that there are some cases when IPv4 Unicast NLRI is not sent out to Adj-RIB-Out (Pre-Policy) even though the peering is IPv4 Unicast. One simple example is NLRI received from iBGP peers is not advertised to other iBGP peers. Some implementation also does not forward NLRIs from eBGP peer to another eBGP peer if the AS_Path Path Attribute in ingress BGP Update includes the same AS number than what is the BGP AS of the eBGP egress peer. BGP Path Attributes are not modified when programmed from Loc-RIB into Adj-RIB-Out (Pre-Policy). L-101, in our example, sends information to Adj-RIB-Out (Pre) of the eBGP peers S-11 and S-12 (not shown in the figure).

Adj-RIB-Out (Pre) to Adj-RIB-Out (Post)

The Adj-RIB-Out (Pre-Policy) equals the Loc-RIB but it only includes routes that are eligible for each neighbor. L-101 send an NLRI about 192.168.31.101/32 from the Adj-RIB-Out (Pre-Policy) to Adj-RIB-Out (Post-Policy) through the BGP Policy-Engine (Outbound Policy). During this process the NLRI itself might be included in some aggregate address, its BGP Path_Attributes might be modified, or new Path_Attributes cloud be added (e.g. communities). The NLRI might even be filtered out from the BGP Update. In our case, L-101 doesn't modify or filter routes in any way, both Adj-RIB-Out tables are equal. The Next-Hop IP Address in Path Attribute MP_REACH_NLRI is set as an IP address that is used for BGP peering when L-101 sends BGP Update to S-11.

Adj-RIB-In (Post) to Adj-RIB-In (Pre)

When S-11 receives the BGP Update about 192.168.31.101/32 from L-101, it installs the NLRI into Adj-RIB-In (Pre-Policy) without any modification. Then the NLRI is sent through the Policy-Engine (Inbound Policy) to Adj-RIB-In (Post-Policy). During the process, there might be some modifications like adding Local-Preference, Weight, or filtering based on some Path Attribute.

Adj-RIB-In (Pre) to Loc-RIB

Loc-RIB contains the NLRIs received from Adj-RIB-In (Post-Policy). The same NLRI might be received from several BGP peers and all of them are installed into Loc-RIB but only one of them is selected as the best route. In the case of BGP ECMP there might be several BGP peers installed as a next-hop (multipathing) and traffic to the destination is flow-based load-balanced between next-hops. The BGP Best Path Selection process compares all NLRIs which has valid Next-Hop (found in RIB) and doesn't have the same local AS in its AS_Path Path Attribute. The latter one is the BGP loop prevention mechanism. After selecting best path eligible NLRIs, the best path selection process compares each NLRIs Path Attribute in this order (1) Highest Weight, (2) Highest Local-Preference, (3) prefer locally originated prefixes, (4) Shortest AS_Path attribute length, (5) prefer IGP < EGP < Incomplete, (6) lowest MED, (7). In the case of each Path Attributes are equal the decision process prefers (8) eBGP over iBGP, (9) the smallest IGP metric to Next-Hop, (10), and as a last step prefer the path through the neighbor that has the lowest BGP RID. From the S-11 perspective, there is only one path to 192.168.31.101/32 via L-101.

Loc-RIB to RIB

This process is simple, routes installed into Loc-RIB are installed into RIB if there are no better route sources for the specific route. Note! BGP does not flood BGP Updates to adjacent BGP peers, instead, it constructs BGP Updates only routes installed into its RIB, no matter how they are ended up there. This means that ingress BGP Updates are processed like described in this section and then reconstructed when sending to adjacent BGP speakers.

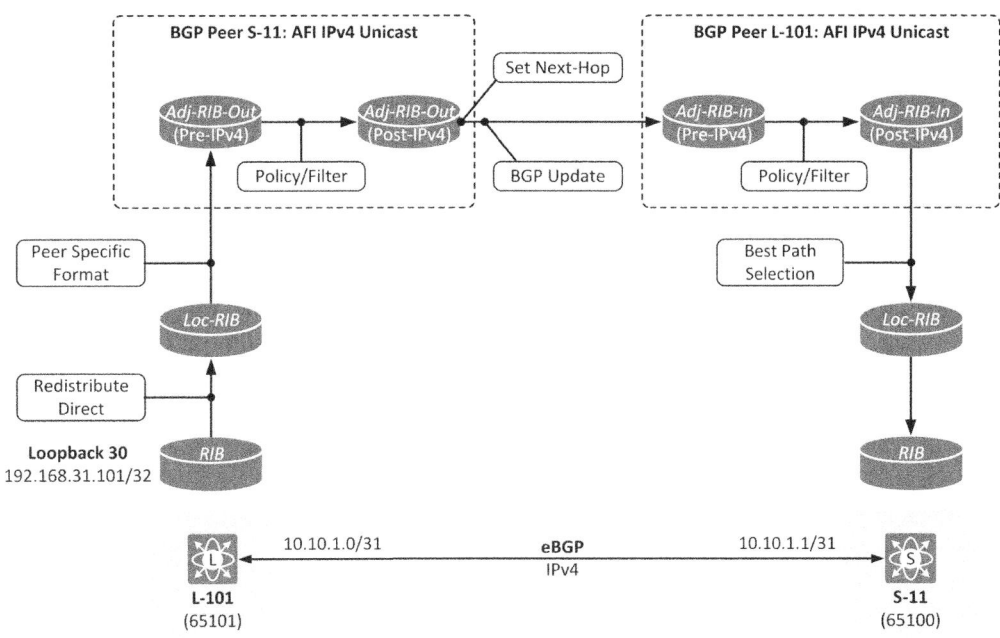

Figure 2-4: *BGP NLRI Advertisement Process.*

Example 2-4 shows the RIB entry about 192.168.31.101 in L-101.

```
L-101# sh ip route 192.168.31.101 | sec 192
192.168.31.101/32, ubest/mbest: 2/0, attached
    *via 192.168.31.101, Lo30, [0/0], 01:43:30, local
    *via 192.168.31.101, Lo30, [0/0], 01:43:30, direct
```
Example 2-4: *The RIB of L-101.*

Example 2-5 shows BGP Loc-RIB about the same IP address. The NLRI is advertised to both spine switches: S-11 (10.10.1.1), and S-12 (10.10.1.3).

```
L-101# sh ip bgp 192.168.31.101
BGP routing table information for VRF default, address family IPv4 Unicast
BGP routing table entry for 192.168.31.101/32, version 2
Paths: (1 available, best #1)
Flags: (0x080002) (high32 00000000) on xmit-list, is not in urib
Multipath: eBGP

  Advertised path-id 1
  Path type: redist, path is valid, is best path, no labeled nexthop
  AS-Path: NONE, path locally originated
    0.0.0.0 (metric 0) from 0.0.0.0 (192.168.0.101)
      Origin incomplete, MED 0, localpref 100, weight 32768

  Path-id 1 advertised to peers:
    10.10.1.1         10.10.1.3
```
Example 2-5: *The RIB of L-101.*

Capture 2-10 illustrates the BGP Update sent by L-101 to S-11. The ORIGIN Path Attribute is incomplete because the route is redistributed into BGP. AS_PATH Path Attribute is set to 65101. The Path Attribute MULTI_EXIT_DISC is set to zero. The Path Attribute MP_REACH_NLRI carries the actual routing information. It describes the destination network/host IP address and its next-hop. Because BGP runs over TCP, all messages are also expected to be acknowledged by the receiver.

```
Internet Protocol Version 4, Src: 10.10.1.0, Dst: 10.10.1.1
Transmission Control Protocol, Src Port:29243, Dst Port:179, Seq:90, Ack:328, Len: 109
Border Gateway Protocol - UPDATE Message
    Marker: ffffffffffffffffffffffffffffffff
    Length: 61
    Type: UPDATE Message (2)
    Withdrawn Routes Length: 0
    Total Path Attribute Length: 38
    Path attributes
        Path Attribute - ORIGIN: INCOMPLETE
            Flags: 0x40, Transitive, Well-known, Complete
            Type Code: ORIGIN (1)
            Length: 1
            Origin: INCOMPLETE (2)
        Path Attribute - AS_PATH: 65101
            Flags: 0x40, Transitive, Well-known, Complete
            Type Code: AS_PATH (2)
            Length: 6
            AS Path segment: 65101
        Path Attribute - MULTI_EXIT_DISC: 0
            Flags: 0x80, Optional, Non-transitive, Complete
            Type Code: MULTI_EXIT_DISC (4)
            Length: 4
            Multiple exit discriminator: 0
        Path Attribute - MP_REACH_NLRI
            Flags: 0x90, Optional, Extended-Length, Non-transitive, Complete
            Type Code: MP_REACH_NLRI (14)
            Length: 14
            Address family identifier (AFI): IPv4 (1)
            Subsequent address family identifier (SAFI): Unicast (1)
            Next hop network address (4 bytes)
                Next Hop: 10.10.1.0
            Number of Subnetwork points of attachment (SNPA): 0
            Network layer reachability information (5 bytes)
                192.168.31.101/32
```

Capture 2-10: *BGP Update Message sent by L-101.*

Example 2-6 shows that S-11 has installed the NLRI in its Loc-RIB. Note that the Weight attribute is set to zero by default while in originating router L-101 it was set to 32768. The NLRI information is also advertised to all eBGP peers of S-11: L-102 (10.10.1.4), SS-1 (10.10.10.1), and SS-2 (10.10.10.3)

```
S-11# sh ip bgp 192.168.31.101
BGP routing table information for VRF default, address family IPv4 Unicast
BGP routing table entry for 192.168.31.101/32, version 9
Paths: (1 available, best #1)
Flags: (0x8008001a) (high32 00000000) on xmit-list, is in urib, is best urib rou
te, is in HW
Multipath: eBGP

  Advertised path-id 1
  Path type: external, path is valid, is best path, no labeled nexthop, in rib
  AS-Path: 65101 , path sourced external to AS
    10.10.1.0 (metric 0) from 10.10.1.0 (192.168.0.101)
      Origin incomplete, MED 0, localpref 100, weight 0

  Path-id 1 advertised to peers:
    10.10.1.4          10.10.10.1         10.10.10.3
```

Example 2-6: *BGP table entry about 192.168.31.101 on S-11 Loc-RIB.*

Example 2-7 shows that S-11 has installed routing information about 192.168.31.101/32 into the RIB.

```
S-11# sh ip route 192.168.31.101
IP Route Table for VRF "default"
'*' denotes best ucast next-hop
'**' denotes best mcast next-hop
'[x/y]' denotes [preference/metric]
'%<string>' in via output denotes VRF <string>

192.168.31.101/32, ubest/mbest: 1/0
   *via 10.10.1.0, [20/0], 00:05:06, bgp-65100, external, tag 65101
```

Example 2-7: *RIB entry about 192.168.31.101 on RIB of S-11.*

Example 2-8 shows that L-202 located in remote Pod-2 has two equal-cost paths to destination 192.168.31.101/32

```
L-202# sh ip route 192.168.31.101
IP Route Table for VRF "default"
'*' denotes best ucast next-hop
'**' denotes best mcast next-hop
'[x/y]' denotes [preference/metric]
'%<string>' in via output denotes VRF <string>

192.168.31.101/32, ubest/mbest: 2/0
   *via 10.10.2.5, [20/0], 02:17:03, bgp-65202, external, tag 65200
   *via 10.10.2.7, [20/0], 02:17:03, bgp-65202, external, tag 65200
```

Example 2-8: *RIB entry about 192.168.31.101 on RIB of L-102.*

BGP Update: Unreachable Destination

Figure 2-5 illustrates the Inter-Switch link failure event between S-11 and L-101. The reaction time depends on the type of link failure and how fast S-11 notifies and reacts to it. If the failure is for example only in a fiber's Transmit pair or some odd SFP failure and reaction is based on HoldDown and Keepalive timers, the reaction time might take some time. However, using Bidirectional Forwarding Detection (BFD) between BGP neighbors, the failure is noticed almost immediately. Using BFD is the best practice. When S-11 notices that the link where the route to 192.168.31.101/32 was received is down, it checks the BGP Loc-RIB if the destination is available through some other BGP peer. In our case, L-101 was the only route source, so the BGP process notifies the RIB to remove the route learned from the BGP. When the route is removed from the RIB and Loc-RIB, S-11 withdraws the route from al of its peers. When BGP neighbors receive the BGP Update with MP-UNREACH-NLRI Path Attribute, they remove the destination described in the "withdrawn routes" attribute.

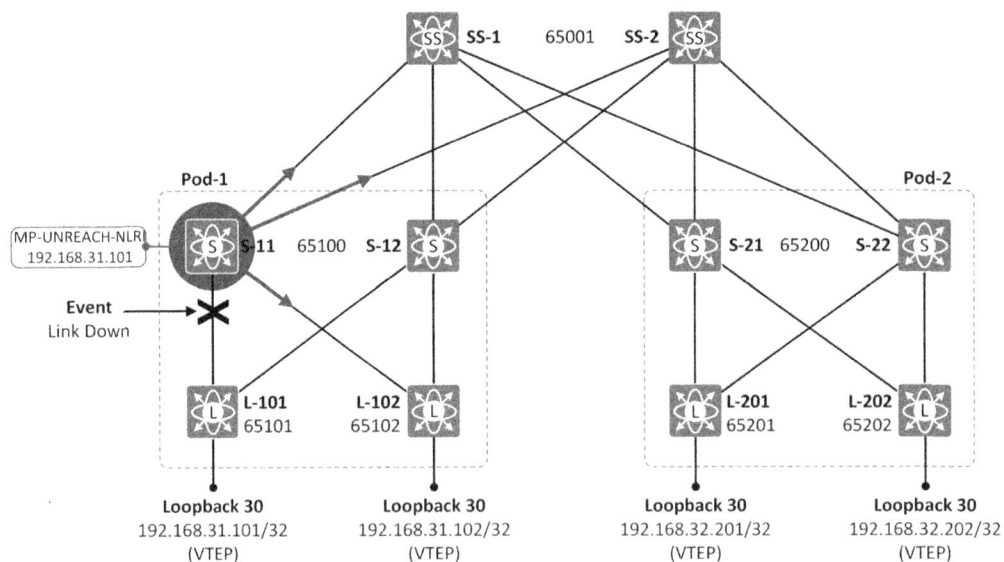

Figure 2-5: *S-11 Reaction to Link-Failure Event.*

The capture 2-11 shows the BGP Update message with MP-UNREACH-NLRI Path Attribute sent by S-11 to SS-1.

```
Internet Protocol Version 4, Src: 10.10.10.0, Dst: 10.10.10.1
Transmission Control Protocol, Src Port: 179, Dst Port: 21728, Seq: 20, Ack: 1, Len:35
Border Gateway Protocol - UPDATE Message
    Marker: ffffffffffffffffffffffffffffffff
    Length: 35
    Type: UPDATE Message (2)
    Withdrawn Routes Length: 0
    Total Path Attribute Length: 12
    Path attributes
        Path Attribute - MP_UNREACH_NLRI
            Flags: 0x90, Optional, Extended-Length, Non-transitive, Complete
            Type Code: MP_UNREACH_NLRI (15)
            Length: 8
            Address family identifier (AFI): IPv4 (1)
            Subsequent address family identifier (SAFI): Unicast (1)
            Withdrawn routes (5 bytes)
                192.168.31.101/32
                    MP Unreach NLRI prefix length: 32
                    MP Unreach NLRI IPv4 prefix: 192.168.31.101
```

Capture 2-11: *The IP address 192.168.31.101/32 was withdrawn by S-11.*

MRAI Timer

The *MinRouteAdvertisementInterval* Timer (MRAI) defines the time of how often NLRI advertisement/withdrawn received from one peer about the same destination can be sent to another peer. This timer is peer specific. RFC 4271 states that the iBGP timer should be faster than eBGP because inside an area w need faster convergence time. However, in the modern Datacenter, MRAI should be set to zero for both peering types [BGP MRAI]. Nexus switches use MRAI value zero by default and it can't be changed.

BGP AS-Path Prepend

There are several options to remove BGP Speaker from the data-path in a controlled manner, the neighbors can put in shut-down mode, the BGP process can be isolated or AS-Path advertised by the router can be prepended. The focus of this section is in AS-Path prepending solution. The example 2-9 shows that in the normal situation SS-1 has two equal paths to 192.168.31.101/32.

```
SS-1# sh ip bgp 192.168.31.101
BGP routing table information for VRF default, address family IPv4 Unicast
BGP routing table entry for 192.168.31.101/32, version 12
Paths: (2 available, best #1)
Flags: (0x8008001a) (high32 00000000) on xmit-list, is in urib, is best urib route, is
in HW
Multipath: eBGP

  Advertised path-id 1
  Path type: external, path is valid, is best path, no labeled nexthop, in rib
  AS-Path: 65100 65101 , path sourced external to AS
    10.10.10.4 (metric 0) from 10.10.10.4 (192.168.0.12)
      Origin incomplete, MED not set, localpref 100, weight 0

  Path type: external, path is valid, not best reason: newer EBGP path, multipath, no
labeled nexthop, in rib
  AS-Path: 65100 65101 , path sourced external to AS
    10.10.10.0 (metric 0) from 10.10.10.0 (192.168.0.11)
      Origin incomplete, MED not set, localpref 100, weight 0

  Path-id 1 advertised to peers:
    10.10.20.0         10.10.20.4
```

Example 2-10: *BGP Loc-RIB about 192.168.31.101 SS-1.*

And both routes are also installed into the RIB.

```
SS-1# sh ip route 192.168.31.101
IP Route Table for VRF "default"
'*' denotes best ucast next-hop
'**' denotes best mcast next-hop
'[x/y]' denotes [preference/metric]
'%<string>' in via output denotes VRF <string>

192.168.31.101/32, ubest/mbest: 2/0
    *via 10.10.10.0, [20/0], 00:01:01, bgp-65001, external, tag 65100
    *via 10.10.10.4, [20/0], 00:19:16, bgp-65001, external, tag 65100
```

Example 2-11: *RIB of SS-1.*

Example 2-11 shows the AS-Path prepend related configuration on S-11.

```
route-map AS-PATH-PREP-GIR permit 10
  set as-path prepend 65100 65100
!
router bgp 65100
  router-id 192.168.0.11
  bestpath as-path multipath-relax
  address-family ipv4 unicast
    maximum-paths 8
  neighbor 10.10.0.0/16 remote-as route-map Dynamic-BGP-AS-List
    address-family ipv4 unicast
      route-map AS-PATH-PREP-GIR out
```

Example 2-11: *AS-Path Prepend Configuration on S-11.*

As a reaction to configuration, S-11 generates a new BGP Update about all of its BGP learned routes prepended with AS-Path attribute 65101 65101.

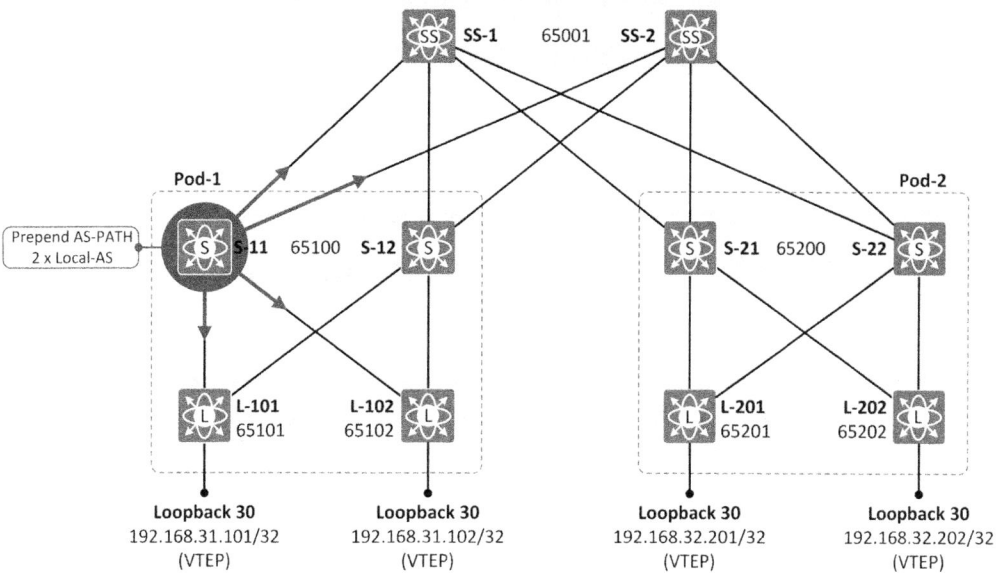

Figure 2-6: *AS-Path prepend on S-22.*

Now the route received from S-11 has AS-Path: 65100 65100 65100 65101 while the route received from S-12 has AS-Path: 65100 65101 and it is selected as the best path due to the shorter AS-Path list.

```
SS-1# sh ip bgp 192.168.31.101
BGP routing table information for VRF default, address family IPv4 Unicast
BGP routing table entry for 192.168.31.101/32, version 14
Paths: (2 available, best #1)
Flags: (0x8008001a) (high32 00000000) on xmit-list, is in urib, is best urib route, is
in HW
Multipath: eBGP

  Advertised path-id 1
  Path type: external, path is valid, is best path, no labeled nexthop, in rib
  AS-Path: 65100 65101 , path sourced external to AS
    10.10.10.4 (metric 0) from 10.10.10.4 (192.168.0.12)
      Origin incomplete, MED not set, localpref 100, weight 0

  Path type: external, path is valid, not best reason: AS Path, no labeled nexthop
  AS-Path: 65100 65100 65100 65101 , path sourced external to AS
    10.10.10.0 (metric 0) from 10.10.10.0 (192.168.0.11)
      Origin incomplete, MED not set, localpref 100, weight 0

  Path-id 1 advertised to peers:
    10.10.20.0          10.10.20.4
```

Example 2-12: *BGP Loc-RIB about 192.168.31.101 in SS-1.*

The route via S-11 is removed from the RIB and the IP address 192.168.31.101 is only available through the S-12.

```
SS-1# sh ip route 192.168.31.101
IP Route Table for VRF "default"
'*' denotes best ucast next-hop
'**' denotes best mcast next-hop
'[x/y]' denotes [preference/metric]
'%<string>' in via output denotes VRF <string>

192.168.31.101/32, ubest/mbest: 1/0
    *via 10.10.10.4, [20/0], 00:14:59, bgp-65001, external, tag 65100
```
Example 2-13: *RIB about 192.168.31.101 in SS-1.*

Example 2-14 shows that L-202 in Pod-2 still use ECMP to the destination because S-21 and S-22 receive update from both SuperSpines. This means that L-202 can send data to 192.168.31.101 with a 1:2 oversubscription ratio. This means that in a failure scenario there might be 50% packet loss. With three switches in the Spine and Super Spine layer, the oversubscription ratio will reduce down to 2:3 which gives us a 33% percent packet loss.

```
L-202# sh ip bgp 192.168.31.101
BGP routing table information for VRF default, address family IPv4 Unicast
BGP routing table entry for 192.168.31.101/32, version 7
Paths: (2 available, best #2)
Flags: (0x8008001a) (high32 00000000) on xmit-list, is in urib, is best urib route, is in HW
Multipath: eBGP

  Path type: external, path is valid, not best reason: newer EBGP path, multipath, no labeled nexthop, in rib
    AS-Path: 65200 65001 65100 65101 , path sourced external to AS
    10.10.2.7 (metric 0) from 10.10.2.7 (192.168.0.22)
      Origin incomplete, MED not set, localpref 100, weight 0

  Advertised path-id 1
  Path type: external, path is valid, is best path, no labeled nexthop, in rib
    AS-Path: 65200 65001 65100 65101 , path sourced external to AS
    10.10.2.5 (metric 0) from 10.10.2.5 (192.168.0.21)
      Origin incomplete, MED not set, localpref 100, weight 0

  Path-id 1 not advertised to any peer
```
Example 2-14: *BGP Loc-RIB about 192.168.31.101 in L-202.*

OSPF and BGP Comparison

Underlay Network should offer reliable IP connectivity between VTEP switches. By saying reliable I mean (a) enough redundant bandwidth (ECMP), (b) fast failure detection and recovery, (c) non-disruptive maintenance works. Both OSPF as a Link-State Protocol and BGP as Path-Vector Protocol fulfills these requirements, so in that sense, the answer to the question is "both are suitable for Underlay network".

If that answer is not good enough, we can try to find the tiebreaker by comparing the properties and operations of protocols shown in table 2-1. OSPF doesn't use a transport layer protocol as BGP does. This means that one layer of complexity is removed from OSPF. Both protocols have a reliable, somewhat complex adjacency process. BGP Adjacency process is a bit more complex than the OSPF adjacency process because BGP uses TCP as a transport protocol. OSPF routers, within an intra area, have a synchronized LSDB and they all make individual decisions about the best paths based on the metric. BGP in turn trust NLRI information received from adjacent BGP peer and the best path is selected using 13 step comparison based on Path Attributes carried within BGP update. In that sense, the BGP routing decision is based on Administrative policy, not on metrics like in the case of OSPF. Note, RFC 7311 describes how the IGP metric can also be carried within the BGP update. Also, there is a draft "draft-ietf-lsvr-bgp-spf-09" [LSVR-BGP] that describes how Link-State distribution and SPF algorithm used with BGP. The convergence process of BGP is simpler than OSPF. In case of a link failure, BGP withdrawn does not affect the whole fabric like in the case of single area OSPF design. Both OSPF and BGP use reliable information exchange, OSPF LSAs are acknowledged, and because BGP uses TCP as a transport protocol, all its messages including BGP Updates are acknowledged by adjacent BGP speakers. The biggest concern about OSPF is its flooding process where Link-State information is flooded when the Link-State Age is 1800 seconds (half of its lifetime). This, however, can be seen as a problem in Massive Scale Datacenters (MSDC) and can be relaxed by using LSA Group Pacing and OSPF Area structure, so the flooding should not be seen as a problem.

However, we need to remember that so far we have discussed only Control-Plane protocol choice for the Underlay network. The Overlay Network will use BGP, so if we use Link-State protocol in Underlay Network, we end up having the complexities of both protocols into the network. This means that the network operator should understand (a) how these protocols work, and (b) how they interoperate. Is this a problem? It should not be because both protocols have their roles. The benefit of using OSPF is that it has native support for unnumbered interfaces which makes the Inter-Switch link IP addressing design much simpler compared to BGP. Some vendors support BGP Unnumbered solution where IPv6 Link-Local addresses are used as unnumbered source addresses but under the hood that solution adds some complexity. Another benefit of using different protocols in Underlay and Overlay Network is that it makes the troubleshooting process simpler. You can remove Leaf switches from the Overlay Network by shutting down the BGP adjacencies without disturbing an Underlay Network. This naturally can be done with BGP by using peering between loopback addresses in Overlay Network. This though means that we end up having two BGP sessions between two switches. From a configuration perspective using OSPF requires fewer lines than BGP. The task for Underlay Network Control-Plane protocol is to offer IP reachability between Leaf switches which by advertising Loopback Interfaces used by NVE interfaces as a source address in VXLAN tunnel header. In OSPF you simply add the loopback interface into OSPF Area using the command ***router ospf [process-Id] area [Area-Id]*** under loopback interface configuration. In BGP you can use network clauses where you use loopback interface IP address but then you end up having a unique config in each device. You could also redistribute direct networks using neighbor specific route-map where you define the advertised address. The configuration complexity, however, can be automated but the selected solution will affect the automation scrip complexity.

The next chapters explain several design-models where most of them are using OSPF in Underlay. Chapter four, however, introduces two BGP-Only solutions where the first one discusses the model where the Underlay Network BGP used direct peering while the Overlay Network peering is between loopback interfaces. Then it explains the solution where both Underlay and Overlay Networks use direct peering. After reading this book you should make your own decisions which solution fits best with your needs.

Functionality	Link State Protocol OSPF	Path Vector Protocol BGP
Transport	Runs on top of IP: Protocol 89	Runs over TCP: Port 179
Forming Adjacency	- Finding peers based on OSPF Hello to 224.0.0.5 - States: DOWN, INIT, ETART, EXCHANGE, FULL - Validation: Hello/Dead Interval, Mask, Area-Id, Pass Authentication process, Unique RID, Same Network Type, MTU	- Defined Neighbors (Active) - Dynamic Neighbors (Passive) - States: Idle, Connect/Active, OpenSent, OpenReceived, Established - Validation: Pass TCP Three Way Handshake, Peer AS number, Peer Source, TTL, Unique RID
Routing Updates	- Link State Advertisement	- BGP Update messages
Best Path Calculation	- LSDB Synchronization - Individual SPF calculation with Dijkstra algorithm - Support ECMP - Decission based on shortest path/lowest metric	- BGP Update messages - Trust what neighbors are telling. - Support ECMP - Decission based on Administrative Policy - RFC 7311 AIGP
Convergence	- Protocol Failures: HelloTime and HoldTime - Link Failures: BFD - Related Timers: LSA and SPF Throtlling, Flood Pacing, LSA Group Pacing	- Protocol Failures: HelloTime/KeepAlive - Link Failures: BFD - Related Timer: MinRouteAdvertisementTimer (MRAI)
Reliability	- All LSA are acknowledged	- Runs over TCP > All messages are acknowledged
Databases	- Link State Database - LS flooding every 1800 seconds	- Adj-RIB-In (Pre/Post) - Loc-RIB - Adj-RIB-Out (Pre/Post)

Table 2-1: *OSPF and BGP comparison.*

References

[RFC 4271]   Y. Rekhter et al., "A Border Gateway Protocol 4 (BGP-4)", RFC 4271, January 2006.

[RFC 5549]   F. Le Faucheur and E. Rosen, "Advertising IPv4 Network Layer Reachability Information with an IPv6 Next Hop, RFC 5549, May 2009.

[RFC 7311]   P. Mohapatra et al., "The Accumulated IGP Metric Attribute for BGP", RFC 7311, August 2014.

[RFC 7938]   P.Lapukhov et al., "Use of BGP for Routing in Large-Scale Data Centers", RFC 7938, August 2016.

[RFC 8671]   T. Evens et al., "Support for Adj-RIB-Out in the BGP Monitoring Protocol (BMP)", RFC 8671, November 2019.

[BGP-MRAI]   P. Jakma, "Revisions to the BGP 'Minimum Route Advertisement Interval' draft-ietf-idr-mrai-dep-04, September 20, 2011.

[LSRV-BGP]   K. Patel et al., "Shortest Path Routing Extensions for BGP Protocol", draft-ietf-lsvr-bgp-spf-09, May 15, 2020.

Chapter 3: BGP Multi-AS with OSPF Underlay

Introduction

In this design model, all Leaf switches have unique BGP AS numbers. Spine switches within Pod share ASN. Super-Spine switches also share the ASN. In this design approach, Leaf - Spine - Spine-Super are eBGP peers. The reason why Spine switches within Pod have a dedicated shared BGP AS is that this way we remove BGP Path-hunting and achieve valley free routing. This design requires a next-hop retaining for EVPN routes and *retain-route-target-all* command. If both Underlay and Overlay Network are using BGP and peering is done between Inter-Switch links, we can send both IPv4 and EVPN NLRIs within one BGP Update. This also shortens the required configuration. As a trade-off, we are losing the ability to remove switch only from the Overlay Network leaving it still into Underlay Network. BGP Multi-AS design with OSPF using unnumbered interface IP addresses in the Underlay network combined with Dynamic-BGP peering in the Spine layer makes this solution both easy to configure and automate. The additional benefit it gives is that the location of each host attached to the fabric can be tracked based on the unique BGP ASN of advertising leaf.

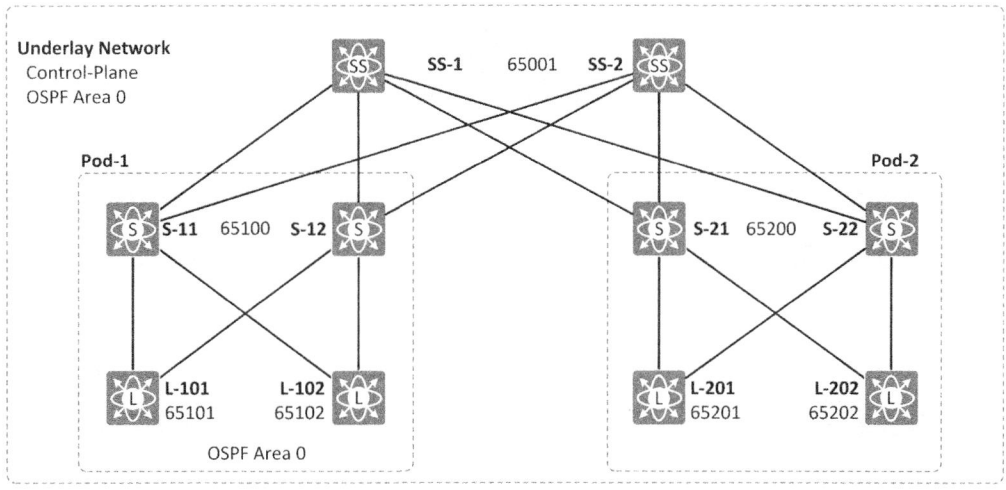

Figure 3-1: *ASN scheme.*

Inter-Switch Link IP addressing

In addition to fast recovery, the beauty of using Link-State Protocols like OSPF in Underlay Network is its native support for Unnumbered interface IP addresses. This is because OSPF runs on top of IP and it uses Multicast messages for finding adjacent OSPF speakers as described in chapter 1. BGP, in turn, runs over TCP and uses Unicast messages for finding adjacent BGP speakers and it doesn't have native support for Unnumbered interface IP address. Some vendors support BGP over Unnumbered Inter-Switch links by using IPv6 ND and Link-Local addressing. That though adds some complexity. Figure 3-1 illustrates the Inter-Switch link IP addressing scheme used in this chapter.

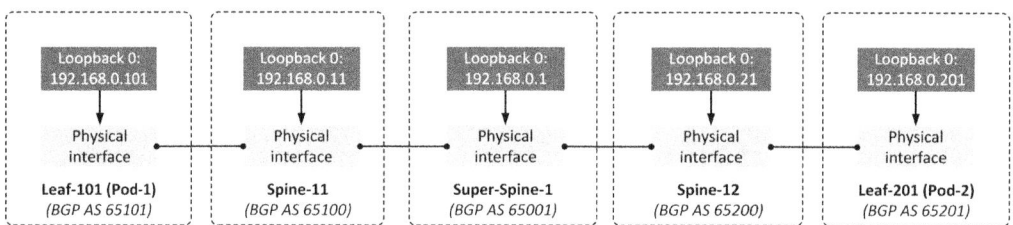

Figure 3-1: *Inter-Switch links IP addressing.*

The configuration example is shown in example 3-1.

```
interface loopback0
  description ** OSPF Unnderlay **
  ip address 192.168.0.101/32
!
interface Ethernet1/1
  no switchport
  mtu 9216
  medium p2p
  ip unnumbered loopback0
  no shutdown
```

Example 3-1: *The IP Address Configuration of Inter-Switch link on Leaf-101.*

Underlay Network Routing with OSPF

OSPF operation in the Underlay network is simple, it exchanges Link-State Update massages with adjacent OSPF speakers, which carries separate Links-State Advertisement (LSAs) about its OSPF enabled links (Loopback Interfaces 0, 15, and 30). Let's take a look at this from the Leaf-101 perspective. It has three Loopback interfaces taken into the OSPF process. The IP address of Loopback 15 is used for Overlay Network BGP L2VPN EVPN peering and BGP messages are sent using these addresses. The IP address of Loopback 30 is used in Control Plane as a Next-Hop for EVPN routes and in Data-plane as destination/source IP addresses in the VXLAN tunnel header. The user traffic is routed by Spine and Super-Spine switches based on this IP address. The IP address of Loopback 0 (Inter-Switch link address) is used for Recursive Next-Hop Resolution (RNH) to resolve where to send VXLAN encapsulated packets.

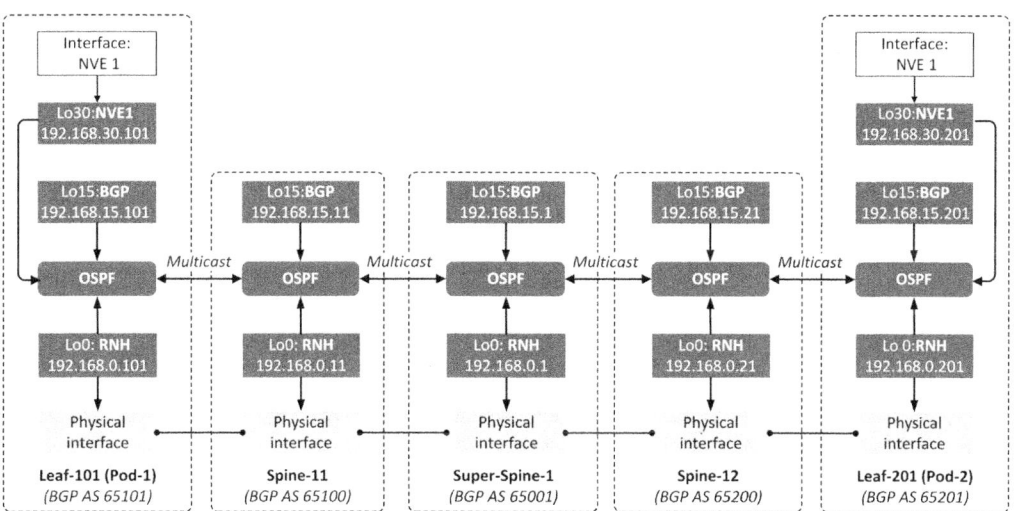

Figure 3-2: *Underlay Network Routing with OSPF.*

Example 3-2 shows commands related to the Underlay Network OSPF.

```
Feature ospf
!
router ospf UNDERLAY-NET
  router-id 192.168.0.101
!
interface loopback15
  description ** BGP EVPN Peering address **
  ip address 192.168.15.101/32
  ip ospf network point-to-point
  ip router ospf UNDERLAY-NET area 0.0.0.0
```

```
!
interface loopback30
  description ** VTEP IP address **
  ip address 192.168.30.101/32
  ip ospf network point-to-point
  ip router ospf UNDERLAY-NET area 0.0.0.0
!
interface Ethernet1/1
  ip unnumbered loopback0
  ip ospf network point-to-point
  no ip ospf passive-interface
  ip router ospf UNDERLAY-NET area 0.0.0.0
```

Example 3-2: *OSPF Configuration on Leaf-101.*

Capture 3-1 shows that BGP Update messages are sent by using BGP peering addresses while the Next-Hop IP address for EVPN NLRI is 192.168.30.101 (= hex: c0 c8 1e 65), which is the IP address used as a source for interface NVE1.

```
Internet Protocol Version 4, Src: 192.168.15.101, Dst: 192.168.15.11
Transmission Control Protocol, Src Port: 15537, Dst Port: 179,
Border Gateway Protocol - UPDATE Message
    Marker: ffffffffffffffffffffffffffffffff
    Length: 126
    Type: UPDATE Message (2)
    Withdrawn Routes Length: 0
    Total Path Attribute Length: 103
    Path attributes
        <snipped>
        Path Attribute - MP_REACH_NLRI
            Flags: 0x90, Optional, Extended-Length, Non-transitive, Complete
            Type Code: MP_REACH_NLRI (14)
            Length: 51
            Address family identifier (AFI): Layer-2 VPN (25)
            Subsequent address family identifier (SAFI): EVPN (70)
            Next hop network address (4 bytes)
            Number of Subnetwork points of attachment (SNPA): 0
            Network layer reachability information (42 bytes)
                EVPN NLRI: MAC Advertisement Route
                    Route Type: MAC Advertisement Route (2)
                    Length: 40
                    Route Distinguisher: 0001c0a80f658009 (192.168.15.101:32777)
                    ESI: 00:00:00:00:00:00:00:00:00:00
                    Ethernet Tag ID: 0
                    MAC Address Length: 48
                    MAC Address: Private_66:68:06 (00:50:79:66:68:06)
                    IP Address Length: 32
                    IPv4 address: 172.16.10.10
                    0000 0000 0111 0101 0011 .... = MPLS Label 1: 1875
                    0000 0000 0111 0101 0111 .... = MPLS Label 2: 1879

0000   50 00 00 08 00 07 50 00 00 01 00 07 08 00 45 c0    P.....P.......E.
<snipped>
0090   04 c0 a8 1e 65 00 02 28 00 01 c0 a8 0f 65 80 09    ....e..(.....e..
<snipped>
```

Capture 3-1: *BGP Update from Leaf-101 to Spine-11.*

Capture 3-2 shows that the Next-Hop address described in the previous BGP message is now used as a destination IP address in the VXLAN tunnel header when pinging from host 172.16.10.40 to 172.16.10.

```
Internet Protocol Version 4, Src: 192.168.30.202, Dst: 192.168.30.101
User Datagram Protocol, Src Port: 51237, Dst Port: 4789
Virtual eXtensible Local Area Network
Ethernet II, Src: 00:50:79:66:68:0e, Dst: 00:50:79:66:68:06
Internet Protocol Version 4, Src: 172.16.10.40, Dst: 172.16.10.10
Internet Control Message Protocol
```

Capture 3-2: VXLAN tunneled *ICMP-reply sent by remote leaf Leaf-201.*

Overlay Network BGP L2VPN EVPN Peering

BGP L2VPN EVPN peering is established between IP addresses of Loopback 15 interfaces. It is also possible to configure BGP peering between the same Loopback IP addresses that are used for Inter-Switch links but then we lose the possibility to isolate the BGP process without disturbing the Underlay network by shutting down the Loopback used for peering. Also, a clear separation of Underlay and Overlay Network is simpler from the troubleshooting perspective.

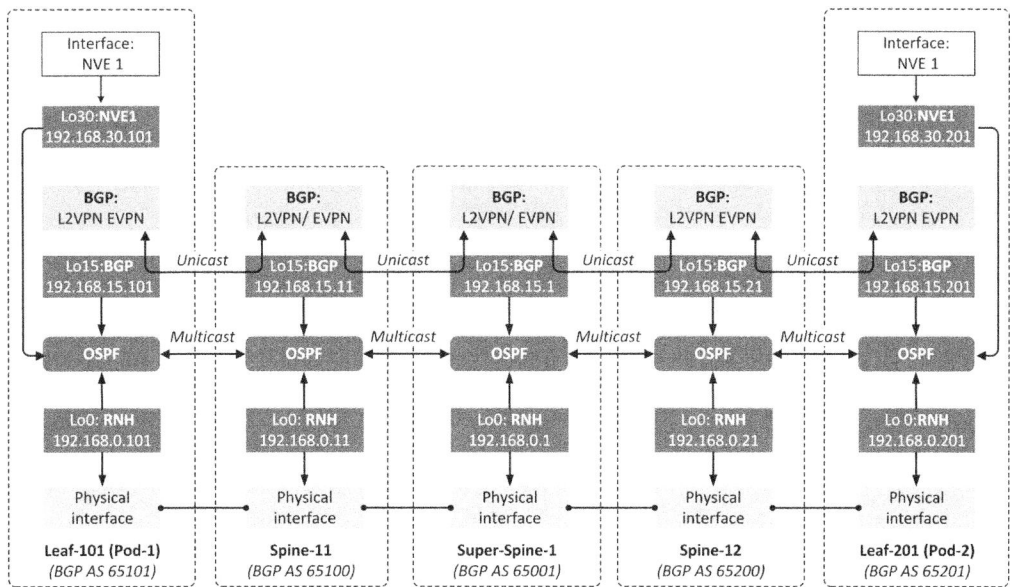

Figure 3-3: *BGP L2VPN EVPN Peering.*

Example 3-4 illustrates the BGP configuration of Leaf-101. TCP SYN and TCP ACK in the BGP three-way negotiation process, as well as BGP Update messages, have default TTL value one. In our example, the eBGP peering is established between IP addresses of interfaces Loopback15. This why the TTL value has to be increased from one to two using the command *ebgp-multihop 2* and the BGP message source IP has to be set to Loopback 15 by using the command *update-source loopback15*. Also, we need to define the peering MP-BGP address-family L2VPN EVPN. Under the address-family configuration, we define that also BGP Extended Communities, like Route-Target, encapsulation type (VXLAN), and Router MAC, will be carried within BGP Updates. Route-Targets used for L2VN and L3VN are auto derived from the routers BGP AS value and the VN-Id. As an example, if VLAN 10 is attached to EVPN instance 10000 in Leaf-101, the auto derived Route-Target (RT) value will be 65101:10000. This RT is then attached to all BGP Updates carrying the EVPN NLRIs. This means that BGP speakers in different AS uses different RT for the same VN-segment which in turn means that Leaf-101 and Leaf-201 have different BGP import/export-policy for the same L2VN and they will not import EVPN NLRI into BGP Loc-RIB by default. The command *rewrite-evpn-rt-asn* changes the ASN part in RT to ASN of receiving router. The ASN part in RT carried in ingress BGP Update has to be the same as the BGP ASN of sending (not originating) BGP peer, otherwise the ASN part is not changed and the NLRI is not imported in BGP Loc-RIB. This is why the command is needed also in Spine and Super-Spine switches. BGP supports multi-pathing. The command *maximum-paths 8* under the "address-family l2vpn evpn" section allows flow-based load-balancing between eight paths that are considered equal from the BGP perspective. Paths that have the same count of ASN but with different ASN listed in the AS Path-List are not valid for ECMP by default. To be a valid ECMP path the ASN has to be the same in the AS Path-List. In our network, this is not the case because Spine switches within Pod share the same ASN. If they belong to different AS, then the ECMP requires the command *bestpath as-path multipath-relax*.

```
router bgp 65101
  router-id 192.168.15.101
  bestpath as-path multipath-relax
  address-family l2vpn evpn
    maximum-paths 8
  neighbor 192.168.15.11
    remote-as 65100
    update-source loopback15
    ebgp-multihop 2
    address-family l2vpn evpn
      send-community
      send-community extended
      rewrite-evpn-rt-asn
```

Example 3-3: *BGP L2VPN EVPN configuration on Leaf-101.*

We are using dynamic BGP neighbor process in Spine switches, where they are passively waiting for TCP SYN packets with the destination port 179 from the subnet 192.168.15.0/24, which is the subnet that we are using for BGP peering in all switches (loopback 15). After a successful TCP three-way handshake process Spine switches verify that the peer ASN received included in the OPEN message is listed as a valid ASN. This solution simplifies the configuration of Spine switches because there is no need for neighbor-specific configuration when some BGP parameters are changed or when new switches are added. The configuration is simple, allowed ASN are defined in a route-map that matches the allowed ASN. Then this route-map is attached to the neighbor configuration. The peer count can be limited by using the command *maximum-peers [peer count]* under the neighbor configuration section. The command *rewrite-evpn-rt-asn* is configured via peer template because it only affects iBGP peering when configured under the neighbor configuration section. The default behavior, when sending BGP Update messages to eBGP peer is to change the next-hop address attribute to the local peering address, in our example to Loopback 30. This will break VXLAN tunnels because the destination IP address in the tunnel header is set based on the next-hop attribute. The Next-Hop can be sent unmodified by using a route-map with the *set ip next-hop unchanged* definition. Additionally, spine switches need to (a) retain RTs, (b) rewrite RTs, and use the BGP multipathing just like in case Leaf switches.

```
route-map Dynamic-BGP-AS-List permit 10
  match as-number 65001, 65002, 65101, 65102
!
route-map RETAIN-NH permit 10
  set ip next-hop unchanged
!
router bgp 65100
  router-id 192.168.15.11
  bestpath as-path multipath-relax
  address-family ipv4 unicast
    maximum-paths 8
  address-family l2vpn evpn
    maximum-paths 8
    retain route-target all
  template peer eBGP-peers
    address-family l2vpn evpn
      rewrite-evpn-rt-asn
  neighbor 192.168.15.0/24 remote-as route-map Dynamic-BGP-AS-List
    inherit peer eBGP-peers
    update-source loopback15
    ebgp-multihop 2
    address-family l2vpn evpn
      send-community
      send-community extended
      route-map RETAIN-NH out
```

Example 3-4: *BGP L2VPN EVPN configuration on Spine-11.*

The configuration of SuperSpine switches uses the same options as what has already been introduced with Leaf and Spine switches.

```
router bgp 65001
  router-id 192.168.15.1
  bestpath as-path multipath-relax
  address-family l2vpn evpn
    maximum-paths 8
    retain route-target all
  neighbor 192.168.15.11
    remote-as 65100
    update-source loopback15
    ebgp-multihop 2
    address-family l2vpn evpn
      send-community
      send-community extended
      route-map RETAIN-NH out
      rewrite-evpn-rt-asn
  neighbor 192.168.15.21
    remote-as 65200
    update-source loopback15
    ebgp-multihop 2
    address-family l2vpn evpn
      send-community
      send-community extended
      route-map RETAIN-NH out
      rewrite-evpn-rt-asn
```

Example 3-5: *BGP L2VPN EVPN configuration on SuperSpine-1.*

Adding L2VN segment

This section explains how the EVPN instance is added to the network. The building blocks needed are shown in figure 3-4. VLAN 10 has Anycast-GW IP 192.168.10.1/24 and it is attached to EVPN with VNI 10010. All SVIs will be using Anycast Gateway MAC 0001:0001:0001. Integrated Routing and Bridging (IRB) function between Inter-VN uses VLAN 77 with IP Forward SVI. Layer 2 Broadcast, Unknown Unicast, and Multicast (L2BUM) forwarding tunnels are established based on EVPN Route-Type 3 (Inclusive Multicast Route).

BGP EVPN Design Consideration 87

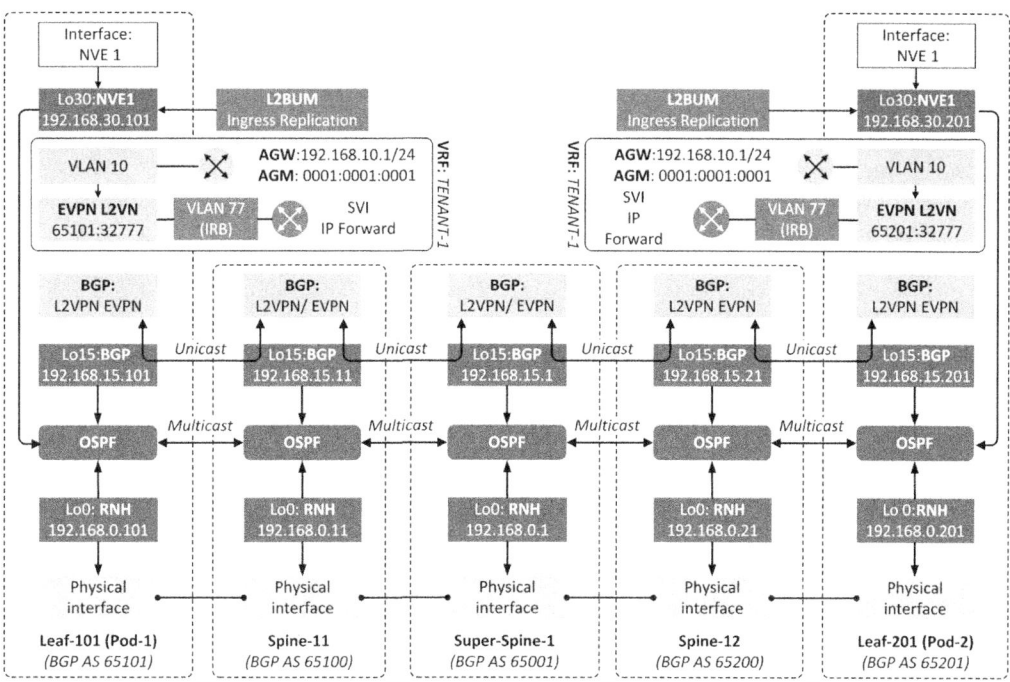

Figure 3-4: *BGP L2VPN EVPN Peering.*

```
fabric forwarding anycast-gateway-mac 0001.0001.0001
!
vlan 1,10,77
vlan 10
  vn-segment 30010
vlan 77
  name IRB-TENANT-1
  vn-segment 30077
!
vrf context TENANT-1
  vni 30077
  rd auto
  address-family ipv4 unicast
    route-target both auto
    route-target both auto evpn
!
interface Vlan10
  no shutdown
  vrf member TENANT-1
  ip address 172.16.10.1/24
  fabric forwarding mode anycast-gateway

interface Vlan77
  description ** IRB-TENANT-1 **
  no shutdown
  mtu 9216
  vrf member TENANT-1
```

```
  ip forward
!
interface nve1
  no shutdown
  host-reachability protocol bgp
  source-interface loopback30
  member vni 30010
    ingress-replication protocol bgp
  member vni 30077 associate-vrf
!
evpn
  vni 30010 l2
    rd auto
    route-target import auto
    route-target export auto
```

Example 3-6: *EVPN Specific Configuration on all leaf switches.*

Routing comparison: Spine Sharing ASN vs. Unique ASN

The purpose of this section is to point out the routing complexity if all switches, including Spine and Super-Spine, have unique ASN. This is done by comparing how the NLRI of the MAC address of Database server 40 (MAC: 0050.7966.680e) is installed into device BRIB first in a shared ASN design model and then with a unique ASN scheme.

Spine Switches Sharing ASN

The Control-Plane operation is not complex in design where all Spine switches within Pod share the same ASN and SuperSpine switches share the same ASN within their layer. Now we are going to take a look at how the MAC Advertisement route about 0050.7966.680e sent by L-202 propagates across the fabric.

Phase 1: L-202 learns MAC and IP address information of Database server 40 when it is booted up. The message could be for example ARP, GARP, or DHCP request. The MAC address information is installed into the MAC address table and L2RIB where it is exported to the BGP process. L-202 builds the BGP Update to which it attaches the mandatory path attributes, as well as EVPN specific information like; Route-targets and encapsulation type extended communities. It also adds VLAN specific Route-Distinguisher. Let's assume that L-202 first sends BGP Update to S-21 (step-1a, time-T_1) and then to S-22 (step-1b, time-T_2).

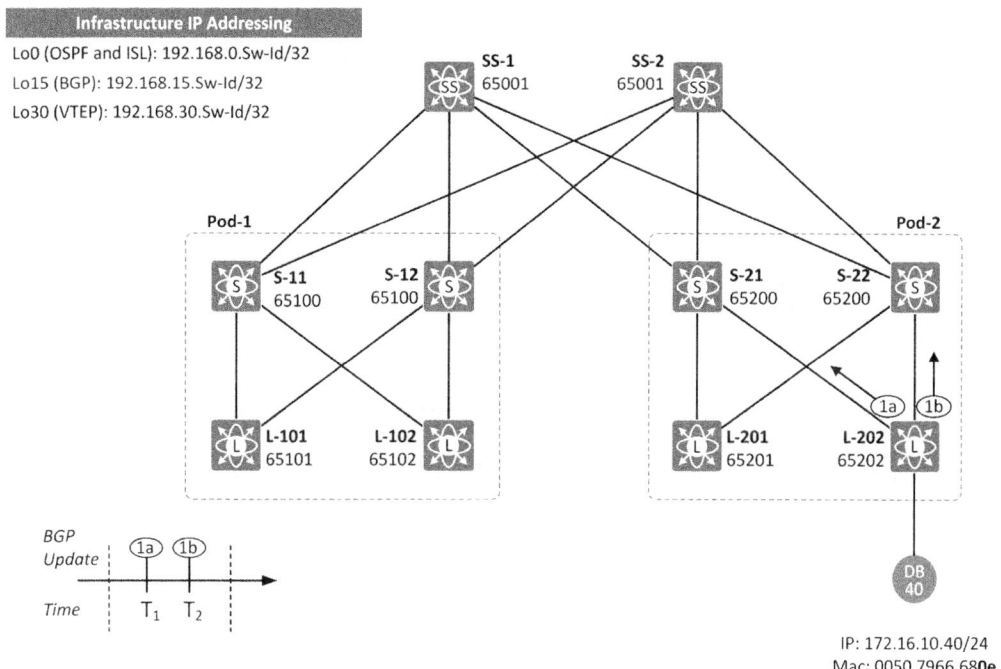

Figure 3-5: *MAC Advertisement Route about 0050.7966.680e – phase 1.*

Phases 2-3: S-21 receives the BGP Update earlier than S-22 because the first BGP Update was sent to S-21 by L-202 in time T_1. After validating the received BGP Update, S-21 installs the NLRI from the Adj-RIB-In into the Loc-RIB and from there through the Adj-RIB-Out to adjacent BGP L2VPN EVPN peers L-201 (time T_3), SS-1 (time T_5), and SS-2 (time T_7). During the update process, S-21 adds its ASN into the path-list. It, however, retains the original Next-Hop address. This is mandatory because the Next-Hop address is used for VXLAN tunneling in Data-Plane. S-22 does the same operation but slightly later than S-21. Remember that the command *retain-route-target all* used in Spine and SuperSpine switches make it possible to advertise original Route-Targets within forwarded BGP Updates (technically BGP Update messages are not forwarded by switches but the NLRI information carried within the received BGP Update is copied into new BGP Update message with some modifications). This means that the MAC Advertisement route is not imported as L2VNI specific entry in BRIB. Spine and SuperSpine switches are not VN aware at all and they do not have L2VN or L3VN entry types in BRIB.

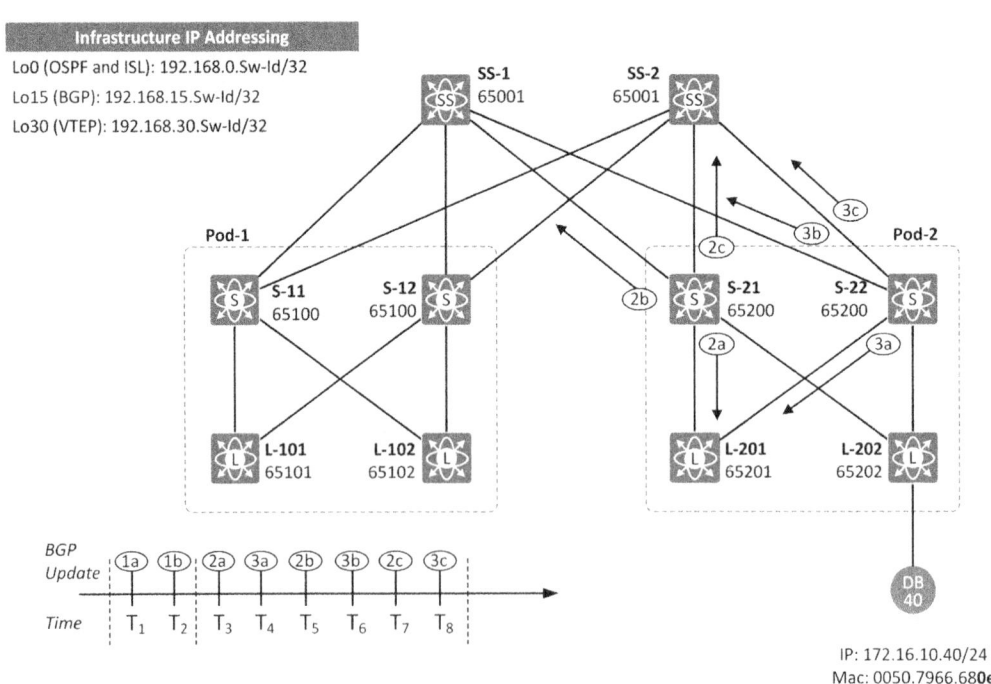

Figure 3-6: *MAC Advertisement Route about 0050.7966.680e – phase 2-3.*

Phases 4-7: SS-1 has received the BGP Update from S-21 earlier than from S-22 and that is why it is selected as the best path and advertised to adjacent BGP L2VPN EVPN peers S-11 (time T_{10}) and S-12 (time T_{12}). The SS-2 does the same process but a bit later than SS-1. S-11 selects the path via SS-1 as the best path because the BGP Update was received earlier from SS-1 than from SS-2. S-11 advertises only the best path to its adjacent BGP L2VPN EVPN speaker L-101 and L-102. S-12 also selects the path via SS-1 as the best path for the same reason than S-11, the BGP Update was received earlier from SS-1. S-12 also advertises only the best route to leaf switches.

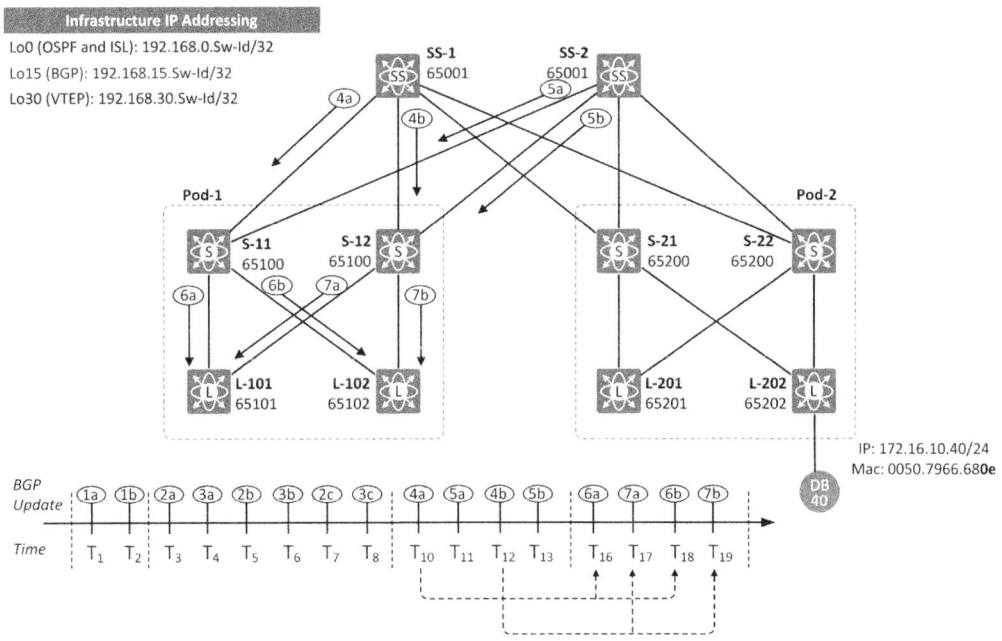

Figure 3-7: *MAC Advertisement Route about 0050.7966.680e – phase 4-7.*

The following examples (3-7 to 3-11) show how the MAC Advertisement Route about 0050.7966.680e is installed into the BGP table. S-21 has only one path while all other switches have two equal, ECMP capable paths to the destination.

```
S-21# sh bgp l2vpn evpn
   Network            Next Hop              Metric      LocPrf    Weight Path
Route Distinguisher: 192.168.15.202:32777
*>e[2]:[0]:[0]:[48]:[0050.7966.680e]:[0]:[0.0.0.0]/216
                     192.168.30.202                                    0 65202 i
```
Example 3-7: *show bgp l2vpn evpn on S-21.*

L-201 has both L2VNI 30010 and L3VNI 30077 which means that it also has an import policy for EVPN routes. The example below shows that L-201 has imported MAC-Only NLRI from Adj-RIB-In into Loc-RIB. During the import process, the RD has been changed from the original 192.168.15.202:32777 to 192.168.15.201:32777. The same process is done during the L3VNI import process.

```
L-201# sh bgp l2vpn evpn
   Network            Next Hop            Metric     LocPrf     Weight Path
Route Distinguisher: 192.168.15.201:32777     (L2VNI 30010)
*>e[2]:[0]:[0]:[48]:[0050.7966.680e]:[0]:[0.0.0.0]/216
                      192.168.30.202                                   0 65200 65202 i
Route Distinguisher: 192.168.15.202:32777
*>e[2]:[0]:[0]:[48]:[0050.7966.680e]:[0]:[0.0.0.0]/216
                      192.168.30.202                                   0 65200 65202 i
* e                   192.168.30.202                                   0 65200 65202 i
Route Distinguisher: 192.168.15.201:3     (L3VNI 30077)
*>e[2]:[0]:[0]:[48]:[0050.7966.680e]:[32]:[172.16.10.40]/272
                      192.168.30.202                                   0 65200 65202 i
```
Example 3-8: *show bgp l2vpn evpn on L-201.*

Examples 3-9 and 3-10 show that both SS-1 and S-11 in Pod-1 has two paths in their BGP table and that the upper one is marked as the best path.

```
SS-1# sh bgp l2vpn evpn
   Network            Next Hop            Metric     LocPrf     Weight Path
Route Distinguisher: 192.168.15.202:32777
*>e[2]:[0]:[0]:[48]:[0050.7966.680e]:[0]:[0.0.0.0]/216
                      192.168.30.202                                   0 65200 65202 i
* e                   192.168.30.202                                   0 65200 65202 i
```
Example 3-9: *show bgp l2vpn evpn on SS-1.*

```
S-11# sh bgp l2vpn evpn
   Network            Next Hop            Metric     LocPrf     Weight Path
Route Distinguisher: 192.168.15.202:32777
*>e[2]:[0]:[0]:[48]:[0050.7966.680e]:[0]:[0.0.0.0]/216
                      192.168.30.202                                   0 65001 65200 65202 i
* e                   192.168.30.202                                   0 65001 65200 65202 i
```
Example 3-10: *show bgp l2vpn evpn on S-11.*

Just like S-201 in Pod-2, L-101 in Pod-1 has imported the NLRI into L2VN/L3VN specific tables with modified RD. Just as a side note, the latter part of the RD specifies the VLAN where the route belongs to (3277 - base value 32767 = 10). Only the best route is imported from Adj-RIB-In where there are two entries, one received from S-11 and the other received from S-12, into Loc-RIB.

```
L-101# sh bgp l2vpn evpn
   Network          Next Hop            Metric     LocPrf     Weight Path
Route Distinguisher: 192.168.15.101:32777       (L2VNI 30010)
*>e[2]:[0]:[0]:[48]:[0050.7966.680e]:[0]:[0.0.0.0]/216
                    192.168.30.202                                 0 65100 65001 65200 65202 i
Route Distinguisher: 192.168.15.202:32777
*>e[2]:[0]:[0]:[48]:[0050.7966.680e]:[0]:[0.0.0.0]/216
                    192.168.30.202                                 0 65100 65001 65200 65202 i
* e                 192.168.30.202                                 0 65100 65001 65200 65202 i
Route Distinguisher: 192.168.15.101:3      (L3VNI 30077)
*>e[2]:[0]:[0]:[48]:[0050.7966.680e]:[32]:[172.16.10.40]/272
                    192.168.30.202                                 0 65100 65001 65200 65202 i
```

Example 3-11: *show bgp l2vpn evpn on L-101.*

Note that even though there is only one entry in the BGP table per RD for both L2VN and L3VN, traffic is load-balanced between S-11 (Destination MAC 50:00:00:08:00:07) and S-12 11 (Destination MAC 50:00:00:05:00:07) as can be seen from ICMP Request messages capture from interface E1/1 and E1/2. The ECMP process will be explained later in a dedicated chapter.

```
Frame 147: 148 bytes on wire (1184 bits), 148 bytes captured (1184 bits) on interface
-, id 0
Ethernet II, Src: 50:00:00:01:00:07 (50:00:00:01:00:07), Dst: 50:00:00:08:00:07
(50:00:00:08:00:07)
Internet Protocol Version 4, Src: 192.168.30.101, Dst: 192.168.30.202
User Datagram Protocol, Src Port: 59756, Dst Port: 4789
Virtual eXtensible Local Area Network
Ethernet II, Src: Private_66:68:06 (00:50:79:66:68:06), Dst: Private_66:68:0e
(00:50:79:66:68:0e)
Internet Protocol Version 4, Src: 172.16.10.10, Dst: 172.16.10.40
Internet Control Message Protocol
```

Capture 3-1: *The first ICMP Request from server 172.16.10.10 to 172.16.10.40.*

```
Frame 148: 148 bytes on wire (1184 bits), 148 bytes captured (1184 bits) on interface
-, id 0
Ethernet II, Src: 50:00:00:01:00:07 (50:00:00:01:00:07), Dst: 50:00:00:05:00:07
(50:00:00:05:00:07)
Internet Protocol Version 4, Src: 192.168.30.101, Dst: 192.168.30.202
User Datagram Protocol, Src Port: 49508, Dst Port: 4789
Virtual eXtensible Local Area Network
Ethernet II, Src: Private_66:68:06 (00:50:79:66:68:06), Dst: Private_66:68:0e
(00:50:79:66:68:0e)
Internet Protocol Version 4, Src: 172.16.10.10, Dst: 172.16.10.40
Internet Control Message Protocol
```

Capture 3-2: *The second ICMP Request from server 172.16.10.10 to 172.16.10.40.*

All Switches in Unique ASN

The Control-Plane operation is much complex in design where all Spines and SuperSpines have unique AS. Figure 3-10 shows the BGP update propagation about the MAC Advertisement route 0050.7966.680e sent by L-202.

Phase 1: This phase is the same as what we saw in Shared design. L-202 learns MAC and IP address information and installs information into the MAC address table and L2RIB. L-202 builds the BGP Update and sends it first to S-21 and then to S-22.

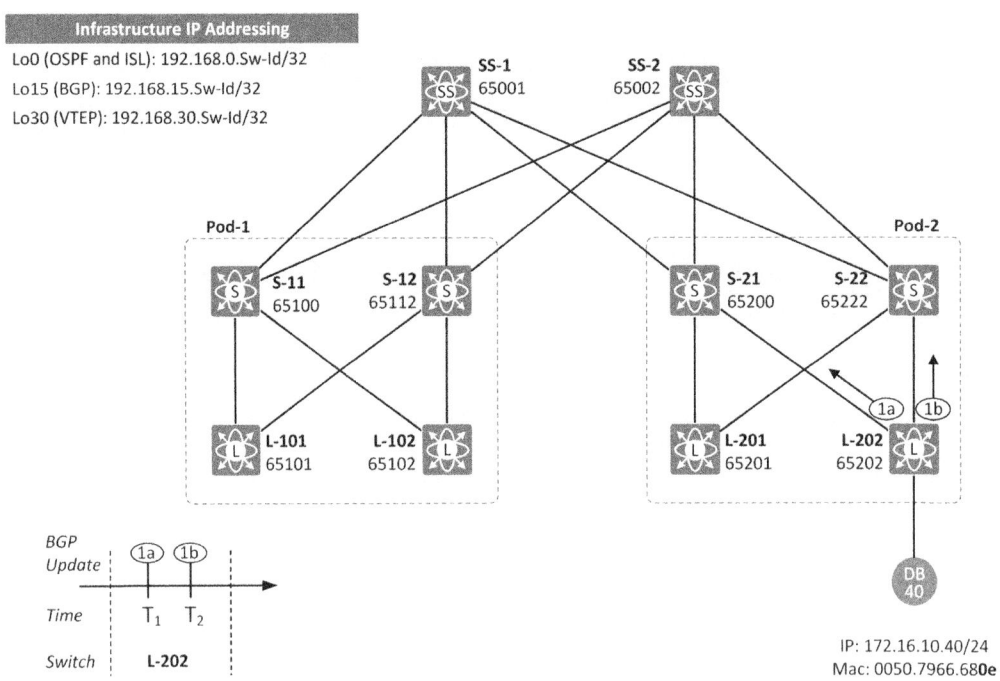

Figure 3-8: *BGP Update from L-202.*

Phases 2-3: These phases are also the same as what we saw in Shared design. S-21 receives the BGP Update earlier than S-22 because the first BGP Update was sent to S-21 by L-202. The MAC Advertisement Route is then advertised to adjacent BGP L2VPN EVPN peers L-201 (time T3), SS-1 (time T5), and SS-2 (time T7). During the update process, S-21 adds its ASN into the path-list. It retains the original Next-Hop address. S-22 does the same operation but slightly later than S-21.

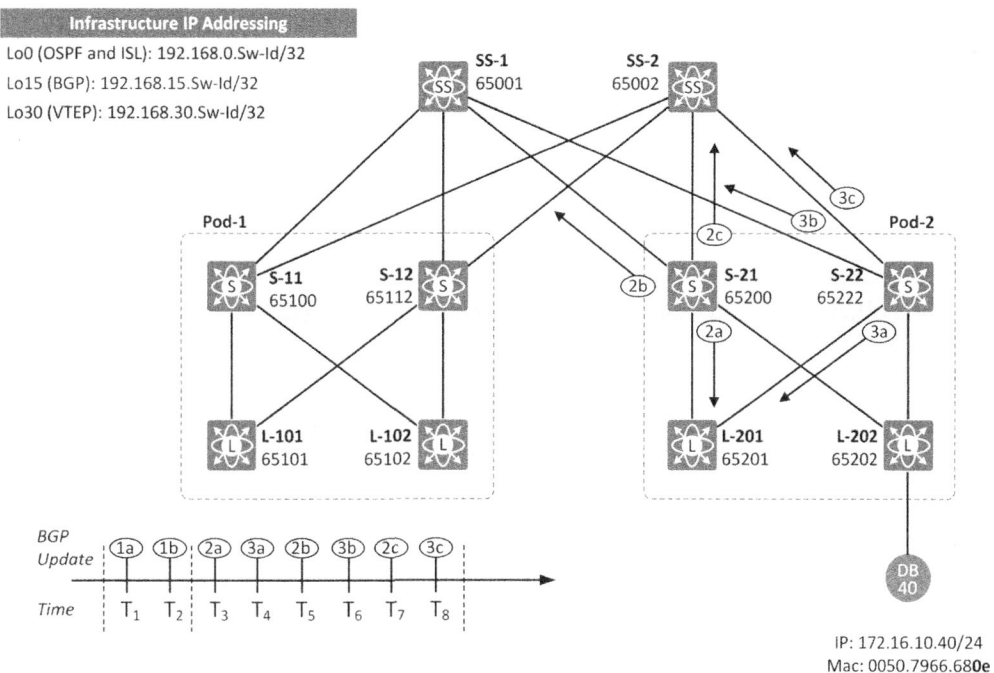

Figure 3-9: *BGP update from S-21 and S-22.*

Phases 4-6: This phase differs from what we saw on the Shared ASN example. L-201 receives BGP Update from slightly earlier from S-21 (time T_3) than from S-22 (time T_4). Based on the tie-breaker "Select Oldest Update" route from S-21 is selected as the best route and advertised to adjacent BGP L2VPN EVPN peer S-22 with local ASN added to the path-list but with original Next-Hop. SS-1 has also received the BGP Update from S-21 earlier than from S-22 and that is why it is selected as the best path and advertised to adjacent BGP L2VPN EVPN peers S-11 (time T_{10}), S-12 (time T_{12}), and S-22 (time T_{14}). The SS-2 does the same process but a bit later than SS-1. As can be seen from the example, MAC Advertisement Route is advertised from SuperSpine back to Spines in Pod-2. The same process is done by L-201. This makes it possible that Leaf-layer within a pod is used as a transit-path in certain failure events. The same applies to the SuperSpine layer, it can be used as a transit-path in for intra-Pod traffic. This may sound like a good solution but the only thing that is achieved is complexity in Control-Plane. The reason for this argument is that there have to be three link failures in our example to L-201 become a transit-path to DB40, S-22 links to both SuperSpine down, and the link between S-21 and L-202 down.

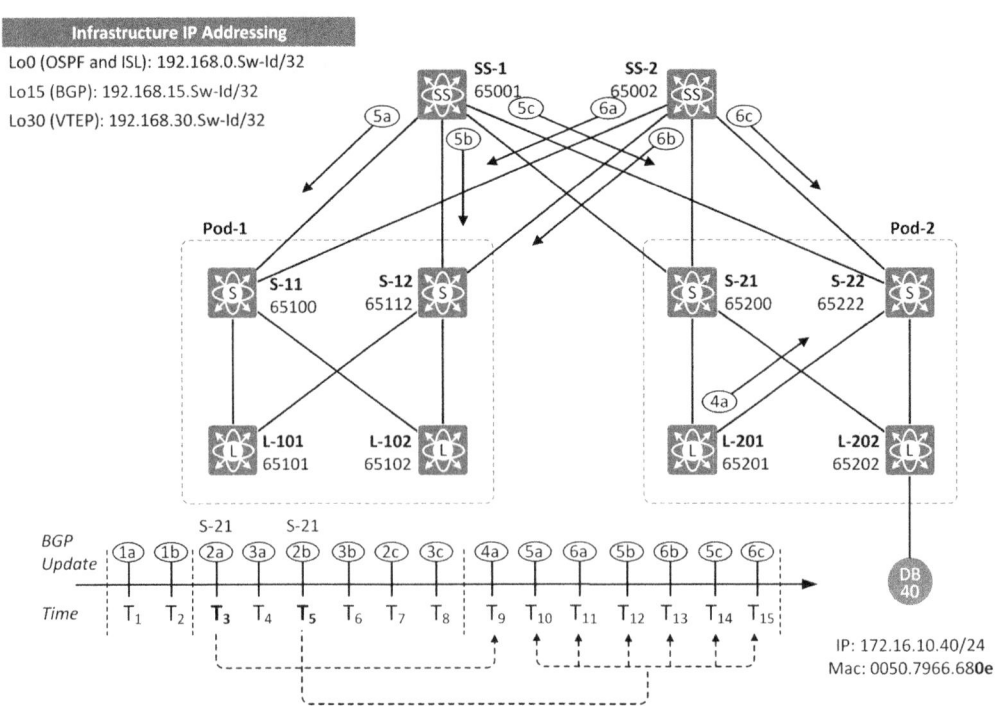

Figure 3-10: *BGP update progress.*

Now it is a good time to check the BRIB in Pod-2 switches. S-21 has only one path to the Database 40 server via L-201. The Next-Hop switch can be identified based on the ASN in the path-list. L-201, SS-1, and SS-2 are not advertised the NLRI to S-21 because they have selected the route advertised by S-21 as the best path.

```
S-21# sh bgp l2vpn evpn
   Network          Next Hop            Metric     LocPrf     Weight Path
Route Distinguisher: 192.168.15.202:32777
*>e[2]:[0]:[0]:[48]:[0050.7966.680e]:[0]:[0.0.0.0]/216
                    192.168.30.202                                  0 65202 i
```
Example 3-12: *BGP table of S-21: Spines in unique ASN.*

Unlike S-21, S-22 has four paths to the destination. The best path is obviously via L-202, while the rest of the three possible paths goes via L-201, SS-1, and SS-2. These three paths are valid for ECMP but at this phase, they are not used.

```
S-22#  sh bgp l2vpn evpn
    Network         Next Hop            Metric     LocPrf     Weight Path
Route Distinguisher: 192.168.15.202:32777
*>e[2]:[0]:[0]:[48]:[0050.7966.680e]:[0]:[0.0.0.0]/216
                    192.168.30.202                                  0 65202 i
*  e                192.168.30.201                                  0 65201 65200 65202 i
*  e                192.168.30.202                                  0 65001 65200 65202 i
*  e                192.168.30.202                                  0 65002 65200 65202 i
```
Example 3-13: *BGP table of S-22: Spines in unique ASN.*

L-201 has two paths to the destination via S-21 and S-22. Both of these paths are valid for ECMP and L-201 can do flow-based load-sharing to the destination.

```
L-201# sh bgp l2vpn evpn
    Network         Next Hop            Metric     LocPrf     Weight Path
Route Distinguisher: 192.168.15.202:32777
*  e[2]:[0]:[0]:[48]:[0050.7966.680e]:[0]:[0.0.0.0]/216
                    192.168.30.202                                  0 65222 65202 i
*>e                 192.168.30.202                                  0 65200 65202 i
```
Example 3-14: *BGP table of L-101: Spines in unique ASN.*

> **Phases 7-8:** The BGP update propagation process continues. S-11 receives the BGP Update from SS-1 earlier than from SS-2, so that route is selected as the best path and advertised to adjacent BGP L2VPN EVPN peers. The same processes apply to S-12.

98 Chapter 3: BGP Multi-AS with OSPF Underlay

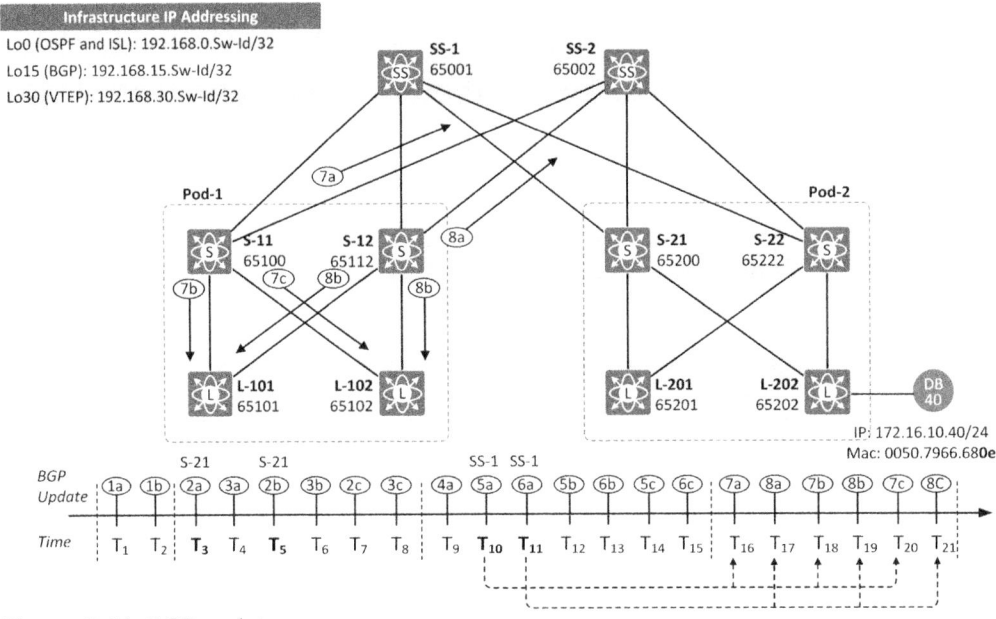

Figure 3-11: *BGP update progress.*

If we now take a look at the BRIB of SS-1, we can see that it has two valid ECMP paths to the destination.

```
SS-1# sh bgp l2vpn evpn
   Network          Next Hop           Metric    LocPrf    Weight Path
Route Distinguisher: 192.168.15.202:32777
* e[2]:[0]:[0]:[48]:[0050.7966.680e]:[0]:[0.0.0.0]/216
                    192.168.30.202                                0 65222 65202 i
*>e                 192.168.30.202                                0 65200 65202 i
```

Example 3-15: *BGP table of SS-1: Spines in unique ASN.*

SS-2, in turn, has four paths to the destination. Notable thing is that the third and fourth paths go via spine switches located in Pod-1.

```
SS-2#  sh bgp l2vpn evpn
Route Distinguisher: 192.168.15.202:32777
*>e[2]:[0]:[0]:[48]:[0050.7966.680e]:[0]:[0.0.0.0]/216
                    192.168.30.202                                0 65200 65202 i
* e                 192.168.30.202                                0 65222 65202 i
* e                 192.168.30.202                                0 65112 65001 65200 65202 i
* e                 192.168.30.202                                0 65100 65001 65200 65202 i
```

Example 3-16: *BGP table of SS-2: Spines in unique ASN.*

Phases 9-10: Both leaf switches in Pod-1 receive BGP Update message first from S-11 and then from S-12. This is why switches also select a path to the destination via S-11 and advertise it to adjacent BGP L2VPN EVPN peers.

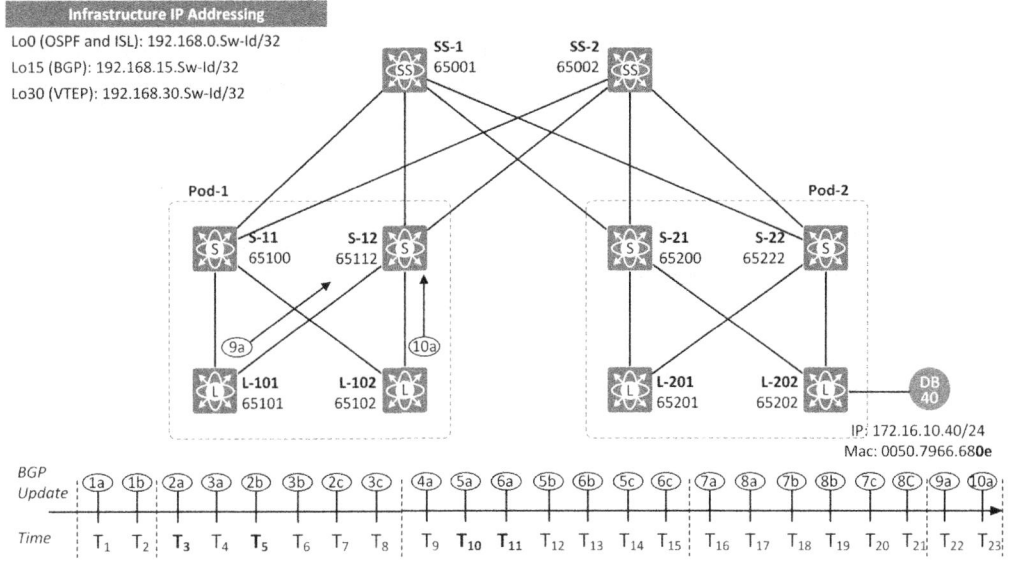

Figure 3-12: *BGP update progress.*

Example 3-17 shows that S-11 has two paths, both ECMP valid, to the destination via SuperSpine switches.

```
S-11# sh bgp l2vpn evpn
Route Distinguisher: 192.168.15.202:32777
*>e[2]:[0]:[0]:[48]:[0050.7966.680e]:[0]:[0.0.0.0]/216
                 192.168.30.202                      0 65001 65200 65202 i
* e              192.168.30.202                      0 65002 65200 65202 i
```
Example 3-17: *BGP table of S-11: Spines in unique ASN (MAC-only).*

Example 3-18, in turn, shows that S-12 has four paths to the destination. The last two paths are received from Leaf-102 and Leaf-101.

```
S-12# sh bgp l2vpn evpn
Route Distinguisher: 192.168.15.202:32777
*>e[2]:[0]:[0]:[48]:[0050.7966.680e]:[0]:[0.0.0.0]/216
                 192.168.30.202                      0 65001 65200 65202 i
* e              192.168.30.202                      0 65002 65200 65202 i
* e              192.168.30.102                      0 65102 65100 65001 65200 65202 i
* e              192.168.30.101                      0 65101 65100 65001 65200 65202 i
```
Example 3-18: *BGP table of S-12: Spines in unique ASN.*

An additional routing complexity can be seen in examples 3-19 and 3-20. The originating switch L-202 has advertised MAC-Only and MAC-IP MAC Advertisement Route within separate BGP Update messages. The timing of these BGP Updates is different and as a result, the BRIB paths to MAC-Only destination are different compared to MAC-IP in S-11 and S-12.

```
S-11# sh bgp l2vpn evpn
*>e[2]:[0]:[0]:[48]:[0050.7966.680e]:[32]:[172.16.10.40]/272
                192.168.30.202                    0 65001 65222 65202 i
* e             192.168.30.202                    0 65002 65222 65202 i
* e             192.168.15.101                    0 65101 65112 65001 65222 65202 i
* e             192.168.15.102                    0 65102 65112 65001 65222 65202 i
```
Example 3-19: *BGP table of S-11: Spines in unique ASN (MAC-IP).*

```
S-12# sh bgp l2vpn evpn
*>e[2]:[0]:[0]:[48]:[0050.7966.680e]:[32]:[172.16.10.40]/272
                192.168.30.202                    0 65001 65222 65202 i
* e             192.168.30.202                    0 65002 65222 65202 i
```
Example 3-20: *BGP table of S-12: Spines in unique ASN (MAC-IP).*

Examples 3-21 and 3-22 describest the BRIBs of L-101 and L-102.

```
L-101# sh bgp l2vpn evpn
Route Distinguisher: 192.168.15.101:32777    (L2VNI 30010)
*>e[2]:[0]:[0]:[48]:[0050.7966.680e]:[0]:[0.0.0.0]/216
                192.168.30.202                    0 65100 65001 65200 65202 i
Route Distinguisher: 192.168.15.202:32777
*>e[2]:[0]:[0]:[48]:[0050.7966.680e]:[0]:[0.0.0.0]/216
                192.168.30.202                    0 65100 65001 65200 65202 i
* e             192.168.30.202                    0 65112 65001 65200 65202 i
Route Distinguisher: 192.168.15.101:3    (L3VNI 30077)
*>e[2]:[0]:[0]:[48]:[0050.7966.680e]:[32]:[172.16.10.40]/272
                192.168.30.202                    0 65112 65001 65222 65202 i
```
Example 3-21: *BGP table of L-101: Spines in unique ASN.*

```
L-102# sh bgp l2vpn evpn
Route Distinguisher: 192.168.15.102:32777    (L2VNI 30010)
*>e[2]:[0]:[0]:[48]:[0050.7966.680e]:[0]:[0.0.0.0]/216
                192.168.30.202                    0 65100 65001 65200 65202 i
Route Distinguisher: 192.168.15.202:32777
*>e[2]:[0]:[0]:[48]:[0050.7966.680e]:[0]:[0.0.0.0]/216
                192.168.30.202                    0 65100 65001 65200 65202 i
* e             192.168.30.202                    0 65112 65001 65200 65202 i
Route Distinguisher: 192.168.15.102:3    (L3VNI 30077)
*>e[2]:[0]:[0]:[48]:[0050.7966.680e]:[32]:[172.16.10.40]/272
                192.168.30.202                    0 65112 65001 65222 65202 i
```
Example 3-22: *BGP table of L-101: Spines in unique ASN.*

BGP EVPN Design Consideration 101

The unique ASN scheme adds complexity to routing convergence. It also allows leaf switches to be used as transit nodes. This, however, requires more than one link/node failures. It is also possible that traffic between hosts within the same Pod goes all the way down to SuperSpine switches and then back to Pod, but once again it requires mode than one link/node failures. The reason for selecting Shared mode over the Unique model should now be obvious.

BGP convergence: Group of Spines in the same AS

Figure 3-5 shows the overall fabric topology with four connected hosts in the leaf layer. Spine switches within a Pod share the same BGP AS. Super Spine switches share also the ASN. Each leaf switch has a dedicated ASN. The focus of this section is to explain how the BGP convergence process when BGP adjacency from Spine-11 perspective when BGP L2VPN EVPN peering to SuperSpine-11 goes down.

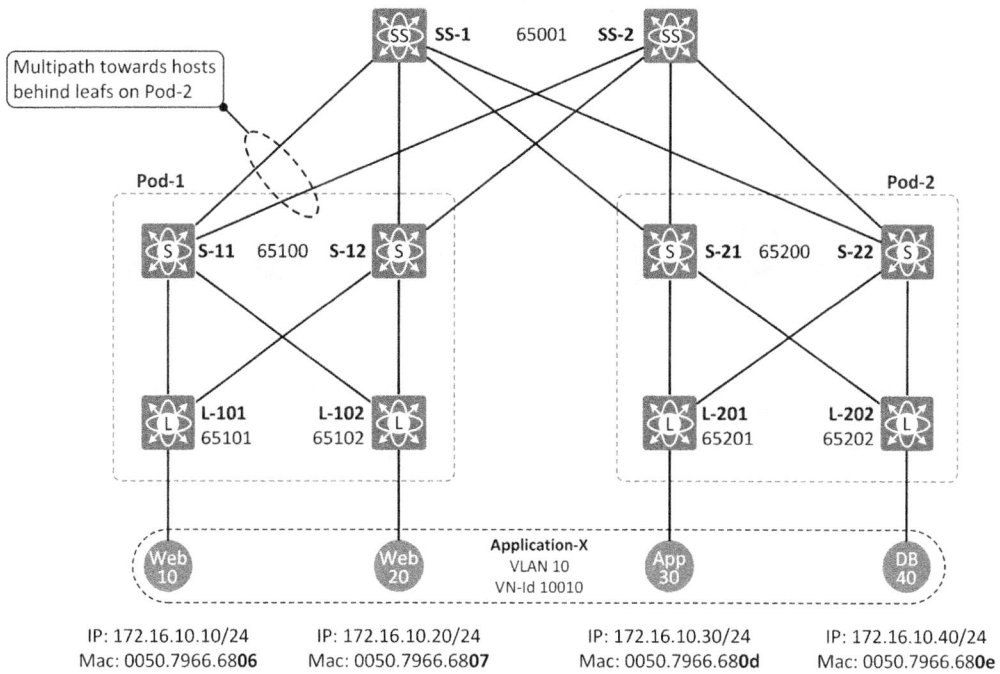

Figure 3-13: *BGP AS Scheme and Connected Hosts.*

The example below shows the BGP table of Spine-11 in a stable situation where all BGP adjacency are up. Spine-11 has installed two routes to the application server 30 (MAC: 0050.7966.680d), with both using Leaf-201 (192.168.15.201) as a next-hop. The output might look a bit confusing because neither route has been marked as multipath with "|" sign. The reason for this is that here the "multipath" does not refer to BGP load-balancing flows to the destination behind one leaf switch. The entry is marked as "multipath" in the case of EVPN ESI multihoming.

```
S-11# sh bgp l2vpn evpn
BGP routing table information for VRF default, address family L2VPN EVPN
BGP table version is 147, Local Router ID is 192.168.15.11
Status: s-suppressed, x-deleted, S-stale, d-dampened, h-history, *-valid, >-best
Path type: i-internal, e-external, c-confed, l-local, a-aggregate, r-redist, I-injected
Origin codes: i - IGP, e - EGP, ? - incomplete, | - multipath, & - backup, 2 - best2

   Network            Next Hop           Metric    LocPrf    Weight Path
Route Distinguisher: 192.168.15.101:32777
*>e[2]:[0]:[0]:[48]:[0050.7966.6806]:[0]:[0.0.0.0]/216
                      192.168.30.101                           0 65101 i
*>e[2]:[0]:[0]:[48]:[0050.7966.6806]:[32]:[172.16.10.10]/272
                      192.168.30.101                           0 65101 i
*>e[3]:[0]:[32]:[192.168.30.101]/88
                      192.168.30.101                           0 65101 i

Route Distinguisher: 192.168.15.102:32777
*>e[2]:[0]:[0]:[48]:[0050.7966.6807]:[0]:[0.0.0.0]/216
                      192.168.30.102                           0 65102 i
*>e[2]:[0]:[0]:[48]:[0050.7966.6807]:[32]:[172.16.10.20]/272
                      192.168.30.102                           0 65102 i
*>e[3]:[0]:[32]:[192.168.30.102]/88
                      192.168.30.102                           0 65102 i

Route Distinguisher: 192.168.15.201:32777
*  e[2]:[0]:[0]:[48]:[0050.7966.680d]:[0]:[0.0.0.0]/216
                      192.168.30.201                           0 65001 65200 65201 i
*>e                   192.168.30.201                           0 65001 65200 65201 i
*  e[2]:[0]:[0]:[48]:[0050.7966.680d]:[32]:[172.16.10.30]/272
                      192.168.30.201                           0 65001 65200 65201 i
*>e                   192.168.30.201                           0 65001 65200 65201 i
*  e[3]:[0]:[32]:[192.168.30.201]/88
                      192.168.30.201                           0 65001 65200 65201 i
*>e                   192.168.30.201                           0 65001 65200 65201 i

Route Distinguisher: 192.168.15.202:32777
*  e[2]:[0]:[0]:[48]:[0050.7966.680e]:[0]:[0.0.0.0]/216
                      192.168.30.202                           0 65001 65200 65202 i
*>e                   192.168.30.202                           0 65001 65200 65202 i
*  e[2]:[0]:[0]:[48]:[0050.7966.680e]:[32]:[172.16.10.40]/272
                      192.168.30.202                           0 65001 65200 65202 i
*>e                   192.168.30.202                           0 65001 65200 65202 i
*  e[3]:[0]:[32]:[192.168.30.202]/88
                      192.168.30.202                           0 65001 65200 65202 i
*>e                   192.168.30.202                           0 65001 65200 65202 i
```

Example 3-23: *show bgp l2vpn evpn on S-11 in Stable Situation.*

Example 3-24 shows that we are using eBGP multipathing. A route has to meet the following requirements in order to participate in an eBGP multipathing; (a) the same count of same ASNs listed in Path-List, (b) same Origin code, (c) same MED, (d) same Local-Preference, and (e) same IGP cost to Next-Hop. In our example, these requirements are met and both routes via SuperSpine-1 and SuperSpine-2 can be used for multipathing. Note that the first requirement about the path-list can be relaxed by using the command *bestpath as-path multipath-relax*. This removes the requirement that ASN listed in Path-ist has to be the same. The NLRI received from SuperSpine-2 is marked as the best path. The reason for that is that it is an older route than the other one. This minimizes the effect of possible route-flapping. But why only one of the routes is marked as the best path if we are using multipathing? The reason is simple, Spine-11 will only advertise the best route to its external peers Leaf-101 and Leaf-102. Note that Spine-11 will not advertise routes back to AS where NLRIs are received from.

```
S-11# sh bgp l2vpn evpn route-type 2
BGP routing table information for VRF default, address family L2VPN EVPN
<snipped>
Route Distinguisher: 192.168.15.201:32777
BGP routing table entry for [2]:[0]:[0]:[48]:[0050.7966.680d]:[0]:[0.0.0.0]/216,
version 147
Paths: (2 available, best #2)
Flags: (0x000202) (high32 00000000) on xmit-list, is not in l2rib/evpn, is not in HW
Multipath: eBGP

  Path type: external, path is valid, not best reason: newer EBGP path, no labeled
nexthop
  AS-Path: 65001 65200 65201 , path sourced external to AS
    192.168.30.201 (metric 121) from 192.168.15.1 (192.168.15.1)
      Origin IGP, MED not set, localpref 100, weight 0
      Received label 30010
      Extcommunity: RT:65100:30010 ENCAP:8

  Advertised path-id 1
  Path type: external, path is valid, is best path, no labeled nexthop
  AS-Path: 65001 65200 65201 , path sourced external to AS
    192.168.30.201 (metric 121) from 192.168.15.2 (192.168.15.2)
      Origin IGP, MED not set, localpref 100, weight 0
      Received label 30010
      Extcommunity: RT:65100:30010 ENCAP:8

  Path-id 1 advertised to peers:
    192.168.15.101    192.168.15.102
<snipped>
```

Example 3-24: *show bgp l2vpn evpn route-type 2 on S-11.*

Figure 3-14 illustrates the situation where BGP peering with Spine-11 is shut down in SuperSpine-11.

104 Chapter 3: BGP Multi-AS with OSPF Underlay

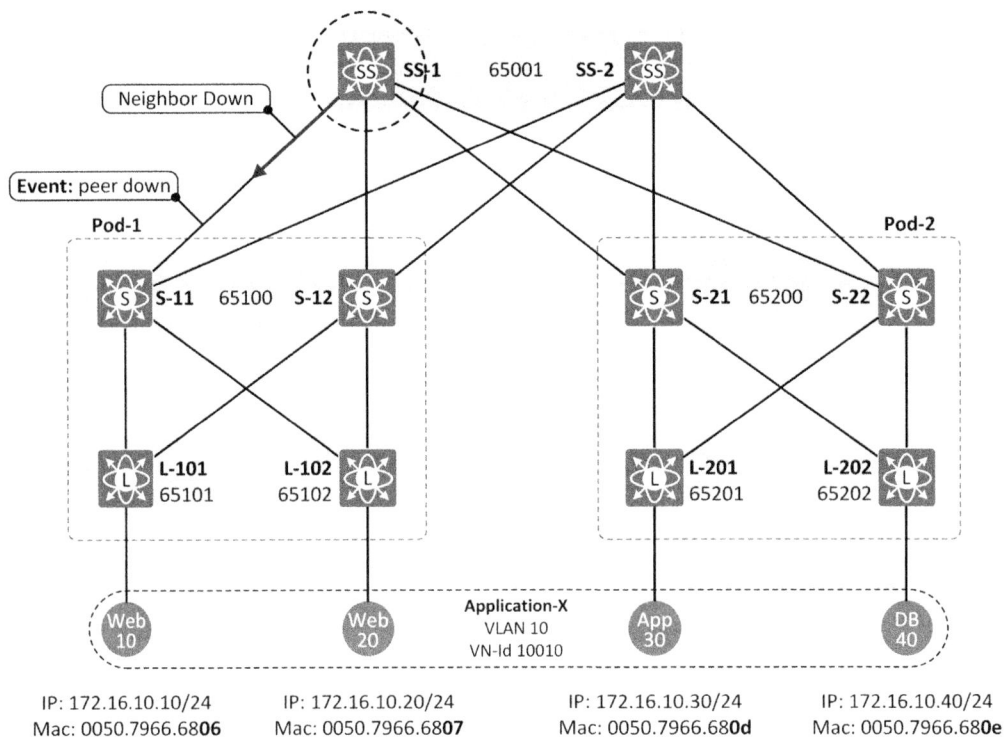

Figure 3-14: *BGP AS Scheme and Connected Hosts.*

The example below describes the reaction to the failure event from Spine-11 point of view. Note that the example only shows events focusing on Application server 30. First, Spine-11 notices that the BGP adjacency to SuperSpine-1 is down. As a reaction, it starts the best path selection process where there is no change to the current situation. Note that since we are using multipathing, there is no RIB update, the Next-Hop 192.168.15.201 for the target hasn't changed.

```
S-11#
2020 Aug  4 17:03:21.278841 bgp:    [2143] (default) RIB: [L2VPN EVPN] Triggering
bestpath selection for
192.168.15.201:32777:[2]:[0]:[0]:[48]:[0050.7966.680d]:[0]:[0.0.0.0]/112 due to peer
down, flags=0x202

2020 Aug  4 17:03:21.280207 bgp:    [2143] (default) RIB: [L2VPN EVPN] Begin select
bestpath for dest 0xce8e29dc
192.168.15.201:32777:[2]:[0]:[0]:[48]:[0050.7966.680d]:[0]:[0.0.0.0]/112,
addpath_crit=0x0, cal_nth=0, install_to_rib=0, flags=0x

2020 Aug  4 17:03:21.280276 bgp:    [2143] (default) RIB: [L2VPN EVPN] Add/delete
192.168.15.201:32777:[2]:[0]:[0]:[48]:[0050.7966.680d]:[0]:[0.0.0.0]/112, flags=0x200,
evi_ctx invalid, in_rib: no

2020 Aug  4 17:03:21.280317 bgp:    [2143] (default) RIB: [L2VPN EVPN] evi_ctx is NULL
(remote RD: 192.168.15.201:32777), no add/del
```

```
2020 Aug  4 17:03:21.280353 bgp:   [2143] (default) RIB: [L2VPN EVPN] Selected
new bestpath
192.168.15.201:32777:[2]:[0]:[0]:[48]:[0050.7966.680d]:[0]:[0.0.0.0]/112
flags=0x200 rid=192.168.15.2 nh=192.168.30.201 bestpath flags=0x40000028

2020 Aug  4 17:03:21.280404 bgp:   [2143] (default) RIB: [L2VPN EVPN]
192.168.15.201:32777:[2]:[0]:[0]:[48]:[0050.7966.680d]:[0]:[0.0.0.0]/112 path#1: set
to rid=192.168.15.2 nh=192.168.30.201 bl=0, flags=0x2, changed=0

2020 Aug  4 17:03:21.280577 bgp:   [2143] (default) RIB: [L2VPN EVPN] Resetting
repopulation flag for
192.168.15.201:32777:[2]:[0]:[0]:[48]:[0050.7966.680d]:[0]:[0.0.0.0]/112 due to no
change in RIB during bestpath selection
```

Example 3-25: *Debug bgp rib on Spine-11, BGP Adjacency with SuperSpine-1 Up -> Down.*

The example below shows the BGP process on Spine-11 when the BGP adjacency with SuperSpine-11 is restored.

```
2020 Aug  4 17:03:45.849433 bgp:   [2143] (default) RIB: [L2VPN EVPN] Triggering
bestpath selection for
192.168.15.201:32777:[2]:[0]:[0]:[48]:[0050.7966.680d]:[0]:[0.0.0.0]/112 due to brib
add resync rib, flags=0x202

2020 Aug  4 17:03:45.849938 bgp:   [2143] (default) RIB: [L2VPN EVPN] evi_ctx is NULL
(remote RD: 192.168.15.201:32777), no add/del

2020 Aug  4 17:03:45.852187 bgp:   [2143] (default) RIB: [L2VPN EVPN] Begin select
bestpath for dest 0xce8e29dc
192.168.15.201:32777:[2]:[0]:[0]:[48]:[0050.7966.680d]:[0]:[0.0.0.0]/112,
addpath_crit=0x0, cal_nth=0, install_to_rib=0, flags=0x

2020 Aug  4 17:03:45.852221 bgp:   [2143] (default) RIB: [L2VPN EVPN] No change (0x200)
in best path for
192.168.15.201:32777:[2]:[0]:[0]:[48]:[0050.7966.680d]:[0]:[0.0.0.0]/112 ,
backup/multipath changed

2020 Aug  4 17:03:45.852259 bgp:   [2143] (default) RIB: [L2VPN EVPN] Add/delete
192.168.15.201:32777:[2]:[0]:[0]:[48]:[0050.7966.680d]:[0]:[0.0.0.0]/112, flags=0x200,
evi_ctx invalid, in_rib: no

2020 Aug  4 17:03:45.852291 bgp:   [2143] (default) RIB: [L2VPN EVPN] evi_ctx is NULL
(remote RD: 192.168.15.201:32777), no add/del
```

Example 3-26: *Debug bgp rib on Spine-11, BGP Adjacency with SuperSpine-1 Down-> Up.*

BGP convergence: All switches in unique AS

This section explains the convergence complexity in design where each switch has a unique ASN. The following example explains the Control-Plane convergence process of S-11 perspective and how it affects the datapath from WEB30 in Pod-1 to DB40 in Pod-2. In the stable stage, L-101 can load balance flows between to DB40 between S-11 and S-12, and S-11 and S-12 can load balance these flows between SS-1 and SS-2.

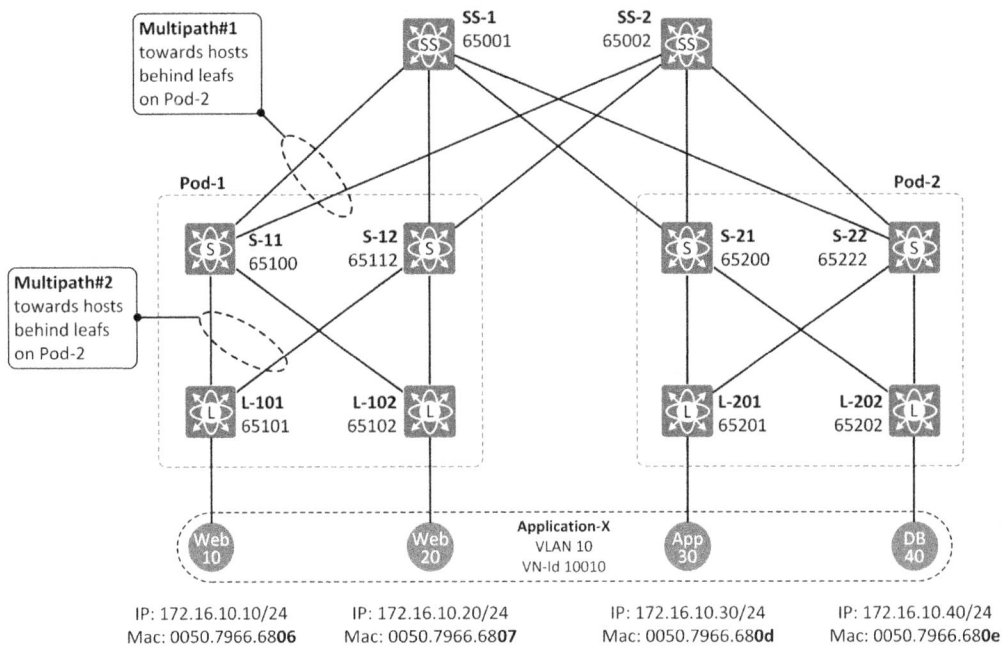

Figure 3-15: *BGP AS Scheme and Connected Hosts.*

We are now focusing on the route to server DB40 (MAC: 0050.7966.680e) from the S-11 perspective. The example below shows that Spine-11 has four possible paths to the server. The leftmost ASN in the path-list describes the peering AS (and the adjacent BGP speaker) from where the NLRI has received. The third path is marked as the best path.

```
S-11# sh bgp l2vpn evpn
BGP routing table information for VRF default, address family L2VPN EVPN
BGP table version is 1319, Local Router ID is 192.168.15.11
Status: s-suppressed, x-deleted, S-stale, d-dampened, h-history, *-valid, >-best
Path type: i-internal, e-external, c-confed, l-local, a-aggregate, r-redist, I-injected
Origin codes: i - IGP, e - EGP, ? - incomplete, | - multipath, & - backup, 2 - best2

    Network              Next Hop            Metric     LocPrf     Weight Path
Route Distinguisher: 192.168.15.101:32777
*>e[2]:[0]:[0]:[48]:[0050.7966.6806]:[0]:[0.0.0.0]/216
                         192.168.30.101                                  0 65101 i
* e                      192.168.30.101                                  0 65102 65112 65101 i
* e                      192.168.30.101                                  0 65002 65112 65101 i
* e                      192.168.30.101                                  0 65001 65112 65101 i
*>e[2]:[0]:[0]:[48]:[0050.7966.6806]:[32]:[172.16.10.10]/272
                         192.168.30.101                                  0 65101 i
* e                      192.168.30.101                                  0 65102 65112 65101 i
* e                      192.168.30.101                                  0 65002 65112 65101 i
* e                      192.168.30.101                                  0 65001 65112 65101 i
*>e[3]:[0]:[32]:[192.168.30.101]/88
                         192.168.30.101                                  0 65101 i
* e                      192.168.30.101                                  0 65102 65112 65101 i
* e                      192.168.30.101                                  0 65002 65112 65101 i
* e                      192.168.30.101                                  0 65001 65112 65101 i

Route Distinguisher: 192.168.15.102:32777
*>e[2]:[0]:[0]:[48]:[0050.7966.6807]:[0]:[0.0.0.0]/216
                         192.168.30.102                                  0 65102 i
*>e[2]:[0]:[0]:[48]:[0050.7966.6807]:[32]:[172.16.10.20]/272
                         192.168.30.102                                  0 65102 i
* e                      192.168.30.102                                  0 65101 65112 65102 i
* e                      192.168.30.102                                  0 65002 65112 65102 i
* e                      192.168.30.102                                  0 65001 65112 65102 i
*>e[3]:[0]:[32]:[192.168.30.102]/88
                         192.168.30.102                                  0 65102 i
* e                      192.168.30.102                                  0 65101 65112 65102 i
* e                      192.168.30.102                                  0 65002 65112 65102 i
* e                      192.168.30.102                                  0 65001 65112 65102 i

Route Distinguisher: 192.168.15.201:32777
* e[2]:[0]:[0]:[48]:[0050.7966.680d]:[0]:[0.0.0.0]/216
                         192.168.30.201                                  0 65102 65112 65002 65222
65201 i
* e                      192.168.30.201                                  0 65101 65112 65002 65222 65201 i
*>e                      192.168.30.201                                  0 65002 65222 65201 i
* e                      192.168.30.201                                  0 65001 65222 65201 i
* e[2]:[0]:[0]:[48]:[0050.7966.680d]:[32]:[172.16.10.30]/272
                         192.168.30.201                                  0 65101 65112 65001 65222 65201 i
* e                      192.168.30.201                                  0 65102 65112 65001 65222 65201 i
*>e                      192.168.30.201                                  0 65002 65200 65201 i
* e                      192.168.30.201                                  0 65001 65222 65201 i
* e[3]:[0]:[32]:[192.168.30.201]/88
                         192.168.30.201                                  0 65101 65112 65001 65222 65201 i
* e                      192.168.30.201                                  0 65102 65112 65001 65222 65201 i
*>e                      192.168.30.201                                  0 65002 65200 65201 i
* e                      192.168.30.201                                  0 65001 65222 65201 i

Route Distinguisher: 192.168.15.202:32777
* e[2]:[0]:[0]:[48]:[0050.7966.680e]:[0]:[0.0.0.0]/216
                         192.168.30.202                                  0 65101 65112 65001 65200 65202 i
* e                      192.168.30.202                                  0 65102 65112 65001 65200 65202 i
*>e                      192.168.30.202                                  0 65002 65200 65202 i
* e                      192.168.30.202                                  0 65001 65200 65202 i
* e[2]:[0]:[0]:[48]:[0050.7966.680e]:[32]:[172.16.10.40]/272
                         192.168.30.202                                  0 65101 65112 65001 65222 65202 i
* e                      192.168.30.202                                  0 65102 65112 65001 65222 65202 i
*>e                      192.168.30.202                                  0 65002 65222 65202 i
* e                      192.168.30.202                                  0 65001 65222 65202 i
```

```
* e[3]:[0]:[32]:[192.168.30.202]/88
                  192.168.30.202                    0 65101 65112 65002 65200 65202 i
* e               192.168.30.202                    0 65102 65112 65002 65200 65202 i
*>e               192.168.30.202                    0 65002 65200 65202 i
* e               192.168.30.202                    0 65001 65200 65202 i
```

Example 3-27: *BGP table of Spine-11 in Stabile Situation.*

The AS path-list is longer in NLRIs received from Leaf-101 and Leaf-102 than what is received from SuperSpine-1 and SuperSpine-2. This means that path via leaf switches are not used in a stable situation and the traffic from servers in Pod-1 to servers in Pod-2 will be load-balanced between SuperSpine-1 and SuperSpine-2. Spine-11 has select the NLRI received from the SuperSpine-2 as a best and it is advertised to BGP neighbors SuperSpine-1, Leaf-101, and Leaf-102.

```
S-11# sh bgp l2vpn evpn 0050.7966.680e
BGP routing table information for VRF default, address family L2VPN EVPN
Route Distinguisher: 192.168.15.202:32777
BGP routing table entry for [2]:[0]:[0]:[48]:[0050.7966.680e]:[0]:[0.0.0.0]/216,
 version 1299
Paths: (4 available, best #3)
Flags: (0x000202) (high32 00000000) on xmit-list, is not in l2rib/evpn, is not in HW
Multipath: eBGP

  Path type: external, path is valid, not best reason: AS Path, no labeled nexthop
  AS-Path: 65101 65112 65001 65200 65202 , path sourced external to AS
    192.168.30.202 (metric 121) from 192.168.15.101 (192.168.15.101)
      Origin IGP, MED not set, localpref 100, weight 0
      Received label 30010
      Extcommunity: RT:65100:30010 ENCAP:8

  Path type: external, path is valid, not best reason: Router Id, no labeled nexthop
  AS-Path: 65102 65112 65001 65200 65202 , path sourced external to AS
    192.168.30.202 (metric 121) from 192.168.15.102 (192.168.15.102)
      Origin IGP, MED not set, localpref 100, weight 0
      Received label 30010
      Extcommunity: RT:65100:30010 ENCAP:8

  Advertised path-id 1
  Path type: external, path is valid, is best path, no labeled nexthop
  AS-Path: 65002 65200 65202 , path sourced external to AS
    192.168.30.202 (metric 121) from 192.168.15.2 (192.168.15.2)
      Origin IGP, MED not set, localpref 100, weight 0
      Received label 30010
      Extcommunity: RT:65100:30010 ENCAP:8

  Path type: external, path is valid, not best reason: newer EBGP path, no labeled
 nexthop
  AS-Path: 65001 65200 65202 , path sourced external to AS
    192.168.30.202 (metric 121) from 192.168.15.1 (192.168.15.1)
      Origin IGP, MED not set, localpref 100, weight 0
      Received label 30010
      Extcommunity: RT:65100:30010 ENCAP:8

  Path-id 1 advertised to peers:
    192.168.15.1        192.168.15.101      192.168.15.102
```

Example 3-28: *BGP table of Spine-11 in Stabile Situation.*

Now the BGP peering to Spine-11 is closed by SuperSpine.

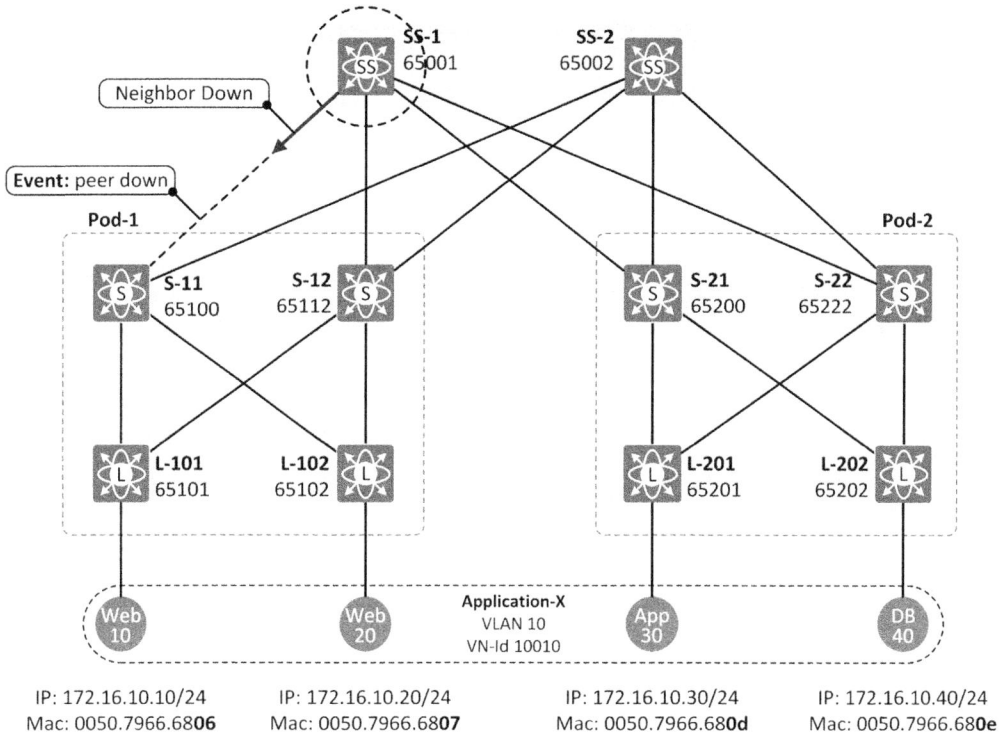

Figure 3-16: *BGP peering down between Spine-11 and SuperSpine-1.*

The result is obvious, due to the neighbor down event, all NLRIs received from SuperSpine-1 are removed from the BGP table. The best path hasn't changed at this stage.

```
S-11# sh bgp l2vpn evpn 0050.7966.680e
BGP routing table information for VRF default, address family L2VPN EVPN
Route Distinguisher: 192.168.15.202:32777
BGP routing table entry for [2]:[0]:[0]:[48]:[0050.7966.680e]:[0]:[0.0.0.0]/216,
version 1328
Paths: (3 available, best #3)
Flags: (0x000202) (high32 00000000) on xmit-list, is not in l2rib/evpn, is not in HW
Multipath: eBGP

  Path type: external, path is valid, not best reason: AS Path, no labeled nexthop
  AS-Path: 65101 65112 65001 65200 65202 , path sourced external to AS
    192.168.30.202 (metric 121) from 192.168.15.101 (192.168.15.101)
      Origin IGP, MED not set, localpref 100, weight 0
      Received label 30010
      Extcommunity: RT:65100:30010 ENCAP:8

  Path type: external, path is valid, not best reason: Router Id, no labeled nexthop
```

```
AS-Path: 65102 65112 65001 65200 65202 , path sourced external to AS
   192.168.30.202 (metric 121) from 192.168.15.102 (192.168.15.102)
      Origin IGP, MED not set, localpref 100, weight 0
      Received label 30010
      Extcommunity: RT:65100:30010 ENCAP:8

Advertised path-id 1
Path type: external, path is valid, is best path, no labeled nexthop
AS-Path: 65002 65200 65202 , path sourced external to AS
   192.168.30.202 (metric 121) from 192.168.15.2 (192.168.15.2)
      Origin IGP, MED not set, localpref 100, weight 0
      Received label 30010
      Extcommunity: RT:65100:30010 ENCAP:8

Path-id 1 advertised to peers:
   192.168.15.101     192.168.15.102
```

Example 3-29: *BGP table of Spine-11: Peer SuperSpine-1 Down.*

Now the BGP peering to Spine-11 is also torn down by SuperSpine-2. This means that Spine-11 is now restricted from the SuperSpine layer. Even though it has the route via L-102 to DB40, either L-101 or L-102 doesn't use it when sending traffic to servers in Pod-2. It still can be used for Intra-Pod traffic forwarding.

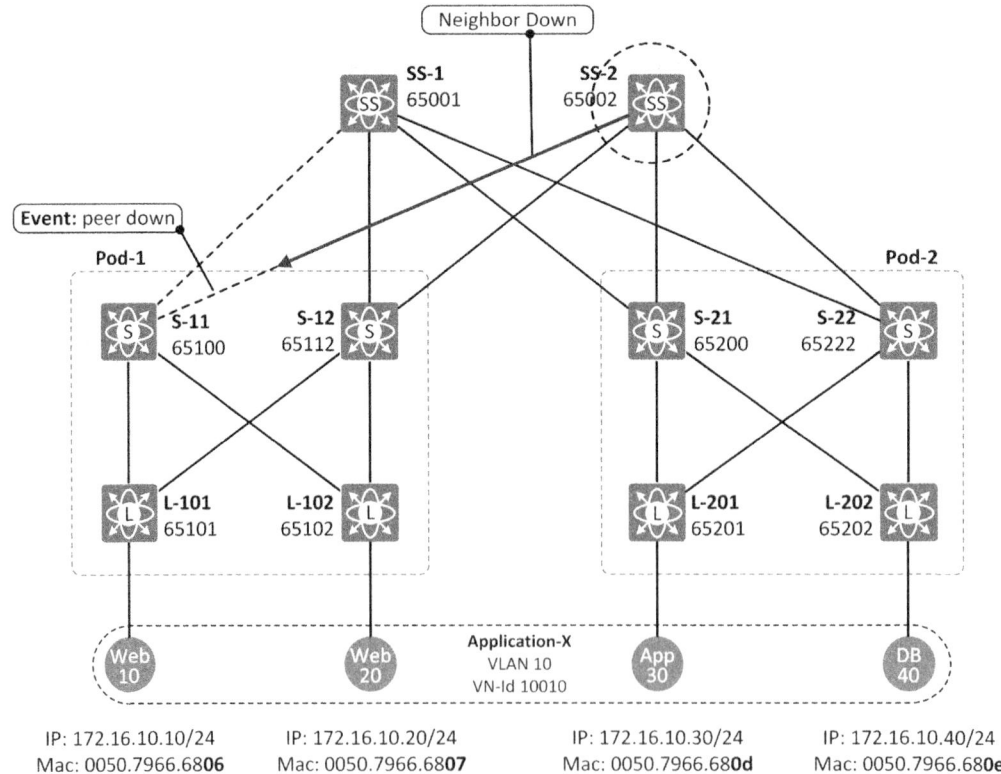

Figure 3-17: *BGP peering down between S-11 and SS-1 as well as S-11 and SS-2.*

Example 3-30 now shows that Spine-11 is still able to forward traffic between hosts in Pod-1 and Pod-2 using leaf layer switches. The path via L-101 is selected as the best path so S-11 only advertises routing information to L-102.

```
S-11# sh bgp l2vpn evpn 0050.7966.680e
BGP routing table information for VRF default, address family L2VPN EVPN
Route Distinguisher: 192.168.15.202:32777
BGP routing table entry for [2]:[0]:[0]:[48]:[0050.7966.680e]:[0]:[0.0.0.0]/216,
version 1339
Paths: (2 available, best #1)
Flags: (0x000202) (high32 00000000) on xmit-list, is not in l2rib/evpn, is not in HW
Multipath: eBGP

  Advertised path-id 1
  Path type: external, path is valid, is best path, no labeled nexthop
  AS-Path: 65101 65112 65001 65200 65202 , path sourced external to AS
    192.168.30.202 (metric 121) from 192.168.15.101 (192.168.15.101)
      Origin IGP, MED not set, localpref 100, weight 0
      Received label 30010
      Extcommunity: RT:65100:30010 ENCAP:8

  Path type: external, path is valid, not best reason: Router Id, no labeled nexthop
  AS-Path: 65102 65112 65001 65200 65202 , path sourced external to AS
    192.168.30.202 (metric 121) from 192.168.15.102 (192.168.15.102)
      Origin IGP, MED not set, localpref 100, weight 0
      Received label 30010
      Extcommunity: RT:65100:30010 ENCAP:8

  Path-id 1 advertised to peers:
    192.168.15.102
```

Example 3-30: *BGP table of Spine-11: Peering to SS-1 and SS-2 are Down.*

When the link between S-11 and L-102 is torn down, the traffic from WEB10 to DB40 is routed via S-11.

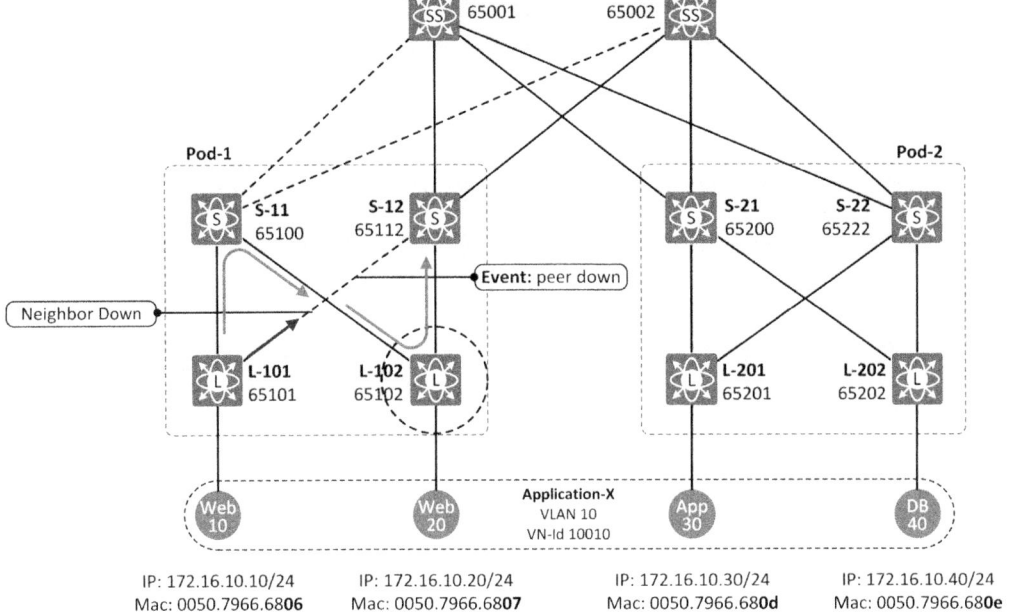

Figure 3-18: *BGP peering down between S-11 and SS-1 as well as S-11 and SS-2.*

This can be verified from the example below.

```
S-11# sh bgp l2vpn evpn 0050.7966.680e
BGP routing table information for VRF default, address family L2VPN EVPN
Route Distinguisher: 192.168.15.202:32777
BGP routing table entry for [2]:[0]:[0]:[48]:[0050.7966.680e]:[0]:[0.0.0.0]/216,
version 1339
Paths: (2 available, best #1)
Flags: (0x000202) (high32 00000000) on xmit-list, is not in l2rib/evpn, is not in HW
Multipath: eBGP

  Advertised path-id 1
  Path type: external, path is valid, is best path, no labeled nexthop
  AS-Path: 65102 65112 65001 65200 65202 , path sourced external to AS
    192.168.30.202 (metric 121) from 192.168.15.102 (192.168.15.102)
      Origin IGP, MED not set, localpref 100, weight 0
      Received label 30010
      Extcommunity: RT:65100:30010 ENCAP:8

  Path-id 1 advertised to peers:
    192.168.15.101
```

Example 3-31: *BGP table of Spine-11: Peering to SS-1, SS-2, and L-102 down.*

As a summary, we can say that even though a unique ASN model offers redundancy, it increases complexity.

Complexity Chart of Multi-ASN Design with OSPF Underlay

The main difference between these two solutions is that when all switches are in unique AS, Failure in the network might launch the Path-Hunting process which increases recovery time. Besides, Valey-Free routing is only achieved with a shared ASN model in Spine and Supre-Spine layer.

Spines in shared ASN – OSPF Underlay

		L	S	SS
Infrastructure IP Addressing				
Native Support for Unnumbered IP	Yes			
Requires subnet per Inter-switch link	No			
Loopback Interface Count		3	2	2
Overlay BGP Adjacency				
Update Source Modification		Yes	Yes	Yes
Increasing TTL (eBGP Multihop)		Yes	Yes	Yes
Support Dynamic-AS in Spine Layer		--	Yes	--
BGP Update Policy				
Retain Route-Targets (retain route-target all)		No	Yes	Yes
Rewrite ASN Part of Route-Target (rewrite-evp-rt-asn)		Yes	Yes	Yes
Requires Unmodified N-H address config (for EVPN)		No	Yes	Yes
Removing BGP Loop Prevention (allow-as in)		No	No	No
Removing BGP Loop Prevention (disable-peer-check)		No	No	No
Requires BGP RR-Cluster in Spine and SuperSpine layer		--	No	No
IPv4/EVPN NLRIs in the same BGP message		No	No	No
Other Considerations				
Possibility to restrict switch from the Overlay Network without disturbing Underlay Network	Yes			

Table 3-1: *Multi-ASN Model Complexity Chart – Spine in Shared ASN.*

All switches in unique ASN - OSPF Underlay

		L	S	SS
Infrastructure IP Addressing				
Native Support for Unnumbered IP	Yes			
Requires subnet per Inter-switch link	No			
Loopback Interface Count		3	2	2
Overlay BGP Adjacency				
Update Source Modification		Yes	Yes	Yes
Increasing TTL (eBGP Multihop)		Yes	Yes	Yes
Support Dynamic-AS in Spine Layer		--	Yes	--
BGP Update Policy				
Retain Route-Targets (retain route-target all)		No	Yes	Yes
Rewrite ASN Part of Route-Target (rewrite-evp-rt-asn)		Yes	Yes	Yes
Requires Unmodified N-H address config (for EVPN)		No	Yes	Yes
Removing BGP Loop Prevention (allow-as in)		No	No	No
Removing BGP Loop Prevention (disable-peer-check)		No	No	No
Requires BGP RR-Cluster in Spine and SuperSpine layer		--	Yes	Yes
IPv4/EVPN NLRIs in the same BGP message		No	No	No
Other Considerations				
Possibility to restrict switch from the Overlay Network without disturbing Underlay Network	Yes			
Path-hunting during convergence				
No Valey-Free routing				

Table 3-2: *Multi-ASN Model Complexity Chart – All switches in Unique ASN.*

References

[RFC 7938]   P.Lapukhov et al., "Use of BGP for Routing in Large-Scale Data Centers", RFC 7938, August 2016.

[RFC 4271]   Y. Rekhter et al., "A Border Gateway Protocol 4 (BGP-4)", RFC 4271, January 2006.

Chapter 4: BGP Only Multi-ASN Design

Introduction

The focus of this chapter is to explain how BGP can be implemented in Underlay and Overlay Network Control-Plane protocol. The first part describes the eBGP peering model where Underlay peerings (IPv4/Unicast) are done between IP addresses used in Inter-Switch Links and Overlay peering (L2VPN/EVPN) is done between logical Loopback interfaces. The second part discusses a model where both Underlay and Overlay peerings are established between IP addresses used in Inter-Switch Links.

Underlay: Direct Peering – Overlay: Loopback

Figure 4-1 illustrates the topology used in this section. I'm using only three switches for simplicity. Underlay Network BGP adjacencies (IPv4 Unicast) are formed between IP addresses used in Inter-Switch Links. IP addresses of Loopback 15 and 30 interfaces are advertised over this peering. Advertisements can be done either under IPv4 Unicast address-family by using network clauses or by using route-maps where advertised interfaces are defined. The latter option fits better for template-based operation because it can be used across all switches.

EVPN specific NLRIs are advertised over an Overlay L2VPN EVPN peering. MAC-Advertisement Routes (EVPN Route-Type 2) used for host reachability are advertised automatically. Inclusive Multicast Routes (EVPN Route-Type 3) and ESI Multihoming (Route-Types 1 and 4) are advertised automatically if used. IP Prefix routes (Route-Type 5) are not advertised without redistributed from other than BGP route sources.

The peering model does not affect Data-Plane encapsulation. However, the failure detection/recovery process is naturally different when using BGP versus OSPF.

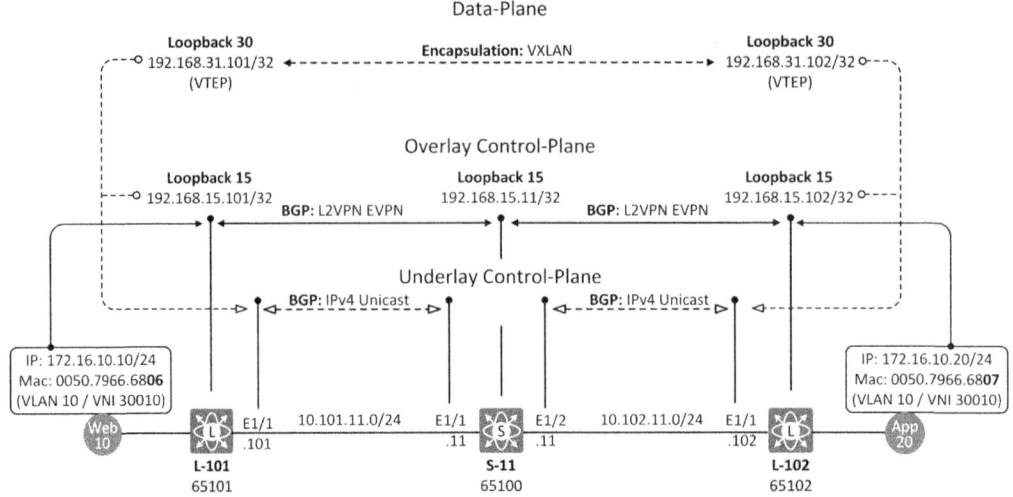

Figure 4-1: *BGP peering down between S-11 and SS-1 as well as S-11 and SS-2.*

Example 4-1 shows the BGP configuration of L-101. There is two neighbor specification to S-11. The first peering is for Underlay Network using address-family IPv4 Unicast for advertising loopback information between interface IP addresses. The second peering is for Overlay Network and its use for EVPN routes. Because it is configured between loopback interfaces.

```
route-map REDISTRIBUTE-LOOPBACK permit 10
  match interface loopback15 loopback30
!
router bgp 65101
  router-id 192.168.15.101
  bestpath as-path multipath-relax
  address-family ipv4 unicast
    redistribute direct route-map REDISTRIBUTE-LOOPBACK
  address-family l2vpn evpn
    maximum-paths 8
    retain route-target all
  neighbor 10.101.11.11
    remote-as 65100
    description ** Underlay BGP Peer **
    address-family ipv4 unicast
  neighbor 192.168.15.11
    remote-as 65100
    description ** BGP Overlay Peer **
    update-source loopback15
    ebgp-multihop 2
    address-family l2vpn evpn
      send-community
      send-community extended
      rewrite-evpn-rt-asn
```

Example 4-1: *BGP configuration on L-101.*

Example 4-2 shows the configuration on S-11. Note, that both Underlay and Overlay BGP adjacency is based on the Dynamic-AS model, where S-11 passively wait for TCP connection to port 179 from neighbors defined in neighbor clause

```
route-map Dynamic-BGP-AS-List permit 10
  match as-number 65001, 65002, 65101, 65102
!
router bgp 65100
  router-id 192.168.15.11
  bestpath as-path multipath-relax
  address-family ipv4 unicast
    maximum-paths 8
  address-family l2vpn evpn
    maximum-paths 8
    nexthop route-map RETAIN-NH
    retain route-target all
  template peer eBGP-peers
    address-family l2vpn evpn
      rewrite-evpn-rt-asn
  neighbor 10.0.0.0/8 remote-as route-map Dynamic-BGP-AS-List
    description ** Underlay BGP Peer **
    address-family ipv4 unicast
  neighbor 192.168.15.0/24 remote-as route-map Dynamic-BGP-AS-List
    inherit peer eBGP-peers
    shutdown
    update-source loopback15
    ebgp-multihop 2
    address-family l2vpn evpn
      send-community
      send-community extended
      route-map RETAIN-NH out
```

Example 4-2: *BGP configuration on S-11.*

Examples 4-3 and 4-4 show that there are two TCP connections between L-101 and S-11. The TCP connection 192.168.15.101:23655 – 192.168.15.11:179 is used for exchange EVPN NLRIs and the second one 10.101.11.101:44588 – 10.101.11.11:179 is used for IPv4 unicast NLRIs. Note that both TCP connections are started by L-101.

```
L-101# show sockets connection tcp | i ESTAB
ESTAB      0      0     192.168.15.101:23655         192.168.15.11:179
ESTAB      0      0     10.101.11.101:44588          10.101.11.11:179
```

Example 4-3: *TCP socket information on L-101.*

```
S-11# show sockets connection tcp | i ESTAB
ESTAB      0      0     192.168.15.11:179            192.168.15.101:23655
ESTAB      0      0     10.101.11.11:179             10.101.11.101:44588
ESTAB      0      0     192.168.15.11:179            192.168.15.102:22330
ESTAB      0      0     10.102.11.11:179             10.102.11.102:56667
```

Example 4-4: *TCP socket information on S-11.*

Example 4-4 shows that L-101 has on BGP IPv4 Unicast peer and it has received three prefixes from it.

```
L-101# sh ip bgp summary
BGP summary information for VRF default, address family IPv4 Unicast
BGP router identifier 192.168.15.101, local AS number 65101
BGP table version is 16, IPv4 Unicast config peers 1, capable peers 1
5 network entries and 5 paths using 1200 bytes of memory
BGP attribute entries [3/492], BGP AS path entries [2/16]
BGP community entries [0/0], BGP clusterlist entries [0/0]

Neighbor        V    AS MsgRcvd MsgSent   TblVer  InQ OutQ Up/Down  State/PfxRcd
10.101.11.11    4 65100      88      85       16    0    0 00:12:03 3
```
Example 4-4: *L-101 BGP IPv4 Unicast peering.*

Example 4-5 shows that L-101 has received NLRIs about Loopback 15 interface of S-11 and L-101, used for Overlay BGP peering. Besides, it has received NLRIs about loopback 30 used for the VTEP address by L-102.

```
L-101# sh ip bgp
BGP routing table information for VRF default, address family IPv4 Unicast
BGP table version is 16, Local Router ID is 192.168.15.101
Status: s-suppressed, x-deleted, S-stale, d-dampened, h-history, *-valid, >-best
Path type: i-internal, e-external, c-confed, l-local, a-aggregate, r-redist, I-
injected
Origin codes: i - IGP, e - EGP, ? - incomplete, | - multipath, & - backup, 2 - best2

   Network            Next Hop           Metric     LocPrf     Weight Path
*>e192.168.15.11/32   10.101.11.11            0                     0 65100 ?
*>r192.168.15.101/32  0.0.0.0                 0        100      32768 ?
*>e192.168.15.102/32  10.101.11.11                                   0 65100 65102 ?
*>r192.168.30.101/32  0.0.0.0                 0        100      32768 ?
*>e192.168.30.102/32  10.101.11.11                                   0 65100 65102 ?
```
Example 4-5: *IPv4 entries in BRIB of L-101.*

Example 4-6 shows that L-101 has BGP L2VPN EVPN peering with S-11 and it has received three EVPN NLRIs from it.

```
L-101# sh bgp l2vpn evpn summary
BGP summary information for VRF default, address family L2VPN EVPN
BGP router identifier 192.168.15.101, local AS number 65101
BGP table version is 123, L2VPN EVPN config peers 2, capable peers 1
10 network entries and 10 paths using 1920 bytes of memory
BGP attribute entries [9/1476], BGP AS path entries [1/10]
BGP community entries [0/0], BGP clusterlist entries [0/0]

Neighbor        V    AS MsgRcvd MsgSent   TblVer  InQ OutQ Up/Down  State/PfxRcd
192.168.15.11   4 65100     159     146      123    0    0 00:12:14 3
```
Example 4-6: *L-101 BGP L2VPN EVPN peering.*

Example 4-7 shows the BRIB entries of L-101. EVPN Route-Types under Route-Distinguishers 192.168.15.102:32777 are received routes. There are two Mac-Advertisement Routes about Database server 40 (0050.7966.6807-172.16.10.20/32), one for MAC-Only and one for MAC-IP NLRI. Also, there is one Inclusive Multicast Route for L2BUM forwarding. EVPN Route-Types under Route-Distinguishers 192.168.15.101:32777 describes the L-101 local routes as well as routes imported from Adj-RIB-In into L2VNI 30010 specific BRIB.

```
L-101# sh bgp l2vpn evpn
BGP routing table information for VRF default, address family L2VPN EVPN
BGP table version is 123, Local Router ID is 192.168.15.101
Status: s-suppressed, x-deleted, S-stale, d-dampened, h-history, *-valid, >-best
Path type: i-internal, e-external, c-confed, l-local, a-aggregate, r-redist, I-
injected
Origin codes: i - IGP, e - EGP, ? - incomplete, | - multipath, & - backup, 2 - best2

   Network            Next Hop            Metric     LocPrf     Weight Path
Route Distinguisher: 192.168.15.101:32777     (L2VNI 30010)
*>l[2]:[0]:[0]:[48]:[0050.7966.6806]:[0]:[0.0.0.0]/216
                      192.168.30.101                    100        32768 i
*>e[2]:[0]:[0]:[48]:[0050.7966.6807]:[0]:[0.0.0.0]/216
                      192.168.30.102                                  0 65100 65102 i
*>l[2]:[0]:[0]:[48]:[0050.7966.6806]:[32]:[172.16.10.10]/272
                      192.168.30.101                    100        32768 i
*>e[2]:[0]:[0]:[48]:[0050.7966.6807]:[32]:[172.16.10.20]/272
                      192.168.30.102                                  0 65100 65102 i
*>l[3]:[0]:[32]:[192.168.30.101]/88
                      192.168.30.101                    100        32768 i
*>e[3]:[0]:[32]:[192.168.30.102]/88
                      192.168.30.102                                  0 65100 65102 i

Route Distinguisher: 192.168.15.102:32777
*>e[2]:[0]:[0]:[48]:[0050.7966.6807]:[0]:[0.0.0.0]/216
                      192.168.30.102                                  0 65100 65102 i
*>e[2]:[0]:[0]:[48]:[0050.7966.6807]:[32]:[172.16.10.20]/272
                      192.168.30.102                                  0 65100 65102 i
*>e[3]:[0]:[32]:[192.168.30.102]/88
                      192.168.30.102                                  0 65100 65102 i

Route Distinguisher: 192.168.15.101:3      (L3VNI 30077)
*>e[2]:[0]:[0]:[48]:[0050.7966.6807]:[32]:[172.16.10.20]/272
                      192.168.30.102                                  0 65100 65102 i
```

Example 4-7: *BRIB of L-101.*

Example 4-8 shows that L-101 NVE peering is up with L-102.

```
L-101# sh nve pee detail
Details of nve Peers:
----------------------------------------
Peer-Ip: 192.168.30.102
    NVE Interface       : nve1
    Peer State          : Up
    Peer Uptime         : 01:05:10
    Router-Mac          : 5000.0002.0007
    Peer First VNI      : 30077
    Time since Create   : 01:05:10
    Configured VNIs     : 30010,30077
    Provision State     : peer-add-complete
    Learnt CP VNIs      : 30010,30077
    vni assignment mode : SYMMETRIC
    Peer Location       : N/A
```

Example 4-8: *NVE peer of L-101.*

Example 4-9 shows that L-101 has installed the MAC address advertised originally by L-102 into the MAC address table of VLAN 10. The example also shows that the MAC address is learned via BGP and that the next-Hop used for that MAC is VTEP used by L-102.

```
L-101# sh l2route evpn mac evi 10

Flags -(Rmac):Router MAC (Stt):Static (L):Local (R):Remote (V):vPC link
(Dup):Duplicate (Spl):Split (Rcv):Recv (AD):Auto-Delete (D):Del Pending
(S):Stale (C):Clear, (Ps):Peer Sync (O):Re-Originated (Nho):NH-Override
(Pf):Permanently-Frozen, (Orp): Orphan

Topology    Mac Address    Prod   Flags       Seq No      Next-Hops
----------  -------------- ------ ----------- ----------  ---------------------------
10          0050.7966.6806 Local  L,          0           Eth1/3
10          0050.7966.6807 BGP    SplRcv      0           192.168.30.102
```

Example 4-9: *MAC Address Table of L-101.*

The packet capture below verifies that Underlay Network IP reachability information is sent over TCP socket 0   10.101.11.101:44588 - 10.101.11.11:179.

BGP EVPN Design Consideration 123

```
Ethernet II, Src: 50:00:00:01:00:07 (50:00:00:01:00:07), Dst: 50:00:00:08:00:07
(50:00:00:08:00:07)
Internet Protocol Version 4, Src: 10.101.11.101, Dst: 10.101.11.11
Transmission Control Protocol, Src Port: 44588, Dst Port: 179, Seq: 90, Ack: 262, Len:
114
Border Gateway Protocol - UPDATE Message
    Marker: ffffffffffffffffffffffffffffffff
    Length: 66
    Type: UPDATE Message (2)
    Withdrawn Routes Length: 0
    Total Path Attribute Length: 43
    Path attributes
Border Gateway Protocol - UPDATE Message
    Marker: ffffffffffffffffffffffffffffffff
    Length: 29
    Type: UPDATE Message (2)
    Withdrawn Routes Length: 0
    Total Path Attribute Length: 6
    Path attributes
Border Gateway Protocol - KEEPALIVE Message
```

Capture 4-1: *TCP socket information on S-11.*

The packet capture below verifies that Overlay Network reachability information (EVPN Route-Types) is sent over TCP socket 192.168.15.101:23655 – 192.168.15.11:179.

```
Ethernet II, Src: 50:00:00:01:00:07 (50:00:00:01:00:07), Dst: 50:00:00:08:00:07
(50:00:00:08:00:07)
Internet Protocol Version 4, Src: 192.168.15.101, Dst: 192.168.15.11
Transmission Control Protocol, Src Port: 23655, Dst Port: 179, Seq: 90, Ack: 478, Len:
376
Border Gateway Protocol - UPDATE Message
    Path attributes
        Path Attribute - ORIGIN: IGP
        Path Attribute - AS_PATH: 65101
        Path Attribute - EXTENDED_COMMUNITIES
            Type Code: EXTENDED_COMMUNITIES (16)
            Length: 16
            Carried extended communities: (2 communities)
                Route Target: 65101:30010 [Transitive 2-Octet AS-Specific]
                Encapsulation: VXLAN Encapsulation [Transitive Opaque]
        Path Attribute - PMSI_TUNNEL_ATTRIBUTE
            Flags: 0xc0, Optional, Transitive, Complete
            Type Code: PMSI_TUNNEL_ATTRIBUTE (22)
            Tunnel Type: Ingress Replication (6)
            0000 0000 0111 0101 0011 .... = MPLS Label: 1875
            Tunnel ID: tunnel end point -> 192.168.30.101
                Tunnel type ingress replication IP end point: 192.168.30.101
        Path Attribute - MP_REACH_NLRI
            Type Code: MP_REACH_NLRI (14)
            Address family identifier (AFI): Layer-2 VPN (25)
            Subsequent address family identifier (SAFI): EVPN (70)
            Next hop network address (4 bytes)
            Number of Subnetwork points of attachment (SNPA): 0
            Network layer reachability information (19 bytes)
                EVPN NLRI: Inclusive Multicast Route
                    Route Type: Inclusive Multicast Route (3)
```

```
                    Length: 17
                    Route Distinguisher: 0001c0a80f658009 (192.168.15.101:32777)
                    Ethernet Tag ID: 0
                    IP Address Length: 32
                    IPv4 address: 192.168.30.101
Border Gateway Protocol - UPDATE Message
    Path attributes
        Path Attribute - ORIGIN: IGP
        Path Attribute - AS_PATH: 65101
        Path Attribute - EXTENDED_COMMUNITIES
            Type Code: EXTENDED_COMMUNITIES (16)
            Length: 32
            Carried extended communities: (4 communities)
                Route Target: 65101:30010 [Transitive 2-Octet AS-Specific]
                Route Target: 65101:30077 [Transitive 2-Octet AS-Specific]
                Encapsulation: VXLAN Encapsulation [Transitive Opaque]
                Unknown subtype 0x03: 0x5000 0x0001 0x0007 [Transitive EVPN]
        Path Attribute - MP_REACH_NLRI
            Address family identifier (AFI): Layer-2 VPN (25)
            Subsequent address family identifier (SAFI): EVPN (70)
            Next hop network address (4 bytes)
            Number of Subnetwork points of attachment (SNPA): 0
            Network layer reachability information (42 bytes)
                EVPN NLRI: MAC Advertisement Route
                    Route Type: MAC Advertisement Route (2)
                    Length: 40
                    Route Distinguisher: 0001c0a80f658009 (192.168.15.101:32777)
                    ESI: 00:00:00:00:00:00:00:00:00:00
                    Ethernet Tag ID: 0
                    MAC Address Length: 48
                    MAC Address: Private_66:68:06 (00:50:79:66:68:06)
                    IP Address Length: 32
                    IPv4 address: 172.16.10.10
                    0000 0000 0111 0101 0011 .... = MPLS Label 1: 1875
                    0000 0000 0111 0101 0111 .... = MPLS Label 2: 1879
Border Gateway Protocol - UPDATE Message
    Path attributes
        Path Attribute - ORIGIN: IGP
        Path Attribute - AS_PATH: 65101
        Path Attribute - EXTENDED_COMMUNITIES
            Type Code: EXTENDED_COMMUNITIES (16)
            Length: 16
            Carried extended communities: (2 communities)
                Route Target: 65101:30010 [Transitive 2-Octet AS-Specific]
                Encapsulation: VXLAN Encapsulation [Transitive Opaque]
        Path Attribute - MP_REACH_NLRI
            Flags: 0x90, Optional, Extended-Length, Non-transitive, Complete
            Type Code: MP_REACH_NLRI (14)
            Length: 44
            Address family identifier (AFI): Layer-2 VPN (25)
            Subsequent address family identifier (SAFI): EVPN (70)
            Next hop network address (4 bytes)
            Number of Subnetwork points of attachment (SNPA): 0
            Network layer reachability information (35 bytes)
                EVPN NLRI: MAC Advertisement Route
                    Route Type: MAC Advertisement Route (2)
                    Length: 33
                    Route Distinguisher: 0001c0a80f658009 (192.168.15.101:32777)
                    ESI: 00:00:00:00:00:00:00:00:00:00
                        ESI Type: ESI 9 bytes value (0)
                        ESI Value: 00 00 00 00 00 00 00 00 00
```

```
                    ESI 9 bytes value: 00 00 00 00 00 00 00 00 00
                    Ethernet Tag ID: 0
                    MAC Address Length: 48
                    MAC Address: Private_66:68:06 (00:50:79:66:68:06)
                    IP Address Length: 0
                    IP Address: NOT INCLUDED
                        [Expert Info (Note/Protocol): IP Address: NOT INCLUDED]
                            [IP Address: NOT INCLUDED]
                            [Severity level: Note]
                            [Group: Protocol]
                    0000 0000 0111 0101 0011 .... = MPLS Label 1: 1875
```

Capture 4-2: *BGP Update from L-101 to S-11.*

Underlay: Direct Peering – Overlay: Direct Peering

This section describes the BGP peering model where both Underlay Network IPv4 Unicast peering and Overlay Network L2VPN EVPN peering is configured directly between IP addresses used in Inter-Switch links.

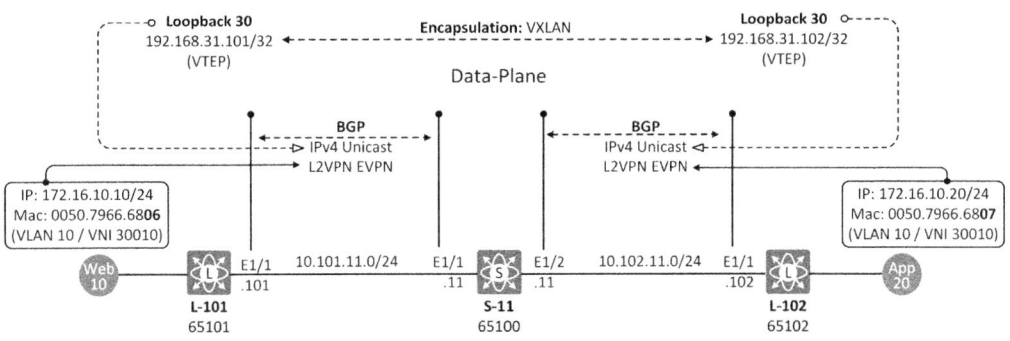

Figure 4-2: *BGP peering down between S-11 and SS-1 as well as S-11 and SS-2.*

The main configuration differences compared to a solution where Overlay BGP peering is done between Loopback IP address are that both AFIs are configured under the same neighbor and there is no need for TTL modification and update source. Besides, there is only one advertised loopback address in leaf switches while there in Spine switches there are no loopback addresses that need to be reachable. This means less configuration, which helps automatization. Examples 4-10 and 4-11 show the BGP configuration of L-101 and S-11.

```
route-map REDISTRIBUTE-LOOPBACK permit 10
  match interface loopback30
!
router bgp 65101
  router-id 192.168.15.101
  bestpath as-path multipath-relax
  address-family ipv4 unicast
    redistribute direct route-map REDISTRIBUTE-LOOPBACK
  address-family l2vpn evpn
    maximum-paths 8
  neighbor 10.101.11.11
    remote-as 65100
    description ** Underlay and Overlay BGP Peer **
    address-family ipv4 unicast
    address-family l2vpn evpn
      send-community
      send-community extended
      rewrite-evpn-rt-asn
```

Example 4-10: *BGP configuration of L-101.*

```
router bgp 65100
  router-id 192.168.15.11
  bestpath as-path multipath-relax
  address-family ipv4 unicast
    maximum-paths 8
  address-family l2vpn evpn
    maximum-paths 8
    nexthop route-map RETAIN-NH
    retain route-target all
  template peer eBGP-peers
    address-family l2vpn evpn
      rewrite-evpn-rt-asn
  neighbor 10.0.0.0/8 remote-as route-map Dynamic-BGP-AS-List
    inherit peer eBGP-peers
    address-family ipv4 unicast
    address-family l2vpn evpn
      send-community
      send-community extended
      route-map RETAIN-NH out
```

Example 4-11: *BGP configuration of S-11.*

Now there is only one TCP connection between L-101 and S-11.

```
L-101# sh sockets connection tcp | i ESTAB
ESTAB     0        0      10.101.11.101:41141             10.101.11.11:179
```

Example 4-12: *TCP socket information on L-101.*

Examples 4-13 and 4-14 show that both BGP peering, IPv4 Unicast and L2VPB EVPN, peering uses the same TCP connection.

```
L-101# sh ip bgp summary
BGP summary information for VRF default, address family IPv4 Unicast
BGP router identifier 192.168.15.101, local AS number 65101
BGP table version is 7, IPv4 Unicast config peers 1, capable peers 1
4 network entries and 4 paths using 960 bytes of memory
BGP attribute entries [2/328], BGP AS path entries [1/10]
BGP community entries [0/0], BGP clusterlist entries [0/0]

Neighbor        V    AS MsgRcvd MsgSent   TblVer  InQ OutQ Up/Down  State/PfxRcd
10.101.11.11    4 65100      23      22        7    0    0 00:03:09 2
```
Example 4-13: *BGP IPv4 Unicast peers of L-101.*

```
L-101# sh bgp l2vpn evpn summary
BGP summary information for VRF default, address family L2VPN EVPN
BGP router identifier 192.168.15.101, local AS number 65101
BGP table version is 78, L2VPN EVPN config peers 3, capable peers 1
10 network entries and 10 paths using 1920 bytes of memory
BGP attribute entries [9/1476], BGP AS path entries [1/10]
BGP community entries [0/0], BGP clusterlist entries [0/0]

Neighbor        V    AS MsgRcvd MsgSent   TblVer  InQ OutQ Up/Down  State/PfxRcd
10.101.11.11    4 65100      23      22       78    0    0 00:03:41 3
```
Example 4-14: *BGP L2VPN EVPN peers of L-101.*

Peering moel has not changed the content of the BRIB, all EVPN routes are still imported into the L2VNI 30010 table under the RD 192.168.15.101:32777.

```
L-101# sh bgp l2vpn evpn
BGP routing table information for VRF default, address family L2VPN EVPN
BGP table version is 78, Local Router ID is 192.168.15.101
Status: s-suppressed, x-deleted, S-stale, d-dampened, h-history, *-valid, >-best
Path type: i-internal, e-external, c-confed, l-local, a-aggregate, r-redist, I-
injected
Origin codes: i - IGP, e - EGP, ? - incomplete, | - multipath, & - backup, 2 - best2

   Network            Next Hop            Metric     LocPrf     Weight Path
Route Distinguisher: 192.168.15.101:32777    (L2VNI 30010)
*>l[2]:[0]:[0]:[48]:[0050.7966.6806]:[0]:[0.0.0.0]/216
                      192.168.30.101                    100        32768 i
*>e[2]:[0]:[0]:[48]:[0050.7966.6807]:[0]:[0.0.0.0]/216
                      192.168.30.102                                   0 65100 65102 i
*>l[2]:[0]:[0]:[48]:[0050.7966.6806]:[32]:[172.16.10.10]/272
                      192.168.30.101                    100        32768 i
*>e[2]:[0]:[0]:[48]:[0050.7966.6807]:[32]:[172.16.10.20]/272
                      192.168.30.102                                   0 65100 65102 i
*>l[3]:[0]:[32]:[192.168.30.101]/88
```

```
                        192.168.30.101                       100        32768 i
*>e[3]:[0]:[32]:[192.168.30.102]/88
                        192.168.30.102                                  0 65100 65102 i

Route Distinguisher: 192.168.15.102:32777
*>e[2]:[0]:[0]:[48]:[0050.7966.6807]:[0]:[0.0.0.0]/216
                        192.168.30.102                                  0 65100 65102 i
*>e[2]:[0]:[0]:[48]:[0050.7966.6807]:[32]:[172.16.10.20]/272
                        192.168.30.102                                  0 65100 65102 i
*>e[3]:[0]:[32]:[192.168.30.102]/88
                        192.168.30.102                                  0 65100 65102 i

Route Distinguisher: 192.168.15.101:3     (L3VNI 30077)
*>e[2]:[0]:[0]:[48]:[0050.7966.6807]:[32]:[172.16.10.20]/272
                        192.168.30.102                                  0 65100 65102 i
```

Example 4-15: *TCP socket information on S-11.*

Besides, NVE peering is UP.

```
L-101# sh nve peer detail
Details of nve Peers:
----------------------------------------
Peer-Ip: 192.168.30.102
    NVE Interface        : nve1
    Peer State           : Up
    Peer Uptime          : 00:04:02
    Router-Mac           : 5000.0002.0007
    Peer First VNI       : 30077
    Time since Create    : 00:04:02
    Configured VNIs      : 30010,30077
    Provision State      : peer-add-complete
    Learnt CP VNIs       : 30010,30077
    vni assignment mode  : SYMMETRIC
    Peer Location        : N/A
```

Example 4-16: *TCP socket information on S-11.*

And the MAC address of the Application Server 20 is installed in the MAC address table.

```
L-101# sh sys int l2fwder mac
Legend:
        * - primary entry, G - Gateway MAC, (R) - Routed MAC, O - Overlay MAC
        age - seconds since last seen,+ - primary entry using vPC Peer-Link,
        (T) - True, (F) - False, C - ControlPlane MAC
   VLAN     MAC Address      Type        age     Secure NTFY Ports
---------+-----------------+--------+---------+------+----+-----------------
G    10    5000.0001.0007   static     -          F    F    sup-eth1(R)
*    10    0050.7966.6806   dynamic   00:08:10    F    F    Eth1/3
*    10    0050.7966.6807   static     -          F    F    nve-peer1 192.168.30.102
     1      1              -00:01:00:01:00:01     -         1
```

Example 4-17: *TCP socket information on S-11.*

The tradeoff for using only one peer for both Underlay and Overlay reachability can be seen from the capture below. All routing information no matter what type of NLRIs we are talking about are advertised within one BGP update. In this kind of very small test environment, it is not a problem, but it can turn to a nightmare in larger installations when doing troubleshooting at 4 a.m.

```
Ethernet II, Src: 50:00:00:01:00:07 (50:00:00:01:00:07), Dst: 50:00:00:08:00:07
(50:00:00:08:00:07)
Internet Protocol Version 4, Src: 10.101.11.101, Dst: 10.101.11.11
Transmission Control Protocol, Src Port: 179, Dst Port: 30237, Seq: 100, Ack: 641,
Len: 423
Border Gateway Protocol - UPDATE Message
    Marker: ffffffffffffffffffffffffffffffff
    Length: 66
    Type: UPDATE Message (2)
    Withdrawn Routes Length: 0
    Total Path Attribute Length: 43
    Path attributes
        Path Attribute - ORIGIN: INCOMPLETE
        Path Attribute - MULTI_EXIT_DISC: 0
        Path Attribute - MP_REACH_NLRI
            Type Code: MP_REACH_NLRI (14)
            Length: 19
            Address family identifier (AFI): IPv4 (1)
            Subsequent address family identifier (SAFI): Unicast (1)
            Next hop network address (4 bytes)
                Next Hop: 10.101.11.101
            Number of Subnetwork points of attachment (SNPA): 0
            Network layer reachability information (10 bytes)
                192.168.15.101/32
                    MP Reach NLRI prefix length: 32
                    MP Reach NLRI IPv4 prefix: 192.168.15.101
                192.168.30.101/32
                    MP Reach NLRI prefix length: 32
                    MP Reach NLRI IPv4 prefix: 192.168.30.101
Border Gateway Protocol - UPDATE Message
    Marker: ffffffffffffffffffffffffffffffff
    Length: 99
    Type: UPDATE Message (2)
    Withdrawn Routes Length: 0
    Total Path Attribute Length: 76
    Path attributes
        Path Attribute - ORIGIN: IGP
        Path Attribute - AS_PATH: 65101
        Path Attribute - EXTENDED_COMMUNITIES
            Type Code: EXTENDED_COMMUNITIES (16)
            Length: 16
            Carried extended communities: (2 communities)
                Route Target: 65101:30010 [Transitive 2-Octet AS-Specific]
                Encapsulation: VXLAN Encapsulation [Transitive Opaque]
        Path Attribute - PMSI_TUNNEL_ATTRIBUTE
            Type Code: PMSI_TUNNEL_ATTRIBUTE (22)
            Length: 9
            Flags: 0
            Tunnel Type: Ingress Replication (6)
            0000 0000 0111 0101 0011 .... = MPLS Label: 1875
            Tunnel ID: tunnel end point -> 192.168.30.101
                Tunnel type ingress replication IP end point: 192.168.30.101
        Path Attribute - MP_REACH_NLRI
```

```
                Type Code: MP_REACH_NLRI (14)
                Length: 28
                Address family identifier (AFI): Layer-2 VPN (25)
                Subsequent address family identifier (SAFI): EVPN (70)
                Next hop network address (4 bytes)
                Number of Subnetwork points of attachment (SNPA): 0
                Network layer reachability information (19 bytes)
                    EVPN NLRI: Inclusive Multicast Route
                        Route Type: Inclusive Multicast Route (3)
                        Length: 17
                        Route Distinguisher: 0001c0a80f658009 (192.168.15.101:32777)
                        Ethernet Tag ID: 0
                        IP Address Length: 32
                        IPv4 address: 192.168.30.101
Border Gateway Protocol - UPDATE Message
    Marker: ffffffffffffffffffffffffffffffff
    Length: 126
    Type: UPDATE Message (2)
    Withdrawn Routes Length: 0
    Total Path Attribute Length: 103
    Path attributes
        Path Attribute - AS_PATH: 65101
        Path Attribute - EXTENDED_COMMUNITIES
            Type Code: EXTENDED_COMMUNITIES (16)
            Length: 32
            Carried extended communities: (4 communities)
                Route Target: 65101:30010 [Transitive 2-Octet AS-Specific]
                Route Target: 65101:30077 [Transitive 2-Octet AS-Specific]
                Encapsulation: VXLAN Encapsulation [Transitive Opaque]
                Unknown subtype 0x03: 0x5000 0x0001 0x0007 [Transitive EVPN]
        Path Attribute - MP_REACH_NLRI
            Length: 51
            Address family identifier (AFI): Layer-2 VPN (25)
            Subsequent address family identifier (SAFI): EVPN (70)
            Next hop network address (4 bytes)
            Number of Subnetwork points of attachment (SNPA): 0
            Network layer reachability information (42 bytes)
                EVPN NLRI: MAC Advertisement Route
                    Route Type: MAC Advertisement Route (2)
                    Length: 40
                    Route Distinguisher: 0001c0a80f658009 (192.168.15.101:32777)
                    ESI: 00:00:00:00:00:00:00:00:00:00
                        ESI Type: ESI 9 bytes value (0)
                        ESI Value: 00 00 00 00 00 00 00 00 00
                        ESI 9 bytes value: 00 00 00 00 00 00 00 00 00
                    Ethernet Tag ID: 0
                    MAC Address Length: 48
                    MAC Address: Private_66:68:06 (00:50:79:66:68:06)
                    IP Address Length: 32
                    IPv4 address: 172.16.10.10
                    0000 0000 0111 0101 0011 .... = MPLS Label 1: 1875
                    0000 0000 0111 0101 0111 .... = MPLS Label 2: 1879
Border Gateway Protocol - UPDATE Message
    Marker: ffffffffffffffffffffffffffffffff
    Length: 103
    Type: UPDATE Message (2)
    Withdrawn Routes Length: 0
    Total Path Attribute Length: 80
    Path attributes
        Path Attribute - ORIGIN: IGP
        Path Attribute - AS_PATH: 65101
```

```
Path Attribute - EXTENDED_COMMUNITIES
    Type Code: EXTENDED_COMMUNITIES (16)
    Length: 16
    Carried extended communities: (2 communities)
        Route Target: 65101:30010 [Transitive 2-Octet AS-Specific]
        Encapsulation: VXLAN Encapsulation [Transitive Opaque]
Path Attribute - MP_REACH_NLRI
    Type Code: MP_REACH_NLRI (14)
    Length: 44
    Address family identifier (AFI): Layer-2 VPN (25)
    Subsequent address family identifier (SAFI): EVPN (70)
    Next hop network address (4 bytes)
    Number of Subnetwork points of attachment (SNPA): 0
    Network layer reachability information (35 bytes)
        EVPN NLRI: MAC Advertisement Route
            Route Type: MAC Advertisement Route (2)
            Length: 33
            Route Distinguisher: 0001c0a80f658009 (192.168.15.101:32777)
            ESI: 00:00:00:00:00:00:00:00:00:00
                ESI Type: ESI 9 bytes value (0)
                ESI Value: 00 00 00 00 00 00 00 00 00
                ESI 9 bytes value: 00 00 00 00 00 00 00 00 00
            Ethernet Tag ID: 0
            MAC Address Length: 48
            MAC Address: Private_66:68:06 (00:50:79:66:68:06)
            IP Address Length: 0
            IP Address: NOT INCLUDED
                [Expert Info (Note/Protocol): IP Address: NOT INCLUDED]
                    [IP Address: NOT INCLUDED]
                    [Severity level: Note]
                    [Group: Protocol]
                0000 0000 0111 0101 0011 .... = MPLS Label 1: 1875
```

Capture 4-3: *BGP Update.*

Complexity Chart Multi-ASN Design with eBGP Underlay

BGP doesn't have native support for peering between Unnumbered Interfaces because it uses TCP as a transport protocol, unlike OSPF that uses Multicast messaging. This is why each Inter-Switch link has an IP subnet. Some vendors take advantage of the IPv6 Neighbor Discovery process and Link-Local addressing but it increases the operational complexity. Direct eBGP peering for both Underlay and Overlay shortens BGP configuration significantly but switches can't be move from Overlay Network without removing it also from the Underlay Network due to one common BGP adjacency for both Underlay and Overlay.

Direct Underlay Peering – Loopback Overlay Peering

	L	S	SS
Infrastructure IP Addressing			
Native Support for Unnumbered IP	No		
Requires subnet per Inter-switch link	Yes		
Loopback Interface Count	3	2	2
Overlay BGP Adjacency			
Update Source Modification	Yes	Yes	Yes
Increasing TTL (eBGP Multihop)	Yes	Yes	Yes
Support Dynamic-AS in Spine Layer	--	Yes	--
BGP Update Policy			
Retain Route-Targets (retain route-target all)	No	Yes	Yes
Rewrite ASN Part of Route-Target (rewrite-evp-rt-asn)	Yes	Yes	Yes
Requires Unmodified N-H address config (for EVPN)	No	Yes	Yes
Removing BGP Loop Prevention (allow-as in)	No	No	No
Removing BGP Loop Prevention (disable-peer-check)	No	No	No
Requires BGP RR-Cluster in Spine and SuperSpine layer	--	Yes	Yes
IPv4/EVPN NLRIs in the same BGP message	No	No	No
Other Considerations			
Possibility to restrict switch from the Overlay Network without disturbing Underlay Network	Yes		
Two TCP sessions, one for both BGP peering, somewhat complex recovery.			
Unique BGP messages for both IPv4 and EVPN NLRIs			

Table 3-1: *Multi-ASN Model Complexity Chart.*

BGP EVPN Design Consideration 133

Direct Underlay Peering – Direct Overlay Peering

		L	S	SS
Infrastructure IP Addressing				
Native Support for Unnumbered IP	No			
Requires subnet per Inter-switch link	Yes			
Loopback Interface Count		2	2	2
Overlay BGP Adjacency				
Update Source Modification		No	No	No
Increasing TTL (eBGP Multihop)		No	No	No
Support Dynamic-AS in Spine Layer		--	Yes	--
BGP Update Policy				
Retain Route-Targets (retain route-target all)		No	Yes	Yes
Rewrite ASN Part of Route-Target (rewrite-evp-rt-asn)		Yes	Yes	Yes
Requires Unmodified N-H address config (for EVPN)		No	Yes	Yes
Removing BGP Loop Prevention (allow-as in)		No	No	No
Removing BGP Loop Prevention (disable-peer-check)		No	No	No
Requires BGP RR-Cluster in Spine and SuperSpine layer		--	Yes	Yes
IPv4/EVPN NLRIs in the same BGP message		Yes	Yes	Yes
Other Considerations				
Possibility to restrict switch from the Overlay Network without disturbing Underlay Network	No			
Common TCP session for both Underlay and Overlay BGP peering				
Both IPv4 and EVPN NLRIs sent within the same BGP message				

Table 3-1: *Multi-ASN Model Complexity Chart.*

Chapter 5: Single AS Model with OSPF Underlay

Introduction

This chapter explains how to use the Single-ASN model in VXLAN Fabric. In this model, all switches share the same ASN, and Spine and SuperSpine switches are BGP Route-Reflectors. In our example, all Inter-Switch links are configured with Unnumbered Loopback 0 interface IP address, which is also used as OSPF RID. In addition to the advertisement of Loopback interfaces 15 (Overlay Control-Plane) and 30 (VTEP), also Loopback 0 is advertised to OSPF peers. This is because it is used as a next-hop address in Underlay routing and even if we are using numbered interface addressing, Loopback 0 should be advertised. This is because OSPF LSU packets that carry LS information are identified by OSPF RID and it makes troubleshooting easier if that address is accessible.

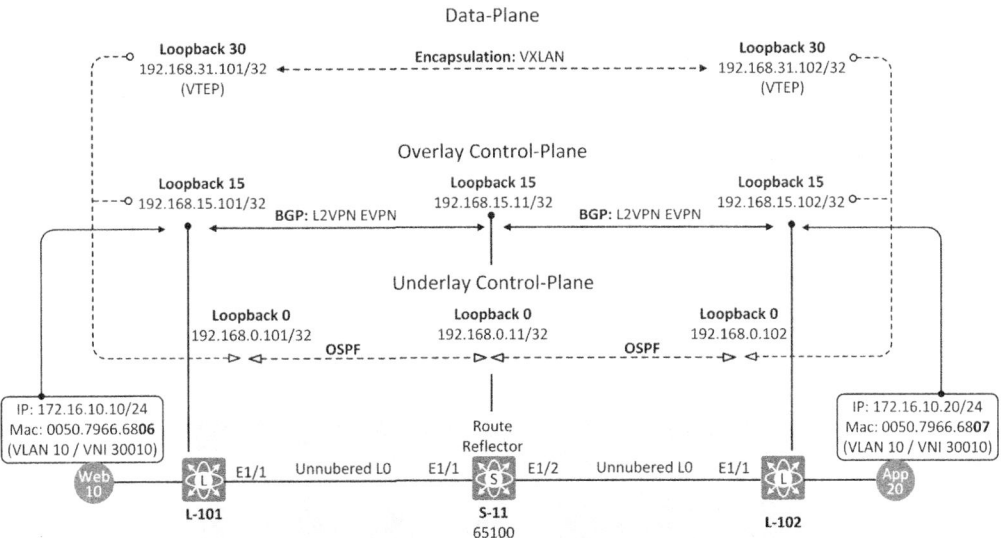

Figure 5-1: *BGP Peering Model Comparison.*

Figure 5-2 shows the overall topology where leaf switches are Route-Reflector clients to Spine switches and Spine switches are Route-Reflector clients for SuperSpine switches and the other way around.

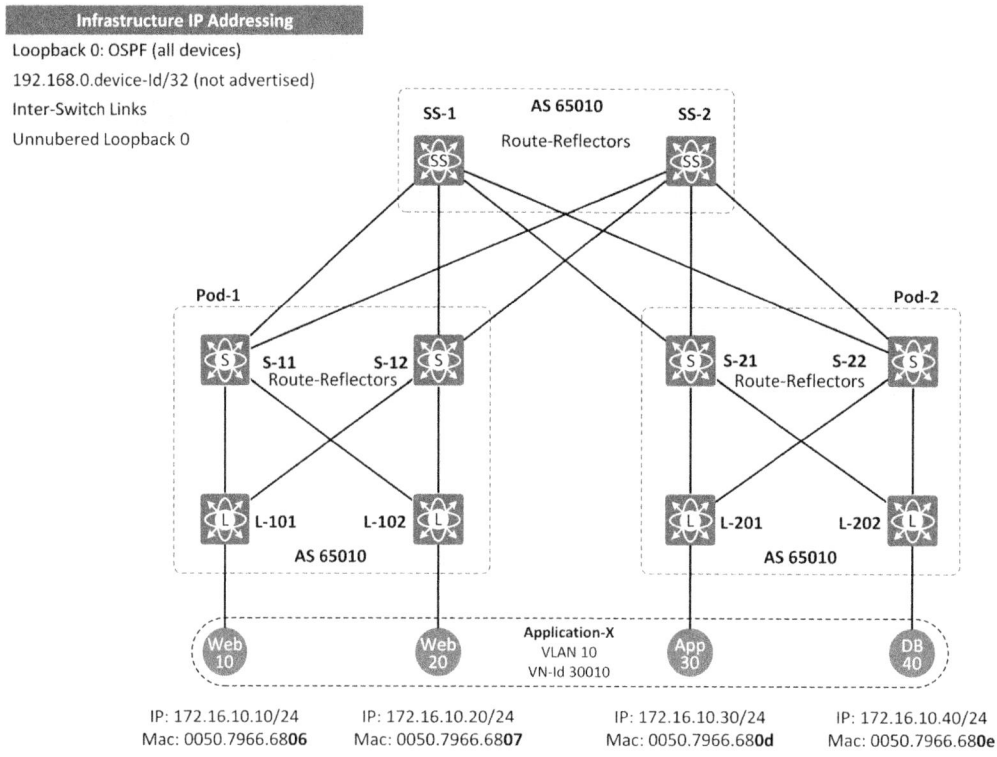

Figure 5-2: *Overal topology.*

Configuration

BGP Policy and BGP Update Configuration

Leaf Switches

The example below shows the BGP configurations of L-101. BGP L2VPN EVPN peering is configured to both S-11 and S-12 between interface Loopback 15. Due to internal BGP peering, there no need for TTL adjustment.

```
router bgp 65100
  router-id 192.168.15.101
  address-family l2vpn evpn
    maximum-paths 8
  neighbor 192.168.15.11
    remote-as 65100
    update-source loopback15
    address-family l2vpn evpn
      send-community
      send-community extended
  neighbor 192.168.15.12
    remote-as 65100
    update-source loopback15
    address-family l2vpn evpn
      send-community
      send-community extended
```

Example 5-1: *L-101 BGP configurations.*

Spine Switches

Examples 5-2 and 5-3 illustrate the BGP configuration of S-11 and S-12. At the time of writing, the command *route-reflector-client* is effective only when configured under the *template peer* group. In theory, all other session parameters can also be configured under the same template peer group but it does not shorten the configuration.

```
router bgp 65100
  router-id 192.168.15.11
  address-family l2vpn evpn
    maximum-paths 8
  template peer RR-Clients
    address-family l2vpn evpn
      route-reflector-client
  neighbor 192.168.15.0/24 remote-as route-map Dynamic-BGP-AS-List
    inherit peer RR-Clients
    update-source loopback15
    address-family l2vpn evpn
      send-community
      send-community extended
```

Example 5-2: *S-11 BGP configurations.*

```
router bgp 65100
  router-id 192.168.15.12
  address-family l2vpn evpn
    maximum-paths 8
  template peer RR-Clients
    address-family l2vpn evpn
      route-reflector-client
  neighbor 192.168.15.0/24 remote-as route-map Dynamic-BGP-AS-List
    inherit peer RR-Clients
    update-source loopback15
    address-family l2vpn evpn
      send-community
      send-community extended
```

Example 5-3: *S-12 BGP configurations.*

Super-Spine Switches

BGP peering in SS-1 and SS-2 is done statically because the dynamic-AS solution passively waits for TCP connection to destination port 179 and if both Spine and SuperSpine switches use it, there will never be any BGP adjacency. All session parameters are configured under the template peer group. This way the only required neighbor specific sub-command is ***inherit peer RR-Clients***

```
no router bgp 65100
router bgp 65100
  router-id 192.168.15.1
  address-family l2vpn evpn
    maximum-paths 8
  template peer RR-Clients
    remote-as 65100
    update-source loopback15
    address-family l2vpn evpn
      send-community
      send-community extended
      route-reflector-client
  neighbor 192.168.15.11
    inherit peer RR-Clients
  neighbor 192.168.15.12
    inherit peer RR-Clients
  neighbor 192.168.15.21
    inherit peer RR-Clients
  neighbor 192.168.15.22
    inherit peer RR-Clients
```

Example 5-4: *SS-1 BGP configurations.*

The BGP configuration of SS-2 is identical compared to the SS-1 BGP configuration. The only difference is the BGP Router-Id.

```
no router bgp 65100
router bgp 65100
  router-id 192.168.15.2
  address-family l2vpn evpn
    maximum-paths 8
  template peer RR-Clients
    remote-as 65100
    update-source loopback15
    address-family l2vpn evpn
      send-community
      send-community extended
      route-reflector-client
  neighbor 192.168.15.11
    inherit peer RR-Clients
  neighbor 192.168.15.12
    inherit peer RR-Clients
  neighbor 192.168.15.21
    inherit peer RR-Clients
  neighbor 192.168.15.22
    inherit peer RR-Clients
```

Example 5-5: *SS-2 BGP configurations.*

If we now test Data-Plane by pinging from Web10 (172.16.10.10) to DB40 (172.16.10.40) we can see that everything seems to be Ok.

```
Web10> ping 172.16.10.40

84 bytes from 172.16.10.40 icmp_seq=1 ttl=64 time=30.197 ms
84 bytes from 172.16.10.40 icmp_seq=2 ttl=64 time=34.186 ms
84 bytes from 172.16.10.40 icmp_seq=3 ttl=64 time=38.163 ms
84 bytes from 172.16.10.40 icmp_seq=4 ttl=64 time=35.794 ms
84 bytes from 172.16.10.40 icmp_seq=5 ttl=64 time=47.291 ms
```

Example 5-6: *Pinging from Web10 to DB40.*

Verification

BGP L2VPN EVPN Peering

Examples 5-7 and 5-8 show that both L-101 and L-102 are established BGP L2VPN EVPN peering with both spine switches and that they have received nine EVPN NLRIs.

```
L-101# sh bgp l2vpn evpn summary
<snipped>

Neighbor        V    AS MsgRcvd MsgSent   TblVer  InQ OutQ Up/Down  State/PfxRcd
192.168.15.11   4 65100     426     171      759    0    0 02:19:28 9
192.168.15.12   4 65100     426     171      759    0    0 02:19:37 9
```
Example 5-7: *show bgp l2vpn evpn summary command on L-101.*

```
L-102# sh bgp l2vpn evpn summary
<snipped>

Neighbor        V    AS MsgRcvd MsgSent   TblVer  InQ OutQ Up/Down  State/PfxRcd
192.168.15.11   4 65100     524     233      881    0    0 03:07:49 9
192.168.15.12   4 65100     529     239      881    0    0 03:06:36 9
```
Example 5-8: *show bgp l2vpn evpn summary command on L-102.*

BGP Table Verification

The example below verifies that L-101 has received three EVPN MAC-Advertisement Routes originated by leaf switches (L-102, L201, and L-202) from both spine switches. L-101 has also received EVPN Inclusive Multicast Routes from the same switch.

```
L-101# sh bgp l2vpn evpn
<snipped>
Status: s-suppressed, x-deleted, S-stale, d-dampened, h-history, *-valid, >-best
Path type: i-internal, e-external, c-confed, l-local, a-aggregate, r-redist, I-
injected
Origin codes: i - IGP, e - EGP, ? - incomplete, | - multipath, & - backup, 2 - b
est2

   Network          Next Hop            Metric     LocPrf     Weight Path
Route Distinguisher: 192.168.15.101:32777    (L2VNI 30010)
*>l[2]:[0]:[0]:[48]:[0050.7966.6806]:[0]:[0.0.0.0]/216
                    192.168.30.101                 100        32768 i
*>i[2]:[0]:[0]:[48]:[0050.7966.6807]:[0]:[0.0.0.0]/216
                    192.168.30.102                 100            0 i
*>i[2]:[0]:[0]:[48]:[0050.7966.680d]:[0]:[0.0.0.0]/216
                    192.168.30.201                 100            0 i
```

```
*>i[2]:[0]:[0]:[48]:[0050.7966.680e]:[0]:[0.0.0.0]/216
                      192.168.30.202              100           0 i
*>l[2]:[0]:[0]:[48]:[0050.7966.6806]:[32]:[172.16.10.10]/272
                      192.168.30.101              100       32768 i
*>i[2]:[0]:[0]:[48]:[0050.7966.6807]:[32]:[172.16.10.20]/272
                      192.168.30.102              100           0 i
*>i[2]:[0]:[0]:[48]:[0050.7966.680d]:[32]:[172.16.10.30]/272
                      192.168.30.201              100           0 i
*>i[2]:[0]:[0]:[48]:[0050.7966.680e]:[32]:[172.16.10.40]/272
                      192.168.30.202              100           0 i
*>l[3]:[0]:[32]:[192.168.30.101]/88
                      192.168.30.101              100       32768 i
*>i[3]:[0]:[32]:[192.168.30.102]/88
                      192.168.30.102              100           0 i
*>i[3]:[0]:[32]:[192.168.30.201]/88
                      192.168.30.201              100           0 i
*>i[3]:[0]:[32]:[192.168.30.202]/88
                      192.168.30.202              100           0 i
Route Distinguisher: 192.168.15.102:32777
*  i[2]:[0]:[0]:[48]:[0050.7966.6807]:[0]:[0.0.0.0]/216
                      192.168.30.102              100           0 i
*>i                   192.168.30.102              100           0 i
*>i[2]:[0]:[0]:[48]:[0050.7966.6807]:[32]:[172.16.10.20]/272
                      192.168.30.102              100           0 i
*  i                  192.168.30.102              100           0 i
*>i[3]:[0]:[32]:[192.168.30.102]/88
                      192.168.30.102              100           0 i
*  i                  192.168.30.102              100           0 i
Route Distinguisher: 192.168.15.201:32777
*  i[2]:[0]:[0]:[48]:[0050.7966.680d]:[0]:[0.0.0.0]/216
                      192.168.30.201              100           0 i
*>i                   192.168.30.201              100           0 i
*>i[2]:[0]:[0]:[48]:[0050.7966.680d]:[32]:[172.16.10.30]/272
                      192.168.30.201              100           0 i
*  i                  192.168.30.201              100           0 i
*>i[3]:[0]:[32]:[192.168.30.201]/88
                      192.168.30.201              100           0 i
*  i                  192.168.30.201              100           0 i
Route Distinguisher: 192.168.15.202:32777
*  i[2]:[0]:[0]:[48]:[0050.7966.680e]:[0]:[0.0.0.0]/216
                      192.168.30.202              100           0 i
*>i                   192.168.30.202              100           0 i
*>i[2]:[0]:[0]:[48]:[0050.7966.680e]:[32]:[172.16.10.40]/272
                      192.168.30.202              100           0 i
*  i                  192.168.30.202              100           0 i
*>i[3]:[0]:[32]:[192.168.30.202]/88
                      192.168.30.202              100           0 i
*  i                  192.168.30.202              100           0 i
Route Distinguisher: 192.168.15.101:3     (L3VNI 30077)
*>i[2]:[0]:[0]:[48]:[0050.7966.6807]:[32]:[172.16.10.20]/272
                      192.168.30.102              100           0 i
*>i[2]:[0]:[0]:[48]:[0050.7966.680d]:[32]:[172.16.10.30]/272
                      192.168.30.201              100           0 i
*>i[2]:[0]:[0]:[48]:[0050.7966.680e]:[32]:[172.16.10.40]/272
                      192.168.30.202              100           0 i
```

Example 5-9: *show bgp l2vpn evpn command on L-101.*

Inconsistency Problem with Received Route Count

Examples 5-10 and 5-11 show that both L-101 and L-102 are established BGP L2VPN EVPN peering. However, the received EVPN route count is different, S-11 has received 6 EVPN routes from both SS-1 and SS-2 while S-12 has received 12.

```
S-11# sh bgp l2vpn evpn summary
BGP summary information for VRF default, address family L2VPN EVPN
BGP router identifier 192.168.15.11, local AS number 65100
BGP table version is 669, L2VPN EVPN config peers 5, capable peers 4
12 network entries and 18 paths using 3600 bytes of memory
BGP attribute entries [17/2788], BGP AS path entries [0/0]
BGP community entries [0/0], BGP clusterlist entries [4/32]

Neighbor         V    AS MsgRcvd MsgSent   TblVer  InQ OutQ Up/Down   State/PfxRcd
192.168.15.1     4 65100     54      31      669    0    0 00:17:35 6
192.168.15.2     4 65100    527     277      669    0    0 00:13:32 6
192.168.15.101   4 65100    202     256      669    0    0 02:20:55 3
192.168.15.102   4 65100    278     334      669    0    0 03:08:48 3
```
Example 5-10: *show bgp l2vpn evpn summary command on S-11.*

```
S-12# sh bgp l2vpn evpn summary
BGP summary information for VRF default, address family L2VPN EVPN
BGP router identifier 192.168.15.12, local AS number 65100
BGP table version is 725, L2VPN EVPN config peers 5, capable peers 4
12 network entries and 30 paths using 5040 bytes of memory
BGP attribute entries [29/4756], BGP AS path entries [0/0]
BGP community entries [0/0], BGP clusterlist entries [8/64]

Neighbor         V    AS MsgRcvd MsgSent   TblVer  InQ OutQ Up/Down   State/PfxRcd
192.168.15.1     4 65100     72      38      725    0    0 00:16:42 12
192.168.15.2     4 65100    527     270      725    0    0 00:13:55 12
192.168.15.101   4 65100    202     244      725    0    0 02:21:29 3
192.168.15.102   4 65100    268     313      725    0    0 03:07:59 3
```
Example 5-11: *show bgp l2vpn evpn summary command on S-12.*

The same inconsistency applies to SuperSpine switches as can be seen in examples 5-12 and 5-13.

```
SS-1# sh bgp l2vpn evpn summary
BGP summary information for VRF default, address family L2VPN EVPN
BGP router identifier 192.168.15.1, local AS number 65100
BGP table version is 106, L2VPN EVPN config peers 4, capable peers 4
12 network entries and 24 paths using 4320 bytes of memory
BGP attribute entries [24/3936], BGP AS path entries [0/0]
BGP community entries [0/0], BGP clusterlist entries [8/32]

Neighbor         V    AS MsgRcvd MsgSent   TblVer  InQ OutQ Up/Down   State/PfxRcd
192.168.15.11    4 65100     51      39      106    0    0 00:19:33 6
192.168.15.12    4 65100     83      40      106    0    0 00:18:16 6
192.168.15.21    4 65100     53      34      106    0    0 00:19:46 6
192.168.15.22    4 65100     67      40      106    0    0 00:19:33 6
```
Example 5-12: *show bgp l2vpn evpn summary command on SS-1.*

BGP EVPN Design Consideration

```
SS-2# sh bgp l2vpn evpn summary
BGP summary information for VRF default, address family L2VPN EVPN
BGP router identifier 192.168.15.2, local AS number 65100
BGP table version is 105, L2VPN EVPN config peers 4, capable peers 4
12 network entries and 48 paths using 7200 bytes of memory
BGP attribute entries [48/7872], BGP AS path entries [0/0]
BGP community entries [0/0], BGP clusterlist entries [16/128]

Neighbor         V    AS MsgRcvd MsgSent   TblVer  InQ OutQ Up/Down  State/PfxRcd
192.168.15.11    4 65100      52      30      105    0    0 00:15:37 12
192.168.15.12    4 65100      55      30      105    0    0 00:15:35 12
192.168.15.21    4 65100      47      29      105    0    0 00:15:35 12
192.168.15.22    4 65100      58      27      105    0    0 00:15:36 12
```

Example 5-13: *show bgp l2vpn evpn summary command on SS-2.*

The next two examples also verify this inconsistency.

```
SS-1# sh bgp l2vpn evpn
BGP routing table information for VRF default, address family L2VPN EVPN
BGP table version is 135, Local Router ID is 192.168.15.1
Status: s-suppressed, x-deleted, S-stale, d-dampened, h-history, *-valid, >-best
Path type: i-internal, e-external, c-confed, l-local, a-aggregate, r-redist, I-
injected
Origin codes: i - IGP, e - EGP, ? - incomplete, | - multipath, & - backup, 2 - best2

   Network            Next Hop            Metric     LocPrf     Weight Path
Route Distinguisher: 192.168.15.101:32777
* i[2]:[0]:[0]:[48]:[0050.7966.6806]:[0]:[0.0.0.0]/216
                      192.168.30.101                 100             0 i
*>i                   192.168.30.101                 100             0 i
* i[2]:[0]:[0]:[48]:[0050.7966.6806]:[32]:[172.16.10.10]/272
                      192.168.30.101                 100             0 i
*>i                   192.168.30.101                 100             0 i
* i[3]:[0]:[32]:[192.168.30.101]/88
                      192.168.30.101                 100             0 i
*>i                   192.168.30.101                 100             0 i

Route Distinguisher: 192.168.15.102:32777
* i[2]:[0]:[0]:[48]:[0050.7966.6807]:[0]:[0.0.0.0]/216
                      192.168.30.102                 100             0 i
*>i                   192.168.30.102                 100             0 i
* i[2]:[0]:[0]:[48]:[0050.7966.6807]:[32]:[172.16.10.20]/272
                      192.168.30.102                 100             0 i
*>i                   192.168.30.102                 100             0 i
* i[3]:[0]:[32]:[192.168.30.102]/88
                      192.168.30.102                 100             0 i
*>i                   192.168.30.102                 100             0 i

Route Distinguisher: 192.168.15.201:32777
* i[2]:[0]:[0]:[48]:[0050.7966.680d]:[0]:[0.0.0.0]/216
                      192.168.30.201                 100             0 i
*>i                   192.168.30.201                 100             0 i
* i[2]:[0]:[0]:[48]:[0050.7966.680d]:[32]:[172.16.10.30]/272
                      192.168.30.201                 100             0 i
*>i                   192.168.30.201                 100             0 i
```

```
*  i[3]:[0]:[32]:[192.168.30.201]/88
                        192.168.30.201                  100             0 i
*>i                     192.168.30.201                  100             0 i

Route Distinguisher: 192.168.15.202:32777
*>i[2]:[0]:[0]:[48]:[0050.7966.680e]:[0]:[0.0.0.0]/216
                        192.168.30.202                  100             0 i
*  i                    192.168.30.202                  100             0 i
*  i[2]:[0]:[0]:[48]:[0050.7966.680e]:[32]:[172.16.10.40]/272
                        192.168.30.202                  100             0 i
*>i                     192.168.30.202                  100             0 i
*  i[3]:[0]:[32]:[192.168.30.202]/88
                        192.168.30.202                  100             0 i
*>i                     192.168.30.202                  100             0 i
```

Example 5-14: *show bgp l2vpn evpn command on SS-1.*

```
SS-2# sh bgp l2vpn evpn
BGP routing table information for VRF default, address family L2VPN EVPN
BGP table version is 137, Local Router ID is 192.168.15.2
Status: s-suppressed, x-deleted, S-stale, d-dampened, h-history, *-valid, >-best
Path type: i-internal, e-external, c-confed, l-local, a-aggregate, r-redist, I-
injected
Origin codes: i - IGP, e - EGP, ? - incomplete, | - multipath, & - backup, 2 - best2

   Network             Next Hop            Metric      LocPrf     Weight Path
Route Distinguisher: 192.168.15.101:32777
*  i[2]:[0]:[0]:[48]:[0050.7966.6806]:[0]:[0.0.0.0]/216
                        192.168.30.101                  100             0 i
*  i                    192.168.30.101                  100             0 i
*  i                    192.168.30.101                  100             0 i
*>i                     192.168.30.101                  100             0 i
*  i[2]:[0]:[0]:[48]:[0050.7966.6806]:[32]:[172.16.10.10]/272
                        192.168.30.101                  100             0 i
*  i                    192.168.30.101                  100             0 i
*  i                    192.168.30.101                  100             0 i
*>i                     192.168.30.101                  100             0 i
*  i[3]:[0]:[32]:[192.168.30.101]/88
                        192.168.30.101                  100             0 i
*  i                    192.168.30.101                  100             0 i
*  i                    192.168.30.101                  100             0 i
*>i                     192.168.30.101                  100             0 i

Route Distinguisher: 192.168.15.102:32777
*  i[2]:[0]:[0]:[48]:[0050.7966.6807]:[0]:[0.0.0.0]/216
                        192.168.30.102                  100             0 i
*  i                    192.168.30.102                  100             0 i
*  i                    192.168.30.102                  100             0 i
*>i                     192.168.30.102                  100             0 i
*  i[2]:[0]:[0]:[48]:[0050.7966.6807]:[32]:[172.16.10.20]/272
                        192.168.30.102                  100             0 i
*  i                    192.168.30.102                  100             0 i
*  i                    192.168.30.102                  100             0 i
*>i                     192.168.30.102                  100             0 i
*  i[3]:[0]:[32]:[192.168.30.102]/88
                        192.168.30.102                  100             0 i
*  i                    192.168.30.102                  100             0 i
*  i                    192.168.30.102                  100             0 i
```

```
*>i                     192.168.30.102                 100         0 i

Route Distinguisher: 192.168.15.201:32777
* i[2]:[0]:[0]:[48]:[0050.7966.680d]:[0]:[0.0.0.0]/216
                        192.168.30.201                 100         0 i
*>i                     192.168.30.201                 100         0 i
* i                     192.168.30.201                 100         0 i
* i                     192.168.30.201                 100         0 i
* i[2]:[0]:[0]:[48]:[0050.7966.680d]:[32]:[172.16.10.30]/272
                        192.168.30.201                 100         0 i
*>i                     192.168.30.201                 100         0 i
* i                     192.168.30.201                 100         0 i
* i                     192.168.30.201                 100         0 i
* i[3]:[0]:[32]:[192.168.30.201]/88
                        192.168.30.201                 100         0 i
*>i                     192.168.30.201                 100         0 i
* i                     192.168.30.201                 100         0 i
* i                     192.168.30.201                 100         0 i

Route Distinguisher: 192.168.15.202:32777
* i[2]:[0]:[0]:[48]:[0050.7966.680e]:[0]:[0.0.0.0]/216
                        192.168.30.202                 100         0 i
*>i                     192.168.30.202                 100         0 i
* i                     192.168.30.202                 100         0 i
* i                     192.168.30.202                 100         0 i
* i[2]:[0]:[0]:[48]:[0050.7966.680e]:[32]:[172.16.10.40]/272
                        192.168.30.202                 100         0 i
*>i                     192.168.30.202                 100         0 i
* i                     192.168.30.202                 100         0 i
* i                     192.168.30.202                 100         0 i
* i[3]:[0]:[32]:[192.168.30.202]/88
                        192.168.30.202                 100         0 i
*>i                     192.168.30.202                 100         0 i
* i                     192.168.30.202                 100         0 i
* i                     192.168.30.202                 100         0 i
```

Example 5-15: *show bgp l2vpn evpn command on SS-2.*

The reason can be found from the examples below. If we take a look at the Cluster list Path-Attribute (describes the Route-Reflectors that have forwarded the original BGP Update message) on received EVPN MAC advertisement Route about 0050.7966.6806 on SS-1 and SS-2 on SS-1, we can see that there both SS-11 and SS-12 are listed.

```
SS-1# sh bgp l2vpn evpn 0050.7966.6806
BGP routing table information for VRF default, address family L2VPN EVPN
Route Distinguisher: 192.168.15.101:32777
BGP routing table entry for [2]:[0]:[0]:[48]:[0050.7966.6806]:[0]:[0.0.0.0]/216,
version 106
Paths: (2 available, best #2)
Flags: (0x000202) (high32 00000000) on xmit-list, is not in l2rib/evpn, is not in HW
Multipath: eBGP

  Path type: internal, path is valid, not best reason: Neighbor Address, no labeled
nexthop
    AS-Path: NONE, path sourced internal to AS
      192.168.30.101 (metric 81) from 192.168.15.12 (192.168.15.12)
```

```
            Origin IGP, MED not set, localpref 100, weight 0
            Received label 30010
            Extcommunity: RT:65100:30010 ENCAP:8
            Originator: 192.168.15.101 Cluster list: 192.168.15.12

    Advertised path-id 1
    Path type: internal, path is valid, is best path, no labeled nexthop
    AS-Path: NONE, path sourced internal to AS
        192.168.30.101 (metric 81) from 192.168.15.11 (192.168.15.11)
            Origin IGP, MED not set, localpref 100, weight 0
            Received label 30010
            Extcommunity: RT:65100:30010 ENCAP:8
            Originator: 192.168.15.101 Cluster list: 192.168.15.11

    Path-id 1 advertised to peers:
        192.168.15.12       192.168.15.21       192.168.15.22
BGP routing table entry for [2]:[0]:[0]:[48]:[0050.7966.6806]:[32]:[172.16.10.10]/272,
version 47
Paths: (2 available, best #2)
Flags: (0x000202) (high32 00000000) on xmit-list, is not in l2rib/evpn, is not in HW
Multipath: eBGP

    Path type: internal, path is valid, not best reason: Neighbor Address, no labeled
nexthop
    AS-Path: NONE, path sourced internal to AS
        192.168.30.101 (metric 81) from 192.168.15.12 (192.168.15.12)
            Origin IGP, MED not set, localpref 100, weight 0
            Received label 30010 30077
            Extcommunity: RT:65100:30010 RT:65100:30077 ENCAP:8 Router MAC:5000.0001.0007
            Originator: 192.168.15.101 Cluster list: 192.168.15.12

    Advertised path-id 1
    Path type: internal, path is valid, is best path, no labeled nexthop
    AS-Path: NONE, path sourced internal to AS
        192.168.30.101 (metric 81) from 192.168.15.11 (192.168.15.11)
            Origin IGP, MED not set, localpref 100, weight 0
            Received label 30010 30077
            Extcommunity: RT:65100:30010 RT:65100:30077 ENCAP:8 Router MAC:5000.0001.0007
            Originator: 192.168.15.101 Cluster list: 192.168.15.11

    Path-id 1 advertised to peers:
        192.168.15.12       192.168.15.21       192.168.15.22
```

Example 5-16: *show bgp l2vpn evpn 0050.7966.6806 command on SS-1.*

While in SS-2 we can see that the EVPN MAC Advertisement Route is also received from Spines in Pod-2 with S-11 and S-21 listed in the Cluster list. This simply means that the Route-Reflectors are not configured properly.

```
SS-2# sh bgp l2vpn evpn 0050.7966.6806
BGP routing table information for VRF default, address family L2VPN EVPN
Route Distinguisher: 192.168.15.101:32777
BGP routing table entry for [2]:[0]:[0]:[48]:[0050.7966.6806]:[0]:[0.0.0.0]/216,
version 105
Paths: (4 available, best #4)
Flags: (0x000202) (high32 00000000) on xmit-list, is not in l2rib/evpn, is not in HW
Multipath: eBGP

  Path type: internal, path is valid, not best reason: Neighbor Address, no labeled
nexthop
    AS-Path: NONE, path sourced internal to AS
      192.168.30.101 (metric 81) from 192.168.15.12 (192.168.15.12)
        Origin IGP, MED not set, localpref 100, weight 0
        Received label 30010
        Extcommunity: RT:65100:30010 ENCAP:8
        Originator: 192.168.15.101 Cluster list: 192.168.15.12

  Path type: internal, path is valid, not best reason: RR Cluster Length, no labeled
nexthop
    AS-Path: NONE, path sourced internal to AS
      192.168.30.101 (metric 81) from 192.168.15.21 (192.168.15.21)
        Origin IGP, MED not set, localpref 100, weight 0
        Received label 30010
        Extcommunity: RT:65100:30010 ENCAP:8
        Originator: 192.168.15.101 Cluster list: 192.168.15.21 192.168.15.1
192.168.15.11

  Path type: internal, path is valid, not best reason: RR Cluster Length, no labeled
nexthop
    AS-Path: NONE, path sourced internal to AS
      192.168.30.101 (metric 81) from 192.168.15.22 (192.168.15.22)
        Origin IGP, MED not set, localpref 100, weight 0
        Received label 30010
        Extcommunity: RT:65100:30010 ENCAP:8
        Originator: 192.168.15.101 Cluster list: 192.168.15.22 192.168.15.1
192.168.15.11

  Advertised path-id 1
  Path type: internal, path is valid, is best path, no labeled nexthop
  AS-Path: NONE, path sourced internal to AS
      192.168.30.101 (metric 81) from 192.168.15.11 (192.168.15.11)
        Origin IGP, MED not set, localpref 100, weight 0
        Received label 30010
        Extcommunity: RT:65100:30010 ENCAP:8
        Originator: 192.168.15.101 Cluster list: 192.168.15.11

  Path-id 1 advertised to peers:
      192.168.15.12       192.168.15.21        192.168.15.22
BGP routing table entry for [2]:[0]:[0]:[48]:[0050.7966.6806]:[32]:[172.16.10.10]/272,
version 48
Paths: (4 available, best #4)
Flags: (0x000202) (high32 00000000) on xmit-list, is not in l2rib/evpn, is not in HW
Multipath: eBGP

  Path type: internal, path is valid, not best reason: Neighbor Address, no labeled
nexthop
    AS-Path: NONE, path sourced internal to AS
```

```
     192.168.30.101 (metric 81) from 192.168.15.12 (192.168.15.12)
       Origin IGP, MED not set, localpref 100, weight 0
       Received label 30010 30077
       Extcommunity: RT:65100:30010 RT:65100:30077 ENCAP:8 Router MAC:5000.0001.0007
       Originator: 192.168.15.101 Cluster list: 192.168.15.12

  Path type: internal, path is valid, not best reason: RR Cluster Length, no labeled
nexthop
  AS-Path: NONE, path sourced internal to AS
     192.168.30.101 (metric 81) from 192.168.15.21 (192.168.15.21)
       Origin IGP, MED not set, localpref 100, weight 0
       Received label 30010 30077
       Extcommunity: RT:65100:30010 RT:65100:30077 ENCAP:8 Router MAC:5000.0001.0007
       Originator: 192.168.15.101 Cluster list: 192.168.15.21 192.168.15.1
192.168.15.11

  Path type: internal, path is valid, not best reason: RR Cluster Length, no labeled
nexthop
  AS-Path: NONE, path sourced internal to AS
     192.168.30.101 (metric 81) from 192.168.15.22 (192.168.15.22)
       Origin IGP, MED not set, localpref 100, weight 0
       Received label 30010 30077
       Extcommunity: RT:65100:30010 RT:65100:30077 ENCAP:8 Router MAC:5000.0001.0007
       Originator: 192.168.15.101 Cluster list: 192.168.15.22 192.168.15.1
192.168.15.11

  Advertised path-id 1
  Path type: internal, path is valid, is best path, no labeled nexthop
  AS-Path: NONE, path sourced internal to AS
     192.168.30.101 (metric 81) from 192.168.15.11 (192.168.15.11)
       Origin IGP, MED not set, localpref 100, weight 0
       Received label 30010 30077
       Extcommunity: RT:65100:30010 RT:65100:30077 ENCAP:8 Router MAC:5000.0001.0007
       Originator: 192.168.15.101 Cluster list: 192.168.15.11

  Path-id 1 advertised to peers:
     192.168.15.12         192.168.15.21         192.168.15.22
```
Example 5-17: *show bgp l2vpn evpn 0050.7966.6806 command on SS-2.*

Fixing the Problem

The missing piece in the puzzle is the Cluster-Id. When the BGP speaker receives the BGP Update that has the same Cluster-Id than what it has, it rejects the Update. On the other hand, if the Cluster-Id is different, then the NLRI is accepted and this is exactly what has happened here.

Next, S-11 and S-12 are configured as a RR Cluster with Cluster-Id 192.168.1.1 (examples 5-18 and 5-19), S-21 and S-22 are configured as a RR Cluster with Cluster-Id 192.168.2.1 (examples 5-20 and 5-21), and SS-1 andSS-2 are configured as a RR Cluster with Cluster-Id 192.168.100.1 (examples 5-22 and 5-23). After Cluster-Id has been configured, the

```
router bgp 65100
  router-id 192.168.15.11
  cluster-id 192.168.1.1
  address-family ipv4 unicast
    maximum-paths 8
  address-family l2vpn evpn
    maximum-paths 8
  template peer RR-Clients
    address-family l2vpn evpn
      route-reflector-client
  neighbor 192.168.15.0/24 remote-as route-map Dynamic-BGP-AS-List
    inherit peer RR-Clients
    update-source loopback15
    address-family l2vpn evpn
      send-community
      send-community extended
```

Example 5-18: *RR Cluster-Id on S-11.*

```
router bgp 65100
  router-id 192.168.15.12
  cluster-id 192.168.1.1
  address-family ipv4 unicast
    maximum-paths 8
  address-family l2vpn evpn
    maximum-paths 8
  template peer RR-Clients
    address-family l2vpn evpn
      route-reflector-client
  neighbor 192.168.15.0/24 remote-as route-map Dynamic-BGP-AS-List
    inherit peer RR-Clients
    update-source loopback15
    address-family l2vpn evpn
      send-community
      send-community extended
```

Example 5-19: *RR Cluster-Id on S-12.*

```
router bgp 65100
  router-id 192.168.15.21
  cluster-id 192.168.2.1
  address-family ipv4 unicast
    maximum-paths 8
  address-family l2vpn evpn
    maximum-paths 8
  template peer RR-Clients
    address-family l2vpn evpn
      route-reflector-client
  neighbor 192.168.15.0/24 remote-as route-map Dynamic-BGP-AS-List
    inherit peer RR-Clients
    update-source loopback15
    address-family l2vpn evpn
      send-community extended
```

Example 5-20: *RR Cluster-Id on S-21.*

```
router bgp 65100
  router-id 192.168.15.22
  cluster-id 192.168.2.1
  address-family ipv4 unicast
    maximum-paths 8
  address-family l2vpn evpn
    maximum-paths 8
  template peer RR-Clients
    address-family l2vpn evpn
      route-reflector-client
  neighbor 192.168.15.0/24 remote-as route-map Dynamic-BGP-AS-List
    inherit peer RR-Clients
    update-source loopback15
    address-family l2vpn evpn
      send-community
      send-community extended
```

Example 5-21: *RR Cluster-Id on S-22.*

```
router bgp 65100
  router-id 192.168.15.1
  cluster-id 192.168.100.1
  address-family l2vpn evpn
    maximum-paths 8
  template peer RR-Clients
    remote-as 65100
    update-source loopback15
    address-family l2vpn evpn
      send-community
      send-community extended
      route-reflector-client
  neighbor 192.168.15.11
    inherit peer RR-Clients
  neighbor 192.168.15.12
    inherit peer RR-Clients
  neighbor 192.168.15.21
    inherit peer RR-Clients
  neighbor 192.168.15.22
    inherit peer RR-Clients
```

Example 5-22: *RR Cluster-Id on SS-1.*

```
router bgp 65100
  router-id 192.168.15.2
  cluster-id 192.168.100.1
  address-family l2vpn evpn
    maximum-paths 8
  template peer RR-Clients
    remote-as 65100
    update-source loopback15
    address-family l2vpn evpn
      send-community
```

```
        send-community extended
        route-reflector-client
  neighbor 192.168.15.11
    inherit peer RR-Clients
  neighbor 192.168.15.12
    inherit peer RR-Clients
  neighbor 192.168.15.21
    inherit peer RR-Clients
  neighbor 192.168.15.22
    inherit peer RR-Clients
```
Example 5-23: *RR Cluster-Id on SS-3.*

Re-checking of BGP Tables

The next four examples verify that the problem is now fixed. The reason why I purposely left the Cluster-Id definition out in the first configuration is that I wanted to point out that even though the Data-Plane looks Ok, the Control-Plane should always be checked and verified that it works as it should be.

```
SS-1# sh bgp l2vpn evpn summary
BGP summary information for VRF default, address family L2VPN EVPN
BGP router identifier 192.168.15.1, local AS number 65100
BGP table version is 209, L2VPN EVPN config peers 4, capable peers 4
12 network entries and 24 paths using 4320 bytes of memory
BGP attribute entries [12/1968], BGP AS path entries [0/0]
BGP community entries [0/0], BGP clusterlist entries [4/16]

Neighbor        V    AS MsgRcvd MsgSent   TblVer  InQ OutQ Up/Down  State/PfxRcd
192.168.15.11   4 65100    103      71      209    0    0 00:34:58 6
192.168.15.12   4 65100    150      74      209    0    0 00:33:40 6
192.168.15.21   4 65100    117      67      209    0    0 00:35:11 6
192.168.15.22   4 65100    141      75      209    0    0 00:34:57 6
```
Example 5-24: *show bgp l2vpn evpn summary on SS-1.*

```
SS-2#  sh bgp l2vpn evpn summary
BGP summary information for VRF default, address family L2VPN EVPN
BGP router identifier 192.168.15.2, local AS number 65100
BGP table version is 261, L2VPN EVPN config peers 4, capable peers 4
12 network entries and 24 paths using 4320 bytes of memory
BGP attribute entries [12/1968], BGP AS path entries [0/0]
BGP community entries [0/0], BGP clusterlist entries [4/16]

Neighbor        V    AS MsgRcvd MsgSent   TblVer  InQ OutQ Up/Down  State/PfxRcd
192.168.15.11   4 65100    145      62      261    0    0 00:31:27 6
192.168.15.12   4 65100    147      65      261    0    0 00:31:25 6
192.168.15.21   4 65100    133      62      261    0    0 00:31:25 6
192.168.15.22   4 65100    146      60      261    0    0 00:31:26 6
```
Example 5-25: *show bgp l2vpn evpn summary on SS-2.*

Examples 5-26 and 5-27 verifies that both spines in Pod-1 are now using the same Cluster-Id.

```
SS-1# sh bgp l2vpn evpn 0050.7966.6806
BGP routing table information for VRF default, address family L2VPN EVPN
Route Distinguisher: 192.168.15.101:32777
BGP routing table entry for [2]:[0]:[0]:[48]:[0050.7966.6806]:[0]:[0.0.0.0]/216,
version 195
Paths: (2 available, best #2)
Flags: (0x000202) (high32 00000000) on xmit-list, is not in l2rib/evpn, is not in HW
Multipath: eBGP

  Path type: internal, path is valid, not best reason: Neighbor Address, no labeled
nexthop
  AS-Path: NONE, path sourced internal to AS
    192.168.30.101 (metric 81) from 192.168.15.12 (192.168.15.12)
      Origin IGP, MED not set, localpref 100, weight 0
      Received label 30010
      Extcommunity: RT:65100:30010 ENCAP:8
      Originator: 192.168.15.101 Cluster list: 192.168.1.1

  Advertised path-id 1
  Path type: internal, path is valid, is best path, no labeled nexthop
  AS-Path: NONE, path sourced internal to AS
    192.168.30.101 (metric 81) from 192.168.15.11 (192.168.15.11)
      Origin IGP, MED not set, localpref 100, weight 0
      Received label 30010
      Extcommunity: RT:65100:30010 ENCAP:8
      Originator: 192.168.15.101 Cluster list: 192.168.1.1

  Path-id 1 advertised to peers:
    192.168.15.12       192.168.15.21        192.168.15.22
BGP routing table entry for [2]:[0]:[0]:[48]:[0050.7966.6806]:[32]:[172.16.10.10]/272,
version 169
Paths: (2 available, best #2)
Flags: (0x000202) (high32 00000000) on xmit-list, is not in l2rib/evpn, is not in HW
Multipath: eBGP

  Path type: internal, path is valid, not best reason: Neighbor Address, no labeled
nexthop
  AS-Path: NONE, path sourced internal to AS
    192.168.30.101 (metric 81) from 192.168.15.12 (192.168.15.12)
      Origin IGP, MED not set, localpref 100, weight 0
      Received label 30010 30077
      Extcommunity: RT:65100:30010 RT:65100:30077 ENCAP:8 Router MAC:5000.0001.0007
      Originator: 192.168.15.101 Cluster list: 192.168.1.1

  Advertised path-id 1
  Path type: internal, path is valid, is best path, no labeled nexthop
  AS-Path: NONE, path sourced internal to AS
    192.168.30.101 (metric 81) from 192.168.15.11 (192.168.15.11)
      Origin IGP, MED not set, localpref 100, weight 0
      Received label 30010 30077
      Extcommunity: RT:65100:30010 RT:65100:30077 ENCAP:8 Router MAC:5000.0001.0007
      Originator: 192.168.15.101 Cluster list: 192.168.1.1

  Path-id 1 advertised to peers:
    192.168.15.12       192.168.15.21        192.168.15.22
```

Example 5-26: *show bgp l2vpn evpn on SS-1.*

```
SS-2# sh bgp l2vpn evpn 0050.7966.6806
BGP routing table information for VRF default, address family L2VPN EVPN
Route Distinguisher: 192.168.15.101:32777
BGP routing table entry for [2]:[0]:[0]:[48]:[0050.7966.6806]:[0]:[0.0.0.0]/216,
version 276
Paths: (2 available, best #2)
Flags: (0x000202) (high32 00000000) on xmit-list, is not in l2rib/evpn, is not in HW
Multipath: eBGP

  Path type: internal, path is valid, not best reason: Neighbor Address, no labeled
nexthop
    AS-Path: NONE, path sourced internal to AS
      192.168.30.101 (metric 81) from 192.168.15.12 (192.168.15.12)
        Origin IGP, MED not set, localpref 100, weight 0
        Received label 30010
        Extcommunity: RT:65100:30010 ENCAP:8
        Originator: 192.168.15.101 Cluster list: 192.168.1.1

  Advertised path-id 1
  Path type: internal, path is valid, is best path, no labeled nexthop
    AS-Path: NONE, path sourced internal to AS
      192.168.30.101 (metric 81) from 192.168.15.11 (192.168.15.11)
        Origin IGP, MED not set, localpref 100, weight 0
        Received label 30010
        Extcommunity: RT:65100:30010 ENCAP:8
        Originator: 192.168.15.101 Cluster list: 192.168.1.1

  Path-id 1 advertised to peers:
    192.168.15.12         192.168.15.21         192.168.15.22
BGP routing table entry for [2]:[0]:[0]:[48]:[0050.7966.6806]:[32]:[172.16.10.10]/272,
version 227
Paths: (2 available, best #2)
Flags: (0x000202) (high32 00000000) on xmit-list, is not in l2rib/evpn, is not in HW
Multipath: eBGP

  Path type: internal, path is valid, not best reason: Neighbor Address, no labeled
nexthop
    AS-Path: NONE, path sourced internal to AS
      192.168.30.101 (metric 81) from 192.168.15.12 (192.168.15.12)
        Origin IGP, MED not set, localpref 100, weight 0
        Received label 30010 30077
        Extcommunity: RT:65100:30010 RT:65100:30077 ENCAP:8 Router MAC:5000.0001.0007
        Originator: 192.168.15.101 Cluster list: 192.168.1.1

  Advertised path-id 1
  Path type: internal, path is valid, is best path, no labeled nexthop
    AS-Path: NONE, path sourced internal to AS
      192.168.30.101 (metric 81) from 192.168.15.11 (192.168.15.11)
        Origin IGP, MED not set, localpref 100, weight 0
        Received label 30010 30077
        Extcommunity: RT:65100:30010 RT:65100:30077 ENCAP:8 Router MAC:5000.0001.0007
        Originator: 192.168.15.101 Cluster list: 192.168.1.1

  Path-id 1 advertised to peers:
    192.168.15.12         192.168.15.21         192.168.15.22
```

Example 5-27: *show bgp l2vpn evpn on SS-2.*

NVE Peering

Examples 5-28 and 5-29 show that L-101 has established NVE peering with all other leaf switches.

```
L-101# sh nve peers
Interface Peer-IP                                State LearnType Uptime   Router-Mac
--------- -----------------------------------    ----- --------- -------- ---------------
--
nve1      192.168.30.102                         Up    CP        02:54:35 5000.0002.0007
nve1      192.168.30.201                         Up    CP        02:54:35 5000.000c.0007
nve1      192.168.30.202                         Up    CP        02:54:35 5000.000b.0007
```
Example 5-28: *show nve peers on L-101.*

```
L-101# sh nve peers detail
Details of nve Peers:
------------------------------------------
Peer-Ip: 192.168.30.102
    NVE Interface       : nve1
    Peer State          : Up
    Peer Uptime         : 02:58:32
    Router-Mac          : 5000.0002.0007
    Peer First VNI      : 30077
    Time since Create   : 02:58:32
    Configured VNIs     : 30010,30077
    Provision State     : peer-add-complete
    Learnt CP VNIs      : 30010,30077
    vni assignment mode : SYMMETRIC
    Peer Location       : N/A
Peer-Ip: 192.168.30.201
    NVE Interface       : nve1
    Peer State          : Up
    Peer Uptime         : 02:58:32
    Router-Mac          : 5000.000c.0007
    Peer First VNI      : 30077
    Time since Create   : 02:58:32
    Configured VNIs     : 30010,30077
    Provision State     : peer-add-complete
    Learnt CP VNIs      : 30010,30077
    vni assignment mode : SYMMETRIC
    Peer Location       : N/A
Peer-Ip: 192.168.30.202
    NVE Interface       : nve1
    Peer State          : Up
    Peer Uptime         : 02:58:32
    Router-Mac          : 5000.000b.0007
    Peer First VNI      : 30077
    Time since Create   : 02:58:32
    Configured VNIs     : 30010,30077
    Provision State     : peer-add-complete
    Learnt CP VNIs      : 30010,30077
    vni assignment mode : SYMMETRIC
    Peer Location       : N/A
```
Example 5-29: *show nve peers detail on L-101.*

Examples 5-32 to 5-35 verify the nve peering of L-201.

```
L-201# sh nve peers
Interface Peer-IP                          State  LearnType  Uptime    Router-Mac
---------  ---------------------------     -----  ---------  --------  ---------------
--
nve1       192.168.30.101                  Up     CP         00:06:57  5000.0001.0007
nve1       192.168.30.102                  Up     CP         00:06:57  5000.0002.0007
nve1       192.168.30.202                  Up     CP         00:06:57  5000.000b.0007
```

Example 5-32: *show nve peers on L-201.*

```
L-201# sh nve peers detail
Details of nve Peers:
-----------------------------------------
Peer-Ip: 192.168.30.101
    NVE Interface       : nve1
    Peer State          : Up
    Peer Uptime         : 00:07:01
    Router-Mac          : 5000.0001.0007
    Peer First VNI      : 30077
    Time since Create   : 00:07:01
    Configured VNIs     : 30010,30077
    Provision State     : peer-add-complete
    Learnt CP VNIs      : 30010,30077
    vni assignment mode : SYMMETRIC
    Peer Location       : N/A
Peer-Ip: 192.168.30.102
    NVE Interface       : nve1
    Peer State          : Up
    Peer Uptime         : 00:07:01
    Router-Mac          : 5000.0002.0007
    Peer First VNI      : 30077
    Time since Create   : 00:07:01
    Configured VNIs     : 30010,30077
    Provision State     : peer-add-complete
    Learnt CP VNIs      : 30010,30077
    vni assignment mode : SYMMETRIC
    Peer Location       : N/A
Peer-Ip: 192.168.30.202
    NVE Interface       : nve1
    Peer State          : Up
    Peer Uptime         : 00:07:01
    Router-Mac          : 5000.000b.0007
    Peer First VNI      : 30077
    Time since Create   : 00:07:01
    Configured VNIs     : 30010,30077
    Provision State     : peer-add-complete
    Learnt CP VNIs      : 30010,30077
    vni assignment mode : SYMMETRIC
    Peer Location       : N/A
```

Example 5-33: *show nve peers detail on L-201.*

MAC Address Table and L2RIB

Example 5-30 shows that MAC address information is installed into the VLAN 10 MAC address table. Note that only locally learned MAC Address has an aging time attached to it while MAC addresses learned via BGP does not have an aging time. This is possible because leaf switches will withdraw locally learned MAC and MAC-IP information in case that they are not reachable. The process relies on ARP-table aging times. The default aging time for locally learned ARP-entries is in NX-OS is 1500 seconds, which is 300 seconds shorter than MAC-address aging timer. When the ARP aging timers exceed, the switch checks the presence of the host by sending an ARP-request to the host. If the host response to ARP-request, the switch will reset the aging timer. If the host does not reply, the entry is removed from the ARP-table but kept in the BGP EVPN table for an additional 1800 seconds (MAC aging timer) before the withdrawn message is sent. The MAC address aging timer should be bigger than the ARP aging timer. This is because the ARP refresh process will also update the MAC table and unnecessary flooding can be avoided.

```
L-101# sh sys int l2fwder mac
Legend:
        * - primary entry, G - Gateway MAC, (R) - Routed MAC, O - Overlay MAC
        age - seconds since last seen,+ - primary entry using vPC Peer-Link,
        (T) - True, (F) - False, C - ControlPlane MAC
   VLAN     MAC Address      Type        age     Secure NTFY Ports
---------+-----------------+--------+---------+------+----+------------------
*   10     0050.7966.680d   static      -         F     F   nve-peer2 192.168.30.201
G   77     5000.0001.0007   static      -         F     F   sup-eth1(R)
G   10     5000.0001.0007   static      -         F     F   sup-eth1(R)
*   10     0050.7966.6806   dynamic   00:07:39    F     F   Eth1/3
*   10     0050.7966.680e   static      -         F     F   nve-peer3 192.168.30.202
*   10     0050.7966.6807   static      -         F     F   nve-peer1 192.168.30.102
    1         1             -00:01:00:01:00:01              -         1
```

Example 5-30: *show system internal l2fwder mac on L-101.*

Example 5-31 shows that MAC address information is also installed into the VLAN 10 MAC address table.

```
L-101# sh l2route evpn mac evi 10

Flags -(Rmac):Router MAC (Stt):Static (L):Local (R):Remote (V):vPC link
(Dup):Duplicate (Spl):Split (Rcv):Recv (AD):Auto-Delete (D):Del Pending
(S):Stale (C):Clear, (Ps):Peer Sync (O):Re-Originated (Nho):NH-Override
(Pf):Permanently-Frozen, (Orp): Orphan

Topology    Mac Address      Prod   Flags         Seq No    Next-Hops
----------  --------------   ----   -----------   -------   ------------------
10          0050.7966.6806   Local  L,            0         Eth1/3
10          0050.7966.6807   BGP    SplRcv        0         192.168.30.102
10          0050.7966.680d   BGP    SplRcv        0         192.168.30.201
10          0050.7966.680e   BGP    SplRcv        0         192.168.30.202
```

Example 5-31: *show l2route evpn mac evi 10 on L-101.*

```
L-201# sh sys int l2fwder mac
Legend:
        * - primary entry, G - Gateway MAC, (R) - Routed MAC, O - Overlay MAC
        age - seconds since last seen,+ - primary entry using vPC Peer-Link,
        (T) - True, (F) - False, C - ControlPlane MAC
    VLAN     MAC Address       Type      age        Secure NTFY Ports
---------+-----------------+--------+---------+------+----+------------------
*   10      0050.7966.680d    dynamic   00:00:29    F     F    Eth1/3
*   10      0050.7966.6806    static    -           F     F    nve-peer2 192.168.30.101
*   10      0050.7966.680e    static    -           F     F    nve-peer3 192.168.30.202
*   10      0050.7966.6807    static    -           F     F    nve-peer1 192.168.30.102
G   10      5000.000c.0007    static    -           F     F    sup-eth1(R)
    1           1                     -00:01:00:01:00:01        -         1
```

Example 5-34: *show system internal l2fwder mac on L-201.*

```
L-201# sh l2route evpn mac evi 10

Flags -(Rmac):Router MAC (Stt):Static (L):Local (R):Remote (V):vPC link
(Dup):Duplicate (Spl):Split (Rcv):Recv (AD):Auto-Delete (D):Del Pending
(S):Stale (C):Clear, (Ps):Peer Sync (O):Re-Originated (Nho):NH-Override
(Pf):Permanently-Frozen, (Orp): Orphan

Topology    Mac Address      Prod   Flags         Seq No    Next-Hops
----------  --------------   ----   -----------   -------   ------------------
10          0050.7966.6806   BGP    SplRcv        0         192.168.30.101
10          0050.7966.6807   BGP    SplRcv        0         192.168.30.102
10          0050.7966.680d   Local  L,            0         Eth1/3
10          0050.7966.680e   BGP    SplRcv        0         192.168.30.202
```

Example 5-35: *show l2route evpn mac evi 10 on L-201.*

Data-Plane Testing

Example 5-36 shows that IP connectivity from Web10 to all other servers is Ok.

```
Web10> ping 172.16.10.10

172.16.10.10 icmp_seq=1 ttl=64 time=0.001 ms
172.16.10.10 icmp_seq=2 ttl=64 time=0.001 ms
172.16.10.10 icmp_seq=3 ttl=64 time=0.001 ms
172.16.10.10 icmp_seq=4 ttl=64 time=0.001 ms
172.16.10.10 icmp_seq=5 ttl=64 time=0.001 ms

Web10> ping 172.16.10.20

84 bytes from 172.16.10.20 icmp_seq=1 ttl=64 time=24.921 ms
84 bytes from 172.16.10.20 icmp_seq=2 ttl=64 time=17.254 ms
84 bytes from 172.16.10.20 icmp_seq=3 ttl=64 time=16.029 ms
84 bytes from 172.16.10.20 icmp_seq=4 ttl=64 time=17.258 ms
84 bytes from 172.16.10.20 icmp_seq=5 ttl=64 time=16.105 ms

Web10> ping 172.16.10.30

84 bytes from 172.16.10.30 icmp_seq=1 ttl=64 time=27.169 ms
84 bytes from 172.16.10.30 icmp_seq=2 ttl=64 time=34.708 ms
84 bytes from 172.16.10.30 icmp_seq=3 ttl=64 time=40.292 ms
84 bytes from 172.16.10.30 icmp_seq=4 ttl=64 time=54.666 ms
84 bytes from 172.16.10.30 icmp_seq=5 ttl=64 time=31.623 ms

Web10> ping 172.16.10.40

84 bytes from 172.16.10.40 icmp_seq=1 ttl=64 time=35.745 ms
84 bytes from 172.16.10.40 icmp_seq=2 ttl=64 time=34.945 ms
84 bytes from 172.16.10.40 icmp_seq=3 ttl=64 time=39.421 ms
84 bytes from 172.16.10.40 icmp_seq=4 ttl=64 time=36.304 ms
84 bytes from 172.16.10.40 icmp_seq=5 ttl=64 time=30.065 ms
```

Example 5-36: *Data-Plane testing by pinging from Web10 to all other servers.*

Complexity Chart

This design model is the simplest form of the BGP configuration perspective. It only requirest BGP Route-Reflector Clusters in Spine and Super-Spine layer.

Single-AS Design with OSPF Underlay

		L	S	SS
Infrastructure IP Addressing				
Native Support for Unnumbered IP	Yes			
Requires subnet per Inter-switch link	No			
Loopback Interface Count		3	2	2
Overlay BGP Adjacency				
Update Source Modification		Yes	Yes	Yes
Increasing TTL (eBGP Multihop)		No	No	No
Support Dynamic-AS in Spine Layer		--	Yes	--
BGP Update Policy				
Retain Route-Targets (retain route-target all)		No	No	No
Rewrite ASN Part of Route-Target (rewrite-evp-rt-asn)		No	No	No
Requires Unmodified N-H address config (for EVPN)		No	No	No
Removing BGP Loop Prevention (allow-as in)		No	No	No
Removing BGP Loop Prevention (disable-peer-check)		No	No	No
Requires BGP RR-Cluster in Spine and SuperSpine layer		--	Yes	Yes
IPv4/EVPN NLRIs in the same BGP message		No	No	No
Other Considerations				
Possibility to restrict switch from the Overlay Network without disturbing Underlay Network	Yes			

Table 5-1: *Single-ASN Model Complexity Chart.*

Chapter 6: Hybrid AS Model with OSPF Underlay

Introduction

This chapter discusses the Hybrid-ASN solution where each Pod has its own unique ASN shared between Spine and Leaf switches. SuperSpine switches have the unique ASN they have eBGP peering with Pod Spine switches. ASN 65100 is assigned to Pod-1 and ASN 65200 is assigned to Pod-2. SuperSpine switches belong have ASN 65001. OSPF is used throughout the whole fabric with the Unnumbered interface. Switches within Pods have iBGP L2VPN EVPN peering. Peering between Spine and Super Spine is an eBGP L2VPN EVPN. Spine switches are also BGP Route-Reflectors for internal Leaf switches.

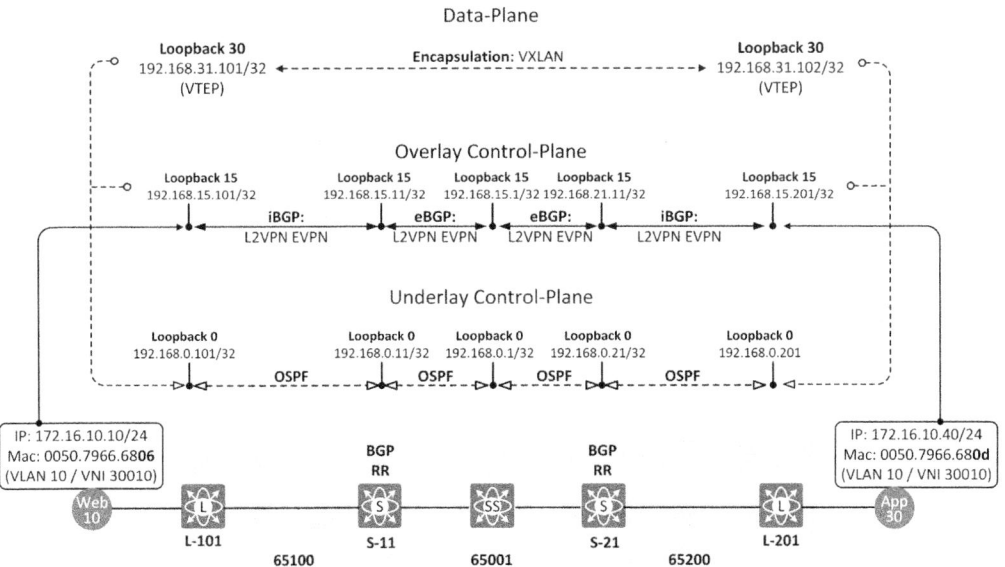

Figure 6-1: *The overall Control-Plane operation in the Hybrid-ASN model.*

Figure 6-2 illustrates the ASN scheme used in this chapter.

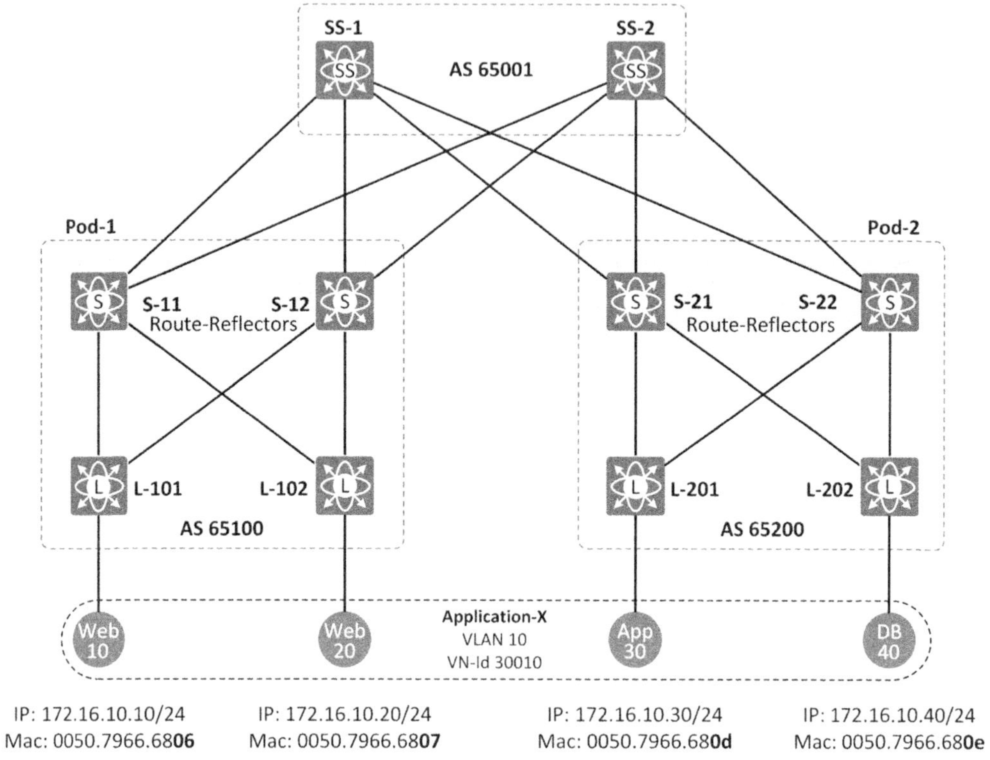

Figure 6-2: *Hybrid ASN Scheme.*

Configuration

Leaf – BGP Policy and BGP Update settings

The example below shows the BGP configuration of L-101. It has BGP L2VPN EVPN peering with both Spines between interface Loopback 15. There is no need for TTL BGP message TTL modification because this is internal peering. Extended communities are required for Route-Targets, VNI, and Tunnel Encapsulation information. L-102 has a similar configuration with the exception that the BGP Router-Id is its IP address of interface Loopback 15.

```
router bgp 65100
  router-id 192.168.15.101
  address-family l2vpn evpn
    maximum-paths 8
  neighbor 192.168.15.11
    remote-as 65100
    update-source loopback15
    address-family l2vpn evpn
      send-community
      send-community extended
  neighbor 192.168.15.12
    remote-as 65100
    update-source loopback15
    address-family l2vpn evpn
      send-community
      send-community extended
evpn
  vni 30010 l2
    rd auto
    route-target import auto
    route-target export auto
vrf context TENANT-1
  rd auto
  address-family ipv4 unicast
    route-target both auto
    route-target both auto evpn
```

Example 6-1: *BGP Configuration of L-101.*

Spine - BGP Adjacency and BGP Update settings

Example 6-2 describes the BGP configuration on S-11. S-11 and S-12 form a BGP RR Cluster so that is why there is the command cluster-id. Spine switches don't have any BGP import policies, that is why we need the command *retain route-target all*. If this command is left out, Spine will forwards BGP Updates but without RT, which in turn means that none of the receiving Leaf switches won't import EVPN NLRIs into VN specific BGP table.

Peering with SuperSpine is external and since we are using peering between Loopback interfaces, TTL has to be increased with the command *ebgp multi-hop 2*. As a side note, this is something that I easily forget when building configs. The next-hop address assigned by originating Leaf switches for EVPN routes has to be sent unmodified by all Spine and SuperSpine switches because receiving Leaf switches will use that next-hop address in Data-Plane as a destination IP in tunnel header when forwarding traffic to host. If the next-hop address is modified during BGP Update propagation, the Data-Plane will be broken. We are using auto RT assignment when exportin EVPN routes to the BGP process by Leaf switches. The first part of auto-generated RT is ASN where the switch is located. This means that switches belonging to different BGP AS will use different RT for the same VN. The command *rewrite-evpn-rt-asn* is needed to modify RT when importing route from Adj-RIB-In (Pre) table. So in our case, when SS-1 receives BGP L2VPN EVPN NLRI from S-11, it changes the ASN part from 65100 to 65001. When it forwards the BGP Update message to spines in Pod-2, it uses RT 65001:30010. The command is needed in every switch because the receiving switch no matter its role does verify that the ASN part on RT is the same that the sending peer ASN used for BGP peering. In practice, this means that S-21, as an example, will accept the EVPN MAC Advertisement route about host Web-10 from SS-1 only if the ASN part in RT Extended Community is 65001. Spine peering with Pod internal Leaf switches is iBGP and that means that there is no next-hop modification when sending BGP Update from SupreSpine switches to Leaf switches. In order to forward BGP Updates between Pod intra Leaf switches Spine switches have a BGP Route-Reflector role where both Spines are using the same Cluster-Id for loop prevention. Cluster-Id is carried as the BGP standard community in BGP Update messages. The configuration could be shortened by using Dynamic-AS but it requires two peering because we are using internal BGP peering with Leaf switches and external peering with SuperSpine switches. This means that there are differences in neighbor policy (ebgp multi-hop, Route-Reflector-Client, Next-Hop modification, rewrite ASN).

```
router bgp 65100
  router-id 192.168.15.11
  cluster-id 192.168.1.1
  address-family l2vpn evpn
    maximum-paths 8
    retain route-target all
  neighbor 192.168.15.1
    remote-as 65001
    update-source loopback15
    ebgp-multihop 2
    address-family l2vpn evpn
      send-community
      send-community extended
```

```
      route-map RETAIN-NH out
      rewrite-evpn-rt-asn
  neighbor 192.168.15.2
    remote-as 65001
    update-source loopback15
    ebgp-multihop 2
    address-family l2vpn evpn
      send-community
      send-community extended
      route-map RETAIN-NH out
      rewrite-evpn-rt-asn
  neighbor 192.168.15.101
    remote-as 65100
    update-source loopback15
    address-family l2vpn evpn
      send-community
      send-community extended
      route-reflector-client
  neighbor 192.168.15.102
    remote-as 65100
    update-source loopback15
    address-family l2vpn evpn
      send-community
      send-community extended
      route-reflector-client
```

Example 6-2: *BGP Configuration of S-11.*

```
router bgp 65100
  router-id 192.168.15.12
  cluster-id 192.168.1.1
  address-family ipv4 unicast
    maximum-paths 8
  address-family l2vpn evpn
    maximum-paths 8
    retain route-target all
  neighbor 192.168.15.1
    remote-as 65001
    update-source loopback15
    ebgp-multihop 2
    address-family l2vpn evpn
      send-community
      send-community extended
      route-map RETAIN-NH out
      rewrite-evpn-rt-asn
  neighbor 192.168.15.2
    remote-as 65001
    update-source loopback15
    ebgp-multihop 2
    address-family l2vpn evpn
      send-community
      send-community extended
      route-map RETAIN-NH out
      rewrite-evpn-rt-asn
```

```
  neighbor 192.168.15.101
    remote-as 65100
    update-source loopback15
    address-family l2vpn evpn
      send-community
      send-community extended
      route-reflector-client
      route-map RETAIN-NH out
  neighbor 192.168.15.102
    remote-as 65100
    update-source loopback15
    address-family l2vpn evpn
      send-community
      send-community extended
      route-reflector-client
```

Example 6-3: *BGP Configuration of S-12.*

SuperSpine - BGP Adjacency and BGP Update settings

Example 6-4 and 6-5 show the BGP configuration of SuperSpine switches SS-1 and SS-2. Because all BGP peerings are external, we are defining Pod specific neighbor policies in a dedicated peer template, one for Pod-1 and the other one for Pod-2. The same rules concerning Route-Targets (retain and rewrite), and next-hop (unmodified) applies to SuperSpine switches than what was discussed with the configuration of the spine switch.

```
router bgp 65001
  router-id 192.168.15.1
  cluster-id 192.168.100.1
  address-family l2vpn evpn
    maximum-paths 8
    retain route-target all
  template peer RR-Clients-Pod-1
    remote-as 65100
    update-source loopback15
    ebgp-multihop 2
    address-family l2vpn evpn
      send-community
      send-community extended
      route-map RETAIN-NH out
      rewrite-evpn-rt-asn
  template peer RR-Clients-Pod-2
    remote-as 65200
    update-source loopback15
    ebgp-multihop 2
    address-family l2vpn evpn
      send-community
      send-community extended
      route-map RETAIN-NH out
      rewrite-evpn-rt-asn
  neighbor 192.168.15.11
```

```
    inherit peer RR-Clients-Pod-1
  neighbor 192.168.15.12
    inherit peer RR-Clients-Pod-1
  neighbor 192.168.15.21
    inherit peer RR-Clients-Pod-2
  neighbor 192.168.15.22
    inherit peer RR-Clients-Pod-2
```

Example 6-4: *BGP Configuration of SS-1.*

```
router bgp 65001
  router-id 192.168.15.2
  cluster-id 192.168.100.1
  address-family l2vpn evpn
    maximum-paths 8
    retain route-target all
  template peer RR-Clients-Pod-1
    remote-as 65100
    update-source loopback15
    ebgp-multihop 2
    address-family l2vpn evpn
      send-community
      send-community extended
      route-map RETAIN-NH out
      rewrite-evpn-rt-asn
  template peer RR-Clients-Pod-2
    remote-as 65200
    update-source loopback15
    ebgp-multihop 2
    address-family l2vpn evpn
      send-community
      send-community extended
      route-map RETAIN-NH out
      rewrite-evpn-rt-asn
  neighbor 192.168.15.11
    inherit peer RR-Clients-Pod-1
  neighbor 192.168.15.12
    inherit peer RR-Clients-Pod-1
  neighbor 192.168.15.21
    inherit peer RR-Clients-Pod-2
  neighbor 192.168.15.22
    inherit peer RR-Clients-Pod-2
```

Example 6-4: *BGP Configuration of SS-2.*

Examples 6-5 and 6-6 show configurations of S-21 and S-22 in Pod-2. They are using the same BGP configuration principles as what was discussed with S-11 in Pod-1.

```
router bgp 65200
  router-id 192.168.15.21
  cluster-id 192.168.2.2
  address-family ipv4 unicast
```

```
    maximum-paths 8
  address-family l2vpn evpn
    maximum-paths 8
    retain route-target all
  neighbor 192.168.15.1
    remote-as 65001
    update-source loopback15
    ebgp-multihop 2
    address-family l2vpn evpn
      send-community
      send-community extended
      route-map RETAIN-NH out
      rewrite-evpn-rt-asn
  neighbor 192.168.15.2
    remote-as 65001
    update-source loopback15
    ebgp-multihop 2
    address-family l2vpn evpn
      send-community
      send-community extended
      route-map RETAIN-NH out
      rewrite-evpn-rt-asn
  neighbor 192.168.15.201
    remote-as 65200
    update-source loopback15
    address-family l2vpn evpn
      send-community
      send-community extended
      route-reflector-client
      route-map RETAIN-NH out
  neighbor 192.168.15.202
    remote-as 65200
    update-source loopback15
    address-family l2vpn evpn
      send-community
      send-community extended
      route-reflector-client
```

Example 6-5: *BGP Configuration of S-21.*

```
router bgp 65200
  router-id 192.168.15.22
  cluster-id 192.168.2.2
  address-family ipv4 unicast
    maximum-paths 8
  address-family l2vpn evpn
    maximum-paths 8
    retain route-target all
  neighbor 192.168.15.1
    remote-as 65001
    update-source loopback15
    ebgp-multihop 2
    address-family l2vpn evpn
```

```
    send-community
    send-community extended
    route-map RETAIN-NH out
    rewrite-evpn-rt-asn
  neighbor 192.168.15.2
    remote-as 65001
    update-source loopback15
    ebgp-multihop 2
    address-family l2vpn evpn
      send-community
      send-community extended
      route-map RETAIN-NH out
      rewrite-evpn-rt-asn
  neighbor 192.168.15.201
    remote-as 65200
    update-source loopback15
    address-family l2vpn evpn
      send-community
      send-community extended
      route-reflector-client
      route-map RETAIN-NH out
  neighbor 192.168.15.202
    remote-as 65200
    update-source loopback15
    address-family l2vpn evpn
      send-community
      send-community extended
      route-reflector-client
```

Example 6-6: *BGP Configuration of S-22.*

Examples 6-7 and 6-8 show the BGP configuration of L-201 and L-202 in Pod-2. They follow the same principles as used in L-101.

```
router bgp 65200
  router-id 192.168.15.201
  address-family l2vpn evpn
    maximum-paths 8
  neighbor 192.168.15.21
    remote-as 65200
    update-source loopback15
    address-family l2vpn evpn
      send-community
      send-community extended
  neighbor 192.168.15.22
    remote-as 65200
    update-source loopback15
    address-family l2vpn evpn
      send-community
      send-community extended
evpn
  vni 30010 l2
    rd auto
    route-target import auto
```

```
    route-target export auto
vrf context TENANT-1
  rd auto
  address-family ipv4 unicast
    route-target both auto
    route-target both auto evpn
```

Example 6-7: *BGP Configuration of L-201.*


```
router bgp 65200
  router-id 192.168.15.202
  address-family l2vpn evpn
    maximum-paths 8
  neighbor 192.168.15.21
    remote-as 65200
    update-source loopback15
    address-family l2vpn evpn
      send-community
      send-community extended
  neighbor 192.168.15.22
    remote-as 65200
    update-source loopback15
    address-family l2vpn evpn
      send-community
      send-community extended
evpn
  vni 30010 l2
    rd auto
    route-target import auto
    route-target export auto
vrf context TENANT-1
  rd auto
  address-family ipv4 unicast
    route-target both auto
    route-target both auto evpn
```

Example 6-8: *BGP Configuration of L-202.*

Verification

Examples 6-9 shows that L-101 has established BGP L2VPN EVPN peering with S-11 and S-12 and it has received nine prefixes from both Spines.

```
L-101# show bgp l2vpn evpn summary
BGP summary information for VRF default, address family L2VPN EVPN
BGP router identifier 192.168.15.101, local AS number 65100
BGP table version is 891, L2VPN EVPN config peers 2, capable peers 2
24 network entries and 33 paths using 5400 bytes of memory
BGP attribute entries [20/3280], BGP AS path entries [1/10]
BGP community entries [0/0], BGP clusterlist entries [1/4]

Neighbor        V    AS MsgRcvd MsgSent   TblVer  InQ OutQ Up/Down  State/PfxRcd
192.168.15.11   4 65100    558     272      891    0    0 01:14:07 9
192.168.15.12   4 65100    538     262      891    0    0 01:14:08 9
```

Example 6-9: *show bgp l2vpn evpn summary on L-101.*

Example 6-10 shows received EVPN MAC Advertisement and Inclusive Multicast Routes in Adj-RIB-In table as well as how they are imported into L2VN and L3 VN specific BGP tables. The benefit of using the Hybrid-AS scheme is that the last ASN in Path-List describes the Pod where the host is located. As a tradeoff, the configuration and Control-Plane operation are more complex compared to the Single-ASN model (despite the BGP RR requirements on Spines). If we take a look at how L-101 sees host DB40 with the MAC address 0050.7966.680e and the IP address 172.16.10.40, we can see that MAC and MAC-IP information is imported into L2VNI 30010 and L3VNI 30077. Path information 65200 tells that at the moment the host is located in Pod-2 (AS 65200).

```
L-101# show bgp l2vpn evpn
BGP routing table information for VRF default, address family L2VPN EVPN
BGP table version is 891, Local Router ID is 192.168.15.101
Status: s-suppressed, x-deleted, S-stale, d-dampened, h-history, *-valid, >-best
Path type: i-internal, e-external, c-confed, l-local, a-aggregate, r-redist, I-
injected
Origin codes: i - IGP, e - EGP, ? - incomplete, | - multipath, & - backup, 2 - best2

   Network            Next Hop            Metric     LocPrf    Weight Path
Route Distinguisher: 192.168.15.101:32777    (L2VNI 30010)
*>l[2]:[0]:[0]:[48]:[0050.7966.6806]:[0]:[0.0.0.0]/216
                      192.168.30.101                  100       32768 i
*>i[2]:[0]:[0]:[48]:[0050.7966.6807]:[0]:[0.0.0.0]/216
                      192.168.30.102                  100           0 i
*>i[2]:[0]:[0]:[48]:[0050.7966.680d]:[0]:[0.0.0.0]/216
                      192.168.30.201                  100           0 65001 65200 i
*>i[2]:[0]:[0]:[48]:[0050.7966.680e]:[0]:[0.0.0.0]/216
                      192.168.30.202                  100           0 65001 65200 i
*>l[2]:[0]:[0]:[48]:[0050.7966.6806]:[32]:[172.16.10.10]/272
                      192.168.30.101                  100       32768 i
*>i[2]:[0]:[0]:[48]:[0050.7966.6807]:[32]:[172.16.10.20]/272
                      192.168.30.102                  100           0 i
*>i[2]:[0]:[0]:[48]:[0050.7966.680d]:[32]:[172.16.10.30]/272
                      192.168.30.201                  100           0 65001 65200 i
*>i[2]:[0]:[0]:[48]:[0050.7966.680e]:[32]:[172.16.10.40]/272
                      192.168.30.202                  100           0 65001 65200 i
*>l[3]:[0]:[32]:[192.168.30.101]/88
                      192.168.30.101                  100       32768 i
```

```
*>i[3]:[0]:[32]:[192.168.30.102]/88
                    192.168.30.102                 100            0 i
*>i[3]:[0]:[32]:[192.168.30.201]/88
                    192.168.30.201                 100            0 65001 65200 i
*>i[3]:[0]:[32]:[192.168.30.202]/88
                    192.168.30.202                 100            0 65001 65200 i

Route Distinguisher: 192.168.15.102:32777
*>i[2]:[0]:[0]:[48]:[0050.7966.6807]:[0]:[0.0.0.0]/216
                    192.168.30.102                 100            0 i
*  i                192.168.30.102                 100            0 i
*  i[2]:[0]:[0]:[48]:[0050.7966.6807]:[32]:[172.16.10.20]/272
                    192.168.30.102                 100            0 i
*>i                 192.168.30.102                 100            0 i
*>i[3]:[0]:[32]:[192.168.30.102]/88
                    192.168.30.102                 100            0 i
*  i                192.168.30.102                 100            0 i

Route Distinguisher: 192.168.15.201:32777
*  i[2]:[0]:[0]:[48]:[0050.7966.680d]:[0]:[0.0.0.0]/216
                    192.168.30.201                 100            0 65001 65200 i
*>i                 192.168.30.201                 100            0 65001 65200 i
*  i[2]:[0]:[0]:[48]:[0050.7966.680d]:[32]:[172.16.10.30]/272
                    192.168.30.201                 100            0 65001 65200 i
*>i                 192.168.30.201                 100            0 65001 65200 i
*  i[3]:[0]:[32]:[192.168.30.201]/88
                    192.168.30.201                 100            0 65001 65200 i
*>i                 192.168.30.201                 100            0 65001 65200 i

Route Distinguisher: 192.168.15.202:32777
*  i[2]:[0]:[0]:[48]:[0050.7966.680e]:[0]:[0.0.0.0]/216
                    192.168.30.202                 100            0 65001 65200 i
*>i                 192.168.30.202                 100            0 65001 65200 i
*  i[2]:[0]:[0]:[48]:[0050.7966.680e]:[32]:[172.16.10.40]/272
                    192.168.30.202                 100            0 65001 65200 i
*>i                 192.168.30.202                 100            0 65001 65200 i
*  i[3]:[0]:[32]:[192.168.30.202]/88
                    192.168.30.202                 100            0 65001 65200 i
*>i                 192.168.30.202                 100            0 65001 65200 i

Route Distinguisher: 192.168.15.101:3     (L3VNI 30077)
*>i[2]:[0]:[0]:[48]:[0050.7966.6807]:[32]:[172.16.10.20]/272
                    192.168.30.102                 100            0 i
*>i[2]:[0]:[0]:[48]:[0050.7966.680d]:[32]:[172.16.10.30]/272
                    192.168.30.201                 100            0 65001 65200 i
*>i[2]:[0]:[0]:[48]:[0050.7966.680e]:[32]:[172.16.10.40]/272
                    192.168.30.202                 100            0 65001 65200 i
```

Example 6-10: *show bgp l2vpn evpn on L-101.*

The example below shows that L-101 has received BGP EVPN MAC Advertisement Route about Database Server 40 (MAC: 0050.7966.680e, IP 172.16.10.40) from both S-11 (192.169.15.11) and S-12 (172.16.15.12), and both NLRIs are installed into Adj-RIB-In with the next-hop 192.168.30.202. From Adj-RIB-In both MAC-Only and MAC-IP information is installed into L2VNI 30010 specific table from the NLRI advertised by S-11 because that one is selected as the best path. As can be seen, the next-hop address towards the destination host is the IP address of the L-202 NVE interface. The actual load-balancing is now based on the Underlay network routing decision. We are using OSPF in this example and there are two equal routes to the destination and Data-Plane load-balancing are done between these two address. If we are using BGP in Underlay, we also need to enable maximum-path under BGP IPv4 AFI in order to do flow-based load-balancing. In other words, BGP EVPN is used to advertise host-based NLRI with their unmodified next-hop, originated by the leaf where the host is connected.

```
L-101# show bgp l2vpn evpn 0050.7966.680e
BGP routing table information for VRF default, address family L2VPN EVPN
Route Distinguisher: 192.168.15.101:32777     (L2VNI 30010)
BGP routing table entry for [2]:[0]:[0]:[48]:[0050.7966.680e]:[0]:[0.0.0.0]/216,
version 884
Paths: (1 available, best #1)
Flags: (0x000212) (high32 00000000) on xmit-list, is in l2rib/evpn, is not in HW
Multipath: eBGP

  Advertised path-id 1
  Path type: internal, path is valid, is best path, no labeled nexthop, in rib
             Imported from
192.168.15.202:32777:[2]:[0]:[0]:[48]:[0050.7966.680e]:[0]:[0.0.0.0]/216
    AS-Path: 65001 65200 , path sourced external to AS
     192.168.30.202 (metric 161) from 192.168.15.11 (192.168.15.11)
       Origin IGP, MED not set, localpref 100, weight 0
       Received label 30010
       Extcommunity: RT:65100:30010 ENCAP:8

  Path-id 1 not advertised to any peer
BGP routing table entry for [2]:[0]:[0]:[48]:[0050.7966.680e]:[32]:[172.16.10.40]/272,
version 553
Paths: (1 available, best #1)
Flags: (0x000212) (high32 00000000) on xmit-list, is in l2rib/evpn, is not in HW
Multipath: eBGP

  Advertised path-id 1
  Path type: internal, path is valid, is best path, no labeled nexthop, in rib
             Imported from
192.168.15.202:32777:[2]:[0]:[0]:[48]:[0050.7966.680e]:[32]:[172.16.10.40]/272
    AS-Path: 65001 65200 , path sourced external to AS
     192.168.30.202 (metric 161) from 192.168.15.11 (192.168.15.11)
       Origin IGP, MED not set, localpref 100, weight 0
       Received label 30010 30077
       Extcommunity: RT:65100:30010 RT:65100:30077 ENCAP:8 Router MAC:5000.000b.0007

  Path-id 1 not advertised to any peer
```

```
Route Distinguisher: 192.168.15.202:32777
BGP routing table entry for [2]:[0]:[0]:[48]:[0050.7966.680e]:[0]:[0.0.0.0]/216,
version 883
Paths: (2 available, best #2)
Flags: (0x000202) (high32 00000000) on xmit-list, is not in l2rib/evpn, is not in HW
Multipath: eBGP

  Path type: internal, path is valid, not best reason: Router Id, no labeled nexthop
  AS-Path: 65001 65200 , path sourced external to AS
    192.168.30.202 (metric 161) from 192.168.15.12 (192.168.15.12)
      Origin IGP, MED not set, localpref 100, weight 0
      Received label 30010
      Extcommunity: RT:65100:30010 ENCAP:8

  Advertised path-id 1
  Path type: internal, path is valid, is best path, no labeled nexthop
             Imported to 1 destination(s)
             Imported paths list: default
  AS-Path: 65001 65200 , path sourced external to AS
    192.168.30.202 (metric 161) from 192.168.15.11 (192.168.15.11)
      Origin IGP, MED not set, localpref 100, weight 0
      Received label 30010
      Extcommunity: RT:65100:30010 ENCAP:8

  Path-id 1 not advertised to any peer
BGP routing table entry for [2]:[0]:[0]:[48]:[0050.7966.680e]:[32]:[172.16.10.40]/272,
version 573
Paths: (2 available, best #2)
Flags: (0x000202) (high32 00000000) on xmit-list, is not in l2rib/evpn, is not in HW
Multipath: eBGP

  Path type: internal, path is valid, not best reason: Router Id, no labeled nexthop
  AS-Path: 65001 65200 , path sourced external to AS
    192.168.30.202 (metric 161) from 192.168.15.12 (192.168.15.12)
      Origin IGP, MED not set, localpref 100, weight 0
      Received label 30010 30077
      Extcommunity: RT:65100:30010 RT:65100:30077 ENCAP:8 Router MAC:5000.000b.0007

  Advertised path-id 1
  Path type: internal, path is valid, is best path, no labeled nexthop
             Imported to 3 destination(s)
             Imported paths list: TENANT-1 default default
  AS-Path: 65001 65200 , path sourced external to AS
    192.168.30.202 (metric 161) from 192.168.15.11 (192.168.15.11)
      Origin IGP, MED not set, localpref 100, weight 0
      Received label 30010 30077
      Extcommunity: RT:65100:30010 RT:65100:30077 ENCAP:8 Router MAC:5000.000b.0007

  Path-id 1 not advertised to any peer

Route Distinguisher: 192.168.15.101:3    (L3VNI 30077)
BGP routing table entry for [2]:[0]:[0]:[48]:[0050.7966.680e]:[32]:[172.16.10.40]/272,
version 554
Paths: (1 available, best #1)
Flags: (0x000202) (high32 00000000) on xmit-list, is not in l2rib/evpn, is not in HW
Multipath: eBGP

  Advertised path-id 1
  Path type: internal, path is valid, is best path, no labeled nexthop
             Imported from
192.168.15.202:32777:[2]:[0]:[0]:[48]:[0050.7966.680e]:[32]:[172.16.10.40]/272
```

```
AS-Path: 65001 65200 , path sourced external to AS
  192.168.30.202 (metric 161) from 192.168.15.11 (192.168.15.11)
    Origin IGP, MED not set, localpref 100, weight 0
    Received label 30010 30077
    Extcommunity: RT:65100:30010 RT:65100:30077 ENCAP:8 Router MAC:5000.000b.0007

Path-id 1 not advertised to any peer
```

Example 6-11: *show bgp l2vpn evpn 0050.7966.680e on L-101.*

Example 6-12 shows that there are two equal-cost paths to 192.168.30.202 marked as next-hop.

```
L-101# sh ip route 192.168.30.202
IP Route Table for VRF "default"
'*' denotes best ucast next-hop
'**' denotes best mcast next-hop
'[x/y]' denotes [preference/metric]
'%<string>' in via output denotes VRF <string>

192.168.30.202/32, ubest/mbest: 2/0
    *via 192.168.0.11, Eth1/1, [110/161], 00:19:09, ospf-UNDERLAY-NET, intra
    *via 192.168.0.12, Eth1/2, [110/161], 00:19:09, ospf-UNDERLAY-NET, intra
```

Example 6-12: *show ip route 192.168.30.202 on L-101.*

The example below shows the L2RIB of L-101. It also verifies that frames to Database Server 40 are sent towards 192.168.30.202. From the example above we can see how the actual encapsulated packet will be sent (Recursive Next-Hop).

```
L-101# show l2route evpn mac evi 10

Flags -(Rmac):Router MAC (Stt):Static (L):Local (R):Remote (V):vPC link
(Dup):Duplicate (Spl):Split (Rcv):Recv (AD):Auto-Delete (D):Del Pending
(S):Stale (C):Clear, (Ps):Peer Sync (O):Re-Originated (Nho):NH-Override
(Pf):Permanently-Frozen, (Orp): Orphan

Topology    Mac Address      Prod    Flags           Seq No      Next-Hops
---------   --------------   ------  -------------   ---------   ----------------------
10          0050.7966.6806   Local   L,              0           Eth1/3
10          0050.7966.6807   BGP     SplRcv          0           192.168.30.102
10          0050.7966.680d   BGP     SplRcv          0           192.168.30.201
10          0050.7966.680e   BGP     SplRcv          0           192.168.30.202
```

Example 6-13: *show l2route evpn mac evi 10 on L-101.*

Example 6-14 shows that the information is received from BGP, the next hop is resolved, the information is sent to the L2FWDER component which sends the information to VLAN 10 MAC Address table, and that traffic to the destination is encapsulated. The encapsulation type is carried within BGP Update as Extended Community Path-Attribute.

```
L-101# sh l2route evpn mac evi 10 detail

<snipped>

Topology    Mac Address      Prod     Flags           Seq No    Next-Hops
---------   --------------   ------   -------------   -------   ----------------------
10          0050.7966.6806 Local    L,              0         Eth1/3
            Route Resolution Type: Regular
            Forwarding State: Resolved
            Sent To: BGP

10          0050.7966.6807 BGP      SplRcv          0         192.168.30.102
            Route Resolution Type: Regular
            Forwarding State: Resolved (PeerID: 1)
            Sent To: L2FWDER
            Encap: 1

10          0050.7966.680d BGP      SplRcv          0         192.168.30.201
            Route Resolution Type: Regular
            Forwarding State: Resolved (PeerID: 2)
            Sent To: L2FWDER
            Encap: 1

10          0050.7966.680e BGP      SplRcv          0         192.168.30.202
            Route Resolution Type: Regular
            Forwarding State: Resolved (PeerID: 3)
            Sent To: L2FWDER
            Encap: 1
```

Example 6-14: *show l2route evpn mac evi 10 detail on L-101.*

Example 6-15 shows the same information from the MAC-IP binding information perspective. Note that the information about localhost 172.16.10.10 is produced by HMM (Host Mobility Manager). HMM keeps track of the host movements. Whenever the leaf switch learns a new MAC-IP binding, the information is installed into ARP-table. HMM notices that there is a new ARP-entry and forwards the information to L2RIB from where it is sent to the BGP process and advertised to other BGP EVPN L2VPN peers. This process is explained in greater detail in my first VXLAN book.

```
L-101# sh l2route evpn mac-ip evi 10
Flags -(Rmac):Router MAC (Stt):Static (L):Local (R):Remote (V):vPC link
(Dup):Duplicate (Spl):Split (Rcv):Recv(D):Del Pending (S):Stale (C):Clear
(Ps):Peer Sync (Ro):Re-Originated (Orp):Orphan
Topology    Mac Address      Host IP                    Prod     Flags       Seq No    Next-Hops
---------   --------------   ------------------------   ------   ---------   -------   ----------------
10          0050.7966.6806 172.16.10.10                 HMM      L,          0         Local
10          0050.7966.6807 172.16.10.20                 BGP      --          0         192.168.30.102
10          0050.7966.680d 172.16.10.30                 BGP      --          0         192.168.30.201
10          0050.7966.680e 172.16.10.40                 BGP      --          0         192.168.30.202
```

Example 6-15: *show l2route evpn mac-ip evi 10 detail on L-101.*

```
L-101# sh l2route evpn mac-ip evi 10 detail
Flags -(Rmac):Router MAC (Stt):Static (L):Local (R):Remote (V):vPC link
(Dup):Duplicate (Spl):Split (Rcv):Recv(D):Del Pending (S):Stale (C):Clear
(Ps):Peer Sync (Ro):Re-Originated (Orp):Orphan
Topology    Mac Address     Host IP                 Prod    Flags       Seq No      Next-Hops
---------   --------------- ---------------         ------  ----------  ----------  ---------------
10          0050.7966.6806  172.16.10.10            HMM     L,          0           Local
            L3-Info: 30077
            Sent To: BGP
10          0050.7966.6807  172.16.10.20            BGP     --          0           192.168.30.102
            encap-type:1
10          0050.7966.680d  172.16.10.30            BGP     --          0           192.168.30.201
            encap-type:1
10          0050.7966.680e  172.16.10.40            BGP     --          0           192.168.30.202
            encap-type:1
```

Example 6-16: *show l2route evpn mac-ip evi 10 detail on L-101.*

The next two examples verify that the Data-Plane is ok and leaf switches can see each other as NVE peers.

```
L-101# sh nve peers
Interface Peer-IP                           State LearnType Uptime   Router-Mac
--------- ---------------                   ----- --------- -------- ---------------
nve1      192.168.30.102                    Up    CP        02:17:19 5000.0002.0007
nve1      192.168.30.201                    Up    CP        01:19:37 5000.000c.0007
nve1      192.168.30.202                    Up    CP        01:19:37 5000.000b.0007
```

Example 6-17: *Show nve peers on L-101.*

```
L-101# sh nve peers detail
Details of nve Peers:
----------------------------------------
Peer-Ip: 192.168.30.102
    NVE Interface          : nve1
    Peer State             : Up
    Peer Uptime            : 02:17:22
    Router-Mac             : 5000.0002.0007
    Peer First VNI         : 30010
    Time since Create      : 02:17:22
    Configured VNIs        : 30010,30077
    Provision State        : peer-add-complete
    Learnt CP VNIs         : 30010,30077
    vni assignment mode    : SYMMETRIC
    Peer Location          : N/A
Peer-Ip: 192.168.30.201
    NVE Interface          : nve1
    Peer State             : Up
    Peer Uptime            : 01:19:40
    Router-Mac             : 5000.000c.0007
    Peer First VNI         : 30010
    Time since Create      : 01:19:40
    Configured VNIs        : 30010,30077
    Provision State        : peer-add-complete
    Learnt CP VNIs         : 30010,30077
    vni assignment mode    : SYMMETRIC
    Peer Location          : N/A
Peer-Ip: 192.168.30.202
```

```
    NVE Interface       : nve1
    Peer State          : Up
    Peer Uptime         : 01:19:40
    Router-Mac          : 5000.000b.0007
    Peer First VNI      : 30010
    Time since Create   : 01:19:40
    Configured VNIs     : 30010,30077
    Provision State     : peer-add-complete
    Learnt CP VNIs      : 30010,30077
    vni assignment mode : SYMMETRIC
    Peer Location       : N/A
```
Example 6-18: *Show nve peers detail on L-101.*

The rest of the show outputs are included in this chapter as an informative source for those readers who are willing to do some own studies.

```
S-11# sh bgp l2vpn evpn summary
BGP summary information for VRF default, address family L2VPN EVPN
BGP router identifier 192.168.15.11, local AS number 65100
BGP table version is 365, L2VPN EVPN config peers 4, capable peers 4
<snipped>

Neighbor          V    AS MsgRcvd MsgSent   TblVer  InQ OutQ Up/Down   State/PfxRcd
192.168.15.1      4 65001    257     179       365    0    0 01:21:06 6
192.168.15.2      4 65001    242     177       365    0    0 01:21:07 6
192.168.15.101    4 65100    196     209       365    0    0 01:19:03 3
192.168.15.102    4 65100    195     207       365    0    0 01:21:06 3
```
Example 6-19: *Show bgp l2vpn evpn summary on S-11.*

```
S-11# sh bgp l2vpn evpn
BGP routing table information for VRF default, address family L2VPN EVPN
BGP table version is 376, Local Router ID is 192.168.15.11
Status: s-suppressed, x-deleted, S-stale, d-dampened, h-history, *-valid, >-best
Path type: i-internal, e-external, c-confed, l-local, a-aggregate, r-redist, I-
injected
Origin codes: i - IGP, e - EGP, ? - incomplete, | - multipath, & - backup, 2 - best2

   Network            Next Hop            Metric     LocPrf     Weight Path
Route Distinguisher: 192.168.15.101:32777
*>i[2]:[0]:[0]:[48]:[0050.7966.6806]:[0]:[0.0.0.0]/216
                      192.168.30.101                   100          0 i
*>i[2]:[0]:[0]:[48]:[0050.7966.6806]:[32]:[172.16.10.10]/272
                      192.168.30.101                   100          0 i
*>i[3]:[0]:[32]:[192.168.30.101]/88
                      192.168.30.101                   100          0 i

Route Distinguisher: 192.168.15.102:32777
*>i[2]:[0]:[0]:[48]:[0050.7966.6807]:[0]:[0.0.0.0]/216
                      192.168.30.102                   100          0 i
*>i[2]:[0]:[0]:[48]:[0050.7966.6807]:[32]:[172.16.10.20]/272
                      192.168.30.102                   100          0 i
*>i[3]:[0]:[32]:[192.168.30.102]/88
                      192.168.30.102                   100          0 i

Route Distinguisher: 192.168.15.201:32777
*  e[2]:[0]:[0]:[48]:[0050.7966.680d]:[0]:[0.0.0.0]/216
```

```
                              192.168.30.201                              0 65001 65200 i
*>e                           192.168.30.201                              0 65001 65200 i
*>e[2]:[0]:[0]:[48]:[0050.7966.680d]:[32]:[172.16.10.30]/272
                              192.168.30.201                              0 65001 65200 i
*  e                          192.168.30.201                              0 65001 65200 i
*>e[3]:[0]:[32]:[192.168.30.201]/88
                              192.168.30.201                              0 65001 65200 i
*  e                          192.168.30.201                              0 65001 65200 i

Route Distinguisher: 192.168.15.202:32777
*>e[2]:[0]:[0]:[48]:[0050.7966.680e]:[0]:[0.0.0.0]/216
                              192.168.30.202                              0 65001 65200 i
*  e                          192.168.30.202                              0 65001 65200 i
*>e[2]:[0]:[0]:[48]:[0050.7966.680e]:[32]:[172.16.10.40]/272
                              192.168.30.202                              0 65001 65200 i
*  e                          192.168.30.202                              0 65001 65200 i
*>e[3]:[0]:[32]:[192.168.30.202]/88
                              192.168.30.202                              0 65001 65200 i
*  e                          192.168.30.202                              0 65001 65200 i
```

Example 6-20: *Show bgp l2vpn evpn on S-11.*

```
S-12# sh bgp l2vpn evpn summary
BGP summary information for VRF default, address family L2VPN EVPN
BGP router identifier 192.168.15.12, local AS number 65100
BGP table version is 359, L2VPN EVPN config peers 4, capable peers 4
12 network entries and 18 paths using 3600 bytes of memory
BGP attribute entries [10/1640], BGP AS path entries [1/10]
BGP community entries [0/0], BGP clusterlist entries [0/0]

Neighbor          V     AS MsgRcvd MsgSent   TblVer  InQ OutQ Up/Down  State/PfxRcd
192.168.15.1      4  65001     259     181      359    0    0 01:21:48 6
192.168.15.2      4  65001     243     178      359    0    0 01:21:48 6
192.168.15.101    4  65100     196     211      359    0    0 01:19:49 3
192.168.15.102    4  65100     196     209      359    0    0 01:21:47 3
```

Example 6-21: *Show bgp l2vpn evpn summary on S-12.*

```
SS-1# sh bgp l2vpn evpn summary
BGP summary information for VRF default, address family L2VPN EVPN
BGP router identifier 192.168.15.1, local AS number 65001
BGP table version is 657, L2VPN EVPN config peers 4, capable peers 4
12 network entries and 24 paths using 4320 bytes of memory
BGP attribute entries [10/1640], BGP AS path entries [2/12]
BGP community entries [0/0], BGP clusterlist entries [0/0]

Neighbor          V     AS MsgRcvd MsgSent   TblVer  InQ OutQ Up/Down  State/PfxRcd
192.168.15.11     4  65100     364     240      657    0    0 01:22:18 6
192.168.15.12     4  65100     345     232      657    0    0 01:22:16 6
192.168.15.21     4  65200     298     220      657    0    0 01:22:26 6
192.168.15.22     4  65200     286     209      657    0    0 01:22:24 6
```

Example 6-22: *Show bgp l2vpn evpn summary on SS-1.*

```
SS-2# sh bgp l2vpn evpn summary
BGP summary information for VRF default, address family L2VPN EVPN
BGP router identifier 192.168.15.2, local AS number 65001
BGP table version is 632, L2VPN EVPN config peers 4, capable peers 4
12 network entries and 24 paths using 4320 bytes of memory
BGP attribute entries [10/1640], BGP AS path entries [2/12]
BGP community entries [0/0], BGP clusterlist entries [0/0]

Neighbor         V    AS MsgRcvd MsgSent   TblVer  InQ OutQ Up/Down  State/PfxRcd
192.168.15.11    4 65100    340     232      632    0    0 01:23:04 6
192.168.15.12    4 65100    330     225      632    0    0 01:23:01 6
192.168.15.21    4 65200    285     215      632    0    0 01:23:12 6
192.168.15.22    4 65200    284     214      632    0    0 01:23:09 6
```

Example 6-23: *Show bgp l2vpn evpn summary on SS-2.*

```
S-21# sh bgp l2vpn evpn summary
BGP summary information for VRF default, address family L2VPN EVPN
BGP router identifier 192.168.15.21, local AS number 65200
BGP table version is 371, L2VPN EVPN config peers 4, capable peers 4
12 network entries and 18 paths using 3600 bytes of memory
BGP attribute entries [10/1640], BGP AS path entries [1/10]
BGP community entries [0/0], BGP clusterlist entries [0/0]

Neighbor         V    AS MsgRcvd MsgSent   TblVer  InQ OutQ Up/Down  State/PfxRcd
192.168.15.1     4 65001    270     181      371    0    0 01:23:31 6
192.168.15.2     4 65001    253     178      371    0    0 01:23:32 6
192.168.15.201   4 65200    184     204      371    0    0 01:23:31 3
192.168.15.202   4 65200    183     205      371    0    0 01:23:32 3
```

Example 6-23: *Show bgp l2vpn evpn summary on S-21.*

```
S-22# sh bgp l2vpn evpn summary
BGP summary information for VRF default, address family L2VPN EVPN
BGP router identifier 192.168.15.22, local AS number 65200
BGP table version is 374, L2VPN EVPN config peers 4, capable peers 4
12 network entries and 18 paths using 3600 bytes of memory
BGP attribute entries [10/1640], BGP AS path entries [1/10]
BGP community entries [0/0], BGP clusterlist entries [0/0]

Neighbor         V    AS MsgRcvd MsgSent   TblVer  InQ OutQ Up/Down  State/PfxRcd
192.168.15.1     4 65001    263     181      374    0    0 01:23:54 6
192.168.15.2     4 65001    246     178      374    0    0 01:23:54 6
192.168.15.201   4 65200    184     203      374    0    0 01:23:54 3
192.168.15.202   4 65200    184     206      374    0    0 01:23:53 3
```

Example 6-24: *Show bgp l2vpn evpn summary on S-22.*

```
L-201# sh bgp l2vpn evpn summary
BGP summary information for VRF default, address family L2VPN EVPN
BGP router identifier 192.168.15.201, local AS number 65200
BGP table version is 982, L2VPN EVPN config peers 2, capable peers 2
24 network entries and 33 paths using 5400 bytes of memory
BGP attribute entries [20/3280], BGP AS path entries [1/10]
BGP community entries [0/0], BGP clusterlist entries [1/4]

Neighbor          V    AS MsgRcvd MsgSent   TblVer  InQ OutQ Up/Down  State/PfxRcd
192.168.15.21     4 65200     494     236      982    0    0 01:25:37 9
192.168.15.22     4 65200     507     238      982    0    0 01:25:35 9
```

Example 6-25: *Show bgp l2vpn evpn summary on L-201.*

```
L-201# sh bgp l2vpn evpn
BGP routing table information for VRF default, address family L2VPN EVPN
BGP table version is 982, Local Router ID is 192.168.15.201
Status: s-suppressed, x-deleted, S-stale, d-dampened, h-history, *-valid, >-best
Path type: i-internal, e-external, c-confed, l-local, a-aggregate, r-redist, I-
injected
Origin codes: i - IGP, e - EGP, ? - incomplete, | - multipath, & - backup, 2 - best2

   Network            Next Hop            Metric     LocPrf     Weight Path
Route Distinguisher: 192.168.15.101:32777
* i[2]:[0]:[0]:[48]:[0050.7966.6806]:[0]:[0.0.0.0]/216
                     192.168.30.101                    100          0 65001 65100 i
*>i                  192.168.30.101                    100          0 65001 65100 i
* i[2]:[0]:[0]:[48]:[0050.7966.6806]:[32]:[172.16.10.10]/272
                     192.168.30.101                    100          0 65001 65100 i
*>i                  192.168.30.101                    100          0 65001 65100 i
* i[3]:[0]:[32]:[192.168.30.101]/88
                     192.168.30.101                    100          0 65001 65100 i
*>i                  192.168.30.101                    100          0 65001 65100 i

Route Distinguisher: 192.168.15.102:32777
* i[2]:[0]:[0]:[48]:[0050.7966.6807]:[0]:[0.0.0.0]/216
                     192.168.30.102                    100          0 65001 65100 i
*>i                  192.168.30.102                    100          0 65001 65100 i
*>i[2]:[0]:[0]:[48]:[0050.7966.6807]:[32]:[172.16.10.20]/272
                     192.168.30.102                    100          0 65001 65100 i
* i                  192.168.30.102                    100          0 65001 65100 i
*>i[3]:[0]:[32]:[192.168.30.102]/88
                     192.168.30.102                    100          0 65001 65100 i
* i                  192.168.30.102                    100          0 65001 65100 i

Route Distinguisher: 192.168.15.201:32777    (L2VNI 30010)
*>i[2]:[0]:[0]:[48]:[0050.7966.6806]:[0]:[0.0.0.0]/216
                     192.168.30.101                    100          0 65001 65100 i
*>i[2]:[0]:[0]:[48]:[0050.7966.6807]:[0]:[0.0.0.0]/216
                     192.168.30.102                    100          0 65001 65100 i
*>l[2]:[0]:[0]:[48]:[0050.7966.680d]:[0]:[0.0.0.0]/216
                     192.168.30.201                    100      32768 i
*>i[2]:[0]:[0]:[48]:[0050.7966.680e]:[0]:[0.0.0.0]/216
                     192.168.30.202                    100          0 i
*>i[2]:[0]:[0]:[48]:[0050.7966.6806]:[32]:[172.16.10.10]/272
```

```
                          192.168.30.101              100         0 65001 65100 i
*>i[2]:[0]:[0]:[48]:[0050.7966.6807]:[32]:[172.16.10.20]/272
                          192.168.30.102              100         0 65001 65100 i
*>l[2]:[0]:[0]:[48]:[0050.7966.680d]:[32]:[172.16.10.30]/272
                          192.168.30.201              100         32768 i
*>i[2]:[0]:[0]:[48]:[0050.7966.680e]:[32]:[172.16.10.40]/272
                          192.168.30.202              100         0 i
*>i[3]:[0]:[32]:[192.168.30.101]/88
                          192.168.30.101              100         0 65001 65100 i
*>i[3]:[0]:[32]:[192.168.30.102]/88
                          192.168.30.102              100         0 65001 65100 i
*>l[3]:[0]:[32]:[192.168.30.201]/88
                          192.168.30.201              100         32768 i
*>i[3]:[0]:[32]:[192.168.30.202]/88
                          192.168.30.202              100         0 i

Route Distinguisher: 192.168.15.202:32777
* i[2]:[0]:[0]:[48]:[0050.7966.680e]:[0]:[0.0.0.0]/216
                          192.168.30.202              100         0 i
*>i                       192.168.30.202              100         0 i
*>i[2]:[0]:[0]:[48]:[0050.7966.680e]:[32]:[172.16.10.40]/272
                          192.168.30.202              100         0 i
* i                       192.168.30.202              100         0 i
*>i[3]:[0]:[32]:[192.168.30.202]/88
                          192.168.30.202              100         0 i
* i                       192.168.30.202              100         0 i

Route Distinguisher: 192.168.15.201:3    (L3VNI 30077)
*>i[2]:[0]:[0]:[48]:[0050.7966.6806]:[32]:[172.16.10.10]/272
                          192.168.30.101              100         0 65001 65100 i
*>i[2]:[0]:[0]:[48]:[0050.7966.6807]:[32]:[172.16.10.20]/272
                          192.168.30.102              100         0 65001 65100 i
*>i[2]:[0]:[0]:[48]:[0050.7966.680e]:[32]:[172.16.10.40]/272
                          192.168.30.202              100         0 i
```

Example 6-26: *Show bgp l2vpn evpn on L-201.*

```
L-201# sh bgp l2vpn evpn 0050.7966.6806
BGP routing table information for VRF default, address family L2VPN EVPN
Route Distinguisher: 192.168.15.101:32777
BGP routing table entry for [2]:[0]:[0]:[48]:[0050.7966.6806]:[0]:[0.0.0.0]/216,
version 968
Paths: (2 available, best #2)
Flags: (0x000202) (high32 00000000) on xmit-list, is not in l2rib/evpn, is not in HW
Multipath: eBGP

  Path type: internal, path is valid, not best reason: Router Id, no labeled nexthop
    AS-Path: 65001 65100 , path sourced external to AS
      192.168.30.101 (metric 161) from 192.168.15.22 (192.168.15.22)
        Origin IGP, MED not set, localpref 100, weight 0
        Received label 30010
        Extcommunity: RT:65200:30010 ENCAP:8

  Advertised path-id 1
  Path type: internal, path is valid, is best path, no labeled nexthop
            Imported to 1 destination(s)
            Imported paths list: default
    AS-Path: 65001 65100 , path sourced external to AS
```

```
     192.168.30.101 (metric 161) from 192.168.15.21 (192.168.15.21)
       Origin IGP, MED not set, localpref 100, weight 0
       Received label 30010
       Extcommunity: RT:65200:30010 ENCAP:8

   Path-id 1 not advertised to any peer
 BGP routing table entry for [2]:[0]:[0]:[48]:[0050.7966.6806]:[32]:[172.16.10.10]/272,
 version 644
 Paths: (2 available, best #2)
 Flags: (0x000202) (high32 00000000) on xmit-list, is not in l2rib/evpn, is not in HW
 Multipath: eBGP

   Path type: internal, path is valid, not best reason: Router Id, no labeled nexthop
   AS-Path: 65001 65100 , path sourced external to AS
     192.168.30.101 (metric 161) from 192.168.15.22 (192.168.15.22)
       Origin IGP, MED not set, localpref 100, weight 0
       Received label 30010 30077
       Extcommunity: RT:65200:30010 RT:65200:30077 ENCAP:8 Router MAC:5000.0001.0007

   Advertised path-id 1
   Path type: internal, path is valid, is best path, no labeled nexthop
               Imported to 3 destination(s)
               Imported paths list: TENANT-1 default default
   AS-Path: 65001 65100 , path sourced external to AS
     192.168.30.101 (metric 161) from 192.168.15.21 (192.168.15.21)
       Origin IGP, MED not set, localpref 100, weight 0
       Received label 30010 30077
       Extcommunity: RT:65200:30010 RT:65200:30077 ENCAP:8 Router MAC:5000.0001.0007

   Path-id 1 not advertised to any peer

 Route Distinguisher: 192.168.15.201:32777     (L2VNI 30010)
 BGP routing table entry for [2]:[0]:[0]:[48]:[0050.7966.6806]:[0]:[0.0.0.0]/216,
 version 969
 Paths: (1 available, best #1)
 Flags: (0x000212) (high32 00000000) on xmit-list, is in l2rib/evpn, is not in HW
 Multipath: eBGP

   Advertised path-id 1
   Path type: internal, path is valid, is best path, no labeled nexthop, in rib
               Imported from
 192.168.15.101:32777:[2]:[0]:[0]:[48]:[0050.7966.6806]:[0]:[0.0.0.0]/216
   AS-Path: 65001 65100 , path sourced external to AS
     192.168.30.101 (metric 161) from 192.168.15.21 (192.168.15.21)
       Origin IGP, MED not set, localpref 100, weight 0
       Received label 30010
       Extcommunity: RT:65200:30010 ENCAP:8

   Path-id 1 not advertised to any peer
 BGP routing table entry for [2]:[0]:[0]:[48]:[0050.7966.6806]:[32]:[172.16.10.10]/272,
 version 640
 Paths: (1 available, best #1)
 Flags: (0x000212) (high32 00000000) on xmit-list, is in l2rib/evpn, is not in HW
 Multipath: eBGP

   Advertised path-id 1
   Path type: internal, path is valid, is best path, no labeled nexthop, in rib
               Imported from
 192.168.15.101:32777:[2]:[0]:[0]:[48]:[0050.7966.6806]:[32]:[172.16.10.10]/272
   AS-Path: 65001 65100 , path sourced external to AS
     192.168.30.101 (metric 161) from 192.168.15.21 (192.168.15.21)
```

```
      Origin IGP, MED not set, localpref 100, weight 0
      Received label 30010 30077
      Extcommunity: RT:65200:30010 RT:65200:30077 ENCAP:8 Router MAC:5000.0001.0007

  Path-id 1 not advertised to any peer

Route Distinguisher: 192.168.15.201:3    (L3VNI 30077)
BGP routing table entry for [2]:[0]:[0]:[48]:[0050.7966.6806]:[32]:[172.16.10.10]/272,
version 641
Paths: (1 available, best #1)
Flags: (0x000202) (high32 00000000) on xmit-list, is not in l2rib/evpn, is not in HW
Multipath: eBGP

  Advertised path-id 1
  Path type: internal, path is valid, is best path, no labeled nexthop
             Imported from
192.168.15.101:32777:[2]:[0]:[0]:[48]:[0050.7966.6806]:[32]:[172.16.10.10]/272
    AS-Path: 65001 65100 , path sourced external to AS
      192.168.30.101 (metric 161) from 192.168.15.21 (192.168.15.21)
        Origin IGP, MED not set, localpref 100, weight 0
        Received label 30010 30077
        Extcommunity: RT:65200:30010 RT:65200:30077 ENCAP:8 Router MAC:5000.0001.0007

  Path-id 1 not advertised to any peer
```

Example 6-27: *show bgp l2vpn evpn 0050.7966.6806 on L-201.*

```
L-201# sh l2route evpn mac evi 10

Flags -(Rmac):Router MAC (Stt):Static (L):Local (R):Remote (V):vPC link
(Dup):Duplicate (Spl):Split (Rcv):Recv (AD):Auto-Delete (D):Del Pending
(S):Stale (C):Clear, (Ps):Peer Sync (O):Re-Originated (Nho):NH-Override
(Pf):Permanently-Frozen, (Orp): Orphan

Topology    Mac Address    Prod    Flags         Seq No     Next-Hops
----------  -------------- ------  ------------  ---------  -------------------
10          0050.7966.6806 BGP     SplRcv        0          192.168.30.101
10          0050.7966.6807 BGP     SplRcv        0          192.168.30.102
10          0050.7966.680d Local   L,            0          Eth1/3
10          0050.7966.680e BGP     SplRcv        0          192.168.30.202
```

Example 6-28: *sh l2route evpn mac evi 10 on L-201.*

```
L-201# sh l2route evpn mac evi 10 detail

Flags -(Rmac):Router MAC (Stt):Static (L):Local (R):Remote (V):vPC link
(Dup):Duplicate (Spl):Split (Rcv):Recv (AD):Auto-Delete (D):Del Pending
(S):Stale (C):Clear, (Ps):Peer Sync (O):Re-Originated (Nho):NH-Override
(Pf):Permanently-Frozen, (Orp): Orphan

Topology    Mac Address    Prod    Flags         Seq No     Next-Hops
----------  -------------- ------  ------------  ---------  -------------------
10          0050.7966.6806 BGP     SplRcv        0          192.168.30.101
                   Route Resolution Type: Regular
                   Forwarding State: Resolved (PeerID: 2)
                   Sent To: L2FWDER
```

```
         Encap: 1

10       0050.7966.6807 BGP     SplRcv         0        192.168.30.102
         Route Resolution Type: Regular
         Forwarding State: Resolved (PeerID: 3)
         Sent To: L2FWDER
         Encap: 1

10       0050.7966.680d Local   L,             0        Eth1/3
         Route Resolution Type: Regular
         Forwarding State: Resolved
         Sent To: BGP

10       0050.7966.680e BGP     SplRcv         0        192.168.30.202
         Route Resolution Type: Regular
         Forwarding State: Resolved (PeerID: 1)
         Sent To: L2FWDER
         Encap: 1
```

Example 6-29: *sh l2route evpn mac evi 10 detail on L-201.*

```
L-201# sh sys int l2fwder mac
Legend:
        * - primary entry, G - Gateway MAC, (R) - Routed MAC, O - Overlay MAC
        age - seconds since last seen,+ - primary entry using vPC Peer-Link,
        (T) - True, (F) - False, C - ControlPlane MAC
    VLAN     MAC Address      Type       age     Secure NTFY Ports
---------+-----------------+----------+---------+------+----+------------------
*   10     0050.7966.680d   dynamic   00:00:01    F      F   Eth1/3
*   10     0050.7966.6806   static       -        F      F   nve-peer2 192.168.30.101
*   10     0050.7966.680e   static       -        F      F   nve-peer1 192.168.30.202
G   77     5000.000c.0007   static       -        F      F   sup-eth1(R)
*   10     0050.7966.6807   static       -        F      F   nve-peer3 192.168.30.102
G   10     5000.000c.0007   static       -        F      F   sup-eth1(R)
    1          1             -00:01:00:01:00:01            -           1
```

Example 6-30: *sh sys int l2fwder mac on L-201.*

```
L-201# sh nve peers
Interface Peer-IP                                 State LearnType Uptime    Router-Mac
--------- --------------------------------------- ----- --------- --------- ----------------
nve1      192.168.30.101                          Up    CP        01:25:58  5000.0001.0007
nve1      192.168.30.102                          Up    CP        01:28:01  5000.0002.0007
nve1      192.168.30.202                          Up    CP        03:24:36  5000.000b.0007
```

Example 6-30: *sh nve peers on L-201.*

```
L-201# sh nve peers detail
Details of nve Peers:
----------------------------------------
Peer-Ip: 192.168.30.101
    NVE Interface        : nve1
    Peer State           : Up
    Peer Uptime          : 01:26:01
    Router-Mac           : 5000.0001.0007
    Peer First VNI       : 30077
    Time since Create    : 01:26:01
    Configured VNIs      : 30010,30077
    Provision State      : peer-add-complete
```

```
      Learnt CP VNIs        : 30010,30077
      vni assignment mode  : SYMMETRIC
      Peer Location        : N/A
Peer-Ip: 192.168.30.102
      NVE Interface        : nve1
      Peer State           : Up
      Peer Uptime          : 01:28:04
      Router-Mac           : 5000.0002.0007
      Peer First VNI       : 30010
      Time since Create    : 01:28:04
      Configured VNIs      : 30010,30077
      Provision State      : peer-add-complete
      Learnt CP VNIs       : 30010,30077
      vni assignment mode  : SYMMETRIC
      Peer Location        : N/A
Peer-Ip: 192.168.30.202
      NVE Interface        : nve1
      Peer State           : Up
      Peer Uptime          : 03:24:39
      Router-Mac           : 5000.000b.0007
      Peer First VNI       : 30010
      Time since Create    : 03:24:39
      Configured VNIs      : 30010,30077
      Provision State      : peer-add-complete
      Learnt CP VNIs       : 30010,30077
      vni assignment mode  : SYMMETRIC
      Peer Location        : N/A
```

Example 6-31: *sh nve peers detail on L-201.*

Complexity Chart of Hybrid-ASN Design

In this design, the BGP design within Pod is the same as in the Single-AS model while Spine and Supre-Spine have eBGP peering.

Direct Underlay Peering – Loopback Overlay Peering

		L	S	SS
Infrastructure IP Addressing				
Native Support for Unnumbered IP	Yes			
Requires subnet per Inter-switch link	No			
Loopback Interface Count		3	2	2
Overlay BGP Adjacency				
Update Source Modification		No	N/Y	Yes
Increasing TTL (eBGP Multihop)		No	N/Y	Yes
Support Dynamic-AS in Spine Layer If used, two Dynamic-AS neighbor section due to different peering type iBGP/eBGP			Yes	
BGP Update Policy				
Retain Route-Targets (retain route-target all)		No	N/Y	Yes
Rewrite ASN Part of Route-Target (rewrite-evp-rt-asn)		No	Yes	Yes
Requires Unmodified N-H address config (for EVPN)		No	N/Y	Yes
Removing BGP Loop Prevention (allow-as in)		No	No	No
Removing BGP Loop Prevention (disable-peer-check)		No	No	No
Requires BGP RR-Cluster in Spine and SuperSpine layer		--	Yes	Yes
IPv4/EVPN NLRIs in the same BGP message		No	No	No
Other Considerations				
Possibility to restrict switch from the Overlay Network without disturbing Underlay Network	Yes			

Table 3-1: *Multi-ASN Model Complexity Chart.*

Chapter 7: Dual-AS Model with OSPF Underlay

Introduction

This chapter discusses of Dual-ASN model where leaf switches within Pod share the ASN and spine switches share their ASN. In our example leaf switches in Pod-1 have ASN 65101 and spine switches have ASN 65100. Leaf switches in Pod-2 have ASN 65201 and spine switches have ASN 65200. SuperSPine switches share the ASN 65001. OSPF is used in Underlay Network. Figure 7-1 illustrates the ASN scheme and BGP L2VPN EVPN requirements. Steps 1a and 1b are related to BGP Adjacency and the rest of the steps to BGP L2VPN EVPN Update messages: (1a) Peering - Update source modification, (1b) increasing TTL on TCP syn and ACK messages and in Update messages, (2) EVPN Route-Target retaining, (3a) Sending BGP L2VPN EVPN Updates without Next-Hop modification, (3b) Sending BGP Updates to eBGP peer with ASN in Path-List where receiver belongs to, (4) rewriting the ASN part on received BGP L2VPN EVPN Update.

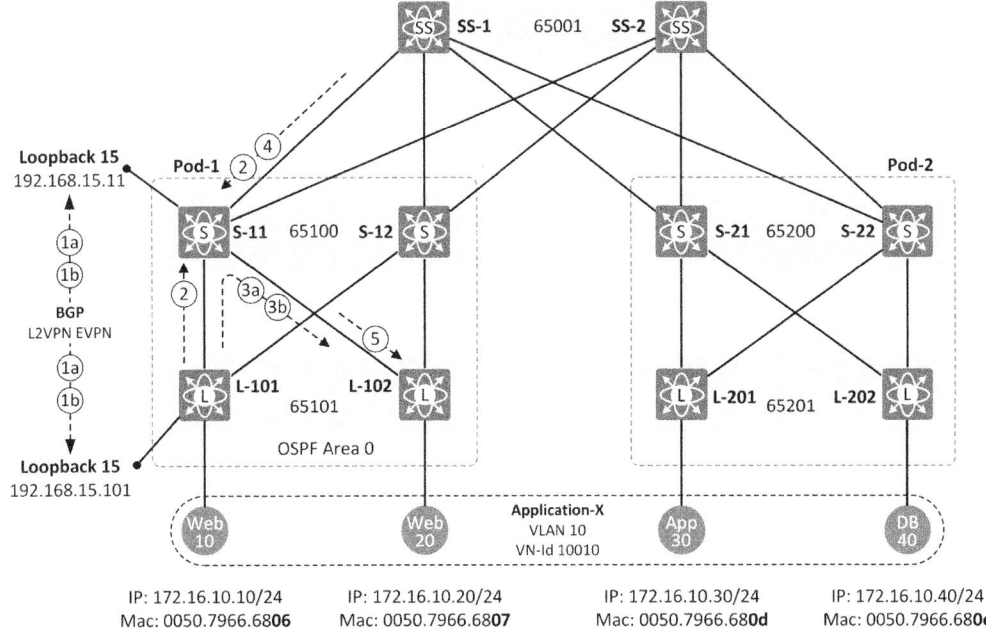

Figure 7-1: *Dual-ASN topology.*

Configuration

BGP Adjacency Policy

When eBGP peering is configured between Loopback Interfaces using the command *update-source loopback 15*, the TTL in TCP SYN and ACK packets are used in TCP Three-Way handshake has to be increased by 2 with the neighbor sub-command *ebgp-multihop 2*. These settings have to be implemented in all eBGP peers.

BGP Update Message Modification

When eBGP is used between BGP L2VPN EVPN peers, three settings have to be modified on Spine switches. *First*, due to lack of import policy, the sub-command *retain route-target all* under the global address l2vpn evpn section makes it possible to spines act as an eBGP route-reflector, meaning it can forward BGP Updates without importing routes from Adj-RIB-In to BGP Loc-RIB. *Second*, he ASN part in EVPN Route-Target has to be changed from received the peer ASN to own ASN with the command *rewrite-evpn-rt-asn*. This command is needed in every switch because the command is effective only when the ASN part in received BGP Update is the same as what is used for BGP peering with that particular BGP peer. *Third*, the Next-Hop path-attribute assigned by ingress VTEP (originating VTEP) into BGP L2VPN EVPN NLRI has to be preserved throughout the advertising process from Ingres VTEP to egress VTEP (remote-VTEP). This Next-Hop is used in the outer IP headers as the destination in Data-Plane when sending data. This requires route-map with *set ip next-hop unchanged* definition, which is then implemented per neighbor basis.

BGP Loop Prevention Adjustment

eBGP has two default loop-prevention mechanisms related to the Dual-AS model. Spine switches don't send BGP Updates to peer that are in the same AS than from where the original update was received. In our example, this means that none of the spine switches doesn't forward BGP Updates between leaf located within the same Pod. This behavior can be relaxed by using the neighbor specific address-family l2vpn evpn sub-command *disable-peer-as-check*. The second loop-prevention mechanism hits when the leaf receives the BGP Update originated by intra-Pod leaf switches because the path-list includes its own ASN. This is only related to leaf switches and can be relaxed by using the neighbor specific address-family l2vpn evpn sub-command *allow-as in*.

Example 7-1 shows the S-11 BGP configuration.

```
route-map RETAIN-NH permit 10
  set ip next-hop unchanged
!
router bgp 65100
  router-id 192.168.15.11
  address-family ipv4 unicast
    maximum-paths 8
  address-family l2vpn evpn
    maximum-paths 8
    retain route-target all
  neighbor 192.168.15.1
    remote-as 65001
    update-source loopback15
    ebgp-multihop 2
    address-family l2vpn evpn
      send-community
      send-community extended
      route-map RETAIN-NH out
      rewrite-evpn-rt-asn
  neighbor 192.168.15.2
    remote-as 65001
    update-source loopback15
    ebgp-multihop 2
    address-family l2vpn evpn
      send-community
      send-community extended
      route-map RETAIN-NH out
      rewrite-evpn-rt-asn
  neighbor 192.168.15.101
    remote-as 65101
    update-source loopback15
    ebgp-multihop 2
```

```
    address-family l2vpn evpn
      disable-peer-as-check
      send-community
      send-community extended
      route-map RETAIN-NH out
  neighbor 192.168.15.102
    remote-as 65101
    update-source loopback15
    ebgp-multihop 2
    address-family l2vpn evpn
      disable-peer-as-check
      send-community
      send-community extended
      route-map RETAIN-NH out
```

Example 7-1: *Spine Configuration.*

Example 7-2 shows the L-101 BGP configurations.

```
router bgp 65101
  router-id 192.168.15.101
  address-family ipv4 unicast
  address-family l2vpn evpn
    maximum-paths 8
    maximum-paths ibgp 8
  neighbor 192.168.15.11
    remote-as 65100
    update-source loopback15
    ebgp-multihop 2
    address-family l2vpn evpn
      allowas-in 3
      send-community
      send-community extended
  neighbor 192.168.15.12
    remote-as 65100
    update-source loopback15
    ebgp-multihop 2
    address-family l2vpn evpn
      allowas-in 3
      send-community
      send-community extended
```

Example 7-2: *Leaf Configuration.*

Verification

BGP peering

The example below shows that L-101 has established BGP peering with both S-11 and S-12 and it has received three EVPN NLRIs from both spines. The reason for the low received NLRI count is that in this chapter, only switches and hosts within Pod-1 are turned on.

```
L-101# sh bgp l2vpn evpn summary
BGP summary information for VRF default, address family L2VPN EVPN
BGP router identifier 192.168.15.101, local AS number 65101
BGP table version is 86, L2VPN EVPN config peers 2, capable peers 2
7 network entries and 10 paths using 1920 bytes of memory
BGP attribute entries [7/1148], BGP AS path entries [1/10]
BGP community entries [0/0], BGP clusterlist entries [0/0]

Neighbor        V    AS MsgRcvd MsgSent   TblVer  InQ OutQ Up/Down       State/PfxRcd
192.168.15.11   4 65100     111      99       86    0    0 01:15:13 3
192.168.15.12   4 65100     111     103       86    0    0 01:15:13 3
```
Example 7-3: *show bgp l2vpn evpn summary on L-101.*

Example 7-4 shows that L-101 has received BGP LVPN EVPN Updates about NLRI about Web20.

BGP table

Example 7-5 shows the BGP table of L-101. Note that NLRI about 172.16.10.20 connected to L-102, has the ASN 65101 in Path-List, which is the same ASN than where L-101 belongs to. The route is learned from external BGP peer and due to normal BGP loop-prevention mechanism this is not allowed but we are allowing own ASN with the command *allow-as* in i.e. we removed one of the loop prevention mechanism which makes this solution vulnerability to routing loops.

```
L-101# sh bgp l2vpn evpn
BGP routing table information for VRF default, address family L2VPN EVPN
BGP table version is 17, Local Router ID is 192.168.15.101
Status: s-suppressed, x-deleted, S-stale, d-dampened, h-history, *-valid, >-best
Path type:  i-internal,  e-external,  c-confed,  l-local,  a-aggregate,  r-redist,  I-injected
Origin codes: i - IGP, e - EGP, ? - incomplete, | - multipath, & - backup, 2 - best2

   Network          Next Hop            Metric     LocPrf     Weight Path
Route Distinguisher: 192.168.15.101:32777    (L2VNI 30010)
*>l[2]:[0]:[0]:[48]:[0050.7966.6806]:[0]:[0.0.0.0]/216
                    192.168.30.101                  100        32768 i
```

```
*>e[2]:[0]:[0]:[48]:[0050.7966.6807]:[0]:[0.0.0.0]/216
                      192.168.30.102                                0 65100 65101 i
*>l[2]:[0]:[0]:[48]:[0050.7966.6806]:[32]:[172.16.10.10]/272
                      192.168.30.101                100       32768 i
*>e[2]:[0]:[0]:[48]:[0050.7966.6807]:[32]:[172.16.10.20]/272
                      192.168.30.102                                0 65100 65101 i
*>l[3]:[0]:[32]:[192.168.30.101]/88
                      192.168.30.101                100       32768 i
*>e[3]:[0]:[32]:[192.168.30.102]/88
                      192.168.30.102                                0 65100 65101 i

Route Distinguisher: 192.168.15.102:32777
* e[2]:[0]:[0]:[48]:[0050.7966.6807]:[0]:[0.0.0.0]/216
                      192.168.30.102                                0 65100 65101 i
*>e                   192.168.30.102                                0 65100 65101 i
* e[2]:[0]:[0]:[48]:[0050.7966.6807]:[32]:[172.16.10.20]/272
                      192.168.30.102                                0 65100 65101 i
*>e                   192.168.30.102                                0 65100 65101 i
* e[3]:[0]:[32]:[192.168.30.102]/88
                      192.168.30.102                                0 65100 65101 i
*>e                   192.168.30.102                                0 65100 65101 i

Route Distinguisher: 192.168.15.101:3     (L3VNI 30077)
*>e[2]:[0]:[0]:[48]:[0050.7966.6807]:[32]:[172.16.10.20]/272
                      192.168.30.102                                0 65100 65101 i
```

Example 7-4: *show bgp l2vpn evpn on L-101.*

Example 7-5 shows detailed information about host Web20 (MAC: 0050.7966.6807 IP: 172.16.10.20).

```
L-101# sh bgp l2vpn evpn 0050.7966.6807
BGP routing table information for VRF default, address family L2VPN EVPN
Route Distinguisher: 192.168.15.101:32777    (L2VNI 30010)
BGP  routing  table  entry  for  [2]:[0]:[0]:[48]:[0050.7966.6807]:[0]:[0.0.0.0]/216,
version 12
Paths: (1 available, best #1)
Flags: (0x000212) (high32 00000000) on xmit-list, is in l2rib/evpn, is not in HW
Multipath: eBGP iBGP

  Advertised path-id 1
  Path type: external, path is valid, is best path, no labeled nexthop, in rib
       Imported                                                              from
192.168.15.102:32777:[2]:[0]:[0]:[48]:[0050.7966.6807]:[0]:[0.0.0.0]/216
    AS-Path: 65100 65101 , path sourced external to AS
      192.168.30.102 (metric 81) from 192.168.15.12 (192.168.15.12)
        Origin IGP, MED not set, localpref 100, weight 0
        Received label 30010
        Extcommunity: RT:65101:30010 ENCAP:8

  Path-id 1 not advertised to any peer
BGP routing table entry for [2]:[0]:[0]:[48]:[0050.7966.6807]:[32]:[172.16.10.20]/272,
version 11
Paths: (1 available, best #1)
Flags: (0x000212) (high32 00000000) on xmit-list, is in l2rib/evpn, is not in HW
Multipath: eBGP iBGP

  Advertised path-id 1
  Path type: external, path is valid, is best path, no labeled nexthop, in rib
```

```
                       Imported                                              from
192.168.15.102:32777:[2]:[0]:[0]:[48]:[0050.7966.6807]:[32]:[172.16.10.20]/272
  AS-Path: 65100 65101 , path sourced external to AS
    192.168.30.102 (metric 81) from 192.168.15.12 (192.168.15.12)
      Origin IGP, MED not set, localpref 100, weight 0
      Received label 30010 30077
      Extcommunity: RT:65101:30010 RT:65101:30077 ENCAP:8 Router MAC:5000.0002.0007

  Path-id 1 not advertised to any peer

Route Distinguisher: 192.168.15.102:32777
BGP routing table entry for  [2]:[0]:[0]:[48]:[0050.7966.6807]:[0]:[0.0.0.0]/216,
version 15
Paths: (2 available, best #2)
Flags: (0x000202) (high32 00000000) on xmit-list, is not in l2rib/evpn, is not in HW
Multipath: eBGP iBGP

  Path type: external, path is valid, not best reason: newer EBGP path, no labeled
nexthop
    AS-Path: 65100 65101 , path sourced external to AS
      192.168.30.102 (metric 81) from 192.168.15.11 (192.168.15.11)
        Origin IGP, MED not set, localpref 100, weight 0
        Received label 30010
        Extcommunity: RT:65101:30010 ENCAP:8

  Advertised path-id 1
  Path type: external, path is valid, is best path, no labeled nexthop
             Imported to 1 destination(s)
             Imported paths list: default
    AS-Path: 65100 65101 , path sourced external to AS
      192.168.30.102 (metric 81) from 192.168.15.12 (192.168.15.12)
        Origin IGP, MED not set, localpref 100, weight 0
        Received label 30010
        Extcommunity: RT:65101:30010 ENCAP:8

  Path-id 1 not advertised to any peer
BGP routing table entry for [2]:[0]:[0]:[48]:[0050.7966.6807]:[32]:[172.16.10.20]/272,
version 14
Paths: (2 available, best #2)
Flags: (0x000202) (high32 00000000) on xmit-list, is not in l2rib/evpn, is not in HW
Multipath: eBGP iBGP

  Path type: external, path is valid, not best reason: newer EBGP path, no labeled
nexthop
    AS-Path: 65100 65101 , path sourced external to AS
      192.168.30.102 (metric 81) from 192.168.15.11 (192.168.15.11)
        Origin IGP, MED not set, localpref 100, weight 0
        Received label 30010 30077
        Extcommunity: RT:65101:30010 RT:65101:30077 ENCAP:8 Router MAC:5000.0002.0007

  Advertised path-id 1
  Path type: external, path is valid, is best path, no labeled nexthop
             Imported to 3 destination(s)
             Imported paths list: default default TENANT-1
    AS-Path: 65100 65101 , path sourced external to AS
      192.168.30.102 (metric 81) from 192.168.15.12 (192.168.15.12)
        Origin IGP, MED not set, localpref 100, weight 0
        Received label 30010 30077
        Extcommunity: RT:65101:30010 RT:65101:30077 ENCAP:8 Router MAC:5000.0002.0007

  Path-id 1 not advertised to any peer
```

```
Route Distinguisher: 192.168.15.101:3    (L3VNI 30077)
BGP routing table entry for [2]:[0]:[0]:[48]:[0050.7966.6807]:[32]:[172.16.10.20]/272,
version 17
Paths: (1 available, best #1)
Flags: (0x000202) (high32 00000000) on xmit-list, is not in l2rib/evpn, is not in HW
Multipath: eBGP iBGP

  Advertised path-id 1
  Path type: external, path is valid, is best path, no labeled nexthop
              Imported                                                                    from
192.168.15.102:32777:[2]:[0]:[0]:[48]:[0050.7966.6807]:[32]:[172.16.10.20]/272
    AS-Path: 65100 65101 , path sourced external to AS
      192.168.30.102 (metric 81) from 192.168.15.12 (192.168.15.12)
        Origin IGP, MED not set, localpref 100, weight 0
        Received label 30010 30077
        Extcommunity: RT:65101:30010 RT:65101:30077 ENCAP:8 Router MAC:5000.0002.0007

  Path-id 1 not advertised to any peer
```
Example 7-5: *show bgp l2vpn evpn 0050.7966.6807 on L-101.*

L2RIB

The example below shows that the MAC address is installed into L2RIB of topology 10 (VNI 30010).

```
L-101# sh l2route evpn mac evi 10
<snipped>
Topology    Mac Address     Prod    Flags            Seq No     Next-Hops
----------- --------------- ------- ---------------- ---------- ----------------------------
10          0050.7966.6806  Local   L,               0          Eth1/3
10          0050.7966.6807  BGP     SplRcv           0          192.168.30.102
```
Example 7-6: *show l2route evpn mac evi 10 on L-101.*

Example 7-7 shows the same information with greater detail.

```
L-101# sh l2route evpn mac evi 10 detail
<snipped>
Topology    Mac Address     Prod    Flags            Seq No     Next-Hops
----------- --------------- ------- ---------------- ---------- ----------------------------
10          0050.7966.6806  Local   L,               0          Eth1/3
            Route Resolution Type: Regular
            Forwarding State: Resolved
            Sent To: BGP

10          0050.7966.6807  BGP     SplRcv           0          192.168.30.102
            Route Resolution Type: Regular
            Forwarding State: Resolved (PeerID: 1)
            Sent To: L2FWDER
         Encap: 1
```
Example 7-7: *show l2route evpn mac evi 10 detail on L-101.*

MAC Address Table

The last example shows that the MAC address is also installed in the VLAN 10 MAC address table.

```
L-101# sh sys int l2fwder mac
<snipped>
     VLAN    MAC Address        Type       age       Secure NTFY Ports
---------+-----------------+---------+----------+------+----+------------------
G    10     5000.0001.0007    static      -          F     F    sup-eth1(R)
*    10     0050.7966.6806    dynamic    0.992774    F     F    Eth1/3
*    10     0050.7966.6807    static      -          F     F    nve-peer1 192.168.30.102
     1         1              -00:01:00:01:00:01     -          1
```

Example 7-8: *show system internal l2fwder mac on L-101.*

Complexity Chart of Hybrid-ASN Design with OSPF Underlay

This model requires disabling two BGP native loop prevention mechanism because leaf switches with Pod belong to the same AS while they have eBGP peering with Spine switches. Besides, rewriting the ASN part on RT is required also in the Leaf layer because Pods are using different ASN.

	L	S	SS
Infrastructure IP Addressing			
Native Support for Unnumbered IP	Yes		
Requires subnet per Inter-switch link	No		
Loopback Interface Count	3	2	2
Overlay BGP Adjacency			
Update Source Modification	Yes	Yes	Yes
Increasing TTL (eBGP Multihop)	Yes	Yes	Yes
Support Dynamic-AS in Spine Layer	Yes	Yes	Yes
BGP Update Policy			
Retain Route-Targets (retain route-target all)	No	Yes	Yes
Rewrite ASN Part of Route-Target (rewrite-evp-rt-asn)	Yes	Yes	Yes
Requires Unmodified N-H address config (for EVPN)	No	Yes	Yes
Removing BGP Loop Prevention (allow-as in)	Yes	Yes	Yes
Removing BGP Loop Prevention (disable-peer-check)	Yes	Yes	Yes
Requires BGP RR-Cluster in Spine and SuperSpine layer	--	Yes	Yes
IPv4/EVPN NLRIs in the same BGP message	No	No	No
Other Considerations			
Possibility to restrict switch from the Overlay Network without disturbing Underlay Network	Yes		

Table 3-1: *Multi-ASN Model Complexity Chart.*

Chapter 8: ESI Multi-Homing

Introduction

This chapter shortly discusses ESI Multi-Homing. The reason why this chapter is included in the book is that the next chapter, chapter 9 discusses Equal Cost Multi-Pathing where BGP L2VPN EVPN ECMP in Overlay Network is related to host Multi-Homing. Figure 8-1 shows the example topology with ESI Multihoming information. There are two hosts connected to Pod-2. Server DB40 (MAC: 0050.7966.680e, IP: 172 16.10.40) is reachable via L-202 only while Server SRV50 (MAC: 0050.7966.6810, IP: 172 16.10.50) is reachable via both L-201 and L-202. The host multihoming solution used in this chapter is based on standard ESI Multi-Homing defined in RFC 7432.

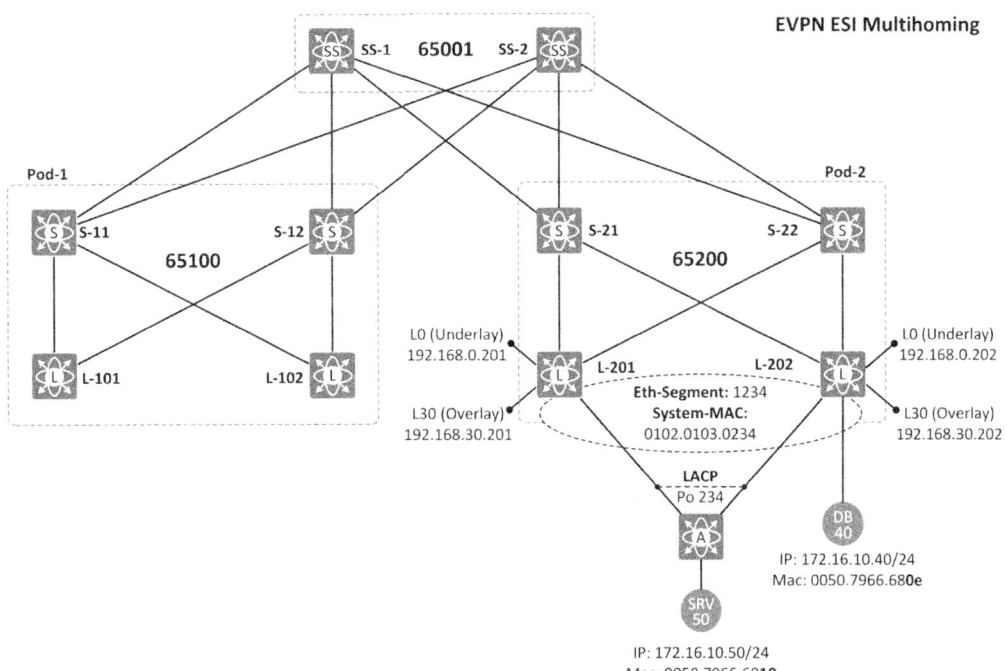

Figure 8-1: *The ESI Multihoming Topology.*

ESI Multihoming Configuration

Example 8-1 shows the configuration related to ESI Multihoming on Pod-2 2 leaf switches L-201 and L-202. The global command *evpn esi multihoming* enables the ESI Multihoming. The command *ethernet-segment 1234* under the Port-Channel configuration defines the Ethernet Segment Local Discriminator (ES LD) and its sub-command *system-mac 0102.0103.0234* defines the system-mac that is used in as an Actor System MAC in LACP messages as well as as a Route-Target value in EVPN Ethernet Segment Route (Route-Type 4) used for per VLAN L2BUM Designator Forwarder (DF) election process. The Ethernet Segment Identifier (ES-Id) is the combination of ES LD and System-MAC with the prefix that defines the segment type, NX-OS uses MAC-based ESI (0x03). In our example, the ESI will be 03.0102.0103.0104.04d2 (HEX 4d2 = BIN 1234). In addition, the command *evpn multihoming core-tracking* is needed in Spine facing interfaces in leaf switches. If the leaf switch loses all of its core connections, it restricts itself from all ethernet segment by shutting down all interfaces attached to Ethernet Segments. This way also multi-homed hosts/switches notice the failure and can remove the restricted leaf switch from the Port-Channel bundle.

Note! The orphan hosts connected to leaf switch that uses ESI Multihoming, are restricted from the network when the leaf switch restricts itself from all Ethernet Segments, even though the ports connected to orphan hosts stay up.

```
evpn esi multihoming
!
spanning-tree domain 1
spanning-tree vlan 1,10,77 priority 4096
!
interface port-channel234
  switchport mode trunk
  switchport trunk allowed vlan 1,10
  ethernet-segment 1234
    system-mac 0102.0103.0234
!
interface Ethernet1/1
  evpn multihoming core-tracking
  medium p2p
  ip unnumbered loopback0
  ip ospf network point-to-point
  no ip ospf passive-interface
  ip router ospf UNDERLAY-NET area 0.0.0.0
```

```
  no shutdown

interface Ethernet1/2
  no switchport
  evpn multihoming core-tracking
  medium p2p
  ip unnumbered loopback0
  ip ospf network point-to-point
  no ip ospf passive-interface
  ip router ospf UNDERLAY-NET area 0.0.0.0
  no shutdown
!
interface Ethernet1/4
  switchport mode trunk
  switchport trunk allowed vlan 1,10
  channel-group 234 mode active
```

Example 8-1: *ESI Multihoming and LACP Configuration on L-201 and L-202.*

Access-Switches are ignorant to Multi-Chassis Port-Channel and the regular Port-Channel configurations are implemented in them.

```
interface port-channel234
  switchport mode trunk
  switchport trunk allowed vlan 10
!
interface Ethernet1/1
  switchport mode trunk
  switchport trunk allowed vlan 10
  channel-group 234 mode active

interface Ethernet1/2
  switchport mode trunk
  switchport trunk allowed vlan 10
  channel-group 234 mode active
!
interface Ethernet1/3
  switchport access vlan 10
```

Example 8-2: *LACP Configuration on Access-SW.*

Designated Forwarder fo L2BUM

Figure 8-2 illustrates the Ethernet Segment Route (Route-Type 4) information originated by L-201 and L-202. The only difference in the address field is the VTEP IP address. The Route-Target Extended Community is the System-MAC address attached to the Ethernet Segment. This value is the same in both switches, so they will import the received NLRI into the BGP table. Switches that don't participate in the ES ignores the NLRI.

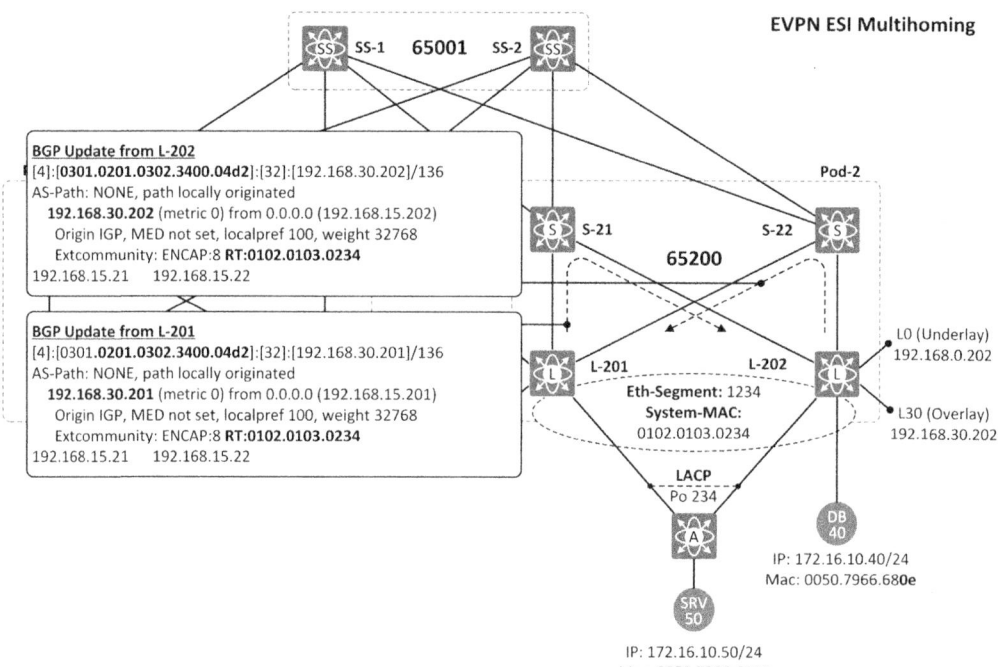

Figure 8-2: *The ESI Multihoming Topology.*

Examples 8-3 and 8-4 illustrates the detailed information about EVPN Route-Type 4. The second high-lighted routing entry describes the NLRIs originated by L-202 and received from both S-21 and S-22 in the Adj-RIB-In table. The best one (from S-21) is imported into Loc-RIB shown under the first high-lighted routing entry. The first one also describes the local NLRI on L-201. Example 8-4 shows the same information from the L-202 perspective.

```
L-201# sh bgp l2vpn evpn route-type 4
BGP routing table information for VRF default, address family L2VPN EVPN
Route Distinguisher: 192.168.15.201:27233     (ES [0301.0201.0302.3400.04d2 0])
BGP routing table entry for [4]:[0301.0201.0302.3400.04d2]:[32]:[192.168.30.201]/136,
<snipped>
Multipath: eBGP

  Advertised path-id 1
  Path type: local, path is valid, is best path, no labeled nexthop
  AS-Path: NONE, path locally originated
     192.168.30.201 (metric 0) from 0.0.0.0 (192.168.15.201)
        Origin IGP, MED not set, localpref 100, weight 32768
        Extcommunity: ENCAP:8 RT:0102.0103.0234

  Path-id 1 advertised to peers:
    192.168.15.21      192.168.15.22
BGP routing table entry for [4]:[0301.0201.0302.3400.04d2]:[32]:[192.168.30.202]/136,
<snipped>
Multipath: eBGP

  Advertised path-id 1
  Path type: internal, path is valid, is best path, no labeled nexthop
            Imported from
192.168.15.202:27233:[4]:[0301.0201.0302.3400.04d2]:[32]:[192.168.30.202]/136
  AS-Path: NONE, path sourced internal to AS
     192.168.30.202 (metric 81) from 192.168.15.21 (192.168.15.21)
        Origin IGP, MED not set, localpref 100, weight 0
        Extcommunity: ENCAP:8 RT:0102.0103.0234
        Originator: 192.168.15.202 Cluster list: 192.168.2.2

  Path-id 1 not advertised to any peer

Route Distinguisher: 192.168.15.202:27233
BGP routing table entry for [4]:[0301.0201.0302.3400.04d2]:[32]:[192.168.30.202]/136,
version 12
Paths: (2 available, best #1)
Flags: (0x000002) (high32 00000000) on xmit-list, is not in l2rib/evpn, is not in HW
Multipath: eBGP

  Advertised path-id 1
  Path type: internal, path is valid, is best path, no labeled nexthop
            Imported to 1 destination(s)
            Imported paths list: default
  AS-Path: NONE, path sourced internal to AS
     192.168.30.202 (metric 81) from 192.168.15.21 (192.168.15.21)
        Origin IGP, MED not set, localpref 100, weight 0
        Extcommunity: ENCAP:8 RT:0102.0103.0234
        Originator: 192.168.15.202 Cluster list: 192.168.2.2

  Path type: internal, path is valid, not best reason: Neighbor Address, no labeled
nexthop
  AS-Path: NONE, path sourced internal to AS
     192.168.30.202 (metric 81) from 192.168.15.22 (192.168.15.22)
        Origin IGP, MED not set, localpref 100, weight 0
        Extcommunity: ENCAP:8 RT:0102.0103.0234
        Originator: 192.168.15.202 Cluster list: 192.168.2.2

  Path-id 1 not advertised to any peer
```

Example 8-3: *EVPN Route-Type 4 on L201.*

```
L-202# sh bgp l2vpn evpn route-type 4
BGP routing table information for VRF default, address family L2VPN EVPN
Route Distinguisher: 192.168.15.201:27233
BGP routing table entry for [4]:[0301.0201.0302.3400.04d2]:[32]:[192.168.30.201]/136,
<snipped>
Multipath: eBGP

  Advertised path-id 1
  Path type: internal, path is valid, is best path, no labeled nexthop
            Imported to 1 destination(s)
            Imported paths list: default
  AS-Path: NONE, path sourced internal to AS
     192.168.30.201 (metric 81) from 192.168.15.21 (192.168.15.21)
        Origin IGP, MED not set, localpref 100, weight 0
        Extcommunity: ENCAP:8 RT:0102.0103.0234
        Originator: 192.168.15.201 Cluster list: 192.168.2.2

  Path type: internal, path is valid, not best reason: Neighbor Address, no labeled
nexthop
  AS-Path: NONE, path sourced internal to AS
     192.168.30.201 (metric 81) from 192.168.15.22 (192.168.15.22)
        Origin IGP, MED not set, localpref 100, weight 0
        Extcommunity: ENCAP:8 RT:0102.0103.0234
        Originator: 192.168.15.201 Cluster list: 192.168.2.2

  Path-id 1 not advertised to any peer

Route Distinguisher: 192.168.15.202:27233    (ES [0301.0201.0302.3400.04d2 0])
BGP routing table entry for [4]:[0301.0201.0302.3400.04d2]:[32]:[192.168.30.201]/136,
<snipped>
Multipath: eBGP

  Advertised path-id 1
  Path type: internal, path is valid, is best path, no labeled nexthop
            Imported from
192.168.15.201:27233:[4]:[0301.0201.0302.3400.04d2]:[32]:[192.168.30.201]/136
  AS-Path: NONE, path sourced internal to AS
     192.168.30.201 (metric 81) from 192.168.15.21 (192.168.15.21)
        Origin IGP, MED not set, localpref 100, weight 0
        Extcommunity: ENCAP:8 RT:0102.0103.0234
        Originator: 192.168.15.201 Cluster list: 192.168.2.2

  Path-id 1 not advertised to any peer
BGP routing table entry for [4]:[0301.0201.0302.3400.04d2]:[32]:[192.168.30.202]/136,
version 9
Paths: (1 available, best #1)
Flags: (0x000002) (high32 00000000) on xmit-list, is not in l2rib/evpn
Multipath: eBGP

  Advertised path-id 1
  Path type: local, path is valid, is best path, no labeled nexthop
  AS-Path: NONE, path locally originated
     192.168.30.202 (metric 0) from 0.0.0.0 (192.168.15.202)
        Origin IGP, MED not set, localpref 100, weight 32768
        Extcommunity: ENCAP:8 RT:0102.0103.0234

  Path-id 1 advertised to peers:
     192.168.15.21        192.168.15.22
```

Example 8-4: *EVPN Route-Type 4 on L202.*

Example 8-5 shows that L-201 is elected as a DF for VLAN 10 and the example 7-6 that L-202 is elected as a DF for VLAN 1. The DF calculation is based on the formula *(VLAN-Id) mod (switch in redundancy group) = DF (switches pointer)*. The ordinal of the switch is set based on their VTEP IP address, the switch with the smallest address gets ordinal zero and the second one gets the ordinal one, and so on. This means that DF for VLAN 10 is calculated: 10 mod 2 = 0, (10 divided by two is five and there is no reminder) > 0 is the ordinal of L-201 (192.168.30.201). DF for VLAN 1 is calculated: 1 mod 2 = 1 (1 divided by 2 is 0 and the remainder is 1).

```
L-201# sh nve ethernet-segment

ESI: 0301.0201.0302.3400.04d2
  Parent interface: port-channel234
  ES State: Up
  Port-channel state: Up
  NVE Interface: nve1
  NVE State: Up
  Host Learning Mode: control-plane
  Active Vlans: 1,10
  DF Vlans: 10
  Active VNIs: 30010
  CC failed for VLANs:
  VLAN CC timer: 0
  Number of ES members: 2
  My ordinal: 0
  DF timer start time: 00:00:00
  Config State: config-applied
  DF List: 192.168.30.201 192.168.30.202
  ES route added to L2RIB: True
  EAD/ES routes added to L2RIB: True
  EAD/EVI route timer age: not running
-----------------------------------------
```
Example 8-5: *Show nve ethernet-segment L-201.*

```
L-202# sh nve ethernet-segment

ESI: 0301.0201.0302.3400.04d2
  Parent interface: port-channel234
  ES State: Up
  Port-channel state: Up
  NVE Interface: nve1
  NVE State: Up
  Host Learning Mode: control-plane
  Active Vlans: 1,10
  DF Vlans: 1
  Active VNIs: 30010
  CC failed for VLANs:
  VLAN CC timer: 0
  Number of ES members: 2
  My ordinal: 1
```

```
DF timer start time: 00:00:00
Config State: config-applied
DF List: 192.168.30.201 192.168.30.202
ES route added to L2RIB: True
EAD/ES routes added to L2RIB: True
EAD/EVI route timer age: not running
----------------------------------------
```

Example 8-6: *Show nve ethernet-segment on L202.*

Mass-Withdraw

The ESI Multi-Homing supports the Mass-Withdrawn process of MAC Advertisement routes. Hosts NLRIs connected to Ethernet Segment are advertised with ESI value. Figure 8-3 shows the BGP Update about NLRI of SRV50 and ESI value used with it. L-201 has sent EVPN Ethernet Auto-Discovery Route (Route-Type 1), where it describes Ethernet segments where it is attached to. The same information is sent also by all other redundancy group switches. Based on Ethernet A-D Route L-101 knows that both L-201 and L-202 share the same ES 0201.0201.0302.3400.04d2. However, these updates are not included in the VLAN Id information (MPLS label set to 0), which is described in Ethernet A-D ES/EVI NLRIs (non-highlighted part in the example 8-7, explained in Load-Balancing section).

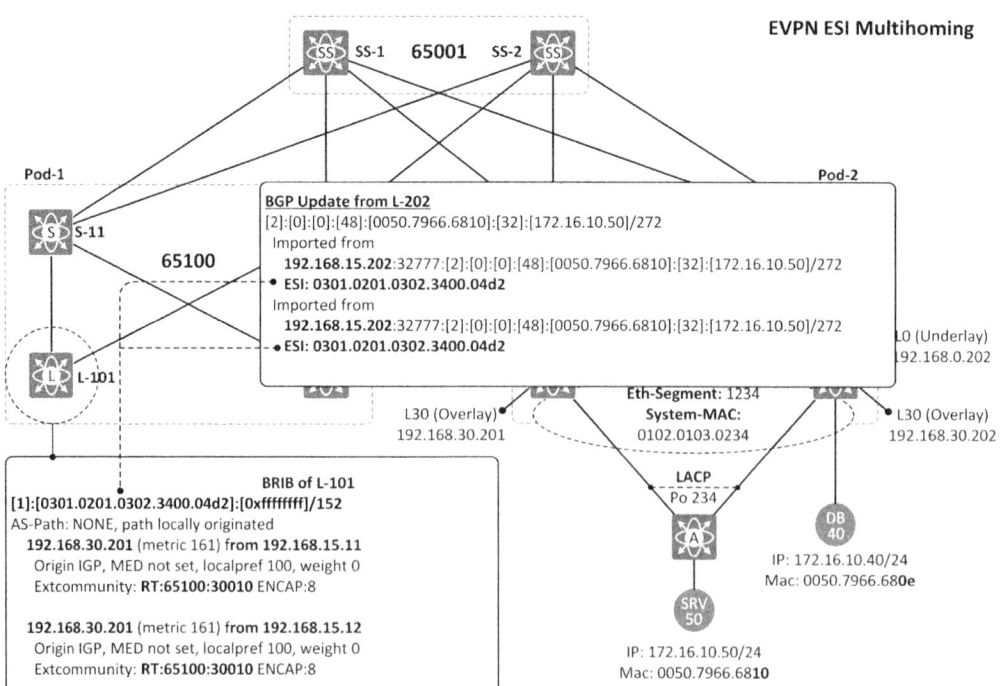

Figure 8-3: *ESI value in EVPN Route-Type 2 and 1.*

When L-201 loses its connection to ES 0201.0201.0302.3400.04d2, it withdraws the ES 0201.0201.0302.3400.04d2 instead of withdrawing each host NLRIs connected to ES. As a reaction, remote leaf L-101 removes all EVPN MAC Advertisement Routes with ES information carried with Withdraw message from its BRIB.

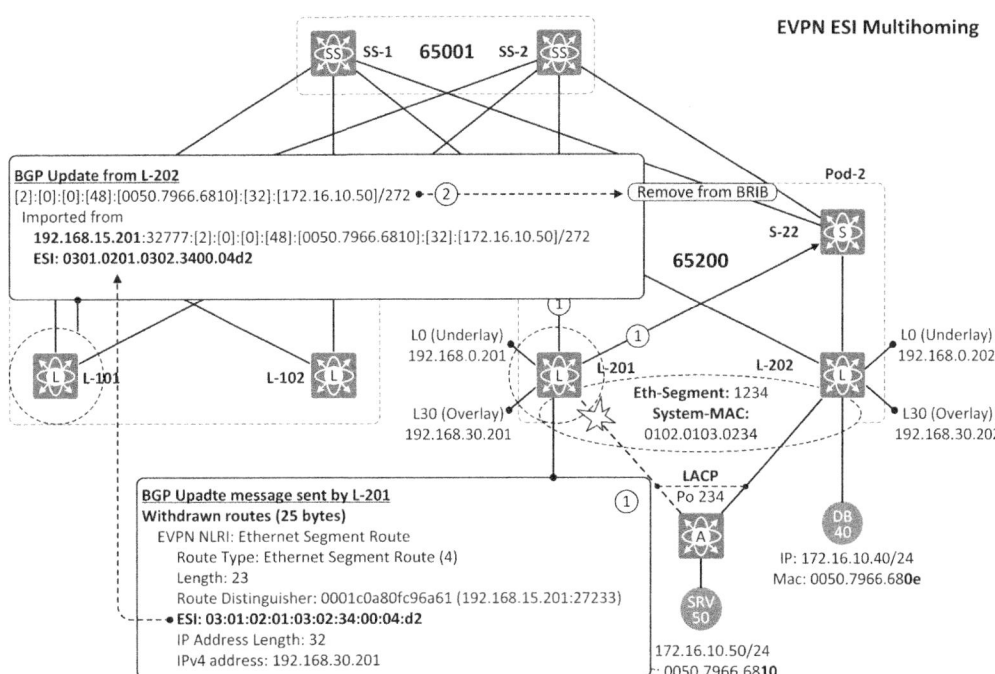

Figure 8-4: *Mass Withdrawn.*

The high-lighted part of the example 8-7 describes the Ethernet A-D ES Routes that are used for enabling the Mass-Withdraw process. Both L-201 and L-202 have advertised the same ES information (last two highlighted parts) and they are both imported into BRIB Under L2VNI 0. So this information is not imported into any particular L2VN.

```
L-101# sh bgp l2vpn evpn route-type 1
BGP routing table information for VRF default, address family L2VPN EVPN
Route Distinguisher: 192.168.15.101:32777    (L2VNI 30010)
BGP routing table entry for [1]:[0301.0201.0302.3400.04d2]:[0x0]/152, version 26
Paths: (2 available, best #1)
Flags: (0x000012) (high32 00000000) on xmit-list, is in l2rib/evpn, is not in HW
Multipath: eBGP iBGP

  Advertised path-id 1
  Path type: internal, path is valid, is best path, no labeled nexthop, in rib
            Imported from
192.168.15.202:32777:[1]:[0301.0201.0302.3400.04d2]:[0x0]/152
```

```
    AS-Path: 65001 65200 , path sourced external to AS
      192.168.30.202 (metric 161) from 192.168.15.11 (192.168.15.11)
        Origin IGP, MED not set, localpref 100, weight 0
        Received label 30010
        Extcommunity: RT:65100:30010 ENCAP:8

  Path type: internal, path is valid, not best reason: Neighbor Address, multipath, no
labeled nexthop, in rib
              Imported from
192.168.15.201:32777:[1]:[0301.0201.0302.3400.04d2]:[0x0]/152
    AS-Path: 65001 65200 , path sourced external to AS
      192.168.30.201 (metric 161) from 192.168.15.11 (192.168.15.11)
        Origin IGP, MED not set, localpref 100, weight 0
        Received label 30010
        Extcommunity: RT:65100:30010 ENCAP:8

  Path-id 1 not advertised to any peer

Route Distinguisher: 192.168.15.101:65534     (L2VNI 0)
BGP routing table entry for [1]:[0301.0201.0302.3400.04d2]:[0xffffffff]/152, version
21
Paths: (2 available, best #1)
Flags: (0x000012) (high32 00000000) on xmit-list, is in l2rib/evpn, is not in HW
Multipath: eBGP iBGP

  Advertised path-id 1
  Path type: internal, path is valid, is best path, no labeled nexthop, in rib
              Imported from
192.168.15.202:118:[1]:[0301.0201.0302.3400.04d2]:[0xffffffff]/152
    AS-Path: 65001 65200 , path sourced external to AS
      192.168.30.202 (metric 161) from 192.168.15.11 (192.168.15.11)
        Origin IGP, MED not set, localpref 100, weight 0
        Received label 0
        Extcommunity: RT:65100:30010 ENCAP:8

  Path type: internal, path is valid, not best reason: Neighbor Address, multipath, no
labeled nexthop, in rib
              Imported from
192.168.15.201:118:[1]:[0301.0201.0302.3400.04d2]:[0xffffffff]/152
    AS-Path: 65001 65200 , path sourced external to AS
      192.168.30.201 (metric 161) from 192.168.15.11 (192.168.15.11)
        Origin IGP, MED not set, localpref 100, weight 0
        Received label 0
        Extcommunity: RT:65100:30010 ENCAP:8

  Path-id 1 not advertised to any peer

Route Distinguisher: 192.168.15.201:118
BGP routing table entry for [1]:[0301.0201.0302.3400.04d2]:[0xffffffff]/152, version
30
Paths: (2 available, best #2)
Flags: (0x000002) (high32 00000000) on xmit-list, is not in l2rib/evpn, is not in HW
Multipath: eBGP iBGP

  Path type: internal, path is valid, not best reason: Router Id, no labeled nexthop
    AS-Path: 65001 65200 , path sourced external to AS
      192.168.30.201 (metric 161) from 192.168.15.12 (192.168.15.12)
        Origin IGP, MED not set, localpref 100, weight 0
        Received label 0
        Extcommunity: RT:65100:30010 ENCAP:8
```

```
    Advertised path-id 1
    Path type: internal, path is valid, is best path, no labeled nexthop
            Imported to 1 destination(s)
            Imported paths list: default
    AS-Path: 65001 65200 , path sourced external to AS
      192.168.30.201 (metric 161) from 192.168.15.11 (192.168.15.11)
        Origin IGP, MED not set, localpref 100, weight 0
        Received label 0
        Extcommunity: RT:65100:30010 ENCAP:8

    Path-id 1 not advertised to any peer

Route Distinguisher: 192.168.15.201:32777
BGP routing table entry for [1]:[0301.0201.0302.3400.04d2]:[0x0]/152, version 32
Paths: (2 available, best #2)
Flags: (0x000002) (high32 00000000) on xmit-list, is not in l2rib/evpn, is not in HW
Multipath: eBGP iBGP

    Path type: internal, path is valid, not best reason: Router Id, no labeled nexthop
    AS-Path: 65001 65200 , path sourced external to AS
      192.168.30.201 (metric 161) from 192.168.15.12 (192.168.15.12)
        Origin IGP, MED not set, localpref 100, weight 0
        Received label 30010
        Extcommunity: RT:65100:30010 ENCAP:8

    Advertised path-id 1
    Path type: internal, path is valid, is best path, no labeled nexthop
            Imported to 1 destination(s)
            Imported paths list: default
    AS-Path: 65001 65200 , path sourced external to AS
      192.168.30.201 (metric 161) from 192.168.15.11 (192.168.15.11)
        Origin IGP, MED not set, localpref 100, weight 0
        Received label 30010
        Extcommunity: RT:65100:30010 ENCAP:8

    Path-id 1 not advertised to any peer

Route Distinguisher: 192.168.15.202:118
BGP routing table entry for [1]:[0301.0201.0302.3400.04d2]:[0xffffffff]/152,version 31
Paths: (2 available, best #2)
Flags: (0x000002) (high32 00000000) on xmit list, is not in l2rib/evpn, is not in HW
Multipath: eBGP iBGP

    Path type: internal, path is valid, not best reason: Router Id, no labeled nexthop
    AS-Path: 65001 65200 , path sourced external to AS
      192.168.30.202 (metric 161) from 192.168.15.12 (192.168.15.12)
        Origin IGP, MED not set, localpref 100, weight 0
        Received label 0
        Extcommunity: RT:65100:30010 ENCAP:8

    Advertised path-id 1
    Path type: internal, path is valid, is best path, no labeled nexthop
            Imported to 1 destination(s)
            Imported paths list: default
    AS-Path: 65001 65200 , path sourced external to AS
      192.168.30.202 (metric 161) from 192.168.15.11 (192.168.15.11)
        Origin IGP, MED not set, localpref 100, weight 0
        Received label 0
        Extcommunity: RT:65100:30010 ENCAP:8

    Path-id 1 not advertised to any peer
```

```
Route Distinguisher: 192.168.15.202:32777
BGP routing table entry for [1]:[0301.0201.0302.3400.04d2]:[0x0]/152, version 33
Paths: (2 available, best #2)
Flags: (0x000002) (high32 00000000) on xmit-list, is not in l2rib/evpn, is not in HW
Multipath: eBGP iBGP

  Path type: internal, path is valid, not best reason: Router Id, no labeled nexthop
  AS-Path: 65001 65200 , path sourced external to AS
    192.168.30.202 (metric 161) from 192.168.15.12 (192.168.15.12)
      Origin IGP, MED not set, localpref 100, weight 0
      Received label 30010
      Extcommunity: RT:65100:30010 ENCAP:8

  Advertised path-id 1
  Path type: internal, path is valid, is best path, no labeled nexthop
          Imported to 1 destination(s)
          Imported paths list: default
  AS-Path: 65001 65200 , path sourced external to AS
    192.168.30.202 (metric 161) from 192.168.15.11 (192.168.15.11)
      Origin IGP, MED not set, localpref 100, weight 0
      Received label 30010
      Extcommunity: RT:65100:30010 ENCAP:8

  Path-id 1 not advertised to any peer
```
Example 8-7: *Show l2vpn evpn route-type12 on L-101.*

Example 8-8 shows the NLRI about SRV50 installed into BRIB of L-101. As can be seen, there is also ES information included in.

```
L-101# sh bgp l2vpn evpn route-type 2
BGP routing table information for VRF default, address family L2VPN EVPN
Route Distinguisher: 192.168.15.101:32777    (L2VNI 30010)
BGP routing table entry for [2]:[0]:[0]:[48]:[0050.7966.6810]:[0]:[0.0.0.0]/216,
version 42
Paths: (1 available, best #1)
Flags: (0x000212) (high32 00000000) on xmit-list, is in l2rib/evpn, is not in HW
Multipath: eBGP iBGP

  Advertised path-id 1
  Path type: internal, path is valid, is best path, no labeled nexthop, in rib
          Imported from
192.168.15.202:32777:[2]:[0]:[0]:[48]:[0050.7966.6810]:[0]:[0.0.0.0]/216
  AS-Path: 65001 65200 , path sourced external to AS
    192.168.30.202 (metric 161) from 192.168.15.11 (192.168.15.11)
      Origin IGP, MED not set, localpref 100, weight 0
      Received label 30010
      Extcommunity: RT:65100:30010 ENCAP:8 MAC Mobility Sequence:00:1

  Path-id 1 not advertised to any peer
BGP routing table entry for [2]:[0]:[0]:[48]:[0050.7966.6810]:[32]:[172.16.10.50]/272,
version 45
Paths: (2 available, best #1)
Flags: (0x000212) (high32 00000000) on xmit-list, is in l2rib/evpn, is not in HW
Multipath: eBGP iBGP

  Advertised path-id 1
  Path type: internal, path is valid, is best path, no labeled nexthop, in rib
```

```
                Imported from
192.168.15.202:32777:[2]:[0]:[0]:[48]:[0050.7966.6810]:[32]:[172.16.10.50]/272
  AS-Path: 65001 65200 , path sourced external to AS
    192.168.30.202 (metric 161) from 192.168.15.11 (192.168.15.11)
      Origin IGP, MED not set, localpref 100, weight 0
      Received label 30010 30077
      Extcommunity: RT:65100:30010 RT:65100:30077 SOO:192.168.15.202:256 ENCAP:8
        Router MAC:5000.000b.0007
      ESI: 0301.0201.0302.3400.04d2

  Path type: internal, path is valid, not best reason: Neighbor Address, multipath, no
labeled nexthop, in rib
                Imported from
192.168.15.201:32777:[2]:[0]:[0]:[48]:[0050.7966.6810]:[32]:[172.16.10.50]/272
  AS-Path: 65001 65200 , path sourced external to AS
    192.168.30.201 (metric 161) from 192.168.15.11 (192.168.15.11)
      Origin IGP, MED not set, localpref 100, weight 0
      Received label 30010 30077
      Extcommunity: RT:65100:30010 RT:65100:30077 ENCAP:8 Router MAC:5000.000c.0007
      ESI: 0301.0201.0302.3400.04d2

  Path-id 1 not advertised to any peer

Route Distinguisher: 192.168.15.201:32777
BGP routing table entry for [2]:[0]:[0]:[48]:[0050.7966.6810]:[32]:[172.16.10.50]/272,
version 40
Paths: (2 available, best #2)
Flags: (0x000202) (high32 00000000) on xmit-list, is not in l2rib/evpn, is not in HW
Multipath: eBGP iBGP

  Path type: internal, path is valid, not best reason: Router Id, no labeled nexthop
  AS-Path: 65001 65200 , path sourced external to AS
    192.168.30.201 (metric 161) from 192.168.15.12 (192.168.15.12)
      Origin IGP, MED not set, localpref 100, weight 0
      Received label 30010 30077
      Extcommunity: RT:65100:30010 RT:65100:30077 ENCAP:8 Router MAC:5000.000c.0007
      ESI: 0301.0201.0302.3400.04d2

  Advertised path-id 1
  Path type: internal, path is valid, is best path, no labeled nexthop
            Imported to 3 destination(s)
            Imported paths list: TENANT-1 default default
  AS-Path: 65001 65200 , path sourced external to AS
    192.168.30.201 (metric 161) from 192.168.15.11 (192.168.15.11)
      Origin IGP, MED not set, localpref 100, weight 0
      Received label 30010 30077
      Extcommunity: RT:65100:30010 RT:65100:30077 ENCAP:8 Router MAC:5000.000c.0007
      ESI: 0301.0201.0302.3400.04d2

  Path-id 1 not advertised to any peer

Route Distinguisher: 192.168.15.202:32777
BGP routing table entry for [2]:[0]:[0]:[48]:[0050.7966.6810]:[0]:[0.0.0.0]/216,
version 43
Paths: (2 available, best #2)
Flags: (0x000202) (high32 00000000) on xmit-list, is not in l2rib/evpn, is not in HW
Multipath: eBGP iBGP

  Path type: internal, path is valid, not best reason: Router Id, no labeled nexthop
  AS-Path: 65001 65200 , path sourced external to AS
    192.168.30.202 (metric 161) from 192.168.15.12 (192.168.15.12)
```

```
          Origin IGP, MED not set, localpref 100, weight 0
          Received label 30010
          Extcommunity: RT:65100:30010 ENCAP:8 MAC Mobility Sequence:00:1

  Advertised path-id 1
  Path type: internal, path is valid, is best path, no labeled nexthop
             Imported to 1 destination(s)
             Imported paths list: default
  AS-Path: 65001 65200 , path sourced external to AS
    192.168.30.202 (metric 161) from 192.168.15.11 (192.168.15.11)
      Origin IGP, MED not set, localpref 100, weight 0
      Received label 30010
      Extcommunity: RT:65100:30010 ENCAP:8 MAC Mobility Sequence:00:1

  Path-id 1 not advertised to any peer
BGP routing table entry for [2]:[0]:[0]:[48]:[0050.7966.6810]:[32]:[172.16.10.50]/272,
version 47
Paths: (2 available, best #2)
Flags: (0x000202) (high32 00000000) on xmit-list, is not in l2rib/evpn, is not in HW
Multipath: eBGP iBGP

  Path type: internal, path is valid, not best reason: Router Id, no labeled nexthop
  AS-Path: 65001 65200 , path sourced external to AS
    192.168.30.202 (metric 161) from 192.168.15.12 (192.168.15.12)
      Origin IGP, MED not set, localpref 100, weight 0
      Received label 30010 30077
      Extcommunity: RT:65100:30010 RT:65100:30077 SOO:192.168.15.202:256 ENCAP:8
          Router MAC:5000.000b.0007
      ESI: 0301.0201.0302.3400.04d2

  Advertised path-id 1
  Path type: internal, path is valid, is best path, no labeled nexthop
             Imported to 3 destination(s)
             Imported paths list: TENANT-1 default default
  AS-Path: 65001 65200 , path sourced external to AS
    192.168.30.202 (metric 161) from 192.168.15.11 (192.168.15.11)
      Origin IGP, MED not set, localpref 100, weight 0
      Received label 30010 30077
      Extcommunity: RT:65100:30010 RT:65100:30077 SOO:192.168.15.202:256 ENCAP:8
          Router MAC:5000.000b.0007
      ESI: 0301.0201.0302.3400.04d2

  Path-id 1 not advertised to any peer

Route Distinguisher: 192.168.15.101:3     (L3VNI 30077)
BGP routing table entry for [2]:[0]:[0]:[48]:[0050.7966.6810]:[32]:[172.16.10.50]/272,
version 46
Paths: (2 available, best #1)
Flags: (0x000202) (high32 00000000) on xmit-list, is not in l2rib/evpn, is not in HW
Multipath: eBGP iBGP

  Advertised path-id 1
  Path type: internal, path is valid, is best path, no labeled nexthop
             Imported from
192.168.15.202:32777:[2]:[0]:[0]:[48]:[0050.7966.6810]:[32]:[172.16.10.50]/272
  AS-Path: 65001 65200 , path sourced external to AS
    192.168.30.202 (metric 161) from 192.168.15.11 (192.168.15.11)
      Origin IGP, MED not set, localpref 100, weight 0
      Received label 30010 30077
      Extcommunity: RT:65100:30010 RT:65100:30077 SOO:192.168.15.202:256 ENCAP:8
          Router MAC:5000.000b.0007
```

```
    ESI: 0301.0201.0302.3400.04d2

  Path type: internal, path is valid, not best reason: Neighbor Address, multipath, no
labeled nexthop
           Imported from
 192.168.15.201:32777:[2]:[0]:[0]:[48]:[0050.7966.6810]:[32]:[172.16.10.50]/272
   AS-Path: 65001 65200 , path sourced external to AS
     192.168.30.201 (metric 161) from 192.168.15.11 (192.168.15.11)
       Origin IGP, MED not set, localpref 100, weight 0
       Received label 30010 30077
       Extcommunity: RT:65100:30010 RT:65100:30077 ENCAP:8 Router MAC:5000.000c.0007
       ESI: 0301.0201.0302.3400.04d2

  Path-id 1 not advertised to any peer
```
Example 8-8: *Show l2vpn evpn route-type 2 on L-101.*

Capture 8-1 shows that as a reaction to ES link failure L-201 withdraws all routes attached to ES 0301.0201.0302.3400.04d2.

```
Internet Protocol Version 4, Src: 192.168.15.201, Dst: 192.168.15.21
Transmission Control Protocol, Src Port: 179, Dst Port: 22290, Seq: 1, Ack: 1, Len: 55
Border Gateway Protocol - UPDATE Message
    Marker: ffffffffffffffffffffffffffffffff
    Length: 55
    Type: UPDATE Message (2)
    Withdrawn Routes Length: 0
    Total Path Attribute Length: 32
    Path attributes
        Path Attribute - MP_UNREACH_NLRI
            Flags: 0x90, Optional, Extended-Length, Non-transitive, Complete
            Type Code: MP_UNREACH_NLRI (15)
            Length: 28
            Address family identifier (AFI): Layer-2 VPN (25)
            Subsequent address family identifier (SAFI): EVPN (70)
            Withdrawn routes (25 bytes)
                EVPN NLRI: Ethernet Segment Route
                    Route Type: Ethernet Segment Route (4)
                    Length: 23
                    Route Distinguisher: 0001c0a80fc96a61 (192.168.15.201:27233)
                    ESI: 03:01:02:01:03:02:34:00:04:d2
                    IP Address Length: 32
                    IPv4 address: 192.168.30.201
```
Capture 8-1: *Withdraw message sent bu L-201 as a reaction ES interface failure.*

Load-Balancing

Example 8-9 is the same as the example 8-7 but this time highlighted parts describe the Ethernet A-D ES/EVI. This NLRI type identifies the Virtual Network that is attached to the described Ethernet Segment and it is used for Load-Balancing. As can be seen from both BRIB entries sent by L-201 and L-202, the MPLS label is set 30010. The RD can't be used because VLAN Ids are locally significant which means that different VLAN can be mapped into the same global VNI. Based on this information remote leaf L-101 knows that ES 0301.0201.0302.3400.04d2 is reachable via _201 and L-202, VN 30010 (where VLAN 10 is locally attached) belongs to that ES and destination which has that ES included in NLRI in BGP table is capable for flow-based Load-Balancing.

```
L-101# sh bgp l2vpn evpn route-type 1
BGP routing table information for VRF default, address family L2VPN EVPN
Route Distinguisher: 192.168.15.101:32777    (L2VNI 30010)
BGP routing table entry for [1]:[0301.0201.0302.3400.04d2]:[0x0]/152, version 26
Paths: (2 available, best #1)
Flags: (0x000012) (high32 00000000) on xmit-list, is in l2rib/evpn, is not in HW
Multipath: eBGP iBGP

  Advertised path-id 1
  Path type: internal, path is valid, is best path, no labeled nexthop, in rib
            Imported from
192.168.15.202:32777:[1]:[0301.0201.0302.3400.04d2]:[0x0]/152
    AS-Path: 65001 65200 , path sourced external to AS
      192.168.30.202 (metric 161) from 192.168.15.11 (192.168.15.11)
        Origin IGP, MED not set, localpref 100, weight 0
        Received label 30010
        Extcommunity: RT:65100:30010 ENCAP:8

  Path type: internal, path is valid, not best reason: Neighbor Address, multipath, no
labeled nexthop, in rib
            Imported from
192.168.15.201:32777:[1]:[0301.0201.0302.3400.04d2]:[0x0]/152
    AS-Path: 65001 65200 , path sourced external to AS
      192.168.30.201 (metric 161) from 192.168.15.11 (192.168.15.11)
        Origin IGP, MED not set, localpref 100, weight 0
        Received label 30010
        Extcommunity: RT:65100:30010 ENCAP:8

  Path-id 1 not advertised to any peer

Route Distinguisher: 192.168.15.101:65534    (L2VNI 0)
BGP routing table entry for [1]:[0301.0201.0302.3400.04d2]:[0xffffffff]/152, version
21
Paths: (2 available, best #1)
Flags: (0x000012) (high32 00000000) on xmit-list, is in l2rib/evpn, is not in HW
Multipath: eBGP iBGP

  Advertised path-id 1
  Path type: internal, path is valid, is best path, no labeled nexthop, in rib
            Imported from
192.168.15.202:118:[1]:[0301.0201.0302.3400.04d2]:[0xffffffff]/152
```

```
  AS-Path: 65001 65200 , path sourced external to AS
    192.168.30.202 (metric 161) from 192.168.15.11 (192.168.15.11)
      Origin IGP, MED not set, localpref 100, weight 0
      Received label 0
      Extcommunity: RT:65100:30010 ENCAP:8

  Path type: internal, path is valid, not best reason: Neighbor Address, multipath, no
labeled nexthop, in rib
            Imported from
192.168.15.201:118:[1]:[0301.0201.0302.3400.04d2]:[0xffffffff]/152
  AS-Path: 65001 65200 , path sourced external to AS
    192.168.30.201 (metric 161) from 192.168.15.11 (192.168.15.11)
      Origin IGP, MED not set, localpref 100, weight 0
      Received label 0
      Extcommunity: RT:65100:30010 ENCAP:8

  Path-id 1 not advertised to any peer

Route Distinguisher: 192.168.15.201:118
BGP routing table entry for [1]:[0301.0201.0302.3400.04d2]:[0xffffffff]/152, version
30
Paths: (2 available, best #2)
Flags: (0x000002) (high32 00000000) on xmit-list, is not in l2rib/evpn, is not in HW
Multipath: eBGP iBGP

  Path type: internal, path is valid, not best reason: Router Id, no labeled nexthop
  AS-Path: 65001 65200 , path sourced external to AS
    192.168.30.201 (metric 161) from 192.168.15.12 (192.168.15.12)
      Origin IGP, MED not set, localpref 100, weight 0
      Received label 0
      Extcommunity: RT:65100:30010 ENCAP:8

  Advertised path-id 1
  Path type: internal, path is valid, is best path, no labeled nexthop
            Imported to 1 destination(s)
            Imported paths list: default
  AS-Path: 65001 65200 , path sourced external to AS
    192.168.30.201 (metric 161) from 192.168.15.11 (192.168.15.11)
      Origin IGP, MED not set, localpref 100, weight 0
      Received label 0
      Extcommunity: RT:65100:30010 ENCAP:8

  Path-id 1 not advertised to any peer

Route Distinguisher: 192.168.15.201:32777
BGP routing table entry for [1]:[0301.0201.0302.3400.04d2]:[0x0]/152, version 32
Paths: (2 available, best #2)
Flags: (0x000002) (high32 00000000) on xmit-list, is not in l2rib/evpn, is not in HW
Multipath: eBGP iBGP

  Path type: internal, path is valid, not best reason: Router Id, no labeled nexthop
  AS-Path: 65001 65200 , path sourced external to AS
    192.168.30.201 (metric 161) from 192.168.15.12 (192.168.15.12)
      Origin IGP, MED not set, localpref 100, weight 0
      Received label 30010
      Extcommunity: RT:65100:30010 ENCAP:8

  Advertised path-id 1
  Path type: internal, path is valid, is best path, no labeled nexthop
            Imported to 1 destination(s)
            Imported paths list: default
```

```
      AS-Path: 65001 65200 , path sourced external to AS
        192.168.30.201 (metric 161) from 192.168.15.11 (192.168.15.11)
          Origin IGP, MED not set, localpref 100, weight 0
          Received label 30010
          Extcommunity: RT:65100:30010 ENCAP:8

      Path-id 1 not advertised to any peer

Route Distinguisher: 192.168.15.202:118
BGP routing table entry for [1]:[0301.0201.0302.3400.04d2]:[0xffffffff]/152,version 31
Paths: (2 available, best #2)
Flags: (0x000002) (high32 00000000) on xmit-list, is not in l2rib/evpn, is not in HW
Multipath: eBGP iBGP

      Path type: internal, path is valid, not best reason: Router Id, no labeled nexthop
      AS-Path: 65001 65200 , path sourced external to AS
        192.168.30.202 (metric 161) from 192.168.15.12 (192.168.15.12)
          Origin IGP, MED not set, localpref 100, weight 0
          Received label 0
          Extcommunity: RT:65100:30010 ENCAP:8

      Advertised path-id 1
      Path type: internal, path is valid, is best path, no labeled nexthop
                Imported to 1 destination(s)
                Imported paths list: default
      AS-Path: 65001 65200 , path sourced external to AS
        192.168.30.202 (metric 161) from 192.168.15.11 (192.168.15.11)
          Origin IGP, MED not set, localpref 100, weight 0
          Received label 0
          Extcommunity: RT:65100:30010 ENCAP:8

      Path-id 1 not advertised to any peer

Route Distinguisher: 192.168.15.202:32777
BGP routing table entry for [1]:[0301.0201.0302.3400.04d2]:[0x0]/152, version 33
Paths: (2 available, best #2)
Flags: (0x000002) (high32 00000000) on xmit-list, is not in l2rib/evpn, is not in HW
Multipath: eBGP iBGP

      Path type: internal, path is valid, not best reason: Router Id, no labeled nexthop
      AS-Path: 65001 65200 , path sourced external to AS
        192.168.30.202 (metric 161) from 192.168.15.12 (192.168.15.12)
          Origin IGP, MED not set, localpref 100, weight 0
          Received label 30010
          Extcommunity: RT:65100:30010 ENCAP:8

      Advertised path-id 1
      Path type: internal, path is valid, is best path, no labeled nexthop
                Imported to 1 destination(s)
                Imported paths list: default
      AS-Path: 65001 65200 , path sourced external to AS
        192.168.30.202 (metric 161) from 192.168.15.11 (192.168.15.11)
          Origin IGP, MED not set, localpref 100, weight 0
          Received label 30010
          Extcommunity: RT:65100:30010 ENCAP:8

      Path-id 1 not advertised to any peer
```

Example 8-9: *Show l2vpn evpn route-type 1 on L-101.*

References

[RFC 7432]   A. Sajassi et al., "BGP MPLS-Based Ethernet VPN", RFC 7432, February 2015.

Building Data Center with VXLAN BGP EVPN – A Cisco NX-OS Perspective
ISBN-10: 1-58714-467-0 – Krattiger Lukas, Shyam Kapadia, and Jansen Davis

Cisco Programmable Fabric with VXLAN BGP EVPN Configuration Guide
https://www.cisco.com/c/en/us/td/docs/switches/datacenter/pf/configuration/guide/b-pf-configuration/IP-Fabric-Underlay-Options.html

Chapter 9: ECMP process

ECMP process

This chapter continues where the previous one ends. Figure 9-1 illustrates the basic ECMP process to SRV50 form L-101 perspective. SRV50 is reachable via two VTEPs (VXLAN Tunnel End Point), L-201: 192.168.30.201, and L-202: 192.168.30.202. When BGP ECMP is enabled on L-101 under L2VPN EVPN AFI, L-101 can load share flows between these two VTEPs. So the first path decision process is done based on the Next-Hop address received within MAC Advertisement Route about SRV50. Let's say that the load sharing algorithm selects VTEP L-201 for the first flow from one of L-101 connected hosts. L-101 does the RNH (Recursive Next-Hop) lookup to find out how to route data to destination 192.168.0.201. Now it will take a routing lookup from the Underlay Network Routing table.

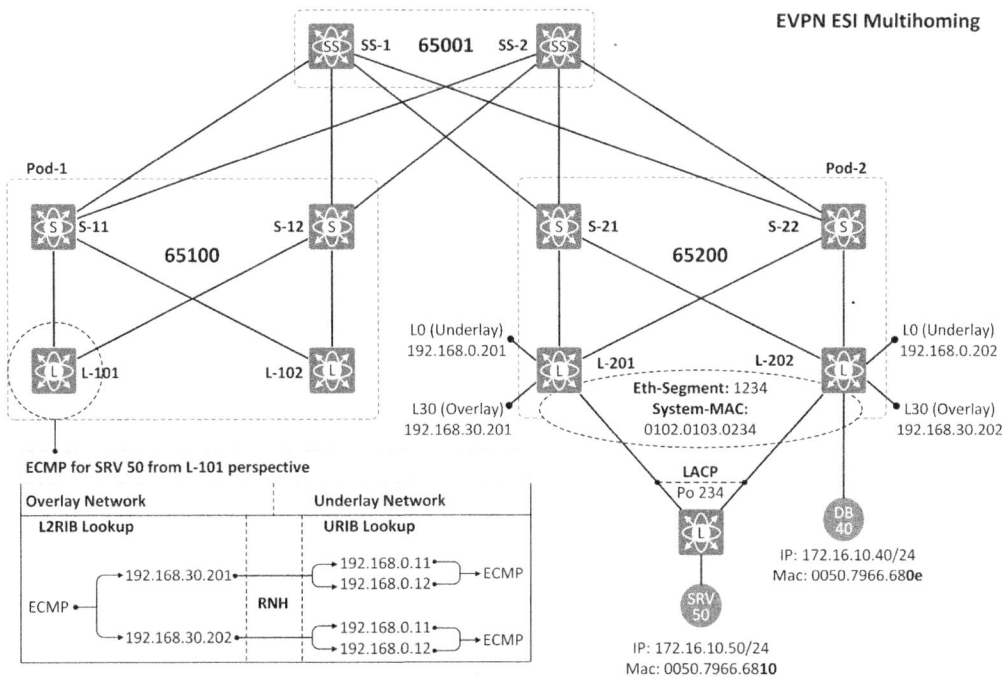

Figure 9-1: *ECMP to SRV50 from L-101 perspective.*

Example 9-1 shows the BGP table of L-101 when BGP multipathing for ibgp is not enabled. L-101 has imported MAC Advertisement Routes about SRV50 received from L-201 and L-202 into Loc-RIB. However, they are not marked as multipath entries with "|" sign.

```
L-101# sh bgp l2vpn evpn
BGP routing table information for VRF default, address family L2VPN EVPN
BGP table version is 86, Local Router ID is 192.168.15.101
Status: s-suppressed, x-deleted, S-stale, d-dampened, h-history, *-valid, >-best
Path type: i-internal, e-external, c-confed, l-local, a-aggregate, r-redist, I-
injected
Origin codes: i - IGP, e - EGP, ? - incomplete, | - multipath, & - backup, 2 - best2

   Network            Next Hop            Metric     LocPrf     Weight Path
Route Distinguisher: 192.168.15.101:32777    (L2VNI 30010)
*>i[1]:[0301.0201.0302.3400.04d2]:[0x0]/152
                      192.168.30.201                 100            0 65001 65200 i
* i                   192.168.30.202                 100            0 65001 65200 i
*>i[2]:[0]:[0]:[48]:[0050.7966.680e]:[0]:[0.0.0.0]/216
                      192.168.30.202                 100            0 65001 65200 i
*>i[2]:[0]:[0]:[48]:[0050.7966.6810]:[0]:[0.0.0.0]/216
                      192.168.30.201                 100            0 65001 65200 i
*>i[2]:[0]:[0]:[48]:[0050.7966.680e]:[32]:[172.16.10.40]/272
                      192.168.30.202                 100            0 65001 65200 i
*>i[2]:[0]:[0]:[48]:[0050.7966.6810]:[32]:[172.16.10.50]/272
                      192.168.30.202                 100            0 65001 65200 i
* i                   192.168.30.201                 100            0 65001 65200 i
*>l[3]:[0]:[32]:[192.168.30.101]/88
                      192.168.30.101                 100        32768 i
*>i[3]:[0]:[32]:[192.168.30.102]/88
                      192.168.30.102                 100            0 i
*>i[3]:[0]:[32]:[192.168.30.201]/88
                      192.168.30.201                 100            0 65001 65200 i
*>i[3]:[0]:[32]:[192.168.30.202]/88
                      192.168.30.202                 100            0 65001 65200 i

Route Distinguisher: 192.168.15.101:65534    (L2VNI 0)
*>i[1]:[0301.0201.0302.3400.04d2]:[0xffffffff]/152
                      192.168.30.201                 100            0 65001 65200 i
* i                   192.168.30.202                 100            0 65001 65200 i

Route Distinguisher: 192.168.15.102:32777
* i[3]:[0]:[32]:[192.168.30.102]/88
                      192.168.30.102                 100            0 i
*>i                   192.168.30.102                 100            0 i

Route Distinguisher: 192.168.15.201:118
* i[1]:[0301.0201.0302.3400.04d2]:[0xffffffff]/152
                      192.168.30.201                 100            0 65001 65200 i
*>i                   192.168.30.201                 100            0 65001 65200 i

Route Distinguisher: 192.168.15.201:32777
* i[1]:[0301.0201.0302.3400.04d2]:[0x0]/152
                      192.168.30.201                 100            0 65001 65200 i
*>i                   192.168.30.201                 100            0 65001 65200 i
* i[2]:[0]:[0]:[48]:[0050.7966.6810]:[0]:[0.0.0.0]/216
                      192.168.30.201                 100            0 65001 65200 i
*>i                   192.168.30.201                 100            0 65001 65200 i
```

```
* i[2]:[0]:[0]:[48]:[0050.7966.6810]:[32]:[172.16.10.50]/272
                    192.168.30.201                  100       0 65001 65200 i
*>i                 192.168.30.201                  100       0 65001 65200 i
* i[3]:[0]:[32]:[192.168.30.201]/88
                    192.168.30.201                  100       0 65001 65200 i
*>i                 192.168.30.201                  100       0 65001 65200 i

Route Distinguisher: 192.168.15.202:118
* i[1]:[0301.0201.0302.3400.04d2]:[0xffffffff]/152
                    192.168.30.202                  100       0 65001 65200 i
*>i                 192.168.30.202                  100       0 65001 65200 i

Route Distinguisher: 192.168.15.202:32777
* i[1]:[0301.0201.0302.3400.04d2]:[0x0]/152
                    192.168.30.202                  100       0 65001 65200 i
*>i                 192.168.30.202                  100       0 65001 65200 i
* i[2]:[0]:[0]:[48]:[0050.7966.680e]:[0]:[0.0.0.0]/216
                    192.168.30.202                  100       0 65001 65200 i
*>i                 192.168.30.202                  100       0 65001 65200 i
* i[2]:[0]:[0]:[48]:[0050.7966.680e]:[32]:[172.16.10.40]/272
                    192.168.30.202                  100       0 65001 65200 i
*>i                 192.168.30.202                  100       0 65001 65200 i
* i[2]:[0]:[0]:[48]:[0050.7966.6810]:[32]:[172.16.10.50]/272
                    192.168.30.202                  100       0 65001 65200 i
*>i                 192.168.30.202                  100       0 65001 65200 i
* i[3]:[0]:[32]:[192.168.30.202]/88
                    192.168.30.202                  100       0 65001 65200 i
*>i                 192.168.30.202                  100       0 65001 65200 i

Route Distinguisher: 192.168.15.101:3     (L3VNI 30077)
*>i[2]:[0]:[0]:[48]:[0050.7966.680e]:[32]:[172.16.10.40]/272
                    192.168.30.202                  100       0 65001 65200 i
*>i[2]:[0]:[0]:[48]:[0050.7966.6810]:[32]:[172.16.10.50]/272
                    192.168.30.202                  100       0 65001 65200 i
* i                 192.168.30.201                  100       0 65001 65200 i
```

Example 9-1: *Show l2vpn evpn on L-101 without BGP maximum-path ibgp command.*

Examples 9-2 verifies that the L2RIB of L-101 has only one next-hop to SRV50 (MAC: 005.79966.6810) about MAC-Only NLRI, and the same applies to MAC-IP NLRI in example 9-3. The server DB40 (005.79966.680e) is single-homed to L-202 so it ok, that it is advertised only by L-202.

```
L-101# sh l2route evpn mac evi 10

Flags -(Rmac):Router MAC (Stt):Static (L):Local (R):Remote (V):vPC link
(Dup):Duplicate (Spl):Split (Rcv):Recv (AD):Auto-Delete (D):Del Pending
(S):Stale (C):Clear, (Ps):Peer Sync (O):Re-Originated (Nho):NH-Override
(Pf):Permanently-Frozen, (Orp): Orphan

Topology   Mac Address      Prod   Flags         Seq No    Next-Hops
---------- ---------------- ------ ------------- --------- --------------------------
10         0050.7966.680e   BGP    SplRcv        0         192.168.30.202
10         0050.7966.6810   BGP    Spl           1         192.168.30.201
```

Example 9-2: *Show l2vpn evpn on L-101 mac evi 10 without BGP maximum-path ibgp command.*

```
L-101(config)# sh l2route evpn mac-ip evi 10
Flags -(Rmac):Router MAC (Stt):Static (L):Local (R):Remote (V):vPC link
(Dup):Duplicate (Spl):Split (Rcv):Recv(D):Del Pending (S):Stale (C):Clear
(Ps):Peer Sync (Ro):Re-Originated (Orp):Orphan
Topology    Mac Address      Host IP           Prod    Flags       Seq No        Next-Hops
-----------  ---------------  -----------------  ------  ----------  -----------  -------------
10          0050.7966.680e   172.16.10.40       BGP     --          0            192.168.30.202
10          0050.7966.6810   172.16.10.50       BGP     --          0            192.168.30.201
```

Example 9-3: *Show l2vpn evpn on L-101 mac-ip evi 10 without BGP maximum-path ibgp command.*

Example 9-4 shows how BGP ECMP for Overlay Network is enabled. The sub-command *maximum-paths ibgp 8* of address-family l2vpn evpn global command states that EVPN NLRIs received from L2VPN EVPN iBGP peers can use 8 ECMP valid paths. Without the "ibgp" definition the ECMP is enabled only for eBGP peers. In our example, both ibgp and ebgp are enabled.

```
router bgp 65100
  router-id 192.168.15.101
  address-family ipv4 unicast
  address-family l2vpn evpn
    maximum-paths 8
    maximum-paths ibgp 8
```

Example 9-4: *BGP ECMP Configuration on L-101.*

Example 9-5 shows that now the entry for SRV50 is marked as a multipath capable route.

```
L-101(config)# sh bgp l2vpn evpn
BGP routing table information for VRF default, address family L2VPN EVPN
BGP table version is 201, Local Router ID is 192.168.15.101
Status: s-suppressed, x-deleted, S-stale, d-dampened, h-history, *-valid, >-best
Path type: i-internal, e-external, c-confed, l-local, a-aggregate, r-redist, I-
injected
Origin codes: i - IGP, e - EGP, ? - incomplete, | - multipath, & - backup, 2 - best2

   Network             Next Hop            Metric     LocPrf     Weight Path
Route Distinguisher: 192.168.15.101:32777    (L2VNI 30010)
*>i[1]:[0301.0201.0302.3400.04d2]:[0x0]/152
                       192.168.30.201                 100           0 65001 65200 i
*|i                    192.168.30.202                 100           0 65001 65200 i
*>i[2]:[0]:[0]:[48]:[0050.7966.680e]:[0]:[0.0.0.0]/216
                       192.168.30.202                 100           0 65001 65200 i
*>i[2]:[0]:[0]:[48]:[0050.7966.680e]:[32]:[172.16.10.40]/272
                       192.168.30.202                 100           0 65001 65200 i
*>i[2]:[0]:[0]:[48]:[0050.7966.6810]:[32]:[172.16.10.50]/272
                       192.168.30.202                 100           0 65001 65200 i
*|i                    192.168.30.201                 100           0 65001 65200 i
*>l[3]:[0]:[32]:[192.168.30.101]/88
                       192.168.30.101                 100           32768 i
*>i[3]:[0]:[32]:[192.168.30.102]/88
                       192.168.30.102                 100           0 i
*>i[3]:[0]:[32]:[192.168.30.201]/88
                       192.168.30.201                 100           0 65001 65200 i
```

```
*>i[3]:[0]:[32]:[192.168.30.202]/88
                         192.168.30.202                   100         0 65001 65200 i

Route Distinguisher: 192.168.15.101:65534    (L2VNI 0)
*>i[1]:[0301.0201.0302.3400.04d2]:[0xffffffff]/152
                         192.168.30.201                   100         0 65001 65200 i
*|i                      192.168.30.202                   100         0 65001 65200 i

Route Distinguisher: 192.168.15.102:32777
*  i[3]:[0]:[32]:[192.168.30.102]/88
                         192.168.30.102                   100         0 i
*>i                      192.168.30.102                   100         0 i

Route Distinguisher: 192.168.15.201:118
*  i[1]:[0301.0201.0302.3400.04d2]:[0xffffffff]/152
                         192.168.30.201                   100         0 65001 65200 i
*>i                      192.168.30.201                   100         0 65001 65200 i

Route Distinguisher: 192.168.15.201:32777
*  i[1]:[0301.0201.0302.3400.04d2]:[0x0]/152
                         192.168.30.201                   100         0 65001 65200 i
*>i                      192.168.30.201                   100         0 65001 65200 i
*  i[2]:[0]:[0]:[48]:[0050.7966.6810]:[32]:[172.16.10.50]/272
                         192.168.30.201                   100         0 65001 65200 i
*>i                      192.168.30.201                   100         0 65001 65200 i
*  i[3]:[0]:[32]:[192.168.30.201]/88
                         192.168.30.201                   100         0 65001 65200 i
*>i                      192.168.30.201                   100         0 65001 65200 i

Route Distinguisher: 192.168.15.202:118
*  i[1]:[0301.0201.0302.3400.04d2]:[0xffffffff]/152
                         192.168.30.202                   100         0 65001 65200 i
*>i                      192.168.30.202                   100         0 65001 65200 i

Route Distinguisher: 192.168.15.202:32777
*  i[1]:[0301.0201.0302.3400.04d2]:[0x0]/152
                         192.168.30.202                   100         0 65001 65200 i
*>i                      192.168.30.202                   100         0 65001 65200 i
*  i[2]:[0]:[0]:[48]:[0050.7966.680e]:[0]:[0.0.0.0]/216
                         192.168.30.202                   100         0 65001 65200 i
*>i                      192.168.30.202                   100         0 65001 65200 i
*  i[2]:[0]:[0]:[48]:[0050.7966.680e]:[32]:[172.16.10.40]/272
                         192.168.30.202                   100         0 65001 65200 i
*>i                      192.168.30.202                   100         0 65001 65200 i
*  i[2]:[0]:[0]:[48]:[0050.7966.6810]:[32]:[172.16.10.50]/272
                         192.168.30.202                   100         0 65001 65200 i
*>i                      192.168.30.202                   100         0 65001 65200 i
*  i[3]:[0]:[32]:[192.168.30.202]/88
                         192.168.30.202                   100         0 65001 65200 i
*>i                      192.168.30.202                   100         0 65001 65200 i

Route Distinguisher: 192.168.15.101:3     (L3VNI 30077)
*>i[2]:[0]:[0]:[48]:[0050.7966.680e]:[32]:[172.16.10.40]/272
                         192.168.30.202                   100         0 65001 65200 i
*>i[2]:[0]:[0]:[48]:[0050.7966.6810]:[32]:[172.16.10.50]/272
                         192.168.30.202                   100         0 65001 65200 i
*|i                      192.168.30.201                   100         0 65001 65200 i
```

Example 9-5: *Show bgp l2vpn evpn on L-101.*

Multipathing can also be verified from the L2RIB. Examples 9-6 and 9-7 show that both MAC-Only and MAC-I NLRIs are reachable via L-201 and L-202. In other words, L-101 does a flow-based load sharing when sending data to SRV50. This is not the whole ECMP story...

```
L-101# sh l2route evpn mac evi 10

Flags -(Rmac):Router MAC (Stt):Static (L):Local (R):Remote (V):vPC link
(Dup):Duplicate (Spl):Split (Rcv):Recv (AD):Auto-Delete (D):Del Pending
(S):Stale (C):Clear, (Ps):Peer Sync (O):Re-Originated (Nho):NH-Override
(Pf):Permanently-Frozen, (Orp): Orphan

Topology    Mac Address      Prod    Flags       Seq No    Next-Hops
---------   --------------   -----   ---------   -------   --------------
10          0050.7966.680e   BGP     SplRcv      0         192.168.30.202
10          0050.7966.6810   BGP     Spl         1         192.168.30.201
                                                           192.168.30.202
```

Example 9-6: *Show l2vpn evpn on L-101 mac evi 10 with BGP maximum-path ibgp command.*

```
L-101(config)# sh l2route evpn mac-ip evi 10
Flags -(Rmac):Router MAC (Stt):Static (L):Local (R):Remote (V):vPC link
(Dup):Duplicate (Spl):Split (Rcv):Recv(D):Del Pending (S):Stale (C):Clear
(Ps):Peer Sync (Ro):Re-Originated (Orp):Orphan
Topology    Mac Address      Host IP         Prod    Flags    Seq No    Next-Hops
---------   --------------   -------------   -----   ------   -------   --------------
10          0050.7966.680e   172.16.10.40    BGP     --       0         192.168.30.202
10          0050.7966.6810   172.16.10.50    BGP     --       0         192.168.30.201
                                                                        192.168.30.202
```

Example 9-7: *Show l2vpn evpn on L-101 mac-ip evi 10 with BGP maximum-path ibgp command.*

The next step for the packet forwarding process, after selecting one of the available ECPN Next-Hop candidates as actual Next-Hop, is to do Recursive Next-Hop Resolution (RNH). Examples 9-8 and 9-9 show that packets to both VTEP addresses can be load shared between S-11 and S-12. Note that we are using OSPF as in Underlay Network Control-Plane.

```
L-101(config)# sh ip route 192.168.30.202
IP Route Table for VRF "default"
'*' denotes best ucast next-hop
'**' denotes best mcast next-hop
'[x/y]' denotes [preference/metric]
'%<string>' in via output denotes VRF <string>

192.168.30.202/32, ubest/mbest: 2/0
    *via 192.168.0.11, Eth1/1, [110/161], 00:24:12, ospf-UNDERLAY-NET, intra
    *via 192.168.0.12, Eth1/2, [110/161], 00:24:12, ospf-UNDERLAY-NET, intra
```

Example 9-8: *Show ip route 192.168.30.202 on L-101.*

```
L-101(config)# sh ip route 192.168.30.201
IP Route Table for VRF "default"
'*' denotes best ucast next-hop
'**' denotes best mcast next-hop
'[x/y]' denotes [preference/metric]
'%<string>' in via output denotes VRF <string>

192.168.30.201/32, ubest/mbest: 2/0
   *via 192.168.0.11, Eth1/1, [110/161], 00:24:17, ospf-UNDERLAY-NET, intra
   *via 192.168.0.12, Eth1/2, [110/161], 00:24:17, ospf-UNDERLAY-NET, intra
```

Example 9-9: *Show ip route 192.168.30.201 on L-101.*

If BGP is used instead of OSPF in Underlay Network the sub-command *maximum-paths* has to be enabled under the IPv4 Unicast address-family in global BGP configuration. The example below is borrowed from chapter 2 (figure 2-11) that is why the VTEP address is 192.168.31.101 instead of 192.168.30.101

```
SS-1# sh ip route 192.168.31.101
IP Route Table for VRF "default"
'*' denotes best ucast next-hop
'**' denotes best mcast next-hop
'[x/y]' denotes [preference/metric]
'%<string>' in via output denotes VRF <string>

192.168.31.101/32, ubest/mbest: 2/0
   *via 10.10.10.0, [20/0], 00:01:01, bgp-65001, external, tag 65100
   *via 10.10.10.4, [20/0], 00:19:16, bgp-65001, external, tag 65100
```

Example 9-10: *Show ip route 192.168.31.201 on L-101.*

The example below shows nve peers learned by L-101.

```
L-101# sh nve peers detail
Details of nve Peers:
----------------------------------------
Peer-Ip: 192.168.30.102
    NVE Interface          : nve1
    Peer State             : Up
    Peer Uptime            : 00:46:44
    Router-Mac             : n/a
    Peer First VNI         : 30010
    Time since Create      : 00:46:44
    Configured VNIs        : 30010,30077
    Provision State        : peer-add-complete
    Learnt CP VNIs         : 30010
    vni assignment mode    : SYMMETRIC
    Peer Location          : N/A
Peer-Ip: 192.168.30.201
    NVE Interface          : nve1
    Peer State             : Up
    Peer Uptime            : 00:31:07
    Router-Mac             : n/a
    Peer First VNI         : 30010
    Time since Create      : 00:31:07
    Configured VNIs        : 30010,30077
    Provision State        : peer-add-complete
    Learnt CP VNIs         : 30010
```

```
        vni assignment mode : SYMMETRIC
        Peer Location       : N/A
Peer-Ip: 192.168.30.202
        NVE Interface       : nve1
        Peer State          : Up
        Peer Uptime         : 00:31:07
        Router-Mac          : 5000.000b.0007
        Peer First VNI      : 30010
        Time since Create   : 00:31:07
        Configured VNIs     : 30010,30077
        Provision State     : peer-add-complete
        Learnt CP VNIs      : 30010,30077
        vni assignment mode : SYMMETRIC
        Peer Location       : N/A
```

Example 9-11: *Show nve peers on L-101.*

The last example shows where the tunnel IP address used as a Next-Hop in Overlay Network tunneling is locally routed i.e. what is their Next-Hop router. The reason why the "Multipath" is marked as "No" is that we are not using BGP in Underlay Network but OSPF, and we are looking for BGP RNH DataBase.

```
L-101# sh bgp l2vpn evpn nexthop-database

Next Hop table for VRF default, address family L2VPN EVPN:
Next-hop trigger-delay(miliseconds)
  Critical: 3000 Non-critical: 10000
IPv4 Next-hop table

IPv4 Unicast Next-hops:

Nexthop: 192.168.30.101, Flags: 0x5, Refcount: 3, IGP cost: 0, Multipath: No
IGP Route type: 0, IGP preference: 0
Attached nexthop: 192.168.30.101, Interface: loopback30
Attached nexthop: 192.168.30.101, Interface: loopback30
Nexthop is attached not-local reachable not-labeled
Nexthop last resolved: 00:49:47, using 192.168.30.101/32
Metric next advertise: Never
RNH epoch: 1

Nexthop: 192.168.30.102, Flags: 0x1, Refcount: 2, IGP cost: 81, Multipath: No
IGP Route type: 0, IGP preference: 110
Attached nexthop: 192.168.0.12, Interface: Ethernet1/2
Attached nexthop: 192.168.0.11, Interface: Ethernet1/1
Nexthop is not-attached not-local reachable not-labeled
Nexthop last resolved: 00:46:47, using 192.168.30.102/32
Metric next advertise: Never
RNH epoch: 1

Nexthop: 192.168.30.201, Flags: 0x1, Refcount: 2, IGP cost: 161, Multipath: No
IGP Route type: 0, IGP preference: 110
Attached nexthop: 192.168.0.12, Interface: Ethernet1/2
Attached nexthop: 192.168.0.11, Interface: Ethernet1/1
Nexthop is not-attached not-local reachable not-labeled
Nexthop last resolved: 00:31:06, using 192.168.30.201/32
Metric next advertise: Never
RNH epoch: 1

Nexthop: 192.168.30.202, Flags: 0x1, Refcount: 6, IGP cost: 161, Multipath: No
```

```
IGP Route type: 0, IGP preference: 110
Attached nexthop: 192.168.0.12, Interface: Ethernet1/2
Attached nexthop: 192.168.0.11, Interface: Ethernet1/1
Nexthop is not-attached not-local reachable not-labeled
Nexthop last resolved: 00:31:06, using 192.168.30.202/32
Metric next advertise: Never
RNH epoch: 1
IPv6 Next-hop table
```

Example 9-12: *Show sh bgp l2vpn evpn nexthop-database on L-101.*

References

[RFC 7908]   K. Sriram et al., "Problem Definition and Classification of BGP Route Leaks", RFC 7908, June 2016.

[VALLEY-FREE]   https://blog.ipspace.net/2018/09/valley-free-routing.html

Chapter 10: L3-Only Inter-Pod Connection

Introduction

So far this book has explained the Pod Inter-Connection model which allows L2 segment stretching between Pods by using Super-Spine switches in the middle of five-stage Clos topology. This chapter discusses L3-Only Pod-Interconnect over MPLS Core Network. Figure 10-1 illustrates the protocols that we are using in this chapter. Within Pods, the Underlay Network routing protocol is OSPF, and the ASN scheme is Single-ASN. The IS-IS is used in MPLS Core Underlay Network, LDP is used for MPLS label distribution, and BGP VPNv4 NLRIs are used for NLRI exchange. This solution supports an end-to-end ECMP, so for the sake of simplicity, all redundancy is removed from this chapter.

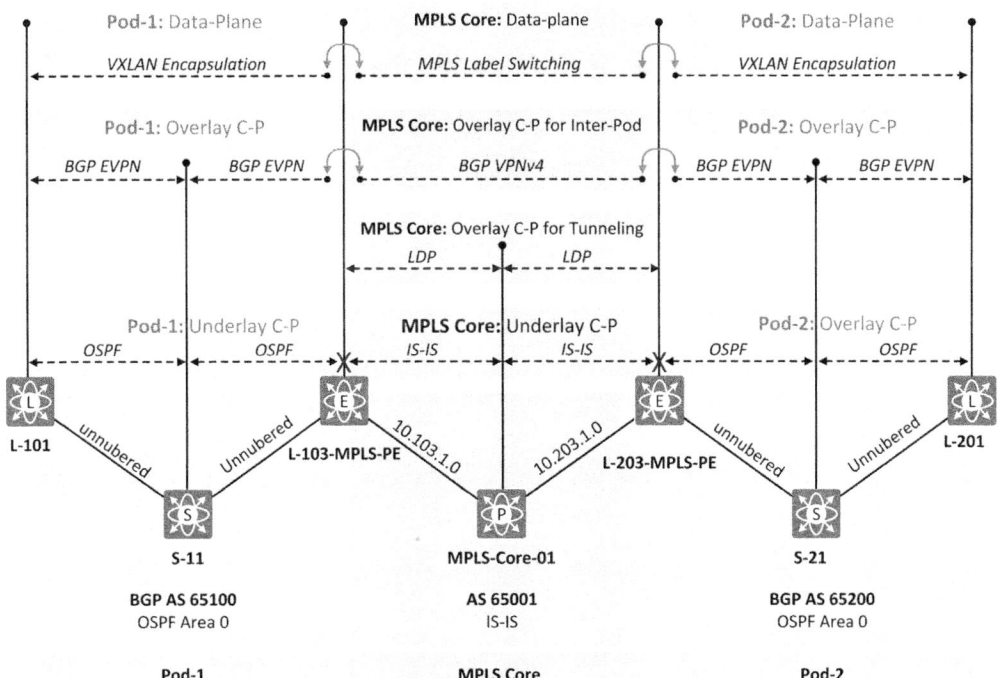

Figure 10-1: *L3-Only Inter-Pod Model.*

MPLS Core Underlay Routing with IS-IS.

The job of an Underlay Network routing protocol in MPLS Core is to advertise IP reachability information related to Core devices in order those to (a) build MPLS Label mapping information used in the Overlay Network for packet forwarding across the MPLS Core and, (b) advertise IP reachability information used for BGP VPNv4 Unicast peering over MPLS Core. Even though using separate IGP in Pod and MPLS core adds some complexity, it also limits the failure domains within Pods. If the same protocols are used within Pods and MPLS Core, there should be some filtering mechanism to prevent unnecessary routing information to leak between domains. With OSPF such filtering requires multi Area structure because within the OSPF area all LSAs are flooded everywhere and this behavior can't be prevented (LSDB has to be identical within OSPF Area). In IS-IS we can use the area model by using L1 and L2 circuits. However, in one protocol model, we might accidentally do something within Pod that affects remote Pod too. With two protocol model that requires redistribution, which shouldn't be done unintentionally (I underline the word shouldn't).

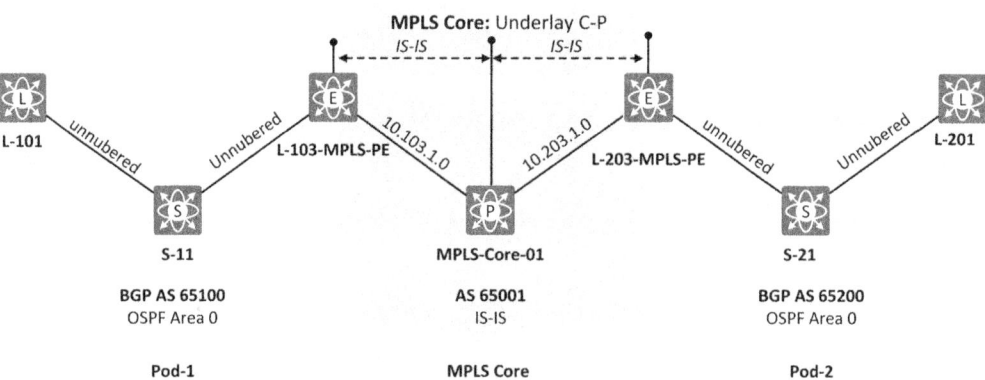

Figure 10-2: *MPLS Core IS-IS Configuration.*

IS-IS Configuration

Example 10-1 shows the minimum configuration needed for IS-IS. The Net address is configured under the router isis section and is IS-IS enabled in MPLS Core facing interface G3 and in Interface Loopback 0 that is later used for MP-BGP VPNv4 peering. There is a lot of fine-tuning option for IS-IS but they are out of the scope of this book.

```
interface Loopback0
 description ** RID/Underlay **
 ip address 192.168.0.103 255.255.255.255
 ip router isis
!
interface GigabitEthernet3
 ip address 10.103.1.103 255.255.255.0
 ip router isis
!
router isis
 net 49.0001.0000.0000.0103.00
 metric-style narrow
!
```

Example 10-1: *MPLS Core Underlay Network Configuration on L-103.*

IS-IS Verification

Examples 10-2 to 10-4 show that MPLS Core devices are IS-IS neighbors. Note that by default they form L1 and L2 peering because we haven't specifically define circuit type.

```
L-103-MPLS-PE#sh isis neighbors

Tag null:
System Id       Type Interface    IP Address      State Holdtime Circuit Id
MPLS-Core-01    L1   Gi3          10.103.1.1      UP    8        MPLS-Core-01.01
MPLS-Core-01    L2   Gi3          10.103.1.1      UP    8        MPLS-Core-01.01
```

Example 10-2: *show isis neighbors on L-103.*

```
L-203-MPLS-PE#sh isis neighbors

Tag null:
System Id       Type Interface    IP Address      State Holdtime Circuit Id
MPLS-Core-01    L1   Gi3          10.203.1.1      UP    9        MPLS-Core-01.
MPLS-Core-01    L2   Gi3          10.203.1.1      UP    9        MPLS-Core-01.
```

Example 10-3: *show isis neighbors on L-203.*

```
MPLS-Core-01#sh isis neighbors

System Id        Type Interface    IP Address      State Holdtime Circuit Id
L-103-MPLS-PE    L1   Gi1          10.103.1.103    UP    23       MPLS-Core-01.
L-103-MPLS-PE    L2   Gi1          10.103.1.103    UP    22       MPLS-Core-01.
L-203-MPLS-PE    L1   Gi3          10.203.1.203    UP    29       MPLS-Core-01.
L-203-MPLS-PE    L2   Gi3          10.203.1.203    UP    28       MPLS-Core-01.
```

Example 10-4: *show isis neighbors on MPLS-Core-01.*

The example below shows the routes that L-103 has learned via IS-IS. The first one is the subnet used in the Inter-Switch link between L-103 and MPLS-Core-01, the second route is the loopback of MPLS-Core-01, and the last one the interface Loopback 0 of L-203 in Pod-2.

```
L-103-MPLS-PE#sh ip route isis
<snipped>

Gateway of last resort is not set

      10.0.0.0/8 is variably subnetted, 3 subnets, 2 masks
i L1     10.203.1.0/24 [115/20] via 10.103.1.1, 00:53:48, GigabitEthernet3
      192.0.1.0/32 is subnetted, 1 subnets
i L1     192.0.1.1 [115/20] via 10.103.1.1, 00:53:48, GigabitEthernet3
      192.168.0.0/32 is subnetted, 4 subnets
i L1     192.168.0.203 [115/30] via 10.103.1.1, 00:53:48, GigabitEthernet3
```

Example 10-5: *show ip route isis on L-103.*

Example 10-6 shows the IS-IS routes on MPLS-Core-01 RIB.

```
MPLS-Core-01#sh ip route isis
<snipped>

Gateway of last resort is not set

      192.168.0.0/32 is subnetted, 2 subnets
i L1     192.168.0.103 [115/20] via 10.103.1.103, 02:06:03, GigabitEthernet1
i L1     192.168.0.203 [115/20] via 10.203.1.203, 02:06:02, GigabitEthernet3
```

Example 10-6: *show ip route isis on MPLS-Core-01.*

The example 10-7 shows the IS-IS route on L-203 RIB.

```
L-203-MPLS-PE#sh ip route isis
<snipped>

Gateway of last resort is not set

      10.0.0.0/8 is variably subnetted, 3 subnets, 2 masks
i L1     10.103.1.0/24 [115/20] via 10.203.1.1, 00:55:24, GigabitEthernet3
      192.0.1.0/32 is subnetted, 1 subnets
i L1     192.0.1.1 [115/20] via 10.203.1.1, 00:55:24, GigabitEthernet3
      192.168.0.0/32 is subnetted, 4 subnets
i L1     192.168.0.103 [115/30] via 10.203.1.1, 00:55:19, GigabitEthernet3
```

Example 10-7: *show ip route isis on L-203.*

MPLS Label Distribution with LDP

Label Distribution Protocol (LDP) is used for exchanging Subnet-to-Label binding information. Each MPLS routers has a Label Information Base (LIB) where they copy all routes from the Routing Information Base (RIB). Routers allocate a local label for every route in LFIB and advertise these Subnet-to-Label binding information using the Label Distribution Protocol (LDP). Received label mapping information is then stored into LIB as an out-label. This means that each route in LFIB has (a) a local label a.k.a *In-Label* and (b) Remote-label a.k.a *Out-Label*. Let's take a look at this from the L-203 perspective. It has received Link State PDU (LSP) about Interface Loopback 0 (192.168.0.103/32) of L-103 flooded by MPLS-Core-01. This information is stored in the IS-IS Database. L-203 runs the Dijkstra algorithm to find the shortest path to 192.168.0.103/32 which naturally is via MPLS-Core-01. It stores the best path to 192.168.0.103/32 into the RIB from where information is copied into the LIB. MPLS-Core has done the same routing process and where it calculates the best path to destination 192.168.0.103/32 and installs the best path into the RIB and copies the information into LIB. Let's say that MPLS-Core-01 allocates local label 17 for 192.168.0.103. this subnet-label binding information is then advertised to L-203 using LDP. MPLS-Core has also received label binding information about the same destination from L-103. Because IP 192.168.0.103/32 is directly connected to L-103, it' allocates the implicit-null label for it and advertises it to MPLS-Core-01.

234 Chapter 10: L3-Only Inter-Pod Connection

At this phase, we have the following LIB information (a) L-203: Out-Label 17 for 192.168.0.103, (b) MPLS-Core-01: In-Label 17 and Out-Label Imp-Null for 192.168.0.103. Now this label mapping information is copied from LIB, which is Control-Plane Database, into LFIB, which in turn is Data-Plane Database. As an example, MPLS-Core-01 creates LFIB entry In-Label 17 > Out-Label Imp-Null (with Next-Hop information). Now when L-203 has data to destination 192.168.0.103, the LFIB lookup says that encapsulate the original data packet with Out-label 17 and send it to MPLS-Core-01. When MPLS-Core-01 received this labeled packet, based on LFIB lookup it pops removes the label 17, and sends the unlabeled packet to L-103 (It does not make RIB lookup at all). It is sent unlabeled because the imp-null label is a special label that is used for signaling the LDP peer that the label binding is about my connected network, so please remove the outer label so I do not have to do that. So what traffic is sent from L-203 to the destination 192.168.0.103? BGP VPNv4 Updates (Control-Plane) and it is also used as a next-hop data from Pod-2 to Pod-1. Figure 10-3 illustrates the LDP peering.

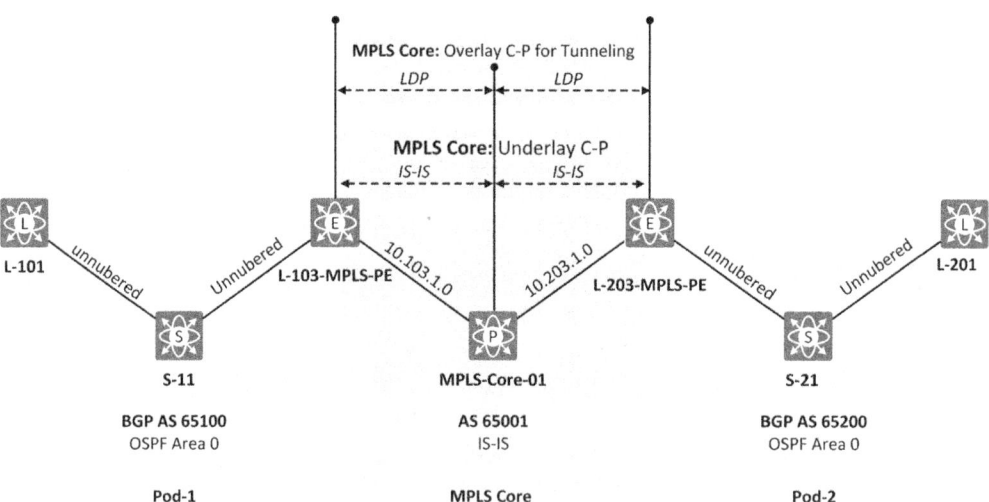

Figure 10-3: *MPLS Core LDP.*

MPLS LDP Configuration

The example below shows the MPLS configuration used in this chapter. There is a lot of options that can be used with LDP such as authentication. For the sake of simplicity, those are left out.

```
interface Loopback0
 description ** RID/Underlay **
 ip address 192.168.0.103 255.255.255.255
 ip router isis
!
interface GigabitEthernet3
 ip address 10.103.1.103 255.255.255.0
 mpls ip
 mpls label protocol ldp
 mpls bgp forwarding
!
mpls ldp router-id Loopback0
```

Example 10-8: *MPLS Configuration on L-103.*

MPLS Verification

Example 10-9 shows that L-103 has established LDP adjacency with MPLS-Core-01 (192.0.1.1) over interface G3 using TCP as a transport protocol.

```
L-103-MPLS-PE#sh mpls ldp neighbor
    Peer LDP Ident: 192.0.1.1:0; Local LDP Ident 192.168.0.103:0
        TCP connection: 192.0.1.1.646 - 192.168.0.103.24040
        State: Oper; Msgs sent/rcvd: 105/97; Downstream
        Up time: 01:18:28
        LDP discovery sources:
          GigabitEthernet3, Src IP addr: 10.103.1.1
        Addresses bound to peer LDP Ident:
          192.0.1.1       10.103.1.1      10.203.1.1
```

Example 10-9: *show mpls ldp neighbor on L-103.*

The next two examples illustrate the LDP peering from MPLS-Core-01 and L-203 perspective. Note that LDP uses TCP as a transport protocol.

```
L-203-MPLS-PE#sh mpls ldp neighbor
    Peer LDP Ident: 192.0.1.1:0; Local LDP Ident 192.168.0.203:0
        TCP connection: 192.0.1.1.646 - 192.168.0.203.28885
        State: Oper; Msgs sent/rcvd: 105/98; Downstream
        Up time: 01:19:11
        LDP discovery sources:
          GigabitEthernet3, Src IP addr: 10.203.1.1
        Addresses bound to peer LDP Ident:
          192.0.1.1        10.103.1.1       10.203.1.1
```

Example 10-10: *show mpls ldp neighbor on MPLS-Core-01.*

```
MPLS-Core-01#sh mpls ldp neighbor
    Peer LDP Ident: 192.168.0.203:0; Local LDP Ident 192.0.1.1:0
        TCP connection: 192.168.0.203.28885 - 192.0.1.1.646
        State: Oper; Msgs sent/rcvd: 99/107; Downstream
        Up time: 01:20:34
        LDP discovery sources:
          GigabitEthernet3, Src IP addr: 10.203.1.203
        Addresses bound to peer LDP Ident:
          10.203.1.203    192.168.0.203    192.168.15.203   192.168.30.203
    Peer LDP Ident: 192.168.0.103:0; Local LDP Ident 192.0.1.1:0
        TCP connection: 192.168.0.103.24040 - 192.0.1.1.646
        State: Oper; Msgs sent/rcvd: 99/107; Downstream
        Up time: 01:20:34
        LDP discovery sources:
          GigabitEthernet1, Src IP addr: 10.103.1.103
        Addresses bound to peer LDP Ident:
          10.103.1.103    192.168.0.103    192.168.15.103   192.168.30.103
```

Example 10-11: *show mpls ldp neighbor on L-203.*

Example 10-12 shows detailed ldp discovery information from the L-203 perspective. 192.168.0.203:0 describes that L-203 is using per-platform label space meaning switches may generate the same label values for the same destination. The xmit/recv means that L-203 has both sent and received LDP hello messages from the peer.

```
L-203-MPLS-PE#sh mpls ldp discovery detail
 Local LDP Identifier:
    192.168.0.203:0
    Discovery Sources:
    Interfaces:
        GigabitEthernet3 (ldp): xmit/recv
            Enabled: Interface config
            Hello interval: 5000 ms; Transport IP addr: 192.168.0.203
            LDP Id: 192.0.1.1:0
              Src IP addr: 10.203.1.1; Transport IP addr: 192.0.1.1
              Hold time: 15 sec; Proposed local/peer: 15/15 sec
              Reachable via 192.0.1.1/32
              Password: not required, none, in use
            Clients: IPv4, mLDP
```

Example 10-12: *show mpls ldp discovery detail on L-203.*

Example 10-13 shows the same information from the MPLS-Core-01 perspective.

```
MPLS-Core-01#sh mpls ldp discovery detail
 Local LDP Identifier:
    192.0.1.1:0
    Discovery Sources:
    Interfaces:
        GigabitEthernet1 (ldp): xmit/recv
            Enabled: Interface config
            Hello interval: 5000 ms; Transport IP addr: 192.0.1.1
            LDP Id: 192.168.0.103:0
              Src IP addr: 10.103.1.103; Transport IP addr: 192.168.0.103
              Hold time: 15 sec; Proposed local/peer: 15/15 sec
              Reachable via 192.168.0.103/32
              Password: not required, none, in use
            Clients: IPv4, mLDP
        GigabitEthernet3 (ldp): xmit/recv
            Enabled: Interface config
            Hello interval: 5000 ms; Transport IP addr: 192.0.1.1
            LDP Id: 192.168.0.203:0
              Src IP addr: 10.203.1.203; Transport IP addr: 192.168.0.203
              Hold time: 15 sec; Proposed local/peer: 15/15 sec
              Reachable via 192.168.0.203/32
              Password: not required, none, in use
            Clients: IPv4, mLDP
```

Example 10-13: *show mpls ldp discovery detail on MPLS-Core-01.*

MPLS Control-Plane Operation - LDP

Example 10-14 shows the Label Distribution process. L-203 generates Implicit-null Label for its IP address 192.168.0.203 (Loopback 0). By doing this it asks the downstream label switch router to remove the top-most tunnel label from the MPLS encapsulated packets. This removes unnecessary label lookup. MPLS-Core-01 receives this binding information and stores it to MPLS LIB (Label Information Base). MPLS-Core-01 itself has assigned label 17 to subnet 192.168.0.203/32 and it advertises it to its LDP peer L-103. It sends the binding information to all of its LDP peers including L-203 but it is left out from the figure. L-103 saves the received binding information into MPLS LIB. This binding information is later used in the MPLS tunnel when forwarding Inter-Pod data.

238 Chapter 10: L3-Only Inter-Pod Connection

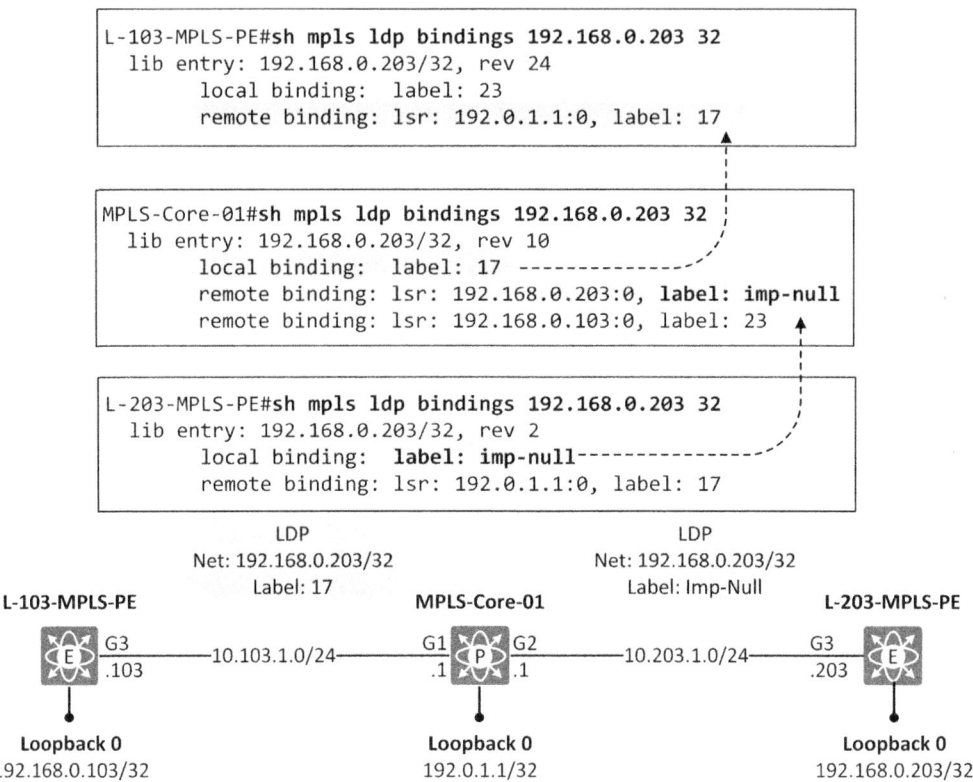

Figure 10-4: *MPLS Core Control-Plane - Label Exchange Process.*

MPLS Data-Plane Operation – Label Switching

Figure 10-5 illustrates the Label Forwarding Information Base (LFIB) of MPLS-Core-01 and L-103. L-103 will use MPLS label 17, learned via LDP from MPLS-Core-01 when sending data towards L-203. When MPLS-Core-01 receives the packet with MPLS label 17, it pops the outer label due to the implicit-null label received from L-203 and forwards the unlabeled packet to L-203.

```
MPLS-Core-01#show mpls forwarding-table 192.168.0.203 32 detail
Local     Outgoing    Prefix              Bytes Label    Outgoing     Next Hop
Label     Label       or Tunnel Id        Switched       interface
17        Pop Label   192.168.0.203/32    14326          Gi3          10.203.1.203
          MAC/Encaps=14/14, MRU=1504, Label Stack{}
          50000014000250000016000288847
          No output feature configured
```

```
L-103-MPLS-PE#sh mpls forwarding-table 192.168.0.203 32 detail
Local     Outgoing    Prefix              Bytes Label    Outgoing     Next Hop
Label     Label       or Tunnel Id        Switched       interface
23        17          192.168.0.203/32    0              Gi3          10.103.1.1
          MAC/Encaps=14/18, MRU=1500, Label Stack{17}
          50000016000050000011000288847 00011000
          No output feature configured
```

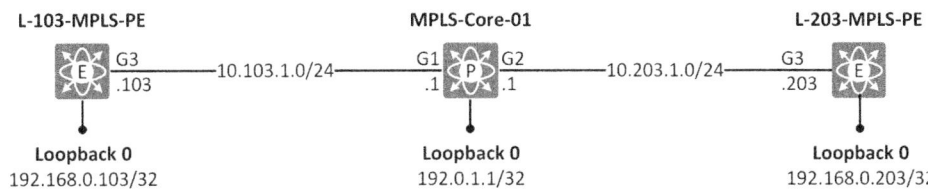

Figure 10-5: *MPLS Core Data-Plane – Label Switching.*

BGP VPNv4 Peering

The NLRI information about internal networks of Pod is exchanged over MPLS Core by using BGP VPNv4 Unicast Address-Family. This information among other NLRIs like prefix, prefix length, and Next-Hop, carries information about VPN Label that is used as a VPN Identifier. In the Data-Plane perspective, this means that TENANT-1 within Pods are identified by VPN X that is used as an inner label when sending Inter-Pod data. The outer label is the label that is received via LDP from the upstream router.

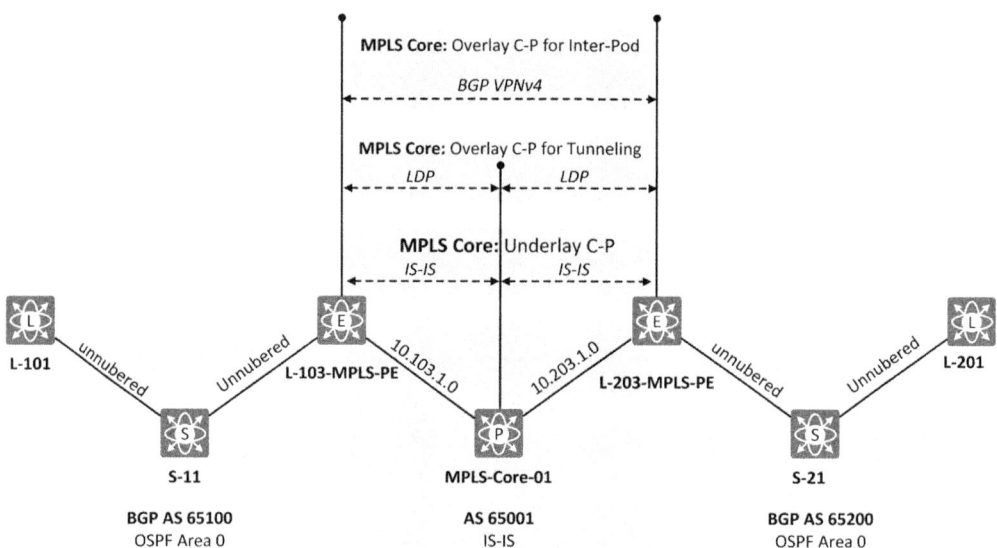

Figure 10-6: *MPLS Core Control-Plane – BGP VPNv4 Unicast Peering.*

BGP VPNv4 Configuration

Example 10-14 shows the BGP VPNv4 configuration on L-103. Because we have eBGP peering over the MPLS network between loopback interfaces, we need to modify the source interface used for peering and increase the TTL value. Because import/export policy in BGP VPNv4 is based on Route-Targets, we need to send extended communities to adjacent BGP VPNv4 peers. Under the address-family vpnv4 section there is the command import l2vpn evpn re-originate that will import BGP Update messages about EVPN routes into the BGP VPNv4 process and send them to BGP VPNv4 peer. BGP ECMP for address-family VPNv4 is activated under the same afi by using the maximum-path command. Because IS-IS has native support for ECMP, we now have ECMP capable MPLS Core network.

```
router bgp 65100
 bgp router-id 192.168.15.103
 bgp log-neighbor-changes
 no bgp default ipv4-unicast
 neighbor 192.168.0.203 remote-as 65200
 neighbor 192.168.0.203 ebgp-multihop 10
 neighbor 192.168.0.203 update-source Loopback0
 !
 !
 address-family vpnv4
  import l2vpn evpn re-originate
  neighbor 192.168.0.203 activate
  neighbor 192.168.0.203 send-community extended
  maximum-paths 8
 exit-address-family
 !
```

Example 10-14: *BGP VPNv4 Configuration on L-103.*

Example 10-15 shows the BGP VPNv4 configuration on L-203.

```
router bgp 65200
 bgp router-id 192.168.15.203
 bgp log-neighbor-changes
 no bgp default ipv4-unicast
 neighbor 192.168.0.103 remote-as 65100
 neighbor 192.168.0.103 ebgp-multihop 10
 neighbor 192.168.0.103 update-source Loopback0
 !
 !
 address-family vpnv4
  import l2vpn evpn re-originate
  neighbor 192.168.0.103 activate
  neighbor 192.168.0.103 send-community extended
  maximum-paths 8
 exit-address-family
```

Example 10-15: *BGP VPNv4 Configuration on L-203.*

BGP VPNv4 Peering Verification

Examples 10-16 and 10-17 verify that L-103 ad L-203 have BGP VPNv4 adjacency. We haven't activated any customer networks neither Pod-1 nor Pod-2, that is why no routes haven't learned at this phase.

```
L-103-MPLS-PE#sh bgp vpnv4 unicast all summary
BGP router identifier 192.168.15.103, local AS number 65100
BGP table version is 1, main routing table version 1

Neighbor        V         AS MsgRcvd MsgSent   TblVer  InQ OutQ Up/Down  State/PfxRcd
192.168.0.203   4      65200     145     147        1    0    0 02:11:18        0
```

Example 10-16: *Show bgp vpnv4 unicast all summry on L-103.*

```
L-203-MPLS-PE#sh bgp vpnv4 unicast all summary
BGP router identifier 192.168.15.203, local AS number 65200
BGP table version is 1, main routing table version 1

Neighbor          V         AS MsgRcvd MsgSent   TblVer  InQ OutQ Up/Down  Statd
192.168.0.103     4      65100     147     146        1    0    0 02:11:48      0
```

Example 10-17: *Show bgp vpnv4 unicast all summry on L-203.*

BGP L2VPN EVPN Peering

The Figure above illustrates the overall BGP peering model. Pod internal peering uses BGP L2VPN EVPN afi and the peering between L-103 and L-203 over MPLS Core uses BGP VPNv4 afi.

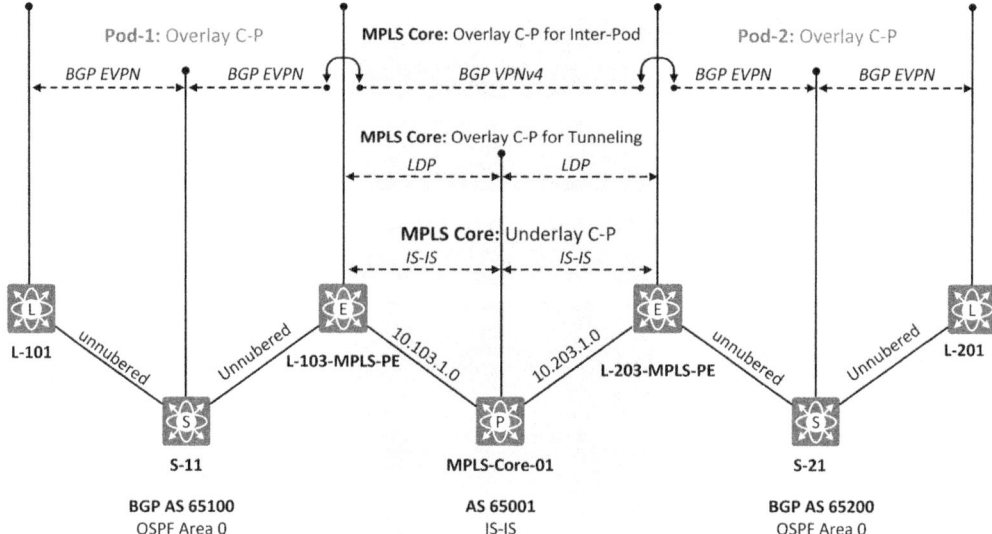

Figure 10-7: Control-Plane Interaction: *EVPN-to-VPNv4-to-EVPN Process.*

BGP VPNv4 Configuration

The only new configuration related to BGP L2VPN EVPN afi on border leafs is the command ***import vpnv4 unicast reoriginate***. This imports BGP VPNv4 NLRI into the BGP L2VPN VPN process. The EVPN Route-Type for Imported NLRIs will be Route-Type 5 (IP Prefix Route), as can be seen later.

```
router bgp 65100
 bgp router-id 192.168.15.103
 bgp log-neighbor-changes
 neighbor 192.168.15.11 remote-as 65100
 neighbor 192.168.15.11 update-source Loopback15
 !
 !
address-family l2vpn evpn
  import vpnv4 unicast re-originate
  neighbor 192.168.15.11 activate
  neighbor 192.168.15.11 send-community both
  maximum-paths 8
 exit-address-family
```

Example 10-17: *Show bgp vpnv4 unicast all summry on L-203.*

```
router bgp 65200
 bgp router-id 192.168.15.203
 bgp log-neighbor-changes
 neighbor 192.168.15.21 remote-as 65200
 neighbor 192.168.15.21 update-source Loopback15
 !
 !
address-family l2vpn evpn
  import vpnv4 unicast re-originate
  neighbor 192.168.15.21 activate
  neighbor 192.168.15.21 send-community both
  maximum-paths 8
 exit-address-family
```

Example 10-17: *Show bgp vpnv4 unicast all summry on L-203.*

BGP L2VPN EVPN Peering Verification

The next two examples verify the BGP L2VPN EVPN peering from border leafs L-103 and L-203 perspective.

```
L-103-MPLS-PE#sh bgp l2vpn evpn summary
BGP router identifier 192.168.15.103, local AS number 65100
BGP table version is 1, main routing table version 1

Neighbor         V          AS MsgRcvd MsgSent   TblVer  InQ OutQ Up/Down
State/PfxRcd
192.168.15.11    4       65100     147     159        1    0    0 02:22:53        0
```

Example 10-18: *Show bgp l2vpn evpn summary on L-103.*

```
L-203-MPLS-PE#sh bgp l2vpn evpn summary
BGP router identifier 192.168.15.203, local AS number 65200
BGP table version is 1, main routing table version 1

Neighbor         V          AS MsgRcvd MsgSent   TblVer  InQ OutQ Up/Down
State/PfxRcd
192.168.15.21    4       65200     147     160        1    0    0 02:22:51        0
```

Example 10-19: *Show bgp l2vpn evpn summary on L-203.*

Adding Tenant to Border Leafs

The next step is adding Tenant into border leafs. We are adding network 172.16.10.0/24 in VRF TENANR-1 in Pod and network 172.16.20.0/24 in the same VRF in Pod-2. We can use the same VLAN-Id and VNI for both subnets because there is no L2 stretching between Pods. L3VNI for TENANT-1 is 30077.

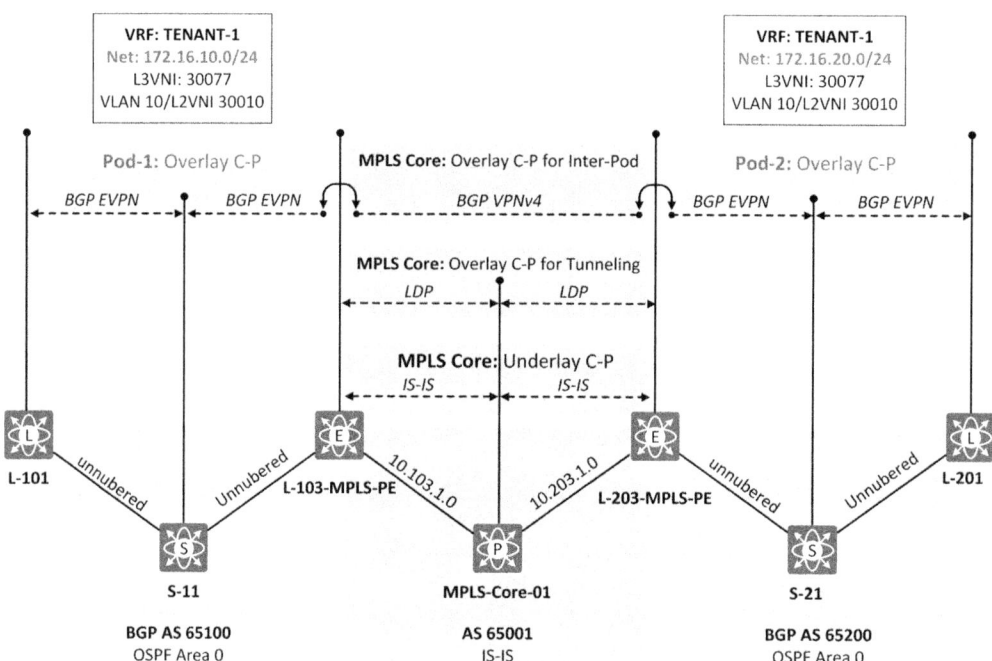

Figure 10-8: Control-Plane Interaction: *EVPN-to-VPNv4-to-EVPN Process*.

Tenant Configuration

I am using CSR1000v as a border leaf so the L2 based configuration slightly differs from NX-OS. Instead of using VLANs, we are using Bridge-Groups. There is no Anycast GW for subnet 172.16.10.0/24 but we are using BDI77 L3VNI IRB (Integrated Routing and Bridging). There are also RT export/import clauses for L3VNI with stitching definition under the address-family section. The border leafs use normal RTs with BGP VPNv4 afi and stitching option with EVPN afi. This means that when BGP Update, carrying VPNv4 NLRI from remote Pod is received by local border leaf it import NLRIs into BGP-Loc RIB as VPNv4 route and then in VXLAN handoff, it attaches the EVPN RT in BGP Update when it is re-originated and advertised into BGP L2VPN EVPN peer.

The same process applies when EVPN NLRIs are imported into BGP Loc-RIB as EVPN entries based on EVPN RT and then advertised to BGP VPNv4 peer with VPNv4 RT. This process can be seen when monitoring Control-Plane in later examples. Note that the L2 Bridge-Group config is not shown in examples. In Appendix A., there is a complete configuration of L-103, L-203, and MPLS-Core-01. Within Pod host IP address are advertised with mask /32, so leaf switches will advertise host IP reachability as unique NLRI. It is not efficient if these updates are passed between Pods and hat is why we are using aggregation in border leaf.

```
L-103-MPLS-PE#sh run vrf TENANT-1
<snipped>
vrf definition TENANT-1
 rd 192.168.15.103:3
 !
 address-family ipv4
  route-target export 65001:10
  route-target import 65001:10
  route-target export 65100:30077 stitching
  route-target import 65100:30077 stitching
 exit-address-family
!
interface BDI77
 mac-address 0077.0077.0077
 vrf forwarding TENANT-1
 ip unnumbered Loopback30
!
router bgp 65100
 !
 address-family ipv4 vrf TENANT-1
  advertise l2vpn evpn
  aggregate-address 172.16.10.0 255.255.255.0 summary-only
 exit-address-family
!
end
```
Example 10-20: *Tenant Configuration on L-103.*

```
L-203-MPLS-PE#sh run vrf TENANT-1
<snipped>
vrf definition TENANT-1
 rd 192.168.15.203:3
 !
 address-family ipv4
  route-target export 65001:10
  route-target import 65001:10
  route-target export 65200:30077 stitching
  route-target import 65200:30077 stitching
 exit-address-family
!
interface BDI77
 mac-address 0077.0077.0077
 vrf forwarding TENANT-1
 ip unnumbered Loopback30
!
router bgp 65200
 !
```

246 Chapter 10: L3-Only Inter-Pod Connection

```
address-family ipv4 vrf TENANT-1
  advertise l2vpn evpn
  aggregate-address 172.16.20.0 255.255.255.0 summary-only
 exit-address-family
!
end
```

Example 10-21: *Tenant Configuration on L-203.*

Verification

Control-Plane: End-to-End Route Propagation

The configuration is now ready. Next, we are going to check the End-to-End Control Plane operation. This is done by power on the Application server App30 (IP: 172.16.20.30/32) connected into L-201 in Pod-2. The next sections explain how IP information eventually ends up into the BGP table of L-101 in Pod-1

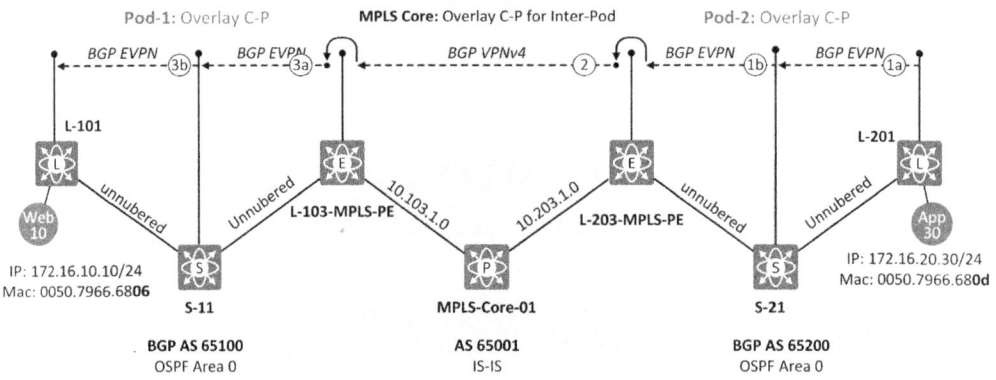

Figure 10-9: *Connecting Hosts to Network.*

Phase 1 (a-b):

Capture 10-1 shows captured BGP Update message originated by L-203 and forwarded by S-21 (BGP RR) to L-203. Because we are using L3-Only Pod interconnect, we are focusing only on L3 information. The IP address is advertised with mask length /32 (host route) and with auto derived Route-Targe 65200:30077, which is used with L3VNI as EVPN MAC-Advertisement Route.

BGP EVPN Design Consideration

```
Internet Protocol Version 4,
 Src: 192.168.15.21, Dst: 192.168.15.203
Transmission Control Protocol,
 Src Port: 179, Dst Port: 12425, Seq: 20, Ack: 39, Len: 141
Border Gateway Protocol - UPDATE Message
        Path Attribute - EXTENDED_COMMUNITIES
            Type Code: EXTENDED_COMMUNITIES (16)
            Length: 32
            Carried extended communities: (4 communities)
                Route Target: 65200:30010 [Transitive 2-Octet AS-Specific]
                Route Target: 65200:30077 [Transitive 2-Octet AS-Specific]
                Unknown subtype 0x03: 0x5000 0x000c 0x0007 [Transitive EVPN]
        Path Attribute - ORIGINATOR_ID: 192.168.15.201
        Path Attribute - CLUSTER_LIST: 192.168.2.2
            Cluster List: 192.168.2.2
                Cluster ID: 192.168.2.2
        Path Attribute - MP_REACH_NLRI
            Type Code: MP_REACH_NLRI (14)
            Length: 51
            Address family identifier (AFI): Layer-2 VPN (25)
            Subsequent address family identifier (SAFI): EVPN (70)
            Next hop network address (4 bytes)
            Number of Subnetwork points of attachment (SNPA): 0
            Network layer reachability information (42 bytes)
                EVPN NLRI: MAC Advertisement Route
                    Route Type: MAC Advertisement Route (2)
                    Length: 40
                    Route Distinguisher: 0001c0a80fc98009 (192.168.15.201:32777)
                    ESI: 00:00:00:00:00:00:00:00:00:00
                        ESI Type: ESI 9 bytes value (0)
                        ESI Value: 00 00 00 00 00 00 00 00
                        ESI 9 bytes value: 00 00 00 00 00 00 00 00 00
                    Ethernet Tag ID: 0
                    MAC Address Length: 48
                    MAC Address: Private_66:68:0d (00:50:79:66:68:0d)
                    IP Address Length: 32
                    IPv4 address: 172.16.20.30
                    0000 0000 0111 0101 0011 .... = MPLS Label 1: 1875
                    0000 0000 0111 0101 0111 .... = MPLS Label 2: 1879
```

Capture 10-1: *EVPN Update sent by S-21 to L-203.*

Phase 2:

Example 10-22 shows the VPNv4 NLRI about 172.16.20.30 imported from EVPN Update. We can see that the EVPN Route-Target is changed from 65200:30077 to 65001:10. Note that the host route is not advertised to any peer because we are using the aggregate only advertisement.

```
L-203-MPLS-PE#sh bgp vpnv4 unicast vrf TENANT-1 172.16.20.30
BGP routing table entry for 192.168.15.203:3:172.16.20.30/32, version 4
Paths: (1 available, best #1, table TENANT-1, Advertisements suppressed by an
aggregate.)
Flag: 0x100
  Not advertised to any peer
  Refresh Epoch 1
  Local, imported path from
[2][192.168.15.201:32777][0][48][00507966680D][32][172.16.20.30]/24
    192.168.30.201 (metric 42) (via default) from 192.168.15.21 (192.168.15.21)
      Origin IGP, localpref 100, valid, internal, best
      Extended Community: RT:65001:10 ENCAP:8 Router MAC:5000.000C.0007
      Originator: 192.168.15.201, Cluster list: 192.168.2.2
      Local vxlan vtep:
        vrf:TENANT-1, vni:30077
        local router mac:0077.0077.0077
        encap:8
        vtep-ip:192.168.30.203
        bdi:BDI77
      Remote VxLAN:
        Topoid 0x1(vrf TENANT-1)
        Remote Router MAC:5000.000C.0007
        Encap 8
        Egress VNI 30077
        RTEP 192.168.30.201
      rx pathid: 0, tx pathid: 0x0
```

Example 10-22: *show bgp vpnv4 unicast vrf TENANT-1 172.16.20.30 on L-203.*

Capture 10-2 shows how the EVPN NLRI information is encoded to VPNv4 NLRI. As a first note, MPLS-Core-01 makes its forwarding decision based topmost MPLS Label which in this example is the Label binding information about IP address 192.168.0.103. So it doesn't look beyond the MPLS label. The prefix 172.16.20.0 is advertised with VPN label 24 (inner label). This label identifies the L3VPN where this prefix belongs to. Note that L3VNI information is not carried within VPNv4 specific updates. We spoke earlier about Route-Target stitching. We can see that EVPN Route-Target 65200:30077 is now changed to 65001:10 so this is how EVPN Route-Targets and VPNv4 Route-Targets are stitched together.

```
Ethernet II, Src: 50:00:00:14:00:02 Dst: 50:00:00:16:00:02
Type: MPLS label switched packet (0x8847)
MultiProtocol Label Switching Header, Label: 16, Exp: 6, S: 1, TTL: 10
Internet Protocol Version 4, Src: 192.168.0.203, Dst: 192.168.0.103
Transmission Control Protocol, Src Port: 179, Dst Port: 38005, Seq: 1, Ack: 1, Border
Gateway Protocol - UPDATE Message
        Path Attribute - MP_REACH_NLRI
            Type Code: MP_REACH_NLRI (14)
            Length: 32
            Address family identifier (AFI): IPv4 (1)
            Subsequent address family identifier (SAFI): Labeled VPN Unicast (128)
            Next hop network address (12 bytes)
                Next Hop: Empty Label Stack RD=0:0 IPv4=192.168.0.203
            Number of Subnetwork points of attachment (SNPA): 0
            Network layer reachability information (15 bytes)
                BGP Prefix
                    Prefix Length: 112
                    Label Stack: 24 (bottom)
                    Route Distinguisher: 192.168.15.203:3
                    MP Reach NLRI IPv4 prefix: 172.16.20.0
        Path Attribute - AS_PATH: 65200
        Path Attribute - AGGREGATOR: AS: 65200 origin: 192.168.15.203
        Path Attribute - ATOMIC_AGGREGATE
        Path Attribute - EXTENDED_COMMUNITIES
            Type Code: EXTENDED_COMMUNITIES (16)
            Length: 8
            Carried extended communities: (1 community)
                Route Target: 65001:10 [Transitive 2-Octet AS-Specific]
```

Capture 10-2: *EVPN Update sent by S-21 to L-203.*

Example 10-22 shows the VPNv4 NLRI about 172.16.20.30 on BGP table entry about of L-103. The route is imported into vrf TENANT-1 Loc-RIB from the Adj-RIB-In based on VPNv4 Route-Target 65001:10.

```
L-103-MPLS-PE#sh bgp vpnv4 unicast vrf TENANT-1 172.16.20.30
BGP routing table entry for 192.168.15.103:3:172.16.20.0/24, version 3
Paths: (1 available, best #1, table TENANT-1)
  Not advertised to any peer
  Refresh Epoch 1
  65200, (aggregated by 65200 192.168.15.203), imported path from
192.168.15.203:3:172.16.20.0/24 (global)
    192.168.0.203 (metric 30) (via default) from 192.168.0.203 (192.168.15.203)
      Origin IGP, metric 0, localpref 100, valid, external, atomic-aggregate, best
      Extended Community: RT:65001:10
      Local vxlan vtep:
        vrf:TENANT-1, vni:30077
        local router mac:0077.0077.0077
        encap:8
        vtep-ip:192.168.30.103
        bdi:BDI77
      mpls labels in/out nolabel/24
      rx pathid: 0, tx pathid: 0x0
```

Example 10-23: *show bgp vpnv4 unicast vrf TENANT-1 172.16.20.30 on L-103.*

Example 10-24 shows how the information is eventually seen by L-101 within Pod-1. The NLRI is EVPN Route-Type 5 (IP Prefix Route). The Next-Hop to the destination is L-103. The Route-Target is now 65100:30077. The change from 65001:10 (VPNv4) to 65100:30077 (EVPN) is done by L-103 (RT stitching).

```
L-101# sh bgp l2vpn evpn 172.16.20.0
BGP routing table information for VRF default, address family L2VPN EVPN
Route Distinguisher: 192.168.15.103:3
BGP routing table entry for [5]:[0]:[0]:[24]:[172.16.20.0]/224, version 5
Paths: (1 available, best #1)
Flags: (0x000002) (high32 00000000) on xmit-list, is not in l2rib/evpn, is not in HW
Multipath: eBGP iBGP

  Advertised path-id 1
  Path type: internal, path is valid, is best path, no labeled nexthop
            Imported to 2 destination(s)
            Imported paths list: TENANT-1 default
  Gateway IP: 0.0.0.0
  AS-Path: 65200 , path sourced external to AS
    192.168.30.103 (metric 81) from 192.168.15.11 (192.168.15.11)
      Origin IGP, MED 0, localpref 100, weight 0
      Aggregated by 192.168.15.203, aggregator AS 65200, atomic-aggregate set
      Received label 30077
      Extcommunity: RT:65100:30077 ENCAP:8 Router MAC:0077.0077.0077
      Originator: 192.168.15.103 Cluster list: 192.168.1.1

  Path-id 1 not advertised to any peer

Route Distinguisher: 192.168.15.101:3    (L3VNI 30077)
BGP routing table entry for [5]:[0]:[0]:[24]:[172.16.20.0]/224, version 6
Paths: (1 available, best #1)
Flags: (0x000002) (high32 00000000) on xmit-list, is not in l2rib/evpn, is not in HW
Multipath: eBGP iBGP

  Advertised path-id 1
  Path type: internal, path is valid, is best path, no labeled nexthop
            Imported from 192.168.15.103:3:[5]:[0]:[0]:[24]:[172.16.20.0]/224
  Gateway IP: 0.0.0.0
  AS-Path: 65200 , path sourced external to AS
    192.168.30.103 (metric 81) from 192.168.15.11 (192.168.15.11)
      Origin IGP, MED 0, localpref 100, weight 0
      Aggregated by 192.168.15.203, aggregator AS 65200, atomic-aggregate set
      Received label 30077
      Extcommunity: RT:65100:30077 ENCAP:8 Router MAC:0077.0077.0077
      Originator: 192.168.15.103 Cluster list: 192.168.1.1

  Path-id 1 not advertised to any peer
```

Example 10-23: *show bgp vpnv4 unicast vrf TENANT-1 172.16.20.30 on L-103.*

Data-Plane: Label Switching Path

In figure 10-10 shows that L-103 has populated CEF entry for destination 172.16.20.0/24 from both RIB and LIB (Label Information Base). We can see that the Next-Hop for destination network 172.16.20.0/24 is L-203 (192.168.0.203). Because the Next-Hop is not directly connected, L-103 has done Recursive Next-Hop resolution. The Next-Hop for 192.168.0.203 is MPLS-Core-01 (10.103.1.1). The labeled binding for the destination 192.168.0.203 is 17. This IP-label binding information was received from MPLS-Core-01 which uses it as a local label for 192.168.0.203. The inner VPN Label is 24, and it is received via BGP VPNv4 Update from L-203. The actual label stack that L-103 will use for MPLS encapsulation when sending packets to the destination is 24, 17.

When MPLS-Core-01 receives the packet with MPLS label 17, it does LFIB (Label Forwarding Information Base) lookup. It has received Imp-Null Label from L-203 and it has generated local label 17 for destination 192.168.0.203, so the LFIB entry tells that the ingress packet with the label 17 will be sent to NH 10.203.1.203 out of interface G2 and the outmost label will be popped out. As a result, L-203 will receive a packet with label 24. Based on that label, it knows to which VPN this packet belongs to.

```
L-203-MPLS-PE#sh ip cef vrf TENANT-1 172.16.20.0 255.255.255.0 detail
172.16.20.0/24, epoch 2, flags [rib only nolabel, rib defined all labels]
  dflt local label info: other/24 [0x2]
  attached to Null0
```

```
MPLS-Core-01#sh mpls forwarding-table labels 17 detail
Local      Outgoing   Prefix              Bytes Label   Outgoing     Next Hop
Label      Label      or Tunnel Id        Switched      interface
17         Pop Label  192.168.0.203/32    43822         Gi3          10.203.1.203
        MAC/Encaps=14/14, MRU=1504, Label Stack{}
        50000014000250000001600028847
        No output feature configured
```

```
L-103-MPLS-PE#sh mpls forwarding-table vrf TENANT-1 172.16.20.0 detail
Local      Outgoing   Prefix              Bytes Label   Outgoing     Next Hop
Label      Label      or Tunnel Id        Switched      interface
None       24         172.16.20.0/24[V]   \
                                          0             Gi3          10.103.1.1
        MAC/Encaps=14/22, MRU=1496, Label Stack{17 24}
        50000016000050000001100028847 0001100000018000
        VPN route: TENANT-1
        No output feature configured
```

```
L-103-MPLS-PE#sh ip cef vrf TENANT-1 172.16.20.0 255.255.255.0 detail
172.16.20.0/24, epoch 2, flags [rib defined all labels]
  recursive via 192.168.0.203 label 24
    nexthop 10.103.1.1 GigabitEthernet3 label 17-(local:23)
```

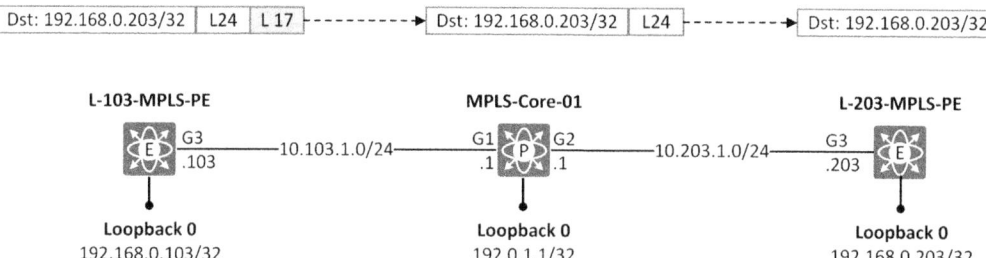

Figure 10-10: *Label Switching Path Verification.*

Data-Plane: ICMP Request

Figure 10-11 summarizes the packet encapsulation process when host 172.16.10.10 in Pod-1 pings host 172.16.20.30 in Pod-2. At step one, L-102 sends the original ICMP Request from Web10 encapsulated with VXLAN headers with VNI 30077. L-103 does MPLS handover where it removes VXLAN headers and encapsulates the packet with MPLS labels and forwards the encapsulated ICMP Request to MPLS-Core-01. MPLS-Core-01 receives the labeled packet, it does LFIB lookup, removes the outer label, and forwards the packet to L-203. L-203 does VXLAN Handover where it removes MPLS headers and encapsulates the packet with VXLAN header and forwards the packet to L-201.

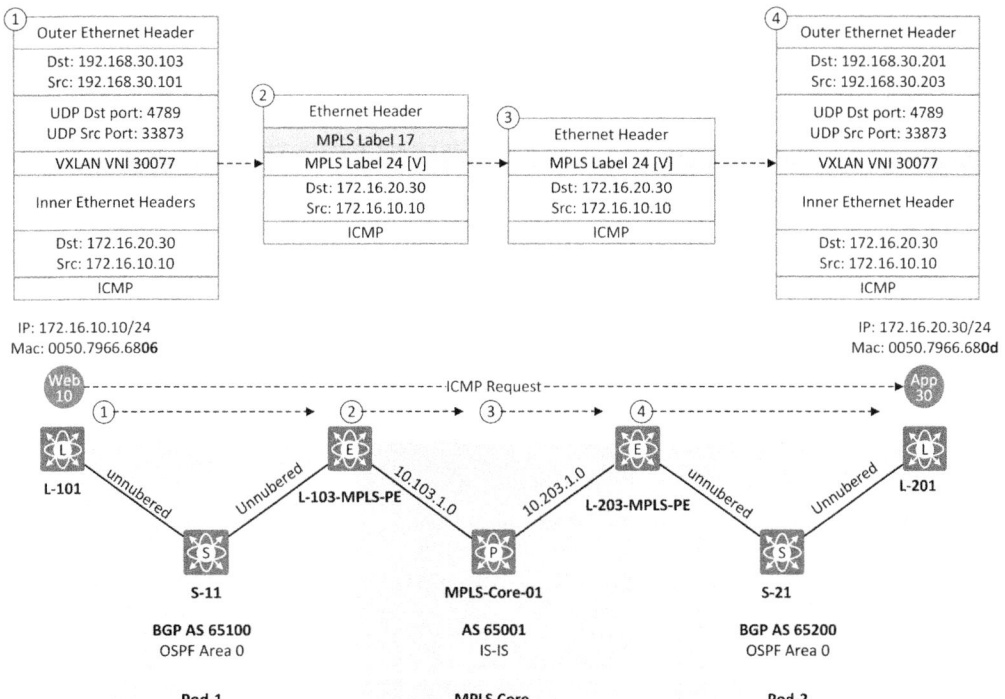

Figure 10-11: *Ping from Web10 to App30.*

Examples 10-24 verifies that there is an IP connectivity between 172.16.10.10 and 172.16.20.30.

```
Web10> ping 172.16.20.30

84 bytes from 172.16.20.30 icmp_seq=1 ttl=59 time=45.206 ms
84 bytes from 172.16.20.30 icmp_seq=2 ttl=59 time=35.885 ms
84 bytes from 172.16.20.30 icmp_seq=3 ttl=59 time=27.089 ms
84 bytes from 172.16.20.30 icmp_seq=4 ttl=59 time=32.390 ms
```

Example 10-24: *ping from 172.16.10.10 to 172.16.20.30.*

Examples 10-25, 10-26, and 10-27 show the packet capture.

```
Ethernet II, Src: 50:00:00:11:00:02, Dst: 50:00:00:16:00:00
MultiProtocol Label Switching Header, Label: 17, Exp: 0, S: 0, TTL: 62
MultiProtocol Label Switching Header, Label: 24, Exp: 0, S: 1, TTL: 62
Internet Protocol Version 4, Src: 172.16.10.10, Dst: 172.16.20.30
Internet Control Message Protocol
```

Capture 10-3: *Capture taken from L-203 MPLS Core Interface.*

```
Ethernet II, Src: 50:00:00:16:00:02, Dst: 50:00:00:14:00:02
MultiProtocol Label Switching Header, Label: 24, Exp: 0, S: 1, TTL: 61
Internet Protocol Version 4, Src: 172.16.10.10, Dst: 172.16.20.30
Internet Control Message Protocol
```

Capture 10-4: *Capture taken from MPLS-Core-01 Interface towards L-203.*

```
Ethernet II, Src: 50:00:00:14:00:00, Dst: 50:00:00:04:00:07
Internet Protocol Version 4, Src: 192.168.30.203, Dst: 192.168.30.201
User Datagram Protocol, Src Port: 33873, Dst Port: 4789
Virtual eXtensible Local Area Network
    Flags: 0x0800, VXLAN Network ID (VNI)
    Group Policy ID: 0
    VXLAN Network Identifier (VNI): 30077
    Reserved: 0
Ethernet II, Src: 00:77:00:77:00:77 (00:77:00:77:00:77), Dst: 50:00:00:0c:00:07
(50:00:00:0c:00:07)
Internet Protocol Version 4, Src: 172.16.10.10, Dst: 172.16.20.30
Internet Control Message Protocol
```

Capture 10-5: *Capture taken from L-203 Fabric Facing Interface.*

Appendix A: Chapter 10 device configurations

```
L-103-MPLS-PE#sh run
version 16.6
!
hostname L-103-MPLS-PE
!
vrf definition TENANT-1
 rd 192.168.15.103:3
 !
 address-family ipv4
  route-target export 65001:10
  route-target import 65001:10
  route-target export 65100:30077 stitching
  route-target import 65100:30077 stitching
 exit-address-family
!
no ip domain lookup
!
redundancy
bridge-domain 10
 member vni 30010
!
bridge-domain 77
 member vni 30077
!
!
interface Loopback0
 description ** RID/Underlay **
 ip address 192.168.0.103 255.255.255.255
 ip router isis
 ip ospf 1 area 0
!
interface Loopback15
 description ** BGP peering **
 ip address 192.168.15.103 255.255.255.255
 ip ospf 1 area 0
!
interface Loopback30
 description ** VTEP/Overlay **
 ip address 192.168.30.103 255.255.255.255
 ip ospf 1 area 0
!
interface GigabitEthernet1
 ip unnumbered Loopback0
 ip ospf network point-to-point
 ip ospf 1 area 0
 negotiation auto
 no mop enabled
```

```
 no mop sysid
!
interface GigabitEthernet2
 ip unnumbered Loopback0
 ip ospf network point-to-point
 ip ospf 1 area 0
 negotiation auto
 no mop enabled
 no mop sysid
!
interface GigabitEthernet3
 ip address 10.103.1.103 255.255.255.0
 ip router isis
 ip ospf network point-to-point
 negotiation auto
 mpls ip
 mpls label protocol ldp
 mpls bgp forwarding
 no mop enabled
 no mop sysid
!
interface GigabitEthernet4
 no ip address
 shutdown
 negotiation auto
 no mop enabled
 no mop sysid
!
interface nve1
 no ip address
 source-interface Loopback30
 host-reachability protocol bgp
 member vni 30077 vrf TENANT-1
 no mop enabled
 no mop sysid
!
interface BDI77
 mac-address 0077.0077.0077
 vrf forwarding TENANT-1
 ip unnumbered Loopback30
 no mop enabled
 no mop sysid
!
router ospf 1
!
router isis
 net 49.0001.0000.0000.0103.00
 metric-style narrow
!
router bgp 65100
 bgp router-id 192.168.15.103
 bgp log-neighbor-changes
 no bgp default ipv4-unicast
 neighbor 192.168.0.203 remote-as 65200
```

```
 neighbor 192.168.0.203 ebgp-multihop 10
 neighbor 192.168.0.203 update-source Loopback0
 neighbor 192.168.15.11 remote-as 65100
 neighbor 192.168.15.11 update-source Loopback15
 !
 address-family ipv4
  aggregate-address 172.16.10.0 255.255.255.0 summary-only
 exit-address-family
 !
 address-family vpnv4
  import l2vpn evpn re-originate
  neighbor 192.168.0.203 activate
  neighbor 192.168.0.203 send-community extended
  maximum-paths 8
 exit-address-family
 !
 address-family l2vpn evpn
  import vpnv4 unicast re-originate
  neighbor 192.168.15.11 activate
  neighbor 192.168.15.11 send-community both
  maximum-paths 8
 exit-address-family
 !
 address-family ipv4 vrf TENANT-1
  advertise l2vpn evpn
  aggregate-address 172.16.10.0 255.255.255.0 summary-only
 exit-address-family
!
!
route-map REDISTRIBUTE-TO-ISIS permit 10
 match interface Loopback0
!
mpls ldp router-id Loopback0
```

```
L-203-MPLS-PE#sh run
!
hostname L-203-MPLS-PE
!
vrf definition TENANT-1
 rd 192.168.15.203:3
 !
 address-family ipv4
  route-target export 65001:10
  route-target import 65001:10
  route-target export 65200:30077 stitching
  route-target import 65200:30077 stitching
 exit-address-family
!
bridge-domain 10
 member vni 30010
!
bridge-domain 77
 member vni 30077
!
```

```
interface Loopback0
 description ** RID/Underlay **
 ip address 192.168.0.203 255.255.255.255
 ip router isis
 ip ospf 1 area 0
!
interface Loopback15
 description ** BGP peering **
 ip address 192.168.15.203 255.255.255.255
 ip ospf 1 area 0
!
interface Loopback30
 description ** VTEP/Overlay **
 ip address 192.168.30.203 255.255.255.255
 ip ospf 1 area 0
!
interface GigabitEthernet1
 ip unnumbered Loopback0
 ip ospf network point-to-point
 ip ospf 1 area 0
 negotiation auto
 no mop enabled
 no mop sysid
!
interface GigabitEthernet2
 ip unnumbered Loopback0
 ip ospf network point-to-point
 ip ospf 1 area 0
 shutdown
 negotiation auto
 no mop enabled
 no mop sysid
!
interface GigabitEthernet3
 ip address 10.203.1.203 255.255.255.0
 ip router isis
 ip ospf network point-to-point
 negotiation auto
 mpls ip
 mpls label protocol ldp
 mpls bgp forwarding
 no mop enabled
 no mop sysid
!
interface GigabitEthernet4
 no ip address
 shutdown
 negotiation auto
 no mop enabled
 no mop sysid
!
interface nve1
 no ip address
 source-interface Loopback30
```

```
 host-reachability protocol bgp
 member vni 30077 vrf TENANT-1
 no mop enabled
 no mop sysid
!
interface BDI77
 mac-address 0077.0077.0077
 vrf forwarding TENANT-1
 ip unnumbered Loopback30
 no mop enabled
 no mop sysid
!
router ospf 1
!
router isis
 net 49.0001.0000.0000.0203.00
 metric-style narrow
!
router bgp 65200
 bgp router-id 192.168.15.203
 bgp log-neighbor-changes
 no bgp default ipv4-unicast
 neighbor 192.168.0.103 remote-as 65100
 neighbor 192.168.0.103 ebgp-multihop 10
 neighbor 192.168.0.103 update-source Loopback0
 neighbor 192.168.15.21 remote-as 65200
 neighbor 192.168.15.21 update-source Loopback15
 !
 address-family ipv4
  aggregate-address 172.16.10.0 255.255.255.0 summary-only
 exit-address-family
 !
 address-family vpnv4
  import l2vpn evpn re-originate
  neighbor 192.168.0.103 activate
  neighbor 192.168.0.103 send-community extended
  maximum-paths 8
 exit-address-family
 !
 address-family l2vpn evpn
  import vpnv4 unicast re-originate
  neighbor 192.168.15.21 activate
  neighbor 192.168.15.21 send-community both
  maximum-paths 8
 exit-address-family
 !
 address-family ipv4 vrf TENANT-1
  advertise l2vpn evpn
  aggregate-address 172.16.20.0 255.255.255.0 summary-only
 exit-address-family
!
mpls ldp router-id Loopback0
```

```
MPLS-Core-01#sh run
hostname MPLS-Core-01
!
interface Loopback0
 ip address 192.0.1.1 255.255.255.255
 ip router isis
 ip ospf 1 area 0
 isis circuit-type level-1
!
interface GigabitEthernet1
 ip address 10.103.1.1 255.255.255.0
 ip router isis
 ip ospf network point-to-point
 negotiation auto
 mpls ip
 mpls label protocol ldp
 mpls bgp forwarding
 no mop enabled
 no mop sysid
!
interface GigabitEthernet2
 no ip address
 negotiation auto
 no mop enabled
 no mop sysid
!
interface GigabitEthernet3
 ip address 10.203.1.1 255.255.255.0
 ip router isis
 ip ospf network point-to-point
 negotiation auto
 mpls ip
 mpls label protocol ldp
 mpls bgp forwarding
 no mop enabled
 no mop sysid
!
interface GigabitEthernet4
 no ip address
 shutdown
 negotiation auto
 no mop enabled
 no mop sysid
!
router ospf 1
!
router isis
 net 49.0001.0000.0000.0001.00
 metric-style narrow
!
mpls ldp router-id Loopback0
```

This book is part of the Network Times handbook series. These are the first two parts.

Printed in Great Britain
by Amazon